Jubilee Manifesto

to a lost friend

Inter-Varsity Press

Jubilee Manifesto

a framework, agenda
& strategy for christian
social reform

edited by
Michael
Schluter
& John
Ashcroft

Inter-Varsity Press
38 De Montfort Street, Leicester LEI 7GP, England
Email: ivp@uccf.org.uk
Website: www.ivpbooks.com

First published 2005

British Library Cataloguing in Publication Data
A catalogue record for this book is available from the British Library.

ISBN–13: 978–1–84474–074–9
ISBN–10: 1–84474–074–9

Set in 10.5/13 pt Dante
Typeset by CRB Associates, Reepham, Norfolk
Printed in Great Britain by MPG Books Ltd, Bodmin, Cornwall

Inter-Varsity Press is the publishing division of the Universities and Colleges Christian
Fellowship (formerly the Inter-Varsity Fellowship), a student movement linking
Christian Unions in universities and colleges throughout Great Britain, and a member
movement of the International Fellowship of Evangelical Students. For more
information about local and national activities write to UCCF, 38 De Montfort Street,
Leicester LEI 7GP, email us at email@uccf.org.uk, or visit the UCCF website at
www.uccf.org.uk.

Contents

About the Jubilee Centre

The Jubilee Centre was founded in 1983 from the conviction that the Bible presents a coherent and relevant alternative to Capitalism, Socialism and other ideologies.

This led the Jubilee Centre to conduct research into the content and application of the biblical social vision and then into a number of campaigns (often in partnership with others) on such issues as Sunday trading (Keep Sunday Special) and credit and debt (Credit Action). It also led to the launch of the Relationships Foundation in 1994 to originate practical initiatives to reform society, based on a relational agenda or Relationism, including criminal justice and health issues, unemployment, business practice and peace-building.

Over recent years the Jubilee Centre's focus has shifted from direct campaigns to concentrate on research, education and providing the foundational material for its campaigning sister organizations. Its research seeks to understand and then apply biblical teaching to contemporary social, political and economic questions. By sharing its work widely, the Jubilee Centre equips Christians in the UK and overseas to influence society according to biblical principles.

The Jubilee Centre publishes the findings of its work regularly. Updates called *Engage* (which include short articles and news) and *Cambridge Papers* (essays of about 4,000 words exploring a contemporary issue) are distributed free of charge each quarter. For further information about the Jubilee Centre, to order or access other publications (most are available free of charge) or to join the free mailing list, please visit: <http://www.jubilee-centre.org> or contact:

Jubilee House,
3 Hooper Street,
Cambridge,
CB1 2NZ
Tel: +44 (0)1223 566319
email: info@jubilee-centre.org

About the authors

John Ashcroft MTh is research director for the Jubilee Centre and for the Relationships Foundation where he is currently leading projects on public-service reform and relational auditing. He holds a degree in theology from Oxford University and a Master of Theology from King's College, London. In addition to writing numerous research papers he has co-authored *Political Christians in a Plural Society* (Jubilee Policy Group, 1993), *Relationships in the NHS* (RSM Press, 2000) and *The Case for Inter-professional Collaboration* (Blackwell, 2005).

Jonathan Burnside PhD is lecturer in Criminal Law at the School of Law, University of Bristol. He is a former Visiting Fellow in Jewish Law at the Oxford Centre for Hebrew and Jewish Studies. He is the author of *The Signs of Sin: Seriousness of Offence in Biblical Law* (Sheffield Academic Press, 2002) and *Religion and Rehabilitation: The Development of Faith-Based Therapeutic Communities in Prison* (Willan, 2004). His work for the Jubilee Centre includes *The Status and Welfare of Immigrants* and a review of the presentation of sexual offences in biblical law. In the early 1990s he spearheaded Relational Justice for the Relationships Foundation. He is editor of the *Relational Justice Bulletin*.

Revd Graham Cole PhD was the Principal of Ridley College, University of Melbourne (1992–2001) and lectured in Christian Thought. He has served as a member of the Council of the University of Melbourne. Recently he was appointed Professor of Biblical and Systematic Theology at Trinity Evangelical Divinity School, Deerfield, Illinois. He has published articles in *Churchman*, *Expository Times*, *Enlightenment and Dissent*, *The Philosopher*, *Tyndale Bulletin*, *Reformed Theological Review*, *Journal of Christian Education* and *Themelios*. He has contributed to a number of books and dictionaries including IVP's *New Dictionary of Christian Ethics and Pastoral Theology*. He has also had poetry published in a number of Australian and American literary journals.

Revd Jeremy Ive PhD holds degrees in History, Philosophy, Politics and Theology from the Universities of Rhodes (Grahamstown, South Africa), Cambridge and London. He trained for the Church of England Ministry at Wycliffe Hall, Oxford, and is currently active in parish ministry in Kent. He was also involved, in different capacities, in the Newick Park Initiative (later Relationships Foundation International and now Concordis International) peace-building programmes in South Africa, Rwanda and Sudan.

Paul Mills PhD graduated in economics at Cambridge University and worked as a researcher at the Jubilee Centre for a year before returning to the University to complete a PhD in economics. He has worked as an economist since 1992 and currently specializes in finance. He is co-author of *Islamic Finance: Theory and Practice* (Palgrave Macmillan). He has been on the writing group of *Cambridge Papers* since 1992 and is on the Jubilee Centre Advisory Board.

Julian Rivers MA, LLM, MIur, PhD, is Senior Lecturer in Law at the University of Bristol, UK. He studied law at Cambridge and Göttingen Universities before appointment to Bristol in 1993. His research interests lie mainly in the area of legal and constitutional theory, with a particular interest in the interplay between law and religion. He translated and wrote an introduction to Robert Alexy's *Theory of Constitutional Rights* (Oxford University Press, 2002) and has contributed to *Law and Religion* (Ashgate, 2000), *Studies in Christian Ethics*, vol. 13, no. 2 (2000), *Law and Religion* (Oxford University Press, 2001), and *Christian Perspectives on the Limits of Law* (Paternoster, 2002). He has been on the writing group of *Cambridge Papers* since 1992 and is a member of the UCCF Trust Board and is on the Advisory Board of the Jubilee Centre.

Michael Schluter PhD is the founder and Chairman of the Jubilee Centre. He is also chairman of the Keep Sunday Special Campaign and the Relationships Foundation. He has a PhD in agricultural economics from Cornell University and worked in East Africa for six years as a consultant for the World Bank and as a research fellow of the International Food Policy Research Institute. Dr Schluter co-authored *The R Factor* (Hodder, 1993) and *The R Option* (Relationships Foundation, 2003). He has been a founding member of a number of social reform initiatives, including the Newick Park Initiative (now called Concordis International), the Keep Sunday Special Campaign, Credit Action, City*life*, Keep Time for Children and Equity for Africa. He has been on the writing group for *Cambridge Papers* since 1992.

Revd Chris Wright PhD is currently International Ministries Director at Langham Partnership International. He also serves as the Advisory Board chairman of the

Jubilee Centre and is honorary president of Crosslinks, an Anglican missionary society. He is the author of several books, including *Living as the People of God* (IVP, 1983), *God's People in God's Land* (Paternoster, 1990) and *Old Testament Ethics for the People of God* (IVP, 2004), as well as commentaries on Deuteronomy and Ezekiel, and for five years was the editor of the journal *Themelios*. After graduating from Cambridge he taught Latin, Greek and Religious Studies in Belfast and then returned to Cambridge to do a PhD. He served in an Anglican parish in Tonbridge, and then taught Old Testament in Union Biblical Seminary, India, for five years. Prior to assuming his current post, he served from 1993 as Principal of All Nations Christian College.

Foreword

How are human beings to flourish? This is both a spiritual and a political question. Politicians wrestle with it and devise manifestoes in the hope of persuading an electorate to vote them into government so that they can turn their policies into law. Their political ambition is to create a society, a community of communities, in which human beings might flourish. Their policies are predicated on a system of values, some implicit, some explicit. The story of those values in Britain, Europe and America twists and turns through history and, to change the metaphor, its threads have been intertwined with the story of Christianity. Along the way these threads have separated into at least two strands, the political and the spiritual. Although at times there were conscious attempts to weave the two together, it seems that in every generation there is need for advocates to speak out and apologists to defend not only the holding together but also the integration of the spiritual and political. Issues of human flourishing raise spiritual as well as political questions. In *Jubilee Manifesto* you will find apologists and advocates who argue the case for an inextricable link between the spiritual and the political, between religious faith and social values, between theology and sociology. To separate the two leads to a double failure, for it is to fail society and to fail God.

The authors of this manifesto find the inspiration and the authority for their spiritual and political ideas in the Bible. Just writing this sentence makes me feel the weight of their task! We live in a culture whose literature, law, music and historic architecture are baptized in the biblical narrative but whose leaders, including its religious ones, make little appeal to the existence let alone the authority of the Bible. Referring to the Bible in public discourse is like pedalling away on an exercise bike and then pressing maximum load! Getting the Bible taken seriously in contemporary debate on social and political issues is an uphill struggle. Even amongst Christians the level of biblical literacy is low and this important document will be a challenge to many even sympathetic readers. The authors recognize the difficulty, but they appeal to the Bible for very good reasons. Anyone who is concerned with the cause of human flourishing could be expected to ask at least two questions: in the history of the human family, is there any example of a human being who has flourished as a true human being, and is there any society whose common life has been so shaped to ensure the flourishing of its members? It is the conviction of the authors that the Bible's relevance and authority reside in its testimony to these two realities: namely, that in the person of Jesus Christ we come face to face with a truly true human being and that in the community of Israel we are given a social paradigm from which we can elicit timeless principles on which to construct a community where human beings might experience their true potential.

Throughout these pages you will see that the principal motif is that of relationship. How we relate in families, as members of communities, as citizens in a state, as a nation and in relation to other nations is the primary question. It is the foundational issue because that is the nature of reality; we are persons in relationship – with each other, with our environment and with God. The touchstone of reality is God. Here we come to the heart of what it is *to be*. God is one God and within his oneness lives a community of three persons in perfect relationship with one another. Here is the model of how to relate. It is an inclusive embracing, an ever-widening circle. The Trinity teases the human imagination while defying human definition. Yet enough of the veil is drawn back for us to glimpse some of the dynamics. In the Gospel of John we see the persons of the Trinity delighting in one another. The Father glorifies the Son, the Son glorifies the Father, the Spirit glorifies the Son.

Here is a mutuality of giving and receiving glory to and from each other. In the Gospel, no-one gives glory to the Spirit for that is left to the church to give glory to the Spirit, the Son and the Father as she is gathered up in the purposes of God to reconcile all things to himself.

The authors of the manifesto argue persuasively that it is God the Holy Trinity who is the beginning and the end, the Alpha and the Omega of all human relatedness. That is why the authors believe that theology is the basis for social policy.

This manifesto is the fruit of over twenty years' study and reflection on holding together the spiritual and the political. As one who has been in the front-line of urban regeneration and community renewal, I welcome this book enthusiastically both personally and on behalf of the church. I particularly welcome the courage of its authors to move from theory to proposing a manifesto with an agenda and a strategy for social reform based on Christian principles. You may not agree with every policy detail; the authors acknowledge the room for disagreement. But you will be challenged with the gauntlet of finding an alternative.

Above all, this is a timely publication. The aggrandizement of Europe presents us with searching questions both about its internal policy as well as its relationship with the rest of the world. Its constitution and its values merit serious critique from a Christian perspective.

In America, political ideology is entwined with religious idealism in a way that leaves many Christians in Britain feeling ill-at-ease as they see Christianity harnessed to a super-nation's political ambitions. There the spiritual and the political are glued together to an extent that makes some believe it best to separate them altogether. Such a division would deny the argument of this manifesto. And in Britain – the nation of Wilberforce and Shaftesbury – are we to conclude that these two examples of the marriage of the spiritual and the political belong firmly and exclusively to our history? Today major political parties increasingly resemble Disraeli's comparison of stagecoaches hurtling along in the same direction, at the same speed, while spraying each other with mud. Has the time come for a new expression of a political idealism rooted in a spiritual understanding of how we as human beings might flourish in relationship with one another? I have begun to say and to pray (and this manifesto encourages me the more so) that God might stir up a new movement determined to do God's will on earth as it is done in heaven. It is the most spiritual and the most political of all prayers to pray 'Your will be done on earth as it is in heaven'. Then will human flourishing be divine.

The Rt. Rev. James Jones
Bishop of Liverpool
November 2004

Preface

This book is written by Christians, primarily for Christians, about the biblical basis for social reform. Its goal, unusually perhaps, is not so much to establish the mandate for such activity, but to lay out the methodology and content for the reform agenda. It assumes that Scripture is the final authority in matters of faith and conduct, including in the word 'conduct' not just personal behaviour but also public policy. It is based on the premise that the Bible is true in what it affirms; where the Bible appears to be silent on a contemporary issue, which is the case in many public-policy debates, the task of Christians is to seek out relevant 'principles' and 'patterns' from the biblical text and apply them to the situation we confront today.

As authors of a book which spans theology and the social sciences, and especially one with such an ambitious title, we are only too aware of our limitations. We regret that we do not have even one woman contributor. For Part 2 of the book especially, we would each ideally be academically qualified not only in theology but in at least one discipline underpinning an area of public policy as well. Only two of us have this double qualification. So it is important for readers to appreciate that the questions we are asking the biblical text are primarily those arising from our experience of working in contemporary academic disciplines and their application to public policy, across a wide range of fields, both in this country and internationally. So this is a book primarily by and for practitioners, rather than a book of theory.

While this book may seem ambitious in the range of its coverage, spanning policy issues as diverse as constitutional structures, economic policy and the criminal justice system, some may wonder why there is so little reference to the environment. This is not because we believe the topic to be unimportant. Rather it is that Jesus summarized the Law as 'love the Lord your God ... [and] love your neighbour as yourself' (Matt. 22:34–40). 'Love of nature' and our teatment of the environment is an outworking, we believe, of these two great commandments. So the Jubilee Centre has wanted to clarify its understanding of them first before undertaking research on the environment. Such research is now a high priority; a significant research project addressing environmental and social sustainability is in its early stages.

We see this book as no more than 'the end of the beginning' for what we believe needs to be a long-term field of research. If our thesis of the centrality of relationships for public policy decisions is accepted, and if biblical revelation provides both norms and extensive reflection on these issues, then our hope is that it may encourage others to push out the boundaries far beyond the place where this initial study has taken us.

It is this sense of opening up a debate which is in part why we have chosen the word 'manifesto' for the title. A manifesto is not the same as a White Paper, or even a Green Paper. It is a series of proposals which invite discussion and response. It is our hope that this book will do exactly that.

At the same time, this work is not mere speculation. Over the last twenty years, we have made a sustained effort to apply the biblical pattern to public life in the UK and beyond. Much of the work is still in its early stages of development, but there have been areas of significant achievement. The lessons from these attempts at applying biblical ideas to public life today are discussed in Part 3.

Our hope is that this book will encourage Christians in all parts of the world, and in all walks of life, to set about the reform of public policy, their workplace and their home life with a fresh sense of purpose and renewed vision. For our task as Christ's disciples is not just to study God's word for society, but also to communicate it and apply it. This task draws us into relationships with those who do not share our faith. Effectiveness in both apologetics and practical social reform requires new ways of communicating and applying the biblical paradigm.

The writing process for the book was more of a collective enterprise than may be apparent from the list of chapter headings, each of which is attributed to just one or two authors. The ideas have developed through extensive discussions among the *Cambridge Papers* writers and Jubilee Centre project teams over a long period. In addition, the authors' group has met four times to discuss the book as a whole. Each chapter has been reviewed and discussed by some or all of the other members of the group. However, the views finally expressed in each chapter are those of the author(s) alone, and should not necessarily be attributed to other members of the group.

We owe so much to so many that it seems invidious to mention any individual. However, we want to thank a few colleagues by name. One is Roy Clements who helped to initiate this enterprise in the 1970s. He had an immense influence on the development of the ideas, and on the lives of many of the authors, over a prolonged period. We are forever grateful for the depth and breadth of his vision over those years. We are also much indebted to Andrew Cameron, Jonathan Chaplin and Gordon McConville for their detailed comments on an earlier draft of the manuscript.

We owe much to the staff of the Jubilee Centre and its associated enterprises for their insights at both a conceptual and practical level over many years. We are grateful, in particular, for the co-ordinating role of Jason Fletcher, manager of the Jubilee Centre, and his searching comments on many earlier drafts. James Williams has played an important role in editing the manuscript and making it both readable and intelligible. The administrative team in Jubilee House have patiently supported the project in countless ways, large and small. The normal caveats regarding authors' final responsibility for content and style apply.

Finally, we would like to thank the trustees, advisory board, prayer partners and donors of the Jubilee Centre and *Cambridge Papers*, and especially members of our immediate families, who have supported this venture over some or all of the last twenty years. Without their sustained commitment to this venture of faith, this book and its associated enterprises would never have come to birth.

Michael Schluter and John Ashcroft
on behalf of the Authors' Group
Cambridge, 2005

1. A new framework for the social order

John Ashcroft and Michael Schluter

The Jubilee Centre's journey

The background to this book is life in Nairobi in the 1970s and the questions Christian students were asking at that time. As Christians, should they be Marxists, following the violent revolution in neighbouring Ethiopia which had brought to an end, as they saw it, centuries of oppression of farmers by feudal landlords? Or should they be Socialists, following the 'ujamaa' socialism of Julius Nyerere in Tanzania who had forced people to live in villages so that they could more easily be provided with access to water and education? Or should they follow the Capitalism of Jomo Kenyatta in Kenya, where land was allocated increasingly without regard to historical or family ties, simply on the basis of 'market forces'? Was the critique of these ideologies to be rooted purely in the social sciences, or did the social vision of the Bible point to an alternative to Marxist and Capitalist theories of development?

The questions being asked in East Africa in the 1970s continue to echo around the globe today. Anti-globalization campaigns suggest that the triumph of democratic Capitalism is not universally accepted, yet little in the way of a convincing alternative is proposed. Current concerns about the environment, social capital, the future of the nation-state and the 'clash of civilizations' suggest that different accounts of the goals of our common life need to be resolved. Human suffering persists, not just in low-income countries but amid the social fragmentation of high-income countries as well. In both contexts there is a relational crisis: not in the sense that all is bad (though, as we shall see, there are plenty of causes for concern) or that we can look back with nostalgia to some golden age in the past, but rather because there are critical choices before us. Personal, organizational and wider social relationships are the key to our well-being: we need to understand the proper nature of these relationships, recognize their importance and value them accordingly. These relationships are under pressure. This may be seen in the time-pressure that weakens relationships in families and organizations, the distorting of relationships in public services through ill-conceived targets, or the impact of highly mobile capital on local economies. The choice before us is, therefore, whether to create a social order that sustains relationships, or to risk their continuing erosion.

The Jubilee Centre was set up in 1983 to study, disseminate and apply a biblical vision for society. This led to a number of reform initiatives. One of the first was a series of consultations involving senior African National Congress (ANC) and Afrikaner figures to look at options for a post-apartheid South Africa in the late 1980s, seeking shared principles for such issues as land reform, constitutional structures, business ownership, urban policy and education. Around the same time UK initiatives were developed to pursue an agenda for strengthening relationships in families and neighbourhoods. This included research and campaigning on such issues as Sunday trading, consumer credit and debt, support for family carers, reform of the criminal justice system and exploring the social impact of labour mobility.[1]

At the time of writing, the Jubilee Centre and its off-shoot charities are involved in peace-building in Sudan, seeking a lasting and just peace for a conflict that has claimed two million lives over the last twenty years; developing community finance initiatives in the UK to tackle pockets of persistent long-term urban unemployment that continue to blight the lives of individuals and families who are excluded from the hopes and prosperity that so many of us take for granted; seeking reform of our public services – sometimes literally a matter of life and death for the most vulnerable; and building a social environment to sustain civic society on which our well-being depends.

This is not a book of political philosophy, but a book for those with an active concern for social reform. It is not just the fruit of thirty years of reflection on biblical teaching relating to political ideologies, but is also the fruit of over twenty years of active engagement in public life in Britain and beyond. It is based on five main convictions:

1. That social reform is an important response to human need, as part of our discipleship and love of both God and neighbour, and as a proper part of the mission of the church in the world.

---

1. Ch. 17 examines the lessons for social reform that can be learned from these initiatives.

2. That the Bible can guide this process, informing our understanding of what constitutes right relationships and offering a paradigm of a relational social order.[2]

3. That our approach to social reform must focus on relationships, both in setting the goals for our lives as individuals and as a society, and in setting the agenda for a social order designed to sustain those relationships.[3]

4. That social reform must be guided and inspired by new ideas that tackle the root systemic causes of social, economic and political problems. Implicit in this conviction is the belief that the '-isms' that shape life today are flawed.

5. That it is important to work with those who do not share our faith, which requires that we create a shared account of the common good.

This last conviction is a product of the journeys that *Jubilee Manifesto* traces. One journey has been from major social issues to discerning the heart of the biblical social vision, drawing on a paradigmatic approach to biblical social ethics. The second, parallel, journey has been to work out how this can be communicated and applied today. In the UK context this has meant addressing the issue of how a vision for social reform can be articulated which is both true to our faith and also provides the basis for engaging with those who are not Christians. In practice, reform requires effective persuasion, not just the assertion of competing truth claims. These two journeys come together around the theme of relationships, a key theme of our faith. Relationships lie at the heart of a biblical social vision, address the core of contemporary social, political and economic problems, and provide a language and agenda which is faithful to the Christian tradition whilst also open and inclusive to those with whom we must work if our concern for social reform is to deliver real change.

The Jubilee Centre's journey, and the different personal journeys of each author are, of course, part of that much wider and longer journey, stretching over millennia, of a community of people learning what it means to 'walk in the ways of the Lord' (Deut. 10:12). With its many tensions and dilemmas it can sometimes feel like walking a tightrope. Faithfulness to Scripture and inclusive engagement with society are not always easy to combine. Ideal visions and pragmatic solutions

---

2. The methodology for this is developed in ch. 5 and applied to individual issues in each chapter of Part 2.

3. Ch. 2 argues that relationships are the core theme of our faith and ch. 3 explores how a concern for relationship informs our understanding of personhood. Ch. 6 discusses the relational values at the heart of the biblical social vision, and ch. 16 introduces the concept of relationism as a framework for social reform.

are hard to hold together. It is hard to combine excellence in biblical studies and secular academic disciplines, professional influence, campaigning and entre-preneurial skill. This is work in progress. The magnitude and breadth of the questions that we address mean that, at least in this volume, the answers cannot be comprehensive. Our priority here is to give an account of the big picture.

There are individuals and organizations in many countries who have similar concerns and whose thinking and action have made a real difference. In the course of our projects we have worked with and learned from many people. This book does not claim to be a comprehensive review of the literature or of Christian contributions to social reform. Rather it presents a case-study in articulating and implementing a reform agenda. Our journey continues and we hope that this book will be part of the process of continuing to learn from as well as supporting others who share a commitment to reform.

Addressing the relational crisis

Part of the case for reform, and our sense of urgency about that task, is based on the extent of human suffering and our understanding of its systemic causes. People die. Lives are blighted. Potential is unfulfilled. Some of the scourges of the past have been addressed, but we face new problems today. Whether we tend towards an optimistic or pessimistic view of the current state of our society and its prospects, we cannot remain heedless of the plight of those who suffer the consequences of social alienation and relationships characterized by neither peace nor justice. Our assessment should be informed by a positive vision which enables us to question whether, both individually and as a society, we have set ourselves the right goals, and to judge how far we fall short.

Think for a moment about the future we set before our children. Will most enjoy a stable family life? Will they be adequately protected if these relation-ships fail? Will all enjoy good health and education? Can all look forward to being included within and contributing to vibrant and cohesive communities? Can they look forward to an old age, confident in their care and security? Is it likely that they will have come to know God and been free to live out their faith? No society has ever fully achieved this. The need for social reform is, then, a perpetual task and not just a judgment on a particular society or age. The case for social reform does not depend on wilful dystopia: we should not hide from problems that do exist, nor be complacent about their potential escalation.

People have mixed experience of relationships. Ambivalence in commitment can result. For every successful partnership, between individuals or organizations, there are the pains, scars and costs of failure. Some see in relationships exciting opportunities, others burdensome responsibilities; ties that bond or ties that bind. The rhetoric of importance is all too easily combined with the reality of neglect. The close links between relationships and values can make for contentious debate. Many people are willing to agree that long-term stable relationships are, in principle, a good thing. But when it comes to defining a 'good' relationship, or what kinds of relationship (if any) should be favoured by public policy, and whether things are getting worse or simply changing, agreement and even rationality can begin to disappear. Evidence can all too easily be marshalled, twisted or ignored to support a wide variety of positions. However, many commentators have charted a steep decline in social capital in the US over the last few decades (e.g. Putnam 2000). Many indicators have come together to paint a worrying picture: less associational activity, lower levels of trust, less community involvement. Measures from the US should not be applied uncritically to the UK. The most recent General Household Survey, however, now includes indicators on social capital in the UK (ONS 2002). This shows, for example, that 20% of people have neither a 'satisfactory friendship network' nor a 'satisfactory relatives network'.[4]

A snapshot of UK indicators gives many causes for concern as well as suggesting that some aspects of social capital are proving resilient, at least for the moment. Behind the percentages is a diversity of experience which includes large pockets of social exclusion. A snapshot also leaves unanswered the question as to whether our social capital is being depleted or renewed. Too many young people are socially excluded, experiencing dysfunctional family relationships and statistically likely to replicate them. The rate of family breakdown is high: 25% of children can expect their parents to separate, with roughly 150,000 children in England and Wales experiencing the divorce of their parents each year; 20% of children live in lone parent households; 23% of conceptions end in abortion; 40% of births are now outside marriage.[5] The prevalence of sexually transmitted diseases is rising rapidly. It is not hard to paint a picture of social fragmentation. We need to see the human and social costs behind the figures. Children's life prospects are stunted. Poverty and disadvantage are perpetuated. Public services are put under potentially unsustainable strain. Social solidarity between generations and between rich and poor is threatened.

The need to reform relationships is not only an issue for the 'West'. Low-income countries have their own well-known litany of problems.[6] Ethnic conflict

---

4. These were defined as seeing or speaking to friends (relatives) at least once a week and having at least one close friend (relative) living nearby.

5. These figures are taken from a review of national statistics in Roberts (2003).

6. Okumu (2002) offers a helpful analysis of the potential for, and obstacles to, an African renaissance.

within and between states, coupled with corruption and weak political structures and institutions, blight the lives of billions of people. Grinding poverty and poor health (not least as a result of AIDS) remain prevalent. Economic development is hampered through problems of trade and debt, access to finance and markets. The pressure on land is intense and the widespread provision of services such as water, health and education is hard to sustain. Looking at these issues from an international perspective reveals the need to reform the ideologies that shape the systems that are the root causes of many of these problems. To the extent that we are influential over, and influenced by, parts of those economic and political systems, the problems of low-income countries are our problems too.

Personal and organizational relationships

Our vision is, at one level, simple. It is that personal, community and organizational relationships matter, and need to be nurtured. But the practice is neither so simple nor agreed. A relationships agenda cuts to the heart of contemporary political, philosophical and economic debates. It is about the kind of society we want to create, the kind of lives we wish to lead. So what content can we give to the potentially nebulous term 'relationships'?

Relationships may be distinguished from mere interactions on the basis of continuity of interaction and knowledge of the person. Thus, bumping into someone in the street does not constitute a relationship. 'Relationships involve a series of interactions between two individuals who know each other, such that each interaction can be influenced both by past interactions and by expectations of interactions in the future' (Hinde 1997: 48). Each of us depends on relationships – not just in a practical sense for everyday work and living, but also emotionally and psychologically. We are 'hard-wired' to thrive in a world of close and supportive relationships. It is in relationships that we find identity, self-worth, security and purpose.

Although 'individuals-in-relationship' are 'the essential component of moral reality' and should be characterized by mutual love (Hill 2002: 126) they are not the only ethically significant relationship. The relationships between individuals and organizations or groups, and between organizations/groups also matter. Indeed, as we shall see in Part 2, much biblical teaching is explicitly about such relationships. This is because individual relationships are set in a social context. Any bi-polar relationship is influenced by a third actor or factor, whether that is primarily a person, a group, or a collection of factors involving many diverse agents.

Participants in dyadic relationships are almost invariably also involved in relationships with other individuals, who in turn may have relationships with each other and with other individuals. Each dyadic relationship is in fact nearly always embedded in a social group, the structure of which provides a further level of complexity. Furthermore this group may interact with other groups within the society, and the relationships, interactions and behaviour of the individuals will be affected by social norms regulating their conduct. (Hinde 1997: 42)

Organizations depend on relationships. Business, for example, can be done only in the context of such relationships as those with customers, suppliers, employees, investors and regulators. Managing and developing these relationships is at the heart of effective business strategy. Similarly, delivery and management of public services involves a wide range of relationships within and between organizations, as well as with the public who are served.

Relationships can be seen as ends in themselves and as means (or, when flawed, as impediments) to achieving those ends. A concern for the well-being of individuals, understood in relational terms, therefore requires us to be concerned with the full range of institutions which shape the relational environment.[7] These are not fully reducible to sets of interpersonal relationships. The relationship between two organizations, for example, or between two departments within a single organization, whilst expressed in a number of interpersonal relationships, has a life and history outside any one interpersonal relationship and may shape the conduct of that relationship significantly. A contract or strategic partnership between two organizations is a relationship between two groups of people. It influences the ethical conduct of many interpersonal relationships. Taking inter-professional collaboration in public services as an example, it is as important to get the structures, policies and working practices of schools and hospitals right as it is to support the development of more effective interpersonal working relationships.[8]

In this context, it is worth explaining why we have not (other than for the practical constraints of space) addressed environmental concerns directly in this book. Humanity is, of course, an organic part of a complex system. The consequences of our interaction with the environment may be severe. These interactions are not in themselves personal relationships but can best be understood by analysing their relational context. We express our love for our Creator by respecting his creation and fulfilling our responsibilities to him. We directly

---

7. Part 2 discusses the substance of a wide range of relationships. A key conclusion, found on pp. 278–279 of ch. 15, is that elements of the proper goals of a nation can be summarized in terms of sustaining five sets of relationships involving God, individuals, extended families, communities and other sub-national groups.

8. The Relationships Foundation, a charity set up by the Jubilee Centre, has done much work in this area. Meads & Ashcroft et al. (2005) offers a detailed study of collaborative relationships in health and social care.

cause others to suffer when they experience the consequences of our neglect of and damage to the environment. Such neglect or damage also affects our relationship with future generations.

The mandate for social reform

Our expectations of social reform should reflect awareness of the different positions and contexts in which both churches and individuals find themselves. We are not all able to pursue social reform in the same way and do not all have the same influence. Yet we should not forget that reform is not our task alone. The people God calls are not always those who may be expected to have the greatest influence (1 Cor. 1:26–29). Reform is not just some discrete campaigning activity (important as this may be), but is, in part, the product of faithfulness in the conduct of our daily life. It is about being a transforming influence in society, not just about participating in formal political processes. So, for example, Christians in positions of professional influence, whether in politics, business or public service, have an opportunity in many small ways to be part of a movement for change in reforming the structures of society. In a time of pragmatic politics where today's beacon or pilot-site can be tomorrow's national policy, the potential to influence policy is widely diffused.

Social reform, seen as part of a long-term movement in changing the values and structures of society, can be distinguished from social action, a response to specific issues or areas of human need. Reform goes beyond alleviating symptoms to addressing causes, and is concerned with the whole of society and not specific parts. Although, for example, much social reform in the nineteenth century was focused on specific issues such as working conditions which, in concrete form, expressed and challenged a wider set of values, institutional reform and not just symptomatic relief was sought. The question we face today is whether our approach to social reform should be to modify and humanize the current structures and systems, or whether we have entered a period where the questions being raised are so fundamental that the guiding assumptions of our approach to economic, social and political life must be revisited.

Our main concern in this book is with the content of the reform agenda, as opposed to the authority by which we engage with society.[9] However, five aspects of the mandate for Christian involvement in social reform are worth noting briefly as the context for this book. These are:

---

9. For the basis for a Christian political theology see, for example, O'Donovan (1996). Hilborn (2004) includes a range of evangelical perspectives on social transformation.

- the lordship of Christ
- an affirmation of creation
- our love of God and neighbour
- our responsibility for our actions
- our concern for mission.

We shall consider each of these briefly in turn.

A key New Testament affirmation is the lordship of Christ. But lord over what? Just the hearts of believers? As Paul writes to the Colossians, surely his lordship is over everybody and everything in heaven and in society (Col. 1:15–20)? The kingdom reaffirms and redeems creation – it is not declared void and irrelevant – and its right ordering still matters. After all, we are taught by Jesus to pray to our heavenly Father, 'your will be done in society as it is in heaven' (Matt. 6:10).[10] Much of what the Old Testament speaks about is concerned with politics and economics. If Jesus' followers are to live 'by every word which proceeds from the mouth of God' (Matt. 4:4, cf. Deut. 8:3), this again points to a Christian mandate to engage with social reform.

The second reason for engagement is love. The Gospels teach us that love requires concern for our neighbour. It would seem odd to relieve the symptoms of injustice but not do what we can to tackle the causes. This is recognized in international development where, for example, fair trade, debt remission and good governance are promoted as opposed to merely distributing humanitarian assistance. Surely the same should be true at home. If it is important for God's people to tackle the symptoms of social distress, it must be important for them to tackle the causes as well. Indeed, Isaiah 58:6–9 is explicit that both must be addressed.

A further factor which should persuade us as Christians to be concerned about what happens in wider society is the possibility that we will be judged not just for our personal response to the gospel, but for the sins of our church, city and country. In the Old Testament whole nations are judged for their collective actions (e.g. Amos 1). In the New Testament Jesus warns of judgment on whole towns such as Bethsaida and Capernaum (Matt. 11:20–24).[11] So perhaps we should expect to be held accountable in some sense for the injustice in our world and should therefore seek to do something about it. To the extent that in global terms

---

10. In Hebrew thought, abstract ideas are often expressed in concrete terms, e.g. conflict becomes sword (Matt. 10:34), and here we believe land/earth is symbolic of the people who live on the land, i.e. society (cf. Amos 8:8).

11. Other examples include Gen. 19; Ezek. 16:49–52; Isa. 58:1–9; Luke 19:14–44 and Rev. 2:1 – 3:22.

we are counted as the rich and powerful, and in some sense the beneficiaries of other people's suffering, then we should consider whether a lack of commitment to reform might be deemed by God to be culpable complacency.

The final aspect of the case for social reform is the link to evangelism. Some Christians see social engagement as a distraction from a Christian's primary task, which is evangelism. If so many people are on their way to hell and eternal separation from God, it is argued, why waste time on improving their material way of life in a world which will ultimately disappear anyway? Matthew 5:11–20 provides an answer. After saying to his disciples that they are to be in the tradition of the prophets, Jesus tells them that they are the salt of society (literally 'the land', see n. 11), that is, that their role, like that of the prophets, is to tackle moral decay. If they fail in that task, people will throw them out as useless. Equally, they are to be the light of the world, so that when people see their good deeds, they will glorify their Father in heaven. Jesus is talking here not about gospel proclamation, but about 'good deeds'. In a world of competing religions, the truth of the message will be assessed as much by what Jesus' disciples do as by what they say.

The credibility of the gospel message is at stake in the reputation of the church. Whether or not people respond to the gospel depends not just on the truth of the message in some abstract sense, nor just on the personal relationship between those who give and receive the message, but on the reputation of the church as a whole. The church as a community is the city on a hill which cannot be hidden, which is meant to be seen (Matt. 5:14–16). The church as a body of God's people ought to have a reputation for both attacking what is wrong and actively promoting what is good, which is what will make its message credible and attractive to outsiders (McIlroy 2004). Without such credibility evangelism will generally yield little lasting fruit.

This link between being active in putting right the injustice in society and national spiritual revival is found often in the prophets, as well as in more recent church history. One of the most striking examples is in the writings of Isaiah. The people are praying for revival; however, through the prophet, God says to his people that the kind of fasting he wants is not self-denial with respect to food, but self-denial in tackling injustice in society (Isa. 58:5–9). Other prophets similarly make it clear that God will not hear people's prayers for renewal if they do not stop their oppression of the poor and other corrupt practices (e.g. Mic. 2:2). In more recent church history in Britain, the spiritual renewal of the Puritan movement went hand in hand with constitutional reform. The social concern of Methodism developed closely with the preaching of Wesley and Whitfield, while the reforms of Wilberforce and Shaftesbury were made possible by, and contributed to, the renewal of the Anglican church. Reform seeks to create an environment in which it is easier to live righteously. It is both reasonable and right to seek to mould a society so as to minimize the conflict between Christ and culture.

A biblical framework

Given this task, how do we discern the agenda for social reform? This book is premised on the belief that we can and should look to the Bible for guidance. This does not mean seeking some neat set of pre-packaged answers, nor that the hard work of the use of reason and creativity are not needed. It does mean that the goals of social reform are not for us to set, but are to be discerned and pursued in obedience to our Creator and Redeemer.

A Christian framework for social reform must not simply buy into other agendas and philosophies whose root values are questionable. It must address the social relationships which are neglected or undermined by secular theories and offer a coherent and inspiring vision. This book sets out the content of an alternative that is drawn from biblical social ethics. The starting point for this approach is the calling of the people of God to be a priestly kingdom and a light to the nations. They were intended to be an example of what it meant for a nation to love. Chapters 4 and 5 describe the basis of this approach in more detail. Reflecting on God's Word is intended to lead us towards wisdom and maturity. It guides our choices but does not make them for us. It is a demanding task, not least because it requires entering into a very different mindset. Our experience, however, has been that it has been worthwhile and productive, shedding new light on contemporary issues and inspiring effective responses. Parts 2 and 3 of this book describe the fruits of these labours.

As the following chapters show, an understanding of key biblical values and concerns such as love, justice and righteousness is fundamentally about relationships. In combination these values cohere in a vision for society with a concern for relationships at its heart. We will argue that the Bible offers a paradigmatic example of a framework of policies and social structures designed to achieve these relational goals. Understanding this paradigm will guide our search for ways to conduct our social, political and economic life which ensure that relationships are sustained rather than undermined.

This focus on relationships results in a comprehensive agenda. We believe, and will seek to demonstrate in the following chapters, that if this agenda is defined by a biblical social vision it will, at times, be radical and distinctive. Transforming society is about getting relationships right. Social reform involves understanding the key relationships in society, articulating a Christian vision for right relationships in this context, and considering how an environment which promotes these right relationships can best be sustained. This involves considering the impact of culture, legislation, organizational structure, working practices and personal lifestyle.

The need for big ideas

Our hermeneutics are inevitably influenced by our goals and the kinds of question that we consequently ask. We should, of course, allow ourselves to be tested as to whether these are the right questions. Social reform needs coherent guiding ideas. These have a number of elements: a vision to inspire; an agenda for action; an analysis of the causes of problems; and the principles and theories which guide a response. People are, however, ambivalent about big ideas. The promise of an inspiring vision and coherent solution is attractive. Few politicians feel comfortable going to the public, openly admitting that big ideas are neither present nor needed. Yet scepticism about big ideas remains. Philosophically, there is scepticism about truth claims and meta-narratives. Universal big ideas seem impossible when truth is relative, rationalities compete, and when the complexity of local systems is inadequately addressed by any one '-ism'. In politics, both left and right have struggled to redefine themselves post-Thatcherism and post-Marxism.

Pragmatic politics – what counts is what works in the quest to 'deliver' – and single-issue campaigns have come to dominate. There may still be a strong and principled commitment to certain outcomes, but less control over the means of achieving those outcomes. In this context John Kay recommends a 'culture of audited experimentation' where a wide variety of solutions are tried and tested, with the role of government being to nurture the blooming of a thousand flowers and playing a part (but not the only part) in the regulatory process of selecting the best and weeding out the worst (Kay 2003).

'Big ideas' should recognize diversity and the limitations of central control, but they are still needed and possible. Big questions are always asked about the forces which shape our lives; satisfactory answers are yet to be found. The future and nature of the nation-state is questioned by writers such as Philip Bobbitt (2003) who raises concerns about what governments can do beyond regulating markets when citizens are subject to forces beyond government control. David Held (Held et al. 1999; 2002) questions whether political philosophies built around the concept of the nation-state can provide political legitimacy for the international relationships and organizations that are needed to deal effectively with global issues.[12] A satisfactory integration of environmental, social and economic concerns remains to be achieved. This is evident, for example, in the concerns about globalization; critique

---

12. For our reflection on some of these issues see chs. 7, 8 and 14.

of consequences is relatively easy, but agreeing on workable alternatives is not. Key issues include the relationship between public and private sectors in the provision of public services, long-term approaches to building trust and social capital, effective regeneration of urban areas and the sustainability of rural areas, and ways of avoiding 'cycles of disadvantage'. Politicians may be wary of proclaiming some big idea as the panacea to all ills, but without some compelling big ideas it will be a rather sickly display of flowers that bloom.

This is in part due to the need for coherence. Many problems are complex and interrelated. Behind individual tragedies such as the death of Victoria Climbié is the need for many areas of service provision to work together.[13] Joined-up government requires joined-up thinking. Single-issue politics neither provides the basis for effective responses to complex interrelated issues, nor builds up the constituency of support for such responses. Without shared big ideas there is the risk that politics can become a sectarian battleground between competing interest groups with short-term horse-trading substituting for effective long-term solutions.

Big ideas are also needed if a positive message and vision are to be communicated. It is relatively easy to set out and unite around a negative agenda. A message of opposition can more easily appear powerful, principled and persuasive. The complexities of workable alternative solutions (far less amenable to emotive soundbites), and the tensions and compromises they require, can be avoided. It is of course important to oppose what is wrong and unjust, but to offer a critique without an alternative is ultimately irresponsible. Relieving suffering and promoting human flourishing requires solutions. Commending our values requires a positive vision and not just 'say no' defensive rearguard campaigns. This is particularly important where social reform draws us into moral arguments over lifestyle.

Christians have shaped responses to such big questions before. The Puritans shaped much republican constitutional thinking – and it is now being more widely acknowledged that their personal devotional reading of Scripture was an important influence on their political views (Ferdon 2004). Victorian Christians engaged with the social implications of industrialization and urbanization. Catholic social teaching and the Personalist movement[14] informed the core values of continental European Christian Democratic political parties. We need similar

---

13. This young girl died of abusive neglect which would have been prevented had the various agencies involved (NHS, social services, police) and the individuals within them worked together effectively. Scott (2005) provides a detailed analysis of the failures in relationships that contributed to her death.

14. See further in ch. 3.

contributions to shaping the agenda today, and this must go beyond pasting secular economic theories into some general theological critique.

This book is written out of a concern that a satisfactory agenda and guiding narrative is not available. Koyzis (2003) offers a helpful survey and critique of contemporary ideologies including liberalism, conservatism, nationalism, democracy and socialism. While each has strengths, all have flaws. Their symptoms are seen in the social, political and economic problems of the world today. The current vacuum in big ideas represents a challenge and an opportunity for the church. The search for new ideas is on. If we do not shape the agenda, others will. If we are silent and ineffective, we risk living in an alien and inhospitable environment which corrodes our own well-being and that of our neighbours. Without a clear agenda our opportunities for involvement will be wasted in fragmented and piecemeal engagement which does not cut to the roots of the problems.

A relational strategy[15]

The agenda we propose must both address the right issues and provide grounds for engagement and co-belligerence with others in order to bring about reform. This brings us back to the theme of relationships as offering both the content of a reform agenda and a strategy for engagement. Our approach to communicating and applying the key themes of the biblical agenda for the social order outlined in Part 2 is shaped by two factors – first by our goals, particularly our view of the proper nature of our commitment to social reform within the overall mission of the church, and second by the political, cultural and eschatological context within which we live and work.

One approach to reform is to focus on evangelism whilst also seeking to provide distinctive Christian service, either within or outside existing structures and institutions. This will involve Christians acting individually as a witness in all areas of their life in society, ensuring that their political views and concerns are effectively represented. It also requires seeking common cause with others where people are willing to work with us on our terms, as well as where specific objectives or concerns happen to coincide.

Whilst this is appropriate and important, the requirements of social reform, and a proper understanding of Christian mission, require Christians at times to do

---

15. This is the focus of ch. 16 which distinguishes an approach focused on the themes of relationships from a relational strategy which has specific normative content derived from the chapters in Part 2.

more. It is essential to reform the structures of society and influence the terms of debate in order to create a society which sustains relationships and within which Christian service and mission can flourish. This requires moving from fighting limited tactical battles to strategic co-belligerence for the common good. It means real engagement with those who are not disposed to listen to the gospel. Explicitly Christian service and witness are vitally important. The church must let the light of its good deeds shine, and the gospel must be verbally proclaimed. But in many places Christians no longer have (or have never had) a privileged position from which to shape the institutions of society. It is in this context that the biblical vision will also need to be commended as a shared vision. This is not on the basis of the real but not universally acknowledged authority of Christ the Lord, but because it is a demonstrably plausible account of human flourishing.

In democratic societies most reform requires majority support. It therefore requires influencing, persuading and working with individuals, groups and organizations who may not share our faith but who do share our concerns. In order to remain true to our own faith as we get involved with those of other faiths and none, we need to consider carefully how we communicate a biblical vision for society. The authority behind it may be rejected and the language may be alien, so we need to find ways by which the norms of right relationships, and the lessons on how to sustain those relationships given to us through the experience of the people of God, can become the basis of a more widely shared vision for society. This is not an alternative to, or substitute for, distinctive and explicit Christian involvement. It complements it but recognizes that effective communication requires some form of translation, and that effective action requires a shared agenda. The language and agenda of relationships addresses both these needs.

Advantages of a relational approach

First, it connects the key theme of the Christian faith with the heart of today's social, economic and political issues. A relational approach, therefore, serves to connect people of different faiths or from different professions around a shared agenda, enabling an effective coalition for change through addressing specific issues. This common ground can be found in unpromising contexts, for the biblical paradigm cuts across many contemporary political divides. So, for example, emphasizing free product markets appeals to the Right, whilst the concern to maintain social solidarity through restrictions on factor markets appeals to the Left. It also offers a middle way between individualistic libertarianism and the more authoritarian strands of communitarianism.

Secondly, our understanding of the nature and importance of relationships aids the discernment and explanation of the rationale behind the paradigm. Biblical teaching serves to guide and inspire what we propose to others (and which we commend as true to our faith) but cannot be presented as the sole justification for policies and actions to those who do not recognize the Bible as in any way authoritative. Other arguments must be employed to commend specific policies. Even where our objective is the proclamation of the gospel, biblical principles must communicate the character of God and not simply appear to be arbitrary commands. We turn to the Bible to open up debate, not close it down. It is in articulating why the Bible teaches what it does that real engagement begins. Thus both reform and apologetics require that we seek to understand the relational rationale behind biblical teaching. This is of particular importance in societies where religious values and truth claims are treated with suspicion, or even hostility.

Thirdly, the theme of relationships captures both the coherence of the vision and the more detailed principles of biblical teaching. It informs public policy and the conduct of our personal lives. Our objectives go beyond articulating a biblical world-view, important though that is for identifying false presuppositions and critiquing secular values. We also need to offer guidance on what the coherent outworking of a Christian world-view might look like. This is the great benefit of the relational translation of the biblical paradigm.

We believe that the relational approach also supports the wider communication of the gospel. Evangelism and Christian ministry take place in the context of relationships. By supporting the development of richer, deeper and more stable relationships it should be easier for Christians, individually and collectively, to witness to Christ. The law remains 'a schoolmaster to bring us to Christ' (Gal. 3:24, AV). John the Baptist models 'pre-evangelism'. The relational dimension of this role is seen in the language of, for example, 'turn[ing] the hearts of the fathers back to their children' (Luke 1:17; Mal. 4:6). Promoting relational values in society helps make people more attuned to the message and values of a relational religion.

Limitations of a relational approach

We should, however, also recognize the limitations of this approach. While the language of relationships is helpful, a secular account of relationships cannot convey the essential message of the gospel. The detailed account of what constitutes 'right relationships' can be defended in relational terms, but we could not derive such values with confidence without reference back to the biblical account of God as Creator and Redeemer, and the implications of our relationship with God for how we should live. A translation of the biblical paradigm into relational language depends on these roots for its fullest content. Without such roots it is likely that many divergent, and sometimes incompatible, articulations will emerge.

Reaching the limits of common values and potential for co-belligerence is not a lack of good will, but a recognition that we are bound by the covenantal love and obligations of our relationship with the One who transcends all social relationships. Our understanding of truth, the limits to our political obedience, our willingness to sacrifice for others, our trust in God's providential action, the belief that judgment is ultimately in God's hands, our understanding of the nature of our calling and the goals we set in our life: these are some of the important aspects of a Christian vision for society which are rooted in faith and cannot be translated adequately into secular terms. Where our commitment to social reform requires us to work with others, relational translation helps. But it must never become a substitute for continuing engagement with biblical teaching, nor be seen as the full account of a Christian concern for society. Nor, of course, does it have the power to bring salvation and forgiveness of sin, or to truly transform lives through the enabling power of the Holy Spirit.

Conclusion

Social reform is needed. Pressured, broken and dysfunctional relationships are both a symptom and cause of social, economic and political problems. The focus of reform should therefore be interpersonal, group and organizational relationships. Social reform, distinguished from service or action, means addressing the causes as well as relieving the symptoms. Institutional change will be a key part of this. Flawed ideologies are part of the problem and we need 'big ideas' to provide a coherent agenda for complex interrelated problems. In response to this need it is important that Christians develop an agenda which is true to their faith and not simply buy into secular theories.

The Bible offers a framework for social reform focused around the theme of relationships. It is an attractive agenda, getting to the heart of the greatest issues we face today. As we shall see, it is closely connected to the core themes of our faith. It also offers the prospect of a shared agenda with wider society as a concern for relationships does not depend on Christian faith. While the language and agenda of relationships serves as a reasonable translation of a Christian social vision, it also opens the prospect of co-belligerence on social issues. Where Christians are a minority, this will be needed if they are to play a part in achieving significant social change. This book is the product of over twenty years of engagement in public life in Britain and other countries. The following chapters describe the lessons from that journey in terms of our understanding of both the content of biblical teaching and how it can be applied.

Part 1 | Framework

Chapter 1 outlined a case for a social reform based around the 'big idea' of relationships, and their nurturing at every level of society. It also introduced a strategy for reform. This section of the book sets out our stall in greater depth. The main focus of the whole work is on the agenda for reform, but for this we need a satisfactory frame, which itself also points to action. So here we introduce and underpin the topical analysis of Part 2 and the practical chapters of Part 3. We seek to answer the following questions: What is needed, conceptually and in practice, to address the problems of contemporary society? How might we go about searching for solutions? Where should we begin looking?

The Christian faith is most fundamentally about relationships, and this is explored in chapter 2. The richest and most profound Christian doctrines – of God and man, of revelation, of sin and salvation – are explained as relational, with profound implications for how the people of God must live.

In chapter 3 we examine some of what Christians have had to say about relationships and persons over the last two millennia, as a result of reflection on the Scriptures, and how these themes have influenced the activities of the church and her impact on society. The strands pursued are the doctrines of the Trinity, of the human person, and the covenant (invigorated at the time of the Reformation).

Christian doctrines are themselves derived from the Bible, as is Christian ethical and social teaching, so in chapter 4 we examine the nature of authority in general and the ethical authority of the Old Testament in particular. We focus on the Old Testament because it is a rich resource for social ethics, yet its relevance is too often neglected and its authority most often contested.

Reforming the institutions of society requires us to move to specific practical proposals which we can commend to those who may not share our faith but may, of necessity, be partners in the reform process. Chapter 5 opens up some of the theoretical issues surrounding how we use the Bible in our discourse about society, social ethics and public policy. We examine the multifaceted character of the ethical teaching of the Bible and defend the use of early Israel as an ethical paradigm.

2. Christianity as a relational religion

Graham Cole

Introduction

In many respects relationships and our stories of them are the keys to life.[1] When asked to introduce ourselves to others we tell our stories. We talk about our parents, our siblings, perhaps our spouses and children if they are part of our story. We mention our friends, especially if there is a possible connection with the person asking the question. We also tell stories about where we grew up (our relation to a particular space) and when we grew up (our relation to a particular time). Those stories are easily analysed in relational terms. We talk about our connections, our links, or put another way, our relationships. We talk diachronically (about our past relationships) and synchronically (about our present relationships). And if we are Christian by conviction we might talk about our relationship to God. For this, Christianity relies in particular on divine revelation about God and ourselves, the Bible. The Bible itself may be construed as a relational book, and to that important idea we will soon turn. Before we do, some attention needs to be given to how Christianity provides a frame of reference within which all of life is to be viewed. Or, put more formally, how the biblical story provides the Christian with a frame of reference.

---

1. For a classic article on the relationship between persons, the personal and story form see Crites (1971).

Christianity's frame of reference

Psychoanalytic thinker, Erich Fromm suggests that religion is 'any system of thought and action shared by a group which gives the individual a frame of reference and an object of devotion' (Fromm 1970: 21).[2] The frame of reference provides the perspectives that inform the practitioner of a given religion's engagement with life. This is an important insight and Christianity is no exception. For the Christian these perspectives are bound up in distinctive stories. Stories of God as Creator and Redeemer, of humanity as lost and in need of rescue, of the divine plan to reclaim an alienated creation through working with a distinctive people Israel and the church for the sake of the whole creation. Once the perspectives found in these stories are assumed in any enquiry they become the Christian's presuppositions for thought and action.

The Bible provides these stories and it is to this famous book that we soon turn our attention. However, before doing so, it is worth asking what our expectations of the Bible should be as far as providing a frame of reference is concerned. If by frame of reference we mean some encyclopaedic coverage of reality that seeks to explain all of human experience from rational thought to art history, from philosophy to the scientific enterprise, to name just a few possibilities, then there will be disappointment. The Bible writers have no interest in such an enterprise, which some call a metaphysic, some a grand theory, and others, like Immanuel Kant, call a *Weltanschauung*, or world-view. The biblical writers are non-postulational; that is to say, show little interest in theorizing grandly about the nature of reality. On the other hand, if by frame of reference we mean an existential interest in who we are, where we come from, what's wrong with us and what future humanity has, then the Bible comes alive with answers. A good case can be made for the canon of Scripture presenting such a frame of reference, which some (e.g. Wilhelm Dilthey) call a *Lebensanschauung* or life-view. Fromm's idea of a frame of reference is akin to this life-view. It is this existential, rather than encyclopaedic, frame of reference that is assumed as the Christian explores the wider questions of human enquiry and examines the nature of life in societies so very different to those of biblical times.

Christianity's relational book

Christianity is a book religion in the sense that its Holy Bible is the source and norm of its ideas of God. In all the Bibles I know the one book is divided into two

---

2. Naugle (2002) provides a more philosophically sophisticated treatment.

parts. The way the two parts are traditionally labelled teaches an important relational message. The first part is the Old Testament and the second is the New Testament. The word 'testament' here is equivalent to 'covenant'. In the biblical literature a covenant is a relationship based on a promise. There are many examples in the Bible. The crucial Old Testament one is God's covenant with Abraham in the book of Genesis. God promises to make Abraham the father of a great nation and to bless the world through him (Gen. 12:1–3). Indeed how the rest of the world treats Abraham will be the test of whether God would bless or curse them. In the New Testament we find that Jesus, the Son of God, is the key player in the outworking of that promise. As God's Son the relationship he enables us to have with God his Father can be described, in contrast to what has gone before, as a new covenant (cf. Luke 22:14–23 and Gal. 3:23 – 4:7). In view of this we could re-describe the two parts as the old relationship and the new relationship. The point is that the very way the Bible is labelled recognizes relationships and their importance.

Indeed the purpose of the inspired literature is to establish and maintain a relationship with God through faith placed in Jesus Christ. In 2 Timothy 3:14–17 we read that Scripture is breathed out by God and is able to make the reader wise for salvation through faith in Christ. This literature has origins in God like no other body of literature. Even so, Scripture is not an end in itself but a means to an end, a covenantal, relational end. Jesus made the same point in his debates with Jewish leaders. He chided them for searching the Scriptures – the Old Testament or relationship is on view – because they thought that they could find eternal life in the text. But the problem was that the text pointed away from itself to a person to be believed in. The text testified to Christ. However, though he stood before them they would not come to him to find life (John 5:36–40). Later in John's account, Jesus comes close to defining the nature of this life. He calls it 'eternal life', and in a prayer to his divine Father he describes this life as a relationship of knowing between the disciple and the father and the Son (John 17:3–5). Scholars suggest that the idea of 'knowing' in this context carries rich relational tones. It is more the language appropriate to knowing one's spouse than knowing a proposition about marriage. Jesus is not speaking simply of an intellectual grasping of who God is, but of a never-ending connection. Not even physical death can break this relationship (John 14:1–3). A philosopher might say that this relationship is more like knowledge by acquaintance than knowledge by description.[3] However, the two forms of knowledge are not antithetical. Indeed, it is hard to imagine a workable marriage relationship without some belief in the

---

3. This distinction was made famous by Bertrand Russell in his *Problems of Philosophy*, reprinted many times since its publication in 1912.

existence of one's partner, and beliefs about both his or her character and value. Knowledge by acquaintance assumes knowledge by description.

What then do these Scriptures say about relationships? Answering this question is the major task in hand. It will lead us to consider the very nature of the Christian God as Trinity – relational on the inside – then to the creature he has made to image him, then to the human predicament of living a life of ruptured relationships that cries out for a relational restoration both for ourselves and for the creation itself. Finally we consider Christianity's relational ethic.

A relational God

The Christian's 'object of devotion' – to use Fromm's words – is the God revealed in the canon of Scripture. In the Old Testament, the oneness of the living God of the Bible is very much on view. The creation story does not present a pantheon of competing deities but the one God who is Maker and Ruler over the historical process (Gen. 1:1 – 2:4a). Indeed the oneness of the Creator and Israel's rescuer is the chief article of Israel's creed: 'Hear, O Israel: The LORD our God the LORD is one. Love the LORD your God with all your heart and with all your soul and with all your strength' (Deut. 6:4–5). This key confession of faith, still so dear to Judaism, is either claiming that God is unique or that he has no rivals. On either reckoning the Lord is the only God there is.

Jesus reaffirmed Israel's confession of the oneness of God (Mark 12:28–34) but takes us further. The one God is complex in oneness. The 'proper' name of God is expanded in the New Testament by Jesus (Matt. 28:18–20) to include Father, Son and Holy Spirit but without losing the oneness (Braaten 1989: 2). Moreover, given the ancient Jewish view that one's name signifies something of one's character, the name of God in its triplex form is not merely designatory but descriptive of what God is really like.

Ultimately, to make sense of the biblical testimony as sketched above would require a non-biblical term, 'Trinity', to capture the complexity. The will-to-relate is true of God *ad intra* (on the inside). God is a relational being, with or without a creation to relate to. The will-to-relate/covenant/commune is in the Godhead in an essential rather than an accidental way. Wonderfully, Trinity means that love did not have a beginning; it has always been (John 17:20–26). The Bible does not present a lonely deity who needed to win friends and influence people. Creation is the overflow of divine love, not divine need. In a world of so many faiths and none, the distinctive relational nature of the Christian God as Trinity is becoming more and more important. Trinity is the only God there is and at the heart of reality is a relational value, love.

Beginning particularly with Karl Barth in the twentieth century there has been amongst theologians a considerable rediscovery of the doctrine of the Trinity.[4] There has been a growing realization that the Trinitarian view of God distinguishes Christianity from the other important Abrahamic faiths such as Judaism and Islam, as well from other major world religions such as Hinduism and Buddhism.

Some Christian theologians see in the doctrine of the Trinity a social programme for today.[5] My own view is that, generally speaking, such approaches fail to be evangelical enough in the classic sense of the word. When the New Testament writers want to inform the consciences of their readers they move to do so from an explicit reference to the Good News. For example, when Paul wants to see an other-centred humility at Philippi he does not refer the readers to an eternal humility of the Son towards the Father in the Godhead, but to the Christ who humbled himself and became obedient even to the point of death in the gospel (Phil. 2:5–11). Again, when Paul calls upon the Ephesian readers to imitate God, they are to imitate how God in Christ forgave us (Eph. 4:32 – 5:2).

In grounding his imperatives on the indicatives of the gospel, Paul was following, whether consciously or not, in the footsteps of Christ himself. Of the four canonical Gospels, none speaks more of the relations between the Father and the Son than that of John. The so-called high-priestly prayer of John 17 is a case in point. In that chapter, Christ speaks of the glory he had with the Father before the world even existed (John 17:5). He prays that the disciples may be one with the Father and the Son as the Son is one with the Father (John 17:20–23). He also speaks of the love between the Father and himself that antedates the creation (v. 24). He prays that the love that the Father has for the Son may be in the disciples (v. 26). Yet when Jesus gives his disciples the new commandment that they are to love one another, he does not invoke the relationship of love between the Father and himself as the paradigm for them to follow (John 13:34). Instead, the disciples are to love one another as Christ has loved them. In the context of chapter 13, with its famous foot-washing episode, what is on view is not only that act of service but also the ultimate washing that the cross would provide. The imitation of Christ and not the imitation of the inner life of the Trinity is the New Testament accent.

What Trinitarian theology[6] helps us see is that, in the Christian frame of reference, the one tri-personal God, who is relational on the inside, is ultimate in reality and value, and that created human persons and their relations as divine

---

4. For literature on the Trinity see Feinberg (2001: 883–884).

5. Knox (1988) and Moltmann (2000) offer divergent examples of the application of Trinitarian theology.

6. For a further discussion of Trinitarian theology, see the next chapter.

image-bearers (more anon) are next to ultimate in reality and value. Such a frame of reference, in general terms, enables the Christian to be humanistic but not a humanist *per se*. Human persons and their relationships really do matter in the scheme of things. Human beings are not simply thrown up by a blind evolutionary process in an impersonal universe that is at the mercy of time and chance. One would expect and hope that Christians would be the great defenders of the human in a world where the value of humans and their relations are at risk not only from the traditional threats of war, oppression, disease, poverty and famine, but also from those who would seek to see the human replaced by the post-human in some kind of techno-utopia.[7] However, as valuable as the concept is for identifying God and underlining the general importance of persons and relationships, the Trinitarian revival has led to an inflation of the social importance of God-as-Trinity. More important for the specifics of social engagement are other biblical motifs, like the kingdom (rule) of God, so central to Jesus' public ministry. It links the Old and New Testaments in a way that the doctrine of the Trinity *ad intra* may not (Peters 1993: 184–186).

A relational humanity

On any Christian view the biblical presentation of humanity as in the image of God is pivotal for understanding who we are. In the history of the discussion of the doctrine of humanity, theologians have isolated three main candidates for the meaning of the biblical phrase 'image of God' (*imago Dei*). The *substance* view accents rationality and moral self-awareness; the *relational* view accents the male–female polarity as an analogue in some sense of God's inner life; the *functional* view emphasizes the task of exercising dominion. In my view these categories are not mutually exclusive. The text itself (Gen. 1:27) does not privilege clearly any one of them. Each view can be articulated in a fashion consistent with the biblical testimony and which illuminates the text. For the purposes of this discussion, however, I will concentrate on the relational and functional understandings of the image of God.

In the light of our discussion of the relational God, we should not be surprised to find that the will-to-relate is a feature of those creatures made in the divine image (Gen. 2:18–23). Our imaging of God is our acting in an appropriate relational way. The unfolding of the Genesis story shows the will-to-relate at work. Adam relates to God his Creator and carries out the creational mandate to

---

7. For a brilliant but chilling article see Ullman (2002): for an exposure of the flaws in such scientism, see Midgley (2002: 76–94).

exercise dominion. Some ecologically concerned criticisms have arisen in response to the Genesis language of dominion and subjugation (Gen. 1:26–29), but the subsequent narrative ought to allay these. Adam tills and cares for the garden zone (Gen. 2:15) and lives *coram Deo* (before God) to use Calvin's great phrase. Adam is no raper of the environment. However, God is not enough to assuage Adam's loneliness, nor are the animals (Gen. 2:18–20). Only an Eve can address this relational need (2:21–25). The language and story-line are simple but the ideas are profound. Some Christians appear to think that a relationship with God should suffice for human contentment. Indeed there was a time in Christian history when individuals in pursuit of God and holiness lived on pillars high above human society in order to do so. Simeon Stylites (c. 390–459 AD), to name just one, became something of an attraction in the ancient world because of this devotion (Cross 1978: 1276). But the Genesis story makes it clear that human beings typically need more than the society of God. We are created to need and love one another. And even Simeon high on his pole could pray for others. Given the Genesis presentation, a non-relational humankind is an aberration.

A relational rupture

The entrance of human sin into the world has disastrous relational consequences. As Genesis 3 unfolds the sad tale of human defection from divine benevolence, the will-to-displace God is the foundational problematic. We see both the will-to-withdraw and the will-to-dominate featuring in the narrative and dialogue. Next Adam and Eve try to hide from God instead of communing as usual (Gen. 3:8). Distance replaces intimacy. Furthermore, Adam will now dominate Eve (3:16) even as she desires to rule him. The environment itself will now resist human dominion and ultimately triumph over human limitations (3:17–19). As for contact with God, this will no longer be easy. Cherubim with flaming swords guard the garden zone (3:23–24). Humankind now lives outside of Eden, as the poet Milton put it, 'Paradise lost'.

What we have been dealing with is called in traditional theology the doctrine of the fall. Adam fell into sin and consequently also fell from his high estate, dragging us with him. French lay-theologian Jacques Ellul has a fresh way of encapsulating the Genesis 3 story. He called it *Le Rupture*. The rupture is far more fruitful in my view as a description of the human predicament outside of Eden. Humankind lives now in the midst of rupture. We find ourselves alienated from God, each other, ourselves and our environment.

I believe it was Charles Maurice de Talleyrand (1754–1838), the French diplomat, who said that without individuals nothing happens and without institutions nothing is preserved. This observation sadly applies not only to what is good but also to what is evil. Humankind's ruptured relationship to God can express itself not only at the individual level but at the institutional as well. The first biblical example of individual sin outside of Eden is the account of Cain killing his brother Abel (Gen. 4). Later in the narrative flow comes the tower of Babel, a societal expression of sin (Gen. 11:1–9). The builders attempt an institutional defence against the judgment of God ('so we may ... not be scattered'). Bad human laws are a feature of many biblical stories, as Shadrach, Meshach and Abednego found out. In that story, the pagan king Nebuchadnezzar institutionalized idolatry through a decree that the three Jews, as servants of the living God, could not obey (Dan. 3). In the story of Babel there is divine judgment. All were scattered. In the story in Daniel there is divine rescue and vindication for the three. The point of parading these biblical examples is to show that alienation from God can be located not only in individuals but also systemically in the ongoing formal and informal patterns of relating in institutional life. Liberation theologians have been particularly concerned to point out and address the problem of structural sin (institutions and laws gone bad) and we are in their debt for doing so, even if at times their analyses seem more sociologically than theologically informed. Moreover, not enough weight is given by them to the problem of individual sin.[8]

The human need for relational connection is far deeper than any educational or technocratic fix will meet. In fact, one of our temptations is to think that if humanity only gets the educational process right then all will be well. This is the Socratic Fallacy – 'to know the truth is to do the truth'. In our Western world, this is wedded to the technocratic fallacy – 'get the technique right and the desired results will follow'. Knowledge is important to human flourishing and technique has its rightful place too. The biblical writers give no grounds for the Christian either to be an obscurantist (anti-knowledge) or a 'Luddite' (anti-technology). But the story of Genesis 3 and the subsequent witness of Scripture tells a story of humankind that requires as the remedy nothing less than a divinely initiated restoration. To the story of that remedy we now turn.

A relational restoration

The Good News that Christianity offers the world is that restoration of our ruptured relationships is possible because of the grace of God. He showers undeserved favour on rebels. Central to God's gracious restoration programme is Jesus Christ. The Eternal Word of God has become flesh, lived a truly human life

---

8. Like Moltmann, liberation theologians see in the Trinity 'the prototype for what society should be' (Boff & Boff 1989: 52).

in obedience to his Father, died our death, was raised to new life taking our humanity with him and shall return to effect the ultimate restoration.

There are many great New Testament images that capture the enormity of Christ's deed of atonement.[9] Indeed, that theological codeword, 'atonement', captures something of the relational heart of the Christian Good News; namely, that Christ's sacrificial death can make God and human beings at-one. For our purposes, Paul's image of reconciliation is particularly illuminating as it is drawn from the world of personal relationships. Through Christ an estrangement is overcome. Indeed, through the grace of God we can be turned from being God's enemies to God's friends (Col. 1:15–23). Jesus' death brings our peace with God and, as we shall see, has cosmic implications. This reconciliation should not be caricatured as though a compassionate Son stands in the breach between an angry Father and a cowering humanity. Rather, as Paul writes to the Corinthian church, God was in Christ reconciling the world to himself (2 Cor. 5:19). Christ's deed seen in these terms provides the frame of reference for Paul's self-description as an ambassador for Christ who entreats his readers to be reconciled to God (2 Cor. 5:20–21). For in Paul's understanding the reconciliation has to be embraced by us before it is effective. The letter to the Hebrews expands our horizons further. Christ offered himself to God through the eternal Spirit according to the important New Testament witness (Heb. 9:13–14). The cross was indeed a Trinitarian event. Since this is the case there are no sound reasons for construing biblical teaching on atonement as advocating divine child-abuse as some of the more radical feminist critics maintain (Brown 1992). However, some crude presentations of the doctrine are open to that charge. I remember being taught that 'grace' is best understood as an acronym: God's Riches At Christ's Expense. Only without a robust Trinitarian theology of the cross are such caricatures of the biblical witness possible.

The New Testament church is one of the great outcomes of this reconciliation. In fact, the peace that Christ's death brings between God and ourselves should be manifested in the unity we have with one another as the body of Christ. Christ's death broke down – or at least it should have – one of the deep estrangements in the ancient world, that between Jew and Gentile (Eph. 2:11–21). Paul's own ministry was an exhibition of that broken wall, as he, a Jew, took the message of Christ to the Gentile world (Eph. 3:1–6). This went both ways, as he organized a collection of monies from Gentile Christians to flow back to help the poor Jerusalem believers (e.g. 2 Cor. 8 – 9). The cross has inter-subjective implications in a multi-ethnic world.

---

9. For an excellent discussion of the biblical testimony in its variety and implications see Stott (1989).

The church should be the community of the reconciled. The relational dimensions of that reconciliation are further underlined by the Christian sacraments of baptism and communion.[10] The Lord of the church mandated both: for communion, see Luke 22:14–23 and 1 Corinthians 11:17–34; for baptism, see Matthew 28:18–20. In the New Testament both baptism and communion are community events. Amongst other things, baptism signifies one's entry into the Body of Christ (the community of reconciled relationships).[11] The Christian does not baptize himself or herself. Others are involved. Likewise, and as the very name 'communion' suggests, the Christian meal is a relational occasion with God by faith and other believers by sight. This event celebrates and reminds Christians of the Good News of Christ's death on our behalf and the promise of his return (1 Cor. 11:26). Indeed, the meal ought to anticipate in a signal way the perfection of communion between God and his people in the world to come, as in the Messianic banquet of Isaiah 25. The apostle Paul makes it clear that participation in the event presupposes that Christians are relating properly towards one another. He was scandalized by the situation in ancient Corinth where a number of Christians in that congregation were trampling all over the importance of relationships (see 1 Cor. 11:17–34) and he had harsh words about the gluttony of some at the meal. The various gifts given to the church by the ascended Christ through the Spirit are not given for personal gain. Paul is quite clear that whether the gift on view is an utterance of wisdom or an utterance of knowledge or faith or healing or miracle-working or prophecy or discernment of spirits or speaking in tongues or the interpretation of tongues – all these are given for the common good (1 Cor. 12:4–11, especially v. 7). Without other-centred behaviour the body won't work. It is no accident, then, that in his discussion of congregational life at Corinth, Paul not only discusses the gifts given to the church and the way they should be exercised to preserve decorum (1 Cor. 12 and 14, respectively) but also writes so eloquently about the love that should shape the exercise of these gifts, making his presentation on Christian love (1 Cor. 13) the bridge between gifting and practice. Without the relational value, love, in operation, then even gifts such as tongues, prophecy and faith are worthless. Not even martyrdom counts without love.

The Christian hope for the people of God is nothing less than an ultimate restoration of the ruptured relationships we experience outside of Eden. This restoration, of which we have only a foretaste in this life, will require nothing less than a new creation. The biblical canon closes on that very theme as the climax

---

10. I understand the sacraments as material signs of spiritual and relational realities. When met with faith they are means of grace used by the Spirit of God.

11. For example, baptism is also an enacted prayer, 'an appeal to God' (1 Pet. 3:21–22).

of the book of Revelation presents a new heavens and a new earth in which God and his people are at home (Rev. 21 – 22). The biblical journey for God's people may have begun in a garden but it ends in a city landscape (compare the first and last chapters of the Bible). Paul nuances the future of creation in a slightly different way when he writes of its rescue from futility (Rom. 8:18–25). Peter adds that this new heavens and new earth will be a place where righteousness is at home (2 Pet. 3:13). To use an Old Testament idiom, we look forward to the *shalom*, or peace, that only the Messiah can finally bring (Isa. 9:6). In a further New Testament idiom, we look forward to the final arrival of the kingdom of right relationships where God's will shall be done on earth as in heaven (Matt. 6:10).[12]

A relational ethic

Fundamental to biblical ethical thought is the notion that relationship brings responsibility. The Ten Commandments, for example, do not locate moral obligation in an abstract set of rules. The obligations – not to worship idols or take God's name in vain, to observe the Sabbath, honour father and mother, not to murder, commit adultery, steal, bear false witness or covet – flow from a relationship that God established with his people through rescuing them from Egyptian oppression (Exod. 20:1–17). New Testament writers like Paul repeat this structure. The obligations of Romans 12 – 15 flow from the relationship established by God with his people through the mercies shown us in Christ in Romans 1 – 11.

This may raise in the minds of some the question of whether this relational seating of obligation only pertains to God's redemptive relationship with some humans. The New Testament leaves us in no doubt on this score. The relationship of the Creator to his creation brings moral obligation with it. To reverence God and give him due glory is the appropriate behaviour of the creature before his or her Maker. This, according to Revelation 14:6–7, is the eternal gospel. Paul presents the reverse of this behaviour in Romans 1:18–32: the pagan idolater who fails to give God his due faces the outworking of this rebellion in his or her lifestyle, which is its own reward or, more accurately still, judgment. In other words, God gives rebels up to the folly of their choices as an expression of his righteous (relationally appropriate) judgment.

---

12. Significantly, in biblical perspective death is the loss of relationship. So in the Genesis story Adam and Eve are driven out of the garden where the tree of life is to be found (Gen. 3:22–24); in Leviticus the evildoer is cut off from his people (Lev. 1:5–8), and final judgment is called separation from God (2 Thess. 1:5–12).

Since relationship brings responsibility, when a New Testament writer like Paul speaks of moral obligation he does not leave it in generalities. What we find in so many of his letters are household codes. He writes of the obligations of masters to slaves and vice versa, of husbands to wives and vice versa, and of children to parents and vice versa (e.g. Eph. 5:22 – 6:9). Christian obedience is worked out along relational lines. The Christian also has a relationship to the governing authorities. In Paul's minimalist vision the governing authorities are God's appointees for justice's sake and for human good. So the proper respect, honour, revenue and taxes are due to them (Rom. 13:1–7). In his letters he does not consider the problem of such authorities turning feral and demanding the allegiance that only God should have. However, in the wider New Testament witness, the book of Revelation envisages that scenario and the Christian's duty is to remain true to the living God even to the point of personal harm (Rev. 13).

Significantly, Jesus summed up moral obligation along relational lines in Matthew 22:34–40. The vertical axis is love for God with all one's heart, soul and mind; the horizontal axis is love for one's neighbour as for oneself. In this passage we see Jesus creatively combining Deuteronomy 6:5 with Leviticus 19:18. His life instantiated such love. He always did the will of his Father in heaven as John's Gospel shows (cf. John 5:30; 14:31 and 17:4) and his compassion for the needy demonstrated his love of neighbour. When the need was teaching, he taught them (Mark 6:30–44), and when the need was food, he fed them (Mark 8:1–10). Compassion for the needy neighbour integrated the ministry of Jesus towards humanity. He expected this quality of love to be the mark of his disciples in their relations with one another (John 13:35). Thus, in understanding the nature of the Christian's mission in the world, a wedge should not be driven between the ministry of the word and the ministry of deeds. To do so is to fall victim to a false polarization that pulls apart the doctrine of God the Creator who cares about his image's creaturely welfare from the doctrine of God the Redeemer who is concerned about rescuing his fallen image.

Paul echoes Jesus in his summing up of human moral obligation towards one's neighbour. Love fulfils the law. What does love of neighbour look like? Such love does not commit adultery with the neighbour's spouse or murder him or her, or steal or covet (Rom. 13:8–10). The commands of the law provide love with eyes to see what to avoid (e.g. idolatry) and what to embrace (e.g. honouring parents). Importantly, the commandments of God for the Christian are to be obeyed in a new location. To use some more Pauline language, the Christian is in Christ not Adam (Rom. 5; 1 Cor. 7; 15). The Christian lives not under Old Testament law *per se* but under grace in Christ. The commandments of God still need to be kept as they give shape to Christian love, as we have seen above. But the commandments are not the basis of relationship with God. Rather they provide directions for the outworking of that relationship in real life. Indeed this was also true of the famous

Ten Commandments found in the older revelation. The ten obligations arise from God's redemptive relationship to Israel (see above). However, with regard to Old Testament commandments the New Testament testimony needs to be carefully noted because the flow of redemptive history and its accompanying revelation have left behind some Old Testament practices. The light of Christ's coming and his cross and resurrection do away with temple worship and the Jewish Sabbath.

The Christian's love is holy love in biblical perspective and should not be confused with mere sentimentality that gushes but does no actual good to and for the other, nor has any real concern for justice. Justice is giving the other his or her due. For Paul that due is love (Rom. 13:8). Christianity espouses a relational ethic.

Conclusions

The Bible provides the Christian with a frame of reference for life and directs the reader to an object of devotion: namely, God – Father, Son and Holy Spirit. The frame of reference reveals Christianity to be a relational religion. We have seen this relationism in Christianity's doctrines which provide the Christian with presuppositions that undergird any attempt to formulate a Christian social vision. It is evident in our understanding of the relational God and humanity as *imago Dei*, in the rupture classically called the fall, and in relational restoration, especially in the reconciliation effected by Christ's death. We have seen the relational accent in the doctrines of the church and the future. We have seen the relational emphasis in the Christian understanding of moral obligation as arising from relationships with God, others and oneself. Indeed the very book that Christians draw their doctrinal models from consists of two testaments that could easily be re-badged as the old relationship and the new. These relational presuppositions have shaped Christian involvement throughout the history of the church. In the next chapter we explore this in more detail with reference to the understanding of God, the human person and the covenant in select strands of the Christian tradition.

3. Relationships in the Christian tradition

Jeremy Ive

Chapter 2 argued that the central tenets of Christianity, for example its concepts of God, humanity and salvation, are ultimately concerned with relationships. Unsurprisingly, then, one finds threads of relational thinking woven deeply into the Christian tradition. While this book develops a novel approach to social ethics, others in the Christian tradition have arrived at complementary or parallel conclusions. By considering some of them we can glean significant insights into a Christian understanding of relationships, position relational thinking historically and strengthen our understanding of how relational concepts might be applied.

This chapter necessarily paints with a broad brush and aims to be illustrative not exhaustive. It will consider aspects of three strands of the Christian tradition that are particularly fruitful for our purposes: the doctrine of the Trinity, the nature of personhood and the Reformed understanding of the covenant.

The doctrine of the Trinity[1]

In both the Eastern (Greek) and Western (Latin) churches, the understanding of the doctrine of God as three persons-in-relation has provided a rich foundation

---

1. The author is indebted to Jason Fletcher for helping make some themes in this chapter more accessible.

for understanding and valuing relationships. That is not say that understanding the Trinity is easy! As Hilary of Poitiers (300–367) observes in his *On the Trinity* (3.1):

> It seems impossible that one object should be both within and without another, or that . . . these Beings can reciprocally contain One Another . . . This is a problem which the wit of man will never solve.[2]

Of course, Bishop Hilary struggled to understand and articulate the very reality he admits cannot be fully understood. Indeed, we would be impoverished had the church not wrestled with how best to express the collective teaching of Scripture about the nature of God, about whom the apostle John could say: 'God *is* love' (1 John 4:8). Here, in the Godhead, is the ultimate rationale for claiming that relationships actually matter. As the Catholic Bishops Conference of England and Wales states in *Cherishing Life* (2004), 'From this mystery [that the one God is three persons] we draw truth for our own relationships' (p. 23).

The problem that confronts any attempt to formulate the doctrine of the Trinity is to be true to the unity and the diversity of God as Trinity. Historically, the diversity of God has been undermined by modalism: the depiction of God in terms of successive appearances by an underlying something, without allowing for the distinctive operation of each of the three persons at any one time. On the other hand, the unity of God has been undermined by subordinationism: the separation of the persons of the Son and the Spirit from the centre of the Godhead, which then tends to be reserved exclusively for the person of the Father. Orthodox Christian teaching has always affirmed that the persons of the Trinity are relationally interdependent as jointly the being of God, and yet each is distinct as a person. Gregory of Nazianzus (329–389) famously expressed the unity and diversity of the Godhead thus: 'No sooner do I conceive of the One than I am illumined by the splendour of the Three; no sooner do I distinguish Them than I am carried back to the One.'[3]

There are two different ways in which the unity and diversity of God have been expressed. The first approach derives from the Latin-speaking West and is known as the method of appropriation. This starts from the unity of God, and then attempts to map out from this the diversity of persons. In other words, it attempts to identify which essential divine attributes belong to each person.

---

2. *A Select Library of Nicene and Post-Nicene Fathers of the Christian Church*, ed. H. Wace and P. Schaff, 14 vols. (New York 1890–1900), Series 2, Vol. 9, p. 264.

3. *Nicene and Post-Nicene Fathers*, Series 2, Vol. 7, p. 712. John Calvin quotes this with approval in a number of places, for example, *Institutes* 1.13.17.

Thomas Aquinas (1225–1274), the most influential theologian of the Western church in the Middle Ages, wrote:

> For the manifestation of our faith it is fitting that the essential attributes [of God] should be appropriated to the persons ... such a manifestation of the divine persons by the use of the essential attributes is called 'appropriation'.[4]

Thomas claimed explicitly, on Augustine's authority, that the essential divine attributes are prior conceptually to the 'persons' of the Trinity. A weakness of this approach is that at the centre of its understanding of God is an unknowable substance that is not capable of being engaged with in personal terms. Furthermore, it does not give any account of the distinctive persons, except as manifestations of an underlying monadic entity.

The second approach is that of *perichoresis* (literally 'mutual making of space'). At the heart of this method is the notion that, as Metropolitan John Zizioulas puts it: 'being is constituted as communion' (Zizioulas 1985: 101). This communion is between concrete and free persons (ibid., 11). It begins with the notion of fully mutual communion, and means that the persons of the Trinity are lovingly bound together in such a way that they are continually giving way to, and enabling one another. Colin Gunton describes *perichoresis* as: 'an ordered but free inter-relational self-formation: God is not simply shapeless, a negatively conceived monad, but eternal interpersonal life' (Gunton 1993: 164).

Perichoresis takes us to the heart of God as persons-in-relationship, putting communion rather than an unknowable something at the heart of who God is, an understanding that is consistent with the vision of Jesus' high-priestly prayer in John 17. It derives from the Greek-speaking East, particularly the insights of the Cappadocian Fathers, and Mother, who described the relationships between the persons of the Trinity as the community of being.[5] Although the Cappadocian Fathers did not themselves use the term *perichoresis* as a noun, it does exemplify their insights about the Trinity (Torrance 2001: 102). Zizioulas notes that Basil of Caesarea was very unhappy with the notion of 'substance' as a description of the unity, and replaced it with the idea of a community of persons (Zizioulas 1985: 134). Basil wrote: 'in the case of the divine and uncompounded nature the union consists in the communion of the Godhead.'[6]

---

4. Thomas Aquinas, *Summa Theologica*, P(1)-Q(39)-A(7). BooksForTheAges, AGES Software, Albany, OR, Version 1.0. © 1997.

5. Basil of Caesarea (c. 330–379), Gregory of Nazianzen (329–389), Gregory of Nyssa (c. 330–395), and Macrina (c. 327–379).

6. *On the Holy Spirit*, 18.45 in *Nicene and Post-Nicene Fathers*, Series 2, Vol. 8, p. 167.

The use of the term with respect to the Trinity seems to have originated in the fifth century (Torrance 2001: 170, n. 9)[7] and was later used by John of Damascus (675–c. 749) who wrote:

> The subsistences [i.e. persons] dwell in one another, in no wise confused but cleaving together, according to the word of the Lord, I am in the father, and the father in Me: nor can one admit difference in will or judgment or energy or power or anything else whatsoever which may produce actual and absolute separation in our case.[8]

It is, then, the love of the persons one for another, which flows out into the relationship of love that God has with the world. Each of the three persons has a distinctive role, but they are so deeply engaged with one another, that they share this role. For example, creation is accomplished by the Father calling all things into being, the Son providing the coherence 'in which all things hold together' (Col. 1:17), and the Spirit moving over the waters and the inchoate creation as the witness and executor of the divine will (Gen. 1:1). Similarly, redemption is accomplished by the Father in sending the Son, who assumed human nature in its fullness in order to accomplish redemption, and by the Spirit in ensuring that the power of sin and death is broken.

Such an understanding of God has implications for our understanding of relationships. First, it leads to a rejection of the final independent significance of the human person, a concept that is rooted in a view of the individual as a distinct entity or substance to whom attributes attach. As Robert Jenson has pointed out, the identification of substance is at root a religious claim: the location of ontological finality in a created entity rather than in the Creator (Jenson 1988: 92). If 'substance' is accorded independent status, it becomes a rival god, that is, it involves a lapse into idolatry. Rather, the significance and meaning accorded to the individual is grounded not in some independent, autonomous substance but in the purposes and work of the triune God in the world and by his call to enter into relationship.

Secondly, the content and experience of true relationships can be understood only in the context of the work of the Father and the Holy Spirit with the Son. The creation of all things in and through the Son, in the power of the Spirit and at the behest of the Father, provides the norms for the operation of all law-spheres, and is the basis for their overall coherence. The alienation of humanity and of the world from God, and of humanity from itself, is overcome in the person and

---

7. See also, Pannenberg (1991), 1:318, nn. 2, 3.
8. John of Damascus, *On the Orthodox Faith*, 1:8, *Nicene and Post-Nicene Fathers*, Series 2, Vol. 9, p. 653.

personality of the Son. As the object of the Father's love, he holds open for us the possibility of true relationships.

Finally, a satisfactory understanding of history can be achieved only on a Trinitarian basis. The direction, richness and harmony of what has been, what is or what will be is related to the continual action of God, overflowing from the love intrinsic to the divine nature. Here the vision of God as triune is a radical challenge to any false complacency, or alternatively to any sense of *ennui* or despair. The greatest surprise of all was the resurrection of Jesus, accomplished by the Holy Spirit, which holds the promise for his transformation of every area of life.[9]

The significance of persons

For Christians (and indeed Jews) through the ages, the human person has held a unique and central significance. Humanity is neither a collection of unrelated individuals nor an undifferentiated mass: created in the image of God, each person is a bearer of infinite value. But how have Christians understood what it means to be a person?

Boethius (480–525) offered a famous and influential definition of the person as *rationabilis naturae individua substantia* ('an individual substance with the rational nature').[10] As noted above, however, the danger with this definition is that the person might be imagined as an independent entity. This was counteracted in the Western tradition by Richard of St Victor (d. 1173), who insisted on understanding persons not as solitary entities, but (drawing on Augustine's insight) as bound to other persons in love.

Thomas Aquinas tried to reconcile the individualism implicit in Boethius's vision with the more communitarian understanding of Richard of St Victor, but the two tendencies were never fully resolved in the West. Pope Pius XI in *Quadragesimo Anno* (1931) summarizes Thomas's view of society as an ordered arrangement of individuals in this way:

> Order, as St. Thomas well explains, is unity arising from the harmonious
> arrangement of many objects; a true, genuine social order demands that the
> various members of a society be united together by some strong bond.[11]

9. Rom. 1:4; 8:2, 11; Eph. 1:20; Phil. 3:10 (where the Holy Spirit is described as 'the power of the resurrection'); 2 Cor. 4:14; 1 Pet. 3:18. See Pannenberg (1977), pp. 170, 172 and (1994), 2:102.

10. Boethius, *De Persona et Duabus Naturis*, c. 2.

11. Paragraph 84; the reference is to Thomas Aquinas, *Contra Gentiles*, 3, 71.

In the twentieth century, Roman Catholic thinkers developed Thomas's insights. This so-called neo-Thomist revival began with the groundbreaking work of Pope Leo XIII (Pope 1878–1903), particularly his famous encyclical *Rerum Novarum* (1891), which dealt with the rights of the worker and cautiously affirmed modern developments in social and political thought such as constitutionalism and democracy (Koyzis 2003: 216). The church's social encyclicals issued since that time are known collectively as Catholic Social Teaching (CST). Its cornerstone is the dignity and social reality of the human being.

Rerum Novarum rejected equally Capitalism's harsh and dehumanizing treatment of workers and the socialist abolition of private property. In doing so, it appealed to Natural Law, that is, the plan and laws of the creator God which he has made immanent in nature, including human nature, and accessible to human reason. With Vatican II there was, in addition, a more direct appeal to the gospel of Jesus Christ focused on the church whose role is to help bring about the reign of God in history and to safeguard the dignity of the human person.[12] In *Justice in the World* (1971), for example, we read: 'Action on behalf of justice and participation in the transformation of the world fully appears to us as a constitutive dimension of the preaching of the Gospel, or, in other worlds, of the Church's mission for the redemption of the human race and its liberation from every oppressive situation.'

The goal of social engagement, as it would be defined in CST, is 'the common good'; that is, the necessary conditions for all people in a community to realize their full potential and fulfil their dignity. Or, *Mater et Magistra* (1961) states: the common good is 'the sum total of those conditions of social living, whereby human beings are enabled more fully and more readily to achieve their own perfection'. There is a clear recognition that such perfection is, as in the Godhead, necessarily relational. In its 1996 statement, *The Common Good and the Catholic Church's Social Teaching*, the Catholic Bishops' Conference of England and Wales notes: 'Communities are brought into being by the participation of individual men and women, responding to [the Triune] impulse towards social relationships – essentially the impulse to love and be loved' (paragraph 18).

Increasingly there was a shift in CST from the direct focus on the problem of exploitation of workers to a call for changes to make human work a genuine means for people to fulfil their humanity and contribute personally to the common good.[13] Towards that end, in *Mater et Magistra*, Pope John XXIII stressed the importance of advancing human dignity in the process of production and the need for greater international equality in and among national economies. In

---

12. *Gaudium et Spes* (1965).

13. Summary of the Bishops of Ontario 1991, 'One Hundred Years of Catholic Social Teaching'.

Laborem Exercens (1981) Pope John Paul II goes on to call for full employment and the proper representation of workers in unions.

In addition, neo-Thomist thinkers developed the notion of 'subsidiarity': decision-making needs to be brought as close as possible to the community concerned – indeed, delegation of power is not to be from top to bottom, but from bottom to top (Chaplin 1996). *Rerum Novarum* defined the relationship between the state and trade unions on the basis of subsidiarity. Pius XI broadened this application to all institutions in *Quadragesimo Anno*:

> Just as it is gravely wrong to take from individuals what they can accomplish by their own initiative and industry and give it to the community, so also it is an injustice and at the same time a grave evil and disturbance of right order to assign to a greater and higher association what lesser and subordinate organizations can do. For every social activity ought of its very nature to furnish help to the members of the body social, and never destroy and absorb them.

This leaves us with an essentially pyramidal understanding of society with the mediating structures such as families, unions and businesses situated a level below the state and with individuals at the base.

Foremost among neo-Thomists was Jacques Maritain (1882–1973), whose social and political philosophy was influential in the development of Christian democracy. Maritain anticipates a new Christendom which sets humanity at the centre, in the light of the humanity which Christ took upon himself. Towards that end, he distinguishes between the state and the body politic. The goal of the body politic (or political society) is the common good, and the state, as the highest part of the body politic, should serve that end (Koyzis 2003: 218). As part of the realization of this goal, the state needs to respect, uphold and promote the rights of the individual, the family and other intermediate associations, according to the principle of subsidiarity. Moreover, political and economic life needs to be guided by the values of social charity and justice (commutative, distributive and legal, as well as contributive, that is, the right of an individual to contribute to society as a whole).

A broader intellectual movement, or philosophical world-view, developed by Roman Catholic thinkers like Maritain and Mournier but also more widely by Protestant and Jewish thinkers in Europe (Macmurray, Oldham, Buber, Scheler) and the US (Calkins, Bowne, Brightman) had a significant influence on CST and merits consideration here. It is known as *personalism* and stresses the central significance of the person in human affairs and relationships of encounter as the means whereby human identity is discovered and defined.

John Macmurray (1891–1976) denounced René Descartes (1596–1650), whose views have largely shaped the modern Western philosophical understanding of the person, for portraying the human being as an egocentric self isolated from the world and others in its own private realm. Macmurray rejected the mechanistic understanding of society and humanity as promoted by Descartes (what Gilbert Ryle called 'a ghost in the machine') as well as the alternative organic picture of reality promoted by G. W. F. Hegel (1770–1831), where the process of history was understood to operate with little room for individual personality. Alongside, but also against both these conceptions, Macmurray argued that action, not thinking, is the basis for what it means to be human.

> The unity of modern problems is the problem of discovering ... a new schema of the Self which shall transcend both the mechanical and the organic schema; and which will enable us to construct ... a civilization whose mechanical and organic structures will be at the service of a personal life, whose meaning and essence is friendship.[14]

For Macmurray, a human being is not a detached observer, but a participant guided by faith in Jesus (Costello 2002). 'The Self is constituted by its relation to the Other ... It has its being in relationship' (Macmurray 1995: 17). Further, 'We become persons in community in virtue of our relations to others. Human life is inherently a common life' (Macmurray 1993: 37). Macmurray's insights were an important antidote to the egoistic and individualist thinking that tended to inform much of Western philosophy, but he did not carry it through into a strong understanding of marriage and the family.

Another personalist, J. H. Oldham (1874–1969), the first Secretary to the World Council of Churches after the Second World War, wrote:

> It is through our responses to other persons that we become persons. It is others who challenge, enlighten and enrich us. There is no such thing as the isolated individual ... Reality is the lived relation. Through sharing in the giving and receiving of mutual being the 'I' becomes real. Reality is an activity in which I share without being able to appropriate it for myself. Where there is no sharing there is no reality. Where there is appropriation by the self there is no reality ... all real life is meeting.[15]

Two prominent twentieth-century Jewish thinkers are also noteworthy. The first, Martin Buber (1878–1965), says: 'The I of the primary word I-Thou makes its

---

14. 'The Unity of Modern Problems', inaugural lecture, Grote Chair of Mind and Logic at University College London, November 1928.
15. Oldham (1942: 31).

appearance as person and becomes conscious of itself as subject ... A person makes his appearance by entering into relation with other persons' (Buber 1937: 62). Emmanuel Levinas (1906–1995), who emphasized the otherness of another person, followed Buber. For him, the ethical 'face to face remains an ultimate situation' (Levinas 1969: 81).

Mixed in with their Jewish background, both Buber and Levinas start from an existential basis: reality is not given but made by us as we experience it. This gives their respective perspectives both strength and weakness. The strength consists in their appreciation of the intensity of the encounter with another person, and the way that person cannot be reduced to an object of intellectual analysis. The weakness is in the lack of any content that can be given to that relationship. This is the paradox that lies at the heart of both their positions.

This is not to say that the resources are not there in the Jewish tradition, based as it is on the Hebrew Bible (the Christian Old Testament); quite the contrary. As will be indicated elsewhere in this book, the notion of covenant, powerfully developed, for example, by Elazar and Cohen does provide a rich basis for ethical life which takes the urgency of the ethical call enunciated by Buber and Levinas together with a vision for relationships rooted in the Hebrew Bible as the basis of who we are and how we are to live.

As with Trinitarian doctrine, personalism and CST, as the tradition which informs one important expression of personalism, is a rich stream of reflection that sheds light on what it means to be a human person. Here we see an emphasis upon the priority of just social relationships, the 'common good' and interpersonal relationships of encounter. That said, a weakness of personalism merits comment. Personalists make a tight distinction between personal and public relationships (Cowburn), personal and role relationships (Anderson) or personal and functional relationships (Macmurray) and maintain that only personal relationships, as central to the dynamic I-Thou encounter, are significant for human well-being. The weakness of this approach is that personalism has little to say about group or organizational relationships or the concerns of public policy. However, such strong distinction does not really work. It seems that all relationships contain both affective (or personal) and functional elements to varying degrees; few are ever purely one or the other. Thus, as argued in chapter 1, public life and working relationships need to be considered as much as private relationships, since both contribute to the development and well-being of the person.

The Reformed understanding of the covenant

In the Reformation, a new basis for understanding relationships from a biblical perspective was rediscovered and developed. This was the concept of *covenant*. It was highly significant in the thinking of the Reformers.[16] Indeed, as Elazar has written: 'The opening of the sixteenth century ushered in the second great age of covenantal politics.'[17] However, it was only from the seventeenth century that covenant theology (or federal theology, from the Latin word for covenant, *foedus*) received systematic treatment.

The Larger Catechecism of Ursinus, who helped draft the Heidelberg Catechecism (1563), the most generally accepted statement of Reformed belief, defines covenant as follows in question 31:

> Q: What is that Covenant? [i.e. 'the gracious covenant newly established with those who believe in Christ']
> A: It is the reconciliation with God gained by the mediation of Christ in which God, because of Christ, promises those who believe in him that he will always be a gracious father and will give them eternal life. They in turn respond to him by accepting his blessings in true faith and, as is fitting for thankful and obedient children, by glorifying him forever.[18]

Out of such a re-awakened theological understanding of the (new) covenant God has made with his people, and more broadly from detailed study of the whole of biblical convenantal theology particularly in the Old Testament, a far-reaching theo-political concept of covenant took shape in Reformed communities. Such a conception recognizes that God does have a unique covenant with his people. However, it also recognizes, as is particularly evident in the creational or Noahide covenant (Gen. 9), that God relates to the whole humanity, not just his people, in a covenantal manner. Elazar comments:

> Humanity's relationships with God, from Adam to the present, are seen as having always been covenantal. Covenants are the means by which God establishes authoritative relations with humanity, reveals his law, and manifests his extraordinarily gracious benevolence in light of man's sinfulness.[19]

---

16. Notably Heinrich Bullinger (1504–1575) in *De Testamento seu Foedere Dei Unico et Aeterno* (Basel, 1537), Zachary Ursinus (1534–1583) in *Summa Theologiae* (1584), and Casper Olevianus (1536–1587) in *De Substantia Foederis Gratuiti inter Deum et Electos* (Geneva, 1585).
17. D. J. Elazar (1996: 147).
18. English translation by F. Klooster and J. Medendorp.
19. Ibid., p. 171.

The covenantal approach as developed within the Reformed tradition,[20] then, involved a distinctive vision of society and the proper relationship between its institutions. Covenant theologians understood the whole community to be fundamentally bound to God as Creator and thence to one another and that this prior relationship to God must govern, order and constrain relationships between individuals and between, and within, social and political institutions. They also conceived of the body politic itself (that is, the people) as standing directly under the sovereignty of God. When combined with an emphasis upon the priesthood of all believers, this directly challenged a top-down, hierarchical vision of society, stressing rather a multi-polar political economy which locates authority in a range of social and political institutions, thus protecting and nurturing the richness of created diversity. The development of this biblical theological basis for thinking about social relationships was a crucial insight and challenged both the individualism and the tendency towards political centralization typical among early modern political theorists.

The radical nature of covenantal thinking can be seen more clearly by comparing it briefly with contemporary alternatives. Jean Bodin (1529/30–1596), for example, shared a Reformed scepticism concerning fallen human nature, but argued that a state must assume sovereign and absolute power in order to ensure the virtue of its subjects and to maintain social order (Allen 1960: 412; Skinner 1978: 287). Similarly, Thomas Hobbes (1588–1679), in *Leviathan*, argued for a strong state to escape the state of nature, where human life was 'solitary, poore, nasty, brutish and short'.[21] Later, Jean-Jacques Rousseau (1712–1778) proceeded from a much more optimistic view of human nature, but his vision for society was thoroughly individualistic:

> His first law is to provide for his own preservation, his first cares are those which he owes to himself; and, as soon as he reaches years of discretion, he is the sole judge of the proper means of preserving himself, and consequently becomes his own master.[22]

Against these, the covenantal understanding, rooted in that prior act of creation which bound humanity to God and one another, advocates a diverse range of social institutions and associations as opposed to political centralization,

---

20. Part 2 goes a long way to defining the contours of the covenant God made with Israel.
21. Hobbes, *Leviathan*, part I, ch. 13 (London: Penguin, 1972), p. 186.
22. 'The Social Contract', in *The Social Contract and Discourses* (London: J. M. Dent and Sons, 1973), Book I, ch. 2, p. 166.

and encourages the active involvement of all citizens in the life of the community.[23]

These insights, along with the expectation that the kingdom of Christ would soon be visibly and finally established, shaped the deep concern in the seventeenth century for the promotion of political rights, fuelling the Dutch revolt against Spain at the beginning of the century, and the conflict between King and Parliament in England leading to civil war (1642–1651) and culminating in the 'Glorious Revolution' of 1688. In Scotland, the Covenanters linked their concern for church order with a struggle for political freedom from the imposition of unconstrained monarchical rule from afar. Samuel Rutherford's *Lex Rex* (1644) provided a powerful clarion call in this struggle. These movements were the precursors for the revolt of the American colonies against the British Crown in the late eighteenth century. The New Englanders who spearheaded this had originally planned to be a 'city set upon a hill' (Matt. 5:14). The first colonists and their powerful English Puritan backers had seen an opportunity for working out the principles of a just order based on relationships unconstrained by the hierarchical oppression of the old European order.

Within this tradition, probably the most explicitly relational thinker in the history of Christian political thought, the German Calvinist Johannes Althusius (1557–1638), merits more detailed treatment. His work is an illustration of the richness of the Reformed political tradition.[24] Althusius published his *Politica Methodice Digesta* (*Systematic Analysis of Politics*) in 1603 in support of the small city-states and self-governing territories of the Holy Roman Empire, which were threatened by the rise of new notions of centralized sovereignty. He began his great work with a striking (re)definition of politics:

> Politics is the art of associating (*consociandi*) men for the purpose of establishing, cultivating, and conserving social life among them. Whence it is called 'symbiotics'. The subject matter of politics is therefore association (*consociatio*), in which the symbiotes pledge themselves each to the other, by explicit or tacit agreement,

---

23. The importance of religious faith to social order was presumed by Reformed theorists. As the acute observer Alexis De Toqueville noted about early nineteenth-century America: 'When the religion of a people is destroyed, doubt gets hold of the higher powers of the intellect and half paralyzes all the others ... men are speedily frightened at the aspect of this unbounded independence. The constant agitation of all surrounding things alarms and exhausts them. As everything is at sea in the sphere of the mind, they determine at least that the mechanism of society shall be firm and fixed' (De Tocqeville, 1972: 21–22).

24. These paragraphs on Althusius are by John Coffey.

to mutual communication of whatever is useful and necessary for the harmonious exercise of social life.[25]

It would not do violence to Althusius to translate his words slightly differently: 'Politics is the art of *relating* ... The subject matter of politics is therefore *relationship*.' He also offers a powerful statement of human interdependence:

> Truly, in living this life no man is self-sufficient, or adequately endowed by nature. For when he is born, destitute of all help, naked and defenceless, as if having lost all his goods in a shipwreck, he is cast forth into the hardships of this life, not able by his own efforts to reach a maternal breast, nor to endure the harshness of his condition, nor to move himself from the place where he was cast forth ... Nor in his adulthood is he able to obtain in and by himself those outward goods he needs for a comfortable and holy life, or to provide by his own energies all the requirements of life ... An aid and remedy for this state of affairs is offered him in symbiotic life, he is led, and almost impelled, to embrace it if he wants to live comfortably and well, even if he merely wants to live. Therein he is called upon to exercise and perform those virtues that are necessarily inactive except in this symbiosis.[26]

For Althusius, only by uniting in associations could people engage in *communicatio* (sharing, exchange) of goods, friendship and law. He differentiated between five types of association: two were private (family, college), whilst three were public (city, province and kingdom). He defended an ascending theory of authority according to which the power grows from the more local to the more general associations, so that the larger institutions rely on the consent of local and voluntary associations below it. He believed that the purpose of the state (or kingdom) was to protect and foster social life as it was expressed in the family, college, city and province. Like Abraham Kuyper after him, Althusius emphasized that each of these associations had their own integrity – indeed, he has been seen as the originator of the neo-Calvinist principle of 'sphere sovereignty'.[27] As a defender of small communities against territorial absolutism he maintained that cities and provinces should possess considerable autonomy as part of a non-federal, quasi-democratic German empire. One of his major goals was to defend the autonomy of cities and provinces against contemporary trends towards the centralization of sovereignty in new nation-states.

---

25. *The Politics of Johannes Althusius*, trans. and abbr. F. S. Carney (London: Eyre and Spottiswoode, 1995), p. 12.
26. Ibid., pp. 12–13.
27. See below, p. 64.

Of particular interest to this book, and although he drew on a wide range of sources, Althusius turned to the Bible for insight, particularly the polity of early Israel, which he treated in his major work.[28] The flourishing of Hebraic studies during the Renaissance and Reformation periods led to a whole series of works on the Jewish polity.[29] There was also a stream of erudite commentaries on the Old Testament text by Reformed divines like Calvin, Junius, Peter Martyr and Johannes Piscator. The role of the Jewish Commonwealth as a model for early modern political theorists has been missed by most historians, but was of vital importance in the late-sixteenth and seventeenth centuries (Boralevi 2002).

Althusius provided a richly textured picture of political community, one that highlights not merely the role of the supreme magistrate, but the whole network of relationships between different levels of society and between governors and people. By starting out from a definition of politics as 'symbiotics' Althusius is able to avoid a reductionist political theory focused entirely on the centralizing state. Instead, he offers a vision with more depth, one that never loses sight of the mediating structures below the level of the state, like families, voluntary associations and local government.

Althusius's theory is remarkable because it combines several elements: political organization is bottom-up, with residual powers located at the lowest possible levels (subsidiarity); the federal body is made up of functional as well as territorial groups (societal federalism); cooperation and consensus are preferred to major-itarian decision-making (consociationalism); and plural group liberties take priority over individual liberties (corporativism). Althusius therefore reminds us that there is an alternative to the dominant Western tradition of the centralized nation-state associated with Jean Bodin and Thomas Hobbes (Hueglin 1992). Too much attention, Hüglin argues, has been devoted to these theorists of centralization;

---

28. Classical writers (Aristotle and Cicero), Fathers (especially Augustine), legal texts (Justinian's *Digest*; Bartolus), Renaissance political writings (Lipsius, Machiavelli's *Discourses*), Spanish Catholic natural law theorists (Vasquez, Mariana), Calvinist constitutionalists (French Huguenots, George Buchanan), and historians of Germany, France and the Netherlands. He also found his inspiration in the ethos of the German guild-towns with their fierce sense of local pride and independence.

29. The Genevan Bonaventure Bertram's *De Politia Judaica* (1574), the Italian Carolus Sigonius's *De Republica Hebraeorum* (1582), the Spanish Catholic Benito Arias Montano's *De Varia Republica, Sive Commentaria in Librum Judicum* (1592), the Huguenot Franciscus Junius's *De Politicae Mosis Observatione* (1602), the Dutchman Petrus Cunaeus's *De Republica Hebraeorum* (1617), and the Lutheran Dietrich Reingkink's *Biblische Polizey* (1653).

not enough to writers like Althusius who envisage less centralized and more devolved forms of polity.

After Althusius, the idea of what Johan Van der Vyver calls 'the internal sovereign authority of social entities' surfaced from time to time on the Continent, for example, in the work of Georg Friedrich Puchta (1798–1846), who spoke of the independence of the church as 'an institution alongside the state' (Van der Vyver 2001: 5–6). The key point in the clear enunciation of systematic Reformed thinking, however, came with the Dutch Christian politician, Groen van Prinsterer (1801–1876) who in 1862 first used the expression *souvereiniteit in eigen sfeer* ('sphere sovereignty') to designate the range of competencies of the church over against the state.

His basic principle of the direct subjection of both church and state to God independently of one another was broadened by Abraham Kuyper (1837–1920), Dutch theologian and statesman who was Prime Minister from 1901–1905 and who founded the Free University of Amsterdam, to embrace all institutions. He said, '[God] did not give all his power to any one institution but gave to every one of these institutions the power that coincided with its nature and calling' (Van der Vyver 2001: 6). In his 1898 Stone Lectures Kuyper set out the view of sphere sovereignty: 'We as Christians must hold that state and society each has its own sphere, or, if you will, its own sovereignty' (Kuyper 1950: 8). He argued for an understanding of:

> *the Sovereignty of the Triune God over the whole cosmos*, in all its spheres and kingdoms, visible and invisible ... In a Calvinistic sense we understand hereby, that the family, the business, science, art and so forth are all social spheres, which do not owe their existence to the state, and which do not derive the law of their life from the superiority of the state, but obey a high authority within their own bosom; an authority which rules, by the grace of God, just as the sovereignty of the state does. (Kuyper 1931: 79, 90–91)

The state does not possess sovereignty in the spheres of (1) personal-social interactions, (2) private business, corporations, guilds, associations, or universities, (3) the home, or (4) communal autonomy.

> In all these four spheres the State-government cannot impose its laws, but must reverence the innate law of life. God rules in these spheres, just as supremely and sovereignly through his chosen virtuosi, as He exercises dominion in the sphere of the State itself, through his chosen magistrates. Bound by its own mandate, therefore, the government may neither ignore nor modify nor disrupt the divine mandate, under which these social spheres stand. The sovereignty, by the grace of God, of the government is here set aside and limited, for God's sake, by another sovereignty, which is equally divine in origin. (Kuyper 1931: 90–91)

Souvereiniteit in eigen kring (1880) presented a theory of societal institutions that showed how school and government, commerce and media, as well as home and ecclesiastic communions, could serve as redemptive vehicles of God's grace. Kuyper's vision was, however, expressed very broadly. The ideas were greatly refined by Hermann Dooyeweerd (1894–1977), who, with his colleague and brother-in-law, Dirk Vollenhoven (1892–1978), traced out a series of modes of the created order – each with its own unique purpose and relational structure.

> For this reason we must emphatically reject the view that the internal structure of an organization can be conceived according to one and the same functional or dialectical 'specific' schema for all types of organized communities. It is immaterial whether this schema is functional-juridical, or socio-psychological or a dialectical synthesis of these two. The internal organization of a church is not merely specifically but radically different from that of a state or that of a modern industrial enterprise. (Dooyeweerd 1969: 283)

Dooyeweerd and Vollenhoven argued that because there are different sorts of relationships, each appropriate to the particular aspect or structure concerned, they all need to be respected and nurtured.

The Reformed or covenantal tradition, then, sets out a vision of a plural social order where no institution or association can be said to encompass the whole of society or be at its pinnacle, all are equally subject to the rule of God. It conceives of a multi-polarity of diverse institutions and associations, each with its own function and authority, which relate to one another on the basis of their specific character. Within this context, the exercise of human personhood can be protected so that the full range of different relationships can flourish and develop. It is an understanding that works out more systematically what the implications of the Trinity are for society as a whole. And, in the case of Althusius, it relates its understanding to the detail of the biblical text, particularly the polity of early Israel.

Conclusion

The Christian tradition is full of rich reflection on the theme of relationships, interpersonal (I-Thou) and social. Exploring the doctrine of the Trinity strengthens our understanding of the relational dynamic at the heart of reality and encourages us to imitate God's character, rejecting the idolatry of individualism. Christian understandings of the human person also yield fruitful insight regarding the priority of relationships of encounter for well-being and, in the case of Catholic Social Teaching more generally, various socio-political outworkings of a commitment to the fundamental dignity and social reality of the human person. The Reformed tradition draws our attention to institutional forms designed to safeguard created social diversity and complexity, which is itself an expression of an underlying commitment to living out the command to love God and neighbour.

These specifically relational insights, however, have often only been partially developed, or mixed with other considerations, and their application has been patchy. With the possible exception of Althusius, a commitment to relationships has not been identified as the organizing principle of biblical social ethics or as the central motif of a Christian social vision, as is proposed in this book. In what follows we shall be setting out in a more comprehensive way the relational vision of the Bible, including how it was worked out in the history of Israel, and how that relational social vision is crucially relevant today. We start by considering the basis on which that vision can be considered authoritative.

4. The ethical authority of the biblical social vision

Chris Wright[1]

Rooted in reality

There are many people, both inside and outside the church, who will argue that the Bible cannot and should not be regarded as having authority in shaping the content of our social and political vision. Should not, because that would be to misunderstand the proper nature of both ethics and the Bible. Cannot, because the texts do not provide the clear, agreed and consistent answers that we seek. Recent debates about homosexuality, for example, have seen the notion scorned that the writings of St Paul, let alone the book of Leviticus, could provide a clear and authoritative basis for sexual ethics today.

Against this scepticism this chapter will argue that the authority of the biblical social vision is rooted in realities to which the Bible bears witness. Ethics is our response to these realities, the detailed working out of which is the task of hermeneutics and ethical construction undertaken by the following chapters of this book. First, the reality of God's identity predicates an ethic of worship and response while God's character predicates an ethic of imitation and reflection. We know and meet this God in the person of the risen Lord to whom all powers are now subject. Just as Israel was called to reflect the character of God in her social life, so too are we called to imitate Christ. The unchanging character of the faithful, just and loving God who created and

---

1. Much of this chapter is also published in C. J. H. Wright (2004: ch. 14).

redeemed us points to an underlying unity of ethic between Old and New Testaments.

Secondly, the reality of the story of God's engagement with creation predicates an ethic of gratitude and mission. In Jesus we see the climax of this story and the guarantee of its conclusion. The story of Israel and Yahweh is also our story, for if we are 'in Christ' then, according to Paul, we are also 'in Abraham' and heirs according to the promise. Our future is the future promised by God to Abraham, achieved by Jesus and to be enjoyed by the whole of redeemed humanity from every tribe, nation, people and language (Rev. 7:9–10). Our lives are to be shaped by the gratitude that looks back to what God has done and the mission that looks forward.

Thirdly, the reality of God's Word, delivered to us in the scriptures of Israel and in the New Testament, carries authority for an ethic of covenantal obedience, for us as for Israel, because, as the epistle to the Hebrews argues, we know the One who said these things (Heb. 10:30). In Jesus we have heard God's final word, the Word made flesh. The disclosure of God, rendered to us in the Old Testament, is now completed by the disclosure rendered to us through the New Testament's portrait and interpretation of Jesus of Nazareth. There are of course discontinuities and developments, but the New Testament authors were in no doubt that behind the Word that came to them through Jesus stood the same God whose word they had received in the scriptures they already possessed. 'We know the One who said . . . ' both identifies the speaker and affirms the abiding relevance of his original words.

Fourthly, the reality of the people of God generates an ethic of paradigm and analogy in which we assume the moral consistency of God and ask 'If this is what God required of them, what, in our different context, does God require of us?' In Jesus we have become part of this people, sharing the comprehensive range of identity and responsibility that was theirs. For through the cross and the gospel of the Messiah Jesus, we have become citizens of God's people, members of God's household, the place of God's dwelling (Eph. 2:11 – 3:13). Such an identity and such a belonging generate an ethical responsibility in the church and the world, which the New Testament spells out in some detail.

What kind of authority?[2]

Given the scepticism about claims to ethical authority, I will first discuss what we should mean by authority. This book focuses on the ethical authority of a

---

2. For a further discussion of what we should mean by the moral authority of Scripture see Rivers (2004).

paradigm[3] for society described in Scripture. It makes considerable reference to the Old Testament in looking for principles of universal moral validity which underlie its culturally specific provisions, recognizing that both Jesus and the New Testament writers point to the continuing relevance of the law and prophets. As the ethical authority of the Old Testament is also most suspect, this chapter focuses on the particular challenges this raises. Can the job of Old Testament ethics be done in such a way that the end product carries any kind of authority? A 'yes' to this will give confidence in regarding a biblical social vision, drawing on the whole canon of Scripture, as authoritative today.

In a survey of contemporary critical scholarship on Old Testament ethics, after appreciation of the positive gains that had been made, I observed that the matter of the ethical authority of biblical texts

> is precisely something which is not adequately tackled in recent critical scholarship ... It is possible to talk about the *power* of the text without really coming to grips with the question of its *authority*. The question is whether the Old Testament carries, for Christians, an authority which *requires* us to hear and respond to its texts as the word of God ... [In much recent writing] the challenge of the Old Testament texts is certainly there, and can be very eloquently expressed. Yet it seems somehow ungrounded in any view of prescriptive normativity. If the Old Testament text is not telling us what we ought to do directly [and it usually isn't], is there any way in which it is telling us what to do at all? And how can we find that out and articulate it? (C. J. H. Wright 1995: 89)

One major difficulty is with the connotations of the word 'authority' itself. In much popular usage it seems to be associated most often with the issuing of commands, based on a military model. Certainly, those who clearly reject the idea of biblical or Old Testament authority in the moral realm usually do so on the grounds that commands, and obedience to commands, are an inadequate, even infantile, basis for ethics. They are not going to be bossed around by the despotic god they perceive in the Old Testament. So in rejecting commands they reject the whole idea of authority. The Old Testament may be an interesting, even helpful (though that is usually stretching it) resource for our reflection on the ethical

---

3. The following chapter explores the concept of a paradigmatic ethic in more detail. In essence it means that early Israel was, intentionally, an example for us of how the relational realities of the created order and the commands to love God and neighbour should shape the life and institutions of a society. It is the coherent interconnectedness of this example that gives it its 'paradigmatic' quality and is to be imitated in other contexts.

problems we face, but the idea that it should exercise some sort of authority over us is regarded at best as quaint and at worst as dangerously fundamentalist.

But even for those of us who affirm our acceptance of 'biblical authority', the association of authority primarily with command does not sit comfortably with the material. The bulk of the Old Testament is not command, either issued to the original addressees and readers or to future generations thereof. It is narrative, poetry, prophecy, song, lament, vision, and so on. What authority lies in those forms of utterance? And furthermore, even such commands as are clearly there in the Old Testament in considerable number were not originally addressed to us. So, if we pursue the military model of authority, going to the Old Testament for commands by which we might take our marching orders for today's problems could be compared to scouring the orders issued by Allied Command in the Second World War for guidance in running the 'war on terrorism'. It's a different world.

One very helpful distinction is that between *authority* and *claim* in any biblical command (O'Donovan 1976). If I am on a crowded street and I hear a policeman call out, 'Move back!' I see his uniform and recognize his authority in giving such a command. His public imperative speech is authorized. But I also have to decide whether or not he is addressing *me*. If not, his command has no claim on my obedience – not because it has no authority (it has), but because I am not the one addressed. His authoritative command has no direct claim on me. However, I also recognize that the authority of the command *would* claim me if I were in a comparable situation to the person actually addressed. So biblical commands carry authority because of the one who gave them whose authority we acknowledge. They claimed the obedience of those to whom they were given in their own historical context. But whether or not they claim *my* obedience depends on many other hermeneutical and contextual factors.

Authority and reality

We are still, however, operating with a military model of authority and I believe we need to widen considerably our understanding of the word. In his majestic *apologia* for evangelical biblical ethics, *Resurrection and Moral Order*, O'Donovan argues that authority is a dimension of reality, which constitutes sufficient and meaningful grounds for action. The created order itself, by virtue of its simple existence or reality, provides an authority structure within which we have freedom to act, both in terms of permission and in terms of a wide range of options (O'Donovan 1986; C. J. H. Wright 1995: ch. 2). Authority is not just a matter of commands; it is also legitimating permission. Authority authorizes; it grants freedom to act within boundaries. Thus, the authorities of my driving licence or my bishop's licence, do not order me every day where I must drive or what sacred service I must render; rather, they authorize me to make those choices for myself, giving me freedom and authority to drive where I wish, to take services, preach, baptize, and so on. In those contexts I am an *authorized* person, liberated by, while still subject to, the authority of the realities that stand behind those documents (the laws of the land and the road; the canons of the church).

Authority, then, is the predicate of reality, the source and boundary of freedom. Now, as O'Donovan argues, the created order itself as a reality is also a structure of authority. A physical brick wall, for example, by its simple real existence constitutes an authority. You have freedom to do what you like on this side of it, or on that side of it. But your freedom ends when you attempt to run through it at high speed. It exerts its authority rather abruptly. Gravity as a force in the physical universe is an authority built into the reality of the way the universe exists. For us humans it authorizes an immense freedom of action on and (subject to the further realities of aero-dynamics), above the surface of the planet. But it also sets limits to that freedom. You may freely choose to step off a cliff, but the authority of gravity will decree it to be the last free choice you make. Reality kicks in.

How do these considerations help our understanding of the authority of the Old Testament (or indeed of the Bible)? If authority is the predicate of reality, then the authority of the canon of Scripture is that it brings us into contact with reality – or several connected realities, each of which has its own intrinsic authority. Reading and knowing the Scriptures causes us to engage with reality. That in turn functions to authorize and to set boundaries around our freedom to act in the world. If this all sounds extremely vague and abstract, it is time to explore in more detail what those realities are and what kind of ethics they generate.[4]

The reality of this God

It is becoming increasingly important in any talk of 'God' to be clear who we are talking about. 'God' is merely an Anglo-Saxon monosyllable that in its origins would more commonly have been plural – the generic term for the deities of northern Europe. The Bible introduces us to the very specific, named and

---

4. I was stimulated in this direction by the observation that the Bible offers us a 'revealed reality rather than a revealed morality' (Gustafson 1984: 140). I would add that the nature of the revealed reality in the Bible is of such a kind (in fact, *sui generis*) that a revealed morality is implicit within it as its authority predicate. But I take Gustafson's point: the Bible is not primarily concerned to give us a moral code but to introduce us to a living Person.

biographied God known as YHWH, the Holy One of Israel (among other titles), the one called Father by Jesus Christ and worshipped as Lord by Israelites, the God confessed as Father, Son and Holy Spirit by Christians.

> Everything depends on our confession of God. The covenanting God of the Bible is not to be understood according to the general category 'god.' Making a theoretical case that this God is unique is not necessary; it is enough to note that in the Bible this God makes a break with all cultural definitions and expectations and stands distant from the other gods who are preoccupied with their rule, their majesty, their well-being in the plush silence of heaven. (Brueggemann 1994: 43–44)

While the Bible does insist that there is much that has been disclosed about this God through the natural world around us (this God's creation), it is fundamentally the texts of Scripture, both testaments, that bring us knowledge of this God. Not only is Yahweh the God 'enthroned upon the praises of Israel' (Ps. 22:3, our own translation), Yahweh is also the God rendered to us by the lips and pens of Israel (Patrick 1981). Yahweh is the reality to which the Old Testament scriptures testify. It is therefore the authority of this God, Yahweh, that the Old Testament scriptures share, because we have no other access to his reality than through these scriptures. This 'rendering of God' in the Old Testament includes both his identity and his character. Each has its authority and impact on ethics.

God's identity

'You were shown these things [the exodus and Sinai experiences]', declares Moses in the rhetoric of Deuteronomy, not so that you might grasp the truth of monotheism, but 'so that you might know ... that *Yahweh* is God in heaven above and on the earth below. There is no other' (Deut. 4:35, 39). The big issue was not merely the *singularity* of deity (though that is important later in Deut. 6:4–5), but the *identity* of the God who had done these spectacular things. It was not just a matter of knowing God, but of knowing Yahweh to be God. In the Old Testament God is to be defined, identified and recognized only as Yahweh.

This underlines the importance of the disclosure of the divine name itself. It is not just a vocable of mysterious pronunciation: 'When Yahweh divulges his name, he identifies himself as the God already known to the fathers and promises a future in which he will continue to be recognized ... Yahweh has an identity which includes a specific biography by which he is recognized in the present and anticipated future' (Patrick 1981: 41). He is the living God, and the proper response on encountering him is humility, worship and obedience – as Moses discovered but Pharaoh rejected (Exod. 5:2). His reality carries its own authority and that authority calls for appropriate response. This was the essence of the challenge Elijah laid before Israel on Mount Carmel. The only god worthy of service is one that is real. Whichever god demonstrates his reality is the one to serve. 'If Yahweh is God, follow him.' The ensuing recognition of Yahweh's reality and identity as God carried its own implications for action. Reality authorizes appropriate response.

Similarly, in the worship of Israel, the acknowledgment of Yahweh carries within it an ethical authority, for it is impossible for Yahweh to be enthroned on the praises of Israel but ignored in the practices of Israel. Israel tried it, but the prophets pointed out that flagrant rebellion in the moral and social realm was tantamount to 'forgetting' Yahweh – in other words, not acknowledging him at all, no matter how fervent their praises.

The reality of the identity of Yahweh implies the authority of an ethics of worship and response. Inasmuch as we encounter the continuing present reality of this same living God in the pages of the Old Testament we encounter that authority also, and are called to respond in worship and obedience.

God's character

Yahweh is without question a character, a *dramatis persona*, in the great drama of the Old Testament. Indeed, as *the* leading character, Yahweh is portrayed in more depth and complexity than any of the human cast, simply because he participates in far more story-lines throughout far more generations than Methuselah had hot dinners. Given the enormous time-span of the literature it is surprising that the character of Yahweh is portrayed with such consistency. Yet that consistency, of course, is not lacking in surprise. Yahweh, as a character in the stories of the Old Testament is constant, but not predictable and certainly not safe.

> The identity of the biblical God is not rigid or static. Rather, he is a *persona* whose identity emerges as dynamic, surprising and occasionally paradoxical, requiring of the reader a dialectical process of recognition. When a depiction borders on inconsistency, the interpreter must grasp it as a surprising manifestation of the one already known. When a depiction is polemical, the interpreter must recognize that the identity of Yahweh involves elements of paradox. (Patrick 1981: 59)

The Old Testament introduces us to this 'Holy Character who is given us on the lips of Israel, who exhibits some constancy, but whose constancy is regularly marked by disjunction and tension' (Brueggemann 1999: 81).

At this point, of course, we could go into a long list of all the qualities and traits that the Hebrew scriptures apply to Yahweh. Such an exercise for a rainy day would be duly instructive and improving. When, however, Moses asked Yahweh to show himself, God was content to utter only a very few of the personality items on his CV, and these became the few that were enduringly linked to Yahweh's name in the narratives, prophecy, praise and prayer of Israel ever after.

'The LORD, the LORD, the compassionate and gracious God, slow to anger, abounding in love and faithfulness, maintaining love to thousands, and forgiving wickedness, rebellion and sin. Yet he does not leave the guilty unpunished; he punishes the children and their children for the sin of the fathers to the third and fourth generation.' (Exod. 34:6–7)

When this primary characterization of Yahweh is encountered in the Old Testament it likewise exudes an authority that calls for the response of reflective attitudes and behaviour. Deuteronomy 10:14–19 is the clearest positive example. If Yahweh is the kind of God who cares for the weak and loves the alien, then you should do likewise. Jonah's disgruntled reaction to God's gracious response to the repentant Ninevites stands in ironic contrast to his own quotation of the Exodus text as a reason for his original rejection of the mission: 'I knew that's what you would go and do,' he complains, 'because that's the kind of God you are. You are a God who typically forgives people and it makes life difficult for us prophets of doom' (see Jon. 4:1–2).

The reality of Yahweh's character implies authority for an ethic of imitation and reflection of that character in human behaviour. We ought to behave in certain ways because that is what Yahweh is like; that reality is sufficient authority.

Some more philosophically minded readers may question if I have not committed the 'naturalistic fallacy' – the point of which is to say that no set of natural facts by themselves generate an obligation. You can't get an *ought* from an *is*. If God is simply a 'fact', that does not produce ethical obligation. My answer, which I learned a long time ago from Keith Ward when he lectured in ethics at Cambridge, is that God is *not* a *natural* fact. Rather, his reality is *sui generis*, not a part of the natural universe. It is of the essence of God's unique reality that it does indeed generate ethical obligation. The reality of the biblical God is a reality that inescapably claims us as human creatures and demands our ethical response. God's reality predicates God's authority.

This needed to be said before moving on to our next point. Because if you can't get an *ought* from an *is*, how much less can you get an *ought* from a *has been*. Yet we are now going to affirm that the very nature of the story rendered to us in the Bible predicates an authority to which we must respond.

The reality of this story

That the Old Testament tells a story needs no defence. More than that, however, the Old Testament tells its story as *the* story, or rather, as a part of that ultimate and universal story that will embrace the whole of creation in its scope. In other words, in reading these texts we are invited to embrace a meta-narrative, a world-view which, like all world-views and meta-narratives, claims to explain the way things are, how they have come to be so, and what they ultimately will be.

The story that engages us in the Old Testament answers the fundamental world-view questions, 'Where are we?' 'Who are we?' 'What's gone wrong?' and 'What is the solution?' We inhabit the earth, which is part of the creation of the one living God, Yahweh. We are human persons made by this God in God's own image, one of God's creatures but unique among them in spiritual and moral relationship and responsibility. Through rebellion and disobedience against our Creator, we have generated the mess that we now see at every level of our lives, relationships and environment. The solution has been initiated by God through the choice and creation of a people, Israel, a people through whom God intends eventually to bring blessing to all nations of the earth, and ultimately to renew the whole creation.

Now the reality of this story is such that it includes us in its scope, for it points to a universal future that embraces all the nations. The Old Testament tells the story which is taken up without question (though not without surprises) in the New Testament. The whole Bible thus tells the story, stretching from Genesis to Revelation, not merely as a good yarn, or even as a classic of epic literature, but fundamentally as a rendering of reality – an account of the universe we inhabit and of the new creation we are destined for. Again, such a rendering of reality carries its intrinsic authority. For if this truly *is* the way things are, if this truly *is* how they have become so, and if this truly *is* where they are going, then there are all kinds of implications for how we ought to respond personally and collectively. At the very least one has to say that if the story ends in the reality of a final moral judgment by this God, as the Bible insists, then human moral choices matter now.

In Old Testament terms, the story had a past and a future and both were important in shaping ethics. Israel's celebration of its *past* is legendary. It was the very stuff of their existence, for it rendered to them not only their own identity and mission, but also that of Yahweh, their God.

> Sing to the LORD, praise his *name*;
>   proclaim his *salvation* day after day.
> Declare his *glory* among the nations,
>   his marvellous *deeds* among all peoples.
> (Ps. 96:2–3, my italics)

The name, salvation and glory of Yahweh were all bound up with 'his marvellous deeds'. He was known through what he had done, and Israel knew that to preserve his identity they must tell the story – whether to themselves or to the nations. For in telling the story stood the rendering of the God who was its prime character. So Israel told the story as a bulwark against idolatry (Deut. 4:9ff.). They told it as an explanation and motivation for the law (Deut. 6:20–25). They told it as a rebuke, to themselves (Ps. 106; Amos 2:9–16; Mic. 6:1–8), or to Yahweh himself (Pss. 44; 89). This story was a comfort and anchor for hope (Jer. 32:17–25).

As a motivation for observing the law, this reminder of the past focused especially on the exodus as the great model *par excellence* of the redeeming love and power of Yahweh. As such it generated an ethic of gratitude that was to be earthed in acts of comparable justice and compassion in Israel's horizontal relationships in the community (e.g. Exod. 22:21; 23:9). The blessings experienced in the story are realities that carry authority. 'Give to him [the released slave] as the LORD your God has blessed you. Remember that you were slaves in Egypt and the LORD your God redeemed you. That is why I give you this command today' (Deut. 15:14–15). The reality of the story carries moral authority.

But the story Israel told had an anticipated *future* right at its beginning. The call of Abraham included the promise that through his descendants God intended to bring blessing to all the nations of the earth. That vision shone with greatly varying degrees of clarity or obscurity at different eras of Israel's life, but there is in many places an awareness of the nations as spectators of what God did in and for Israel, and an awareness that the nations will observe how Israel responded positively or negatively (Deut. 4:5–8; 29:22–28; Ezek. 36:16–23). Ultimately, Israel existed *for the sake of* the nations. There is a teleological thrust to Israel's story. It is the story of a God with a mission and a people with a mission, to be a light to the nations so that ultimately 'all flesh will see the glory of the LORD'. Such a vision, a prophetic reality even if not yet a historically realized one, undoubtedly generated a range of ethical responses. For if this is the future guaranteed by the faithfulness of God, what should be the impact on the way Israel should live now (Isa. 2:1–5, note v. 5)? The question remains authoritative for us, too. For we share the same vision of the future, a future which to the eyes of faith is a reality – 'the substance of things hoped for' – and thereby an ethic-generating authority for those who live in its light. Our mission also is founded on the future inherent in God's promise, the future to which the story leads.

The reality of this story, rendered to us on the pages of the Old Testament, carries authority for an ethic of gratitude in view of God's actions for Israel in the past, and an ethic of missional intentionality in view of God's purposes for humanity in the future.

The reality of this word

There is a revelatory claim that is intrinsic to the Old Testament scriptures. It is possible, of course, to deny the claim – either by denying that these texts are actually revelatory of God (even if God's own reality is accepted), or by denying that there is any god there to be revealed. However, in seeking what, as Christians, we may regard as the authority of the Old Testament, there can be no doubt that such authority is bound up with the reality of this word from this God. It is our affirmation, following the New Testament, that in these texts the real God really spoke and still speaks. And the reality of this God's person and word constitutes an authority that grants freedom and sets boundaries – as the very first story of divine-human encounter illustrates with such profound simplicity.

Revelatory word

Disclosure is at the heart of Israel's faith: 'You were *shown* these things . . . so that you might know . . .' (Deut. 4:32–40); 'He has *shown* you, O man, what is good . . .' (Mic. 6:8);

> 'He has *revealed* his word to Jacob,
>   his laws and decrees to Israel.
> He has done this for no other nation'
> (Ps. 147:19);

> 'I have not *spoken* in secret,
>   from somewhere in a land of darkness;
> I have not said to Jacob's descendants,
>   "Seek me in vain."
> I, the LORD, speak the truth;
>   I declare what is right.'
> (Isa. 45:19, my italics)

The very heart of Israel's creedal faith is addressed to their ears (in explicit contrast to their eyes – 'you saw no form'), as something to be heard and heeded – a disclosure of reality which is both propositional: '*Hear*, O Israel, the LORD your God, the LORD is one', and relational: 'and you shall love the LORD your God with all your heart and with all your soul and with all your strength' (Deut. 6:4–5).

This last text, though in a class of its own, is one of many which seem to me to pull the rug from under the strange idea that revelation in the Bible is personal but not propositional (the subtext being that propositions are somehow cold, abstract and less than personal or relational, which has always struck me as very odd in view of one rather relational use of the word 'propose'). It is hard to imagine a more propositional form of utterance than Deuteronomy 6:4, though the context supplies plenty of other candidates (4:39, for example, or 7:9, or supremely the identity-card of Yahweh, Exod. 34:6–7). Do the Psalms not bristle with revelatory propositions like, 'The earth is Yahweh's and everything in it' (Ps. 24:1)? And the prophets would be left with rather thin books if their propositional disclosures of Yahweh's reality and the reality of Israel's status, failures and future prospects were removed. This is a word which declares, affirms and states, in no uncertain terms. But, as the seamless flow in Deuteronomy 6:4–5 makes clear, the disclosure of reality predicates an authority within which relationship and ethics can flourish. 'The LORD is . . . and you shall love.' There is no dichotomy between the two. Indicative flows into imperative. The same is true of the lavish sprinkling of the simple proposition, 'I am the LORD', through the commands of Leviticus 17 – 26. It is not a case of a 'revealed reality *rather than* a revealed morality', but a revealed reality which by its very nature carries a revealed, but fundamentally responsive and relational, morality.

This familiar combination brings us to consider the *covenantal* nature of Israel's relationship with God and of the authority of 'this word' within it. As we saw earlier, the idea of an authoritative revelation is most often linked (by those who don't like it much) with the direct commands of God. And then this 'command-obedience' mode is frequently castigated as an inferior brand of ethics for which the technical word is 'heteronomy' (obedience to the laws of another). Words like 'arbitrary' seem to pop out of the subconscious thesaurus and bond with 'commands', just as 'blind' does with 'obedience'. Or, in another discourse stable, the 'boo'-words include 'external', 'codes' and 'legalism'. As against such derogatory colouring of the whole vocabulary of command and obedience we need to set the covenantal dynamic of Old Testament faith and ethics (Mouw 1984).

The essence of the covenant relationship as portrayed in the texts of the Old Testament is that it is *relational*, not mechanical, arbitrary or blind. God has acted in this story for the good of this people. The whole relationship is based upon the constantly affirmed realities of Yahweh's love, faithfulness to promises, redeeming power, gracious patience, providence and protection. Predicated upon such realities, the obedience of Israel is framed as a response of love, gratitude, praise and continued blessing. I do what God wants because that is what I most want, too. The relationship between us makes such choices and behaviour natural and joyful. That, at least, is the ideal hope of the covenant. Furthermore, since, as we saw, authority is the source as well as the boundary of freedom, obedience to God's law is seen as fulfilling, satisfying, delightful and, indeed, the hallmark of personal freedom. 'I will walk about in freedom for I have sought out your precepts' (Ps. 119:45, cf. of course, Pss. 1 and 19). Covenantal obedience in relationship to such a God is, simply, the way to life and to living (Deut. 30:11–20).

Furthermore, the covenantal nature of Israel's obedience means that it is precisely *not* blind. On the one hand, it is constantly justified and enlightened on the basis of the wide range of motivational and rationale-providing clauses in the law itself. In line with our definition of authority, these clauses typically point to some *reality* (of God, or of the story so far, or of the nature of life in the land), and say 'because this is so, this is the authority for what you are being told to do, or not do'. In fact, the narrative framework of the Torah (with its past and future orientation), makes this implicit point: the authority of this whole law rests on the reality of this God and this story. On the other hand, Israel's obedience is not blind because it is actually presented as *consenting*, at least in intent. In more than one context, Israel is presented as making the free, informed and deliberate choice to submit to Yahweh as covenant Lord, even, on one occasion, in the face of some sceptical dissuasion (Exod. 24:7; Deut. 5:27–29; 26:17; Josh. 24:14–24). In other words, the authority of Yahweh was an authority freely chosen and submitted to by Israel – not a blind or servile obedience to arbitrary commands. With hindsight, Israel's promise to obey Yahweh may have been optimistic (isn't ours?), but it was certainly not blind, coerced or arbitrary.

Performative word

Finally, the reality of this word is not only revelatory. It is performative. God does things with words (Briggs 2003). The fresh appreciation of this dimension of speech-act in divine utterance (as indeed in many forms of human speech) is welcome, but hardly new. Isaiah 55:10–11 has a thing or two to say about the performative power of this word of God. The amazing fecundity of this word is that it both *refers to* and *generates* reality. Therein lies its double authority. These texts speak of the reality of God, Creator of the universe, Redeemer of Israel, already creating a new heaven and a new earth. But the same texts also deliver to us the love and justice, the will and demands, the judgment and promise, of this God in such a way that we cannot escape their ethical force-field. It is the word of God that brings forth the kind of living that the reality of God requires of us. The word is performative through our performance.

As Psalm 33 so richly reflects, this is a world-transforming word that puts the world to rights (vv. 4–5). It is a world-creating word that calls the world into being (vv. 6–9). It is a world-governing word that runs the world's history according to plan (vv. 10–11). And it is a world-watching word that calls the world universally to account (vv. 13–15). This is the authority structure, rendered to us in the text of the Old Testament, which makes righteous rejoicing, hope-filled fear and patient trust the only appropriate responses to such a word (vv. 1–2, 18–22), and warns those who rely on anything as paltry as great big armies that they have simply lost touch with reality (vv. 16–17).

The reality of this word, delivered to us in the scriptures of Israel, carries authority for an ethic of covenantal obedience, for us as for Israel, for 'we know the One who said' these things (Heb. 10:30).

The reality of this people

The fourth reality rendered by the Old Testament scriptures is that of the people of Israel. Whatever may be our historical reconstruction of the process of their emergence in late Bronze Age and early Iron Age Palestine, the fact remains that they did emerge.[5] Ancient Israel, with its distinctive view of its own election, history and relationship to Yahweh its God, is a historical reality of enormous significance to the history of the rest of humanity. We would know about the people of Israel to some degree, of course, from the material remains of their existence and the references to them in the literature of other contemporary nations. But essentially, it is the Old Testament that renders this people to us, just as it renders to us their God, the Holy One of Israel.

Now it is clear that for the Israelites themselves, the simple reality of their existence as a people constituted an authority for mandating certain forms of ethical behaviour and condemning others. To be an Israelite was to belong to a community of memory and hope and a community of ethical norms. Positively, the concept of holiness was a community ethic with a wide range of implications – social, economic, familial, political, agricultural, judicial, commercial, ritual, and so on (as seen clearly in Lev. 19, for example). Negatively, the conviction that certain things 'are not done in Israel' (even when they actually were), points to the ethical normativity of simply being 'this people'.

Theologically, of course, we could point to many dimensions of the significance of Israel's election, of the missional purpose of God for the nations that is the bottom line of the promise to Abraham, and to their faith that witnessed to the reality of the God they worshipped and whose worship they bequeathed to us. But my point here is simply this: when we consider what ethical authority the Old Testament carries, part of it lies in its witness to the reality of this people as a historical phenomenon. The existence of Israel carried its own ethical authority for those who belonged to that people in the Old Testament period itself. But more than that, the role and mission laid on Israel of being a priesthood in the midst of the nations (Exod. 19:4–6), of being a light to the nations (Isa. 42:6; 49:6, etc.), a visible exemplar of social righteousness to the watching nations (Deut. 4:6–8) – all of these gave the ethics of Israel a wider authoritative relevance than in their own society alone. As discussed in the

---

5. The guild of Old Testament historians remains as divided as ever over their reconstruction of the process by which Israel emerged. For recent surveys of the debate, particularly the archaeological battleground, see Bimson (1989, 2003); Dever (2000, 2001); Long, Baker & Wenham (2002).

following chapter, Israel was intended to function as a paradigm for others. In my view, this is not a hermeneutical ruse imposed upon the Old Testament retrospectively by us, but was part of the intentionality of election from the beginning. To borrow a phrase originally applied to Jesus, Israel is a 'concrete universal' (Spohn 1995).[6] Their concrete existence in history functions, not in spite of its particularity but precisely through and because of it, to disclose the kind of ethical behaviour, attitudes and motivation that God requires universally in human communities.

The reality of this people, rendered to us in the Old Testament scriptures, generates an ethic of paradigm and analogy, in which we assume the moral consistency of God and ask, 'If this is what God required of them, what, in our different context, does God require of us?'

Conclusion

The authority of the Old Testament, and indeed of the whole Bible, is mediated to us through these realities: God's identity, his engagement with creation, his Word and his people. As we read the Old Testament in the light of Christ we are called to respond across the range of our whole ethical environment to these great life-sustaining truths. Reflecting our gratitude for what he has done, and our confident hope in what he is doing, we need to imitate the character of the God we worship in our social as well as our personal lives. The implications of this for the social dynamic that should lie at the heart of our vision for society are explored in more detail in chapter 6. We are called to an ethic of covenantal obedience to the Word God has spoken to us and to learn from the experience of the people of God who, over the centuries, have been guided and instructed as to what it means to walk in the ways of the Lord. How we discern what this means in practice with the respect to the norms that should govern the structure, operation and inter-relationships of the institutions of society, as well as the conduct of our personal lives, is the concern of the following chapter.

---

6. Spohn includes an interesting discussion of a paradigmatic and analogical approach to using the concrete gospel narratives of Jesus in generating Christian ethics, similar to the approach I take to the Old Testament (C. J. H. Wright 2004). He recognizes that what he says of Jesus is also relevant to the Old Testament also: 'I propose that Jesus of Nazareth functions normatively as a *concrete universal*, because his particular story embodies a paradigmatic pattern which has universal moral applicability. (Similarly, the exodus event is the concrete universal which is normative for ethics in the Jewish tradition)' (Spohn 1995: 102).

5. The biblical agenda: issues of interpretation

John Ashcroft

If it is reasonable to turn to the Bible as an authoritative guide to the content of our social vision, what does it offer? The previous chapter suggests a multi-layered ethic drawing on all the genres of Scripture, in both Old and New Testaments, and encompassing our theological understanding of the nature of God as well as the range of commands given to different people in different contexts. It raised the idea of the people of Israel as a paradigmatic example to be followed. This chapter considers the theological appropriateness of a paradigmatic approach and explores how a paradigm should be understood and applied. We start by acknowledging some of the difficulties of hermeneutics and the significance of the context within which we have approached this task. We then consider the nature of biblical ethics, the way in which the Bible can offer paradigmatic examples to shape a framework for social reform, how to assess the relevance of different parts of Scripture to a particular context, and the nature of the principles that can be derived.

Entering the minefield

Over the centuries of their involvement in society Christians have read the Bible in different ways and come to very different conclusions about how we should live. The history of Christian social engagement is littered with the dangers of taking general Christian values such as justice and mercy and adopting contemporary secular economic theories to guide their application. Both free-market and Marxist economics, for example, have been supported by Christians. Looking back over the history of Christian involvement in social reform we can see both republican and monarchist readings of Deuteronomy around the period of the English civil war, or the use of the Bible in the slavery debate to support radical abolitionism, gradualist reform and a defence of slavery.[1]

Even if the argument for the plausibility of authority in biblical ethics is accepted, the problems of unpalatable texts and conflicting conclusions remain. Pleins, for example, argues that that there is not one biblical vision, but several, each representing the different agenda and context of different groups in society (Pleins 2001). He discerns the human voice in the texts we read and the cultural contamination it brings. Thus, in considering the 'bold social programme' of the Holiness Code, he sees in the treatment of women 'the key problematic for the contemporary interpreter, for there is no escaping the fact that the Priestly vision is built on the conscious domination of women as a group, though such is the case throughout much of biblical literature' (Pleins 2001: 68). The criticism should not go unchallenged, but an adequate response in terms of both the interpretation of the texts and their application requires careful hermeneutics.

This book does not seek to provide answers to all the debates that surround hermeneutics. Nevertheless, it is important to explain the approach and the context which have shaped the chapters in Part 2 of the book. Our approach draws on the experience of twenty years of involvement in social reform. It emerges from the need to produce practical and persuasive answers to real questions, and to act on them. The reality of hermeneutics is not just the definitive account of how to understand and apply what the Bible teaches. It is, sometimes, a messy journey, as was that of the people of Israel who were called to be pioneers in walking in the ways of the Lord. Social and economic reform has its classic texts, the expositions of agenda-setting theories, but social reform is also the product of the daily actions and decisions of people working under pressure in communities, schools, business, hospitals, the civil service and other institutions. In those moments of decision, and in those actions which shape our habits and culture, we need to see how to make the connection between our faith and the complexity of the situation we confront. The context of any hermeneutics is important. For the Jubilee Centre, the context of running practical initiatives to tackle unemployment, support organizational development in the NHS, alleviate consumer debt and reform the criminal justice system, among other things, has proved significant in interpreting and applying the biblical text that informs and guides our efforts.

---

1. See Noll (2002) for a more detailed study of the use of the Bible in slavery debates. Ferdon (2004) reviews the use of the Bible in the constitutional debates between 1649 and 1660 in England.

The nature of our engagement in social reform influences the hermeneutical task. For us it is, in part, about persuading people who do not share our faith. Thus, Scripture serves to guide and inspire what we propose to others (and which we commend as true to our faith) but cannot be presented as the sole justification for actions to those who do not recognize Scripture as in any way authoritative. Other arguments must be employed to commend specific policies.[2] Even where our objective is the proclamation of the gospel, biblical principles must communicate the character of God and not simply appear to be arbitrary commands. We turn to the Bible to open up debate, not close it down. It is in articulating why the Bible teaches what it does that real engagement begins. Thus both reform and apologetics require that we seek to understand the rationale behind biblical teaching.

Our objectives go beyond articulating a biblical world-view, important though that is. A world-view approach, with reference to key theological themes such as creation, fall and redemption, offers powerful tools for critique. Identifying false presuppositions and misplaced values is important. However, we also need guidance on what the outworking of a Christian world-view might look like in practice. This means considering the ethical norms that govern the institutions of society and their interrelationships. This is the great benefit of an ethical paradigm and chapter 15 looks specifically at the interconnectedness of the main organizations and spheres of activity within this paradigm, their goals and functions, and the laws that governed or influenced their operation. As chapter 17 illustrates, our own engagement with biblical texts has inspired action. It has provided a vantage point from which to question some of our own cultural assumptions. We remain convinced that the Bible offers a reliable, practical and authoritative guide to what it means to 'love', both individually and collectively as a society.

The nature of biblical ethics

Before considering in more detail what we mean by the concept of an ethical paradigm, and how it is both discerned and applied, we consider a number of aspects of the nature of biblical ethics. The first is that biblical ethics are social ethics. Secondly, that we seek an ethic that is both truly biblical and truly Christian. Thirdly, our approach should be educative and missiological. Fourthly, we must be true to both the consistency and particularity of biblical ethics. Finally, we must capture both the realism and the idealism of biblical ethics.

---

2. For justification of this approach for the world of academia see Marsden (1997).

A social ethic

In their calling to be a priestly nation and a light to the nations, the social ethics of the people of Israel were intended to be an example. These social ethics are more than 'simply a compendium of moral teaching to enable the individual to lead a privately upright life before God' (C. J. H. Wright 2004: 51). The Old Testament is, of course, deeply interested in people's individual moral choices and behaviour. However, the second-person singular address to the individual is in the context of the community. 'God's purpose was not to invent a production line for righteous individuals, but to create a new community of people who in their social life would embody those qualities of righteousness, peace, justice and love which reflect God's own character and were God's original purpose for humanity' (C. J. H. Wright 2004: 51).[3]

Hill, drawing on Carter (1990), advocates an 'interrelationist' understanding of society as a third option to individualist or collectivist accounts. 'For the biblical writers, bi-polar relationships seem to be the basic units of social reality. Neither the individual nor society as a whole seems to be the foundational unit. A completely different account of society is adopted' (Hill 2002: 103). In this context Hill argues that the purpose of social structures is to be understood in terms of the good of relationships, not simply the good of individuals or of society as a whole (ibid. 106). For Hill, this interrelationist understanding of society, coupled with a proper understanding of Christ's authority, allows us to avoid both a social gospel which conflates the kingdom and the world and a pietism that neglects social structures.

> As the patterning of relationships, social structures will not only influence the development of individuals but be influenced by those individuals acting in relationship. The complexities of social change may be daunting but we will not have created and admitted an independent entity that reeks uncontrollable and irresistible havoc on the individual members of society. Social ethics and social change will continue to be realistic possibilities. (ibid., 114)

It is also important not to confuse personal and institutional principles.[4] Turning the other cheek is a good principle to guide our actions when we are wronged personally. It is not a mandate for policies which seek to turn other people's cheeks for them. The underlying values of forgiveness and reconciliation may still guide the goals that policies and institutions seek to achieve, but the

---

3. The nature of these qualities is discussed in ch. 6.
4. See ch. 15 for a definition of institutions and an account of how biblical institutional norms cohere.

direct application of those values may not be appropriate in specific judicial situations. Institutional norms are of special importance for social policy as they have two vital roles.[5] By defining the structure and function of institutions, they determine the political, economic and social system, and are the basis for the *goals* of social policy. These have widespread implications for the welfare of individuals, although norms only affect them indirectly via the institution. Christians concerned with social reform will therefore need to develop a coherent set of such institutional norms.

A Christian ethic

The claim that Jesus is Lord underpins political theology.[6] As Christians, our personal obedience is claimed and all institutions are set under Christ's authority. Chapter 8 considers the implications of this for political authority, while in chapter 13 we see how, in the light of Christ, our understanding of justice and forgiveness are for ever changed. Our understanding of what is truly good is informed by the ethical teaching of the New Testament. An account of what it means to live a life of love would be stunted and impoverished if not guided by the teaching and example of Christ. In the epistles we begin to see in more detail what this account means for our life as a community and the potential for the church to be a transforming presence in the world. In the context of social reform we seek to shape the institutions of a fallen society. The redemption of society is in process but we continue to live with the reality of sin. We need, therefore, wisdom to discern what biblical norms can be legitimately 'enforced' through legislation in a fallen and pluralistic society. Jesus, for example, describes divorce law as being given for the hardness of men's hearts and forcefully sets out the higher standard expected of Christians (Matt. 19:8). It is important that such standards are lived out within the church as a witness to society.

It is through Jesus' teaching that we understand that the Old Testament remains a guide for reforming the institutions of society. However, Christ's authority is not expressed in literal adherence to Old Testament law, as advocated by theonomists.

> Such literal imitation is not only practically impossible (because we do not live in the world of an ancient Near Eastern agrarian economy and tribal culture); it is also theologically impossible (because neither the church nor any modern state stands in exactly the same relationship to God as Israel did in the Old Testament). Such claimed literal imitation in our very different circumstances also fails to take account

---

5. This is discussed in greater detail in Schluter & Clements (1990: 46–48).
6. O'Donovan (1994; 1996) sets out the basis for a Christian political theology.

of how God takes history and culture seriously and embedded his ethical requirements on Israel very specifically in their context. And it mistakenly equates Old Testament ethics more or less exclusively with the law codes and their commands and penalties, whereas, as we have seen, the narratives and all the rest of the Old Testament scriptures are of just as much importance. (C. J. H. Wright 2004: 63)[7]

Nor can we dismiss the Old Testament as ethically irrelevant on the grounds that it has all been fulfilled in Christ and relegated to a dispensation now long past, or because of a jaundiced view of what we see in the Old Testament and the magnitude of the hermeneutical difficulties.

All such neglect of the Old Testament for ethical purposes seems to me impossible to reconcile with either the seal of Jesus' authority on the abiding validity of the law and the prophets (Matthew 5:17–19), or Paul's affirmation that all scripture (meaning the Old Testament) is not only inspired but also profitable for ethical guidance and written for our instruction (2 Timothy 3:16). If Israel was meant to be 'a light to the nations', then that light must be allowed to shine. We have to find some way to let the light penetrate the centuries and illuminate our world. (C. J. H. Wright 2004: 63)

It is by overcoming a false dichotomy between creation and kingdom ethics that we are able to regard the institutional tradition of Israel as ethically normative and Christian (Schluter & Clements 1990). Clines' (1997) analysis of Genesis 1 – 3 supports the idea that relationships between God and humans, and between humans, belong to the purpose of creation. Schmid (1984) and Knierim (1995) emphasize $ṣedeq/ṣĕdāqâ$[8] as a characteristic of God imprinted on the universe itself at creation. A robust Trinitarian theology sees Christ at work both in creation and in securing its redemption though his death and resurrection. The concern for relationships, established in creation and demonstrated in the life of Israel, is fulfilled in Christ. In his account of paradigmatic ethics, Janzen concludes:

To ask whether Old Testament ethics can be abandoned once Jesus has manifested its climax is to ask whether salvation from Egypt, from political-economic oppression, is no longer God's will once salvation has been extended, through Jesus,

---

7. A helpful short critique of the theonomist approach can be found in C. J. H. Wright (2004: 403–408).

8. Usually translated as 'righteousness' but includes salvation and right relationships within the field of meaning. See ch. 6, p. 109 for further discussion.

to embrace the defeat of cosmic powers. It is to ask whether land is no longer to be tended responsibly once we know that an eternal home has been prepared for us. It is to ask whether father and mother should no longer be maintained in dignity once we know that we have new fathers and mothers and brothers and sisters from among those who do the will of God. To truncate God's story like this, though frequently done in the church, was certainly not the gospel of Jesus.
(Janzen 1994: 210)

Educative and missiological

In Christ the universal mission foreshadowed in the Old Testament is brought to its climax. This raises the third point, that our approach should be educative and missiological, for that is the purpose of the texts themselves. The previous chapter has argued that biblical ethics flow from the reality of God and the story of a people with whom he entered into a special relationship as part of his redemptive purpose. The result was not a rule book which prescribes in detail how we should act in every area of life for all time. Indeed, experience shows that our relationships, with either God or each other, cannot flourish where there are rules for every minute aspect of life to which our only response is to obey or disobey. That does not foster wisdom and ethical maturity. 'In Deuteronomy 17:18–20, the written legal text (the Book of the Law) is intended for the king. It is for his instruction, and its primary purpose is to make him wise. In contrast to the legislative model ... the law has, primarily, a sapiential function' (Burnside 2003: 11; cf. Jackson 1989: 246–247). This educative role is also drawn out in Deuteronomy 4:5–8 where observance of the law is expected to prompt other nations to ask 'what other nation is so great as to have such righteous decrees and laws?' Though not given directly to them, the law was given for the benefit of other nations (Ps. 147:20). It was entrusted to Israel, to enable them to live as a light (Isa. 42:6), such that, in the prophetic vision, the law would 'go forth' to the nations, or they would 'come up' to Jerusalem to learn it (Mic. 4:2).

Consistent and particular

Our approach is based on a belief that the ideals by which we should live do not change, and that all Scripture guides us reliably and consistently. There are, of course, different emphases which may exist in some tension. O'Donovan notes that 'if political theologians are to treat ancient Israel's political tradition as normative, they must observe the discipline of treating it as history' (O'Donovan 1996: 27). We must recognize their development as a nation, and not fix upon a single part of that history. We must listen to the voice of the biblical authors themselves, recognizing the applied particularity of individual texts and not apply our own narrative. Goldingay argues that we should not be paralysed by the particularity of the Bible's statements but rather we should 'rejoice in their particularity because it shows us how the will of God was expressed in their context, and we take them as a paradigm for our own ethical construction' (Goldingay 1991: 55).

In entering the minefield of hermeneutics, the most important safeguard is to use all of Scripture,[9] continually, with humility and in community. This precludes working with single themes or isolated principles. 'Justice' or 'stewardship', for example, capture important elements of a biblical vision, but are incomplete in themselves. Taken out of context, a single issue is ripe for misapplication. As we shall see in Part 2, biblical teaching on social, economic and political issues is closely interrelated. For example, criminal justice teaching depends upon and seeks to protect family and community relationships. These, in turn, are influenced and protected by a distinctive approach to economic and political life.

Realistic and idealistic

The poor and vulnerable are not served by naïve idealism. The gritty realism of Old Testament law resonates with many of today's situations – it deals with rape and murder, theft and expropriation, war and rebellion. The implication of this is that in looking for biblical guidance as to how a vision for right relationships might be made incarnate in the life and institutions of contemporary society, the Old Testament may offer relevant examples. The approach to social reform advocated in this book might be described as pragmatic idealism. We should not shirk from a vision of a very different (and better) society. Christians should, as far as possible, live out that higher vision. But, through engaging with the experience of Israel, we can also be guided towards pragmatic solutions which take public policy today in the right direction, while never reaching the perfection to which we aspire.

A paradigmatic ethic

A paradigm is a model or pattern which enables us to look at many different situations while holding on to some single concept or set of governing principles. In a paradigm all the parts bear a relationship to each other and it is this pattern of relationships that we are to learn from. So, we work by analogy from a specific known reality (the paradigm) to a wider or different context in which there are problems to be solved, answers to be found, and choices to be made. It provides a

---

9. We will go on to consider how the importance of drawing on the whole of Scripture is reconciled with the recognition that different parts of Scripture may be particularly instructive or more appropriate in guiding responses to different situations.

framework within which principles can be coherently interpreted, captures the essence of the underlying logic or intention behind individual laws, and provides a practical example of how a set of principles can be combined with specific laws and institutions. Thus, in the following section, in describing Israel as a paradigm we refer not to one selected fixed expression of its national life, but to the pattern of institutional norms, which were expressed with varying degrees of faithfulness over the course of Israel's history.

Israel as a paradigm

A paradigm is more than an example in the way that we might look to America as an example of democratic capitalism, Britain as an example of parliamentary democracy or to continental Europe for an alternative to the Anglo-Saxon approach. Such examples may be informative, but they are not authoritative. The ethical authority of the *paradigm* lies in the decisive finality of Christ's resurrection and in the authority of the God who has called and guided his people to be that paradigm. It expresses underlying norms and, because of the authority both of those norms and of the God who was involved in and responded to their concrete expression, it is authoritative for all people. Rivers (2004) notes two aspects of authority: the political authority which requires obedience and the evidential authority which reliably informs and guides us. Both senses of authority apply to Israel as a paradigm, and careful reasoning is needed to determine in what relevant ways the commands addressed to Israel are addressed to us.

Wright offers fruitful thinking on how to use paradigms. Grammar is one example (if *parler* is the paradigm verb we can use it to get right the endings of other similar verbs), though a little formulaic for the irregular character of real life. He adds other examples, sometimes drawing on the philosophy of science (C. J. H. Wright 2004: 66–69). He cites Kuhn's (1970) use of the term to describe both the constellation of beliefs and values shared by a given community as well as specific exemplary 'concrete puzzle solutions'. Poythress (1988) refers to these as a 'disciplinary matrix' and 'exemplar'. In this book we focus on the extent to which Israel was intended to serve as a paradigmatic example. As we see how Israel worked out the 'puzzle' of living according to their constellation, or matrix, of beliefs, we can find pointers as to how we might solve the puzzle in our context.

It is by looking at how biblical teaching coheres as a model that we are pointed to the vision for society. A starting point for the Jubilee Centre in developing this approach was Jesus' teaching on the greatest commandment (Matt. 22:34–40). His statement that all the Law and the Prophets hang on the commandments to love God and neighbour suggested an organizing principle. It prompts the question as to what in practice it means to love and how a society can be structured to sustain loving relationships. The Jubilee Centre's second research paper set out our first attempt to explore whether the Law and Prophets could provide a set of institutional norms for societies today (Schluter & Clements 1986, 1990).

At the same time, Chris Wright developed the idea of an ethical paradigm from a different starting point, the image of Israel as a kingdom of priests with its connotations of acting as a teacher, model and mediator for the nations (Exod. 19:1–6).

> The social shape of Israel was not an incidental freak of ancient history, nor was it just a temporary, material by-product of their spiritual message. We cannot set aside the social dimension of the Old Testament as a kind of husk, out of which we claim to extract a kernel of spiritual timeless truths. Rather, the social reality of Israel was an integral part of what God had called them into existence for. Theologically, the purpose of Israel's existence was to be a vehicle both for God's revelation and for the blessing of humanity. They were not only the bearers of redemption, but were to be a model of what a redeemed community should be like, living in obedience to God's will. Their social structure, aspirations, principles and policies, so organically related to their covenantal faith in the Lord, were also part of the content of that revelation, part of the pattern of redemption. God's message of redemption through Israel was not just verbal; it was visible and tangible. They, the medium, were themselves part of the message. Simply by existing and being obedient to the covenant law of the Lord, they would raise questions among the nations about the nature of their God and the social justice of their community. (C. J. H. Wright 2004: 62)

Bartholomew also draws on the image of Israel as a priestly nation in his introduction to a dialogue with O'Donovan on the ethical and political use of the Bible. He quotes Durham's description of Israel as 'a display-people, a showcase to the world of how being in covenant with Yahweh changes a people' (Bartholomew et al. 2002: 2) as well as noting the use of the language of royal priesthood in 1 Peter 2:9. He concludes that 'in the Old Testament and the New, the image of a royal priesthood alerts us to God's intention for his people to mediate his presence and light in the good, but fallen, world'.

Paradigmatic cases

This book explores the way in which Israel offers a paradigm of what it means for a society to build into its institutions the concern to love both God and neighbour. Other authors have used the term 'paradigm' to describe *examples* which powerfully bring together a range of beliefs and values. Hanson (1986), for example, suggests that key events such as the exodus were so powerful that they took on a paradigmatic quality guiding how God could be expected to act and how his people should respond. Janzen (1994) suggests that the Bible offers a number of archetypal role-models – composite pictures of an ideal – in much the same way that we may construct an image of a good father or good driver. He goes on to argue that these paradigms are fulfilled in the person of Jesus.

This sense of a concrete example is useful in understanding some aspects of biblical law. There are several genres of biblical literature that should be read in different ways. The corpus of material generally regarded as 'biblical law' is but one of these genres and its interpretation may be guided by the others. A semiotic understanding of biblical law suggests that individual passages may describe paradigmatic cases.[10] It is important that the Hebrew concept of law is not assumed to be the same as modern Western traditions and interpreted in the same manner. Attempts to derive principles which treat the biblical text as, for example, common law are liable to misunderstand the nature and intent of biblical law.

> Modern legal praxis is based on the Rule of Law, that is, the belief that adjudication should be governed by laws and not by people. This legislative model of law, based upon the application of statutes in court, holds that general normative propositions laid down in advance are normally sufficient to deal with every human situation that may arise. The role of the judge is to apply general rules laid down by a higher authority, whether the legislature itself or superior courts in a system of precedents … [T]his Western conception of law is culturally contingent and does not reflect biblical legal praxis. In other words, the idea that judges should see their role as the application of general rules laid down by authority was not the dominant conception of the relationship between legislator and judge in biblical law. (Burnside 2003: 10)

Burnside (2003: 11–15) cites a number of reasons for this:

- The educative role of the law is seen in the depiction of the book of the law given to the king to be read 'all the days of his life so that he may learn to revere the Lord his God and follow carefully all the words of this law and these decrees' (Deut. 17:19).
- Newly appointed judges are charged in general terms to act justly and avoid corruption (Deut. 16:18–20). They are not asked to follow detailed rules and even when local judges need to consult central authorities (17:8–13) there is no reference to any authoritative set of rules that the priests have to apply.
- Executing justice is a matter of exercising Solomonic wisdom, not just the application of rules. This wisdom comes from the fear of the Lord and

---

10. I am indebted to Jonathan Burnside for much of the material in this section. See also Jackson (2000).

understanding of the Torah. This is seen in Solomon's prayer (1 Kgs 3:29) and in Jehoshaphat's appointment of judges (2 Chr. 19:6–7). They are given a general authority to judge according to divinely inspired intuitions of justice.

- The nature of much biblical law takes the form of 'self-executing rules'. The emphasis is on local administration of justice without reliance on legal professions. Biblical law is directed to the people as a form of teaching (see, for example, 2 Chr. 17:7–9) to be implemented by them directly where possible.

The modern approach to jurisprudence is concerned with the proper interpretation of the words and situations a law can cover. Biblical law had a different cultural, social and institutional context. It describes situations, and is intended to prompt the question 'What images do the words of this rule evoke?' This opens the further question as to what similar situations these images bring to mind. Burnside (2002) has taken the case of the thief at night (Exod. 22:2–3) as an example. A literal interpretation involves close examination of the language to identify the range of situations the words cover. The 'imagistic' approach asks the questions: 'What typical images do the words of this rule evoke? What situations does it make you think of?' The further a specific situation departs from the typical situation, the less likely it is that the rule applies and the more room there is for negotiation between the parties (Jackson 1992: 75–82). The purpose of this is to enable simple 'self-help' rules which make it clear in advance what may and may not be done and so enable people to resolve their own disputes. This is also how Jesus taught. In answer to the question 'Who is my neighbour?' Jesus did not offer a set of legal principles to guide the definition of a neighbour. He told the story of the Good Samaritan (Luke 10:25–37) and told the 'expert in the law' to 'go and do likewise'.

Reading law in this way enables those who use the law to learn many things. It communicates values. Understanding, for example, the differing concepts of seriousness of crime in the Old Testament may point to values which should guide our sentencing today. It also suggests different ways of doing things. The structures of a society and the workings of its institutions both express certain values and may be more or less effective in safeguarding and fostering other values. So, for example, biblical teaching on debt touches on issues of power relationships between lender and borrower, the danger that debt becomes a trap for the poor, the risks of presumption on the future, as well as suggesting other ways of ordering the economy and the beneficial consequences of so doing. It is far richer than simply a prescription on what can and cannot be done in seeking repayment of debt.

Living the paradigm

The chapters in Part 2 collectively describe the broad contours of the biblical paradigm. We have not sought in this volume to offer detailed principles to guide policy formation in each of these areas, although each chapter refers to other more detailed studies. Nevertheless, it is important to consider in a little more detail how a paradigm can be applied in practice. We start by considering what we should mean by the term 'principle'.

What should we mean by 'principles'?

We use the term 'principle' here to refer not to a formal legal rule, but to the summary constructs which are our attempt to capture key aspects of biblical teaching, from many parts of the text, in a way that can be brought to bear on contemporary issues. They can be seen as a bridge with one footing fixed in Scripture but constructed differently in order to reach different points on the shifting sands of our contemporary context. As an aid, principles serve to remind us of the key values and guide us in their application rather than to prescribe courses of action directly. They should be derived from the paradigm as a whole, using a rounded semiotic approach, not from isolated texts.

It is vitally important to distinguish principles from policies. A key distinction is that principles are ethical statements whilst policies are the means of achieving those goals. Christians should be willing to propose and campaign for specific policies as part of their social and political engagement, recognizing that disagreement is legitimate. The church, however, should be cautious in committing itself to policies because policies reflect the art of the possible – economically, politically and socially. They will inevitably be time-bound and open to legitimately differing technical judgments relating, for example, to current economic conditions or management theory.

Deriving principles

Our own experience has been that the interpretative cycle of text-paradigm-principle-policy can work in any order and any direction, enabling continual revision of provisional understandings. Sometimes reading texts with the paradigm in mind may alert us to the underlying principles. At other times wrestling with a challenging principle may enrich our understanding of the paradigm. There are also times when deep experience of the issues and contemporary policies helps us to understand the text. Detailed knowledge of the justice system – its strengths as well as its failings – makes it easier to understand the issues which biblical law was seeking to address. Criminologists and economists may be alert to nuances that may be missed easily by biblical scholars, who in turn can help social scientists to appreciate the theological implications of the texts.

To take just one specific example, how do we make the move from biblical teaching on interest to reform of financial institutions?[11] Are the cultural and technological gaps so great that, as Rodd (2001) argues, they represent nothing more than 'distant visions from a strange land'? Should we be content with general principles of justice and mercy and use our God-given intellects to argue about what they should mean today? The number of theories of justice on offer guarantees a lively debate. Or is it reasonable to seek more specific 'principles' capable of guiding choices and communicating values? The difficulties in doing this are well known, though in addressing the difficulties it is important to be clear about the nature of the task.

The process must begin with acknowledgment of our fallibility as interpreters of Scripture. In our dialogue with God our hearing is distorted and our understanding impaired – sometimes wilfully, always unconsciously. This means that the principles we derive should never be imbued with the authority of Scripture. They are our constructs, derived prayerfully, but reflecting our flaws. When studying the particularity of a text, decisions are required about what reflects a particular cultural context or the limits of the possibilities for action at that time and the extent to which an 'ultimate ethic' (Webb 2001) can be discerned within the constrained particularity of the biblical texts. We may, with good reason, doubt the extent to which we can avoid reading our values and priorities into the text. We may also question the differences between our relationships as individuals, church and societies to both God and the world, and the specific nature of Israel's covenantal relationship.

Discerning the underlying intention of any law is not always straightforward, even within the context of a paradigm. Any law may have consequences (either beneficial or harmful) which exceed its intentions. Chapter 13 argues that while Deuteronomy 13:10–11 clearly recognizes the deterrent effects of the death penalty it does not seek to justify the penalty for this reason, nor does it argue in principle that deterrence is a sound justification for penalties. It may however be a welcome side-effect. The jubilee land laws protected family rootedness but also acted as a mechanism for avoiding concentrations of wealth and economic dependency. Both outcomes are almost certainly intended, but it will not always be possible to combine the same set of beneficial consequences and purposes in a single law today. This may require us to seek to discern whether there was a primary intention.

The Bible itself may offer many clues and pointers to the primary intention. Naboth's firm rejection of Ahab's offer to purchase his vineyard for cash or in exchange for another vineyard clearly suggests that land is not simply an

---

11. See ch. 11.

economic asset to be traded (1 Kgs 21). The story of Zelophehad's daughters as a case-study of land inheritance laws illustrates the importance of retaining land within the wider family unit.[12] Both examples suggest that the role of land as a foundation for social relationships, and not just as a means of livelihood, was an important concern of the law. The case of Zelophehad's daughters has been used as an example of movement within biblical material towards the elevation of women in status and rights (Webb 2001: 76–77). However, there is no indication within the text itself that a concern for equality is the driving issue. The biblical paradigm's focus on land and family expresses, rather, the underlying concern to preserve the integrity and cohesiveness of the wider family landholding. This does not, of course, preclude it also being part of a movement towards greater equality or make such an ethical concern inappropriate. It does, however, serve as a warning that if the content of the paradigm is derived from an ethic which is significantly shaped by our contemporary concerns, then the principles we derive may be distorted by this bias.

Lessons from jurisprudence

Some of the concepts from theories of legal reasoning can be helpful in our use and derivation of principles. One example is the concept of the 'ladder of abstraction' to describe the derivation of ever more general principles from a rule (Twining & Miers 1976: 40–47). Taking the jubilee land laws (Lev. 25) as an example, a range of principles reflecting differing degrees of generalization could be derived.

Applying the most specific principle may not be appropriate, but problems also emerge the further up the 'ladder' one moves. In the process of deriving principles, judgments are made about the values and intentions that lay behind the law. Table 1 illustrates the problem that two rather different sets of principles can be derived from the same law. The context of the paradigm is needed to determine the proper balance between a focus on economic justice and the protection of familial roots as a key purpose of this law. Secondly, very general principles can give rise to such a wide range of possible policies that they end up being of limited value. Here it may be helpful to distinguish general principles that summarize the values guiding overall goals, and more specific principles concerned with the means of realizing those goals. Thirdly, they offer no mechanism for resolving conflicts with other principles, as in trying simultaneously to apply principles of justice and mercy. Fourthly, without a clear grasp of the overall paradigm there is a danger of deriving principles and then supporting policies that are contrary to the overall thrust of the law.

---

12. See the discussion in ch. 9, below.

	Ladder A	Ladder B
Level 4	Relationships matter	Justice in economic life
Level 3	The extended family should meet regularly	All economic assets should be redistributed
Level 2	Families should be co-located in a neighbourhood	All property should be redistributed
Level 1	All families should have roots in specific pieces of land	All land should be redistributed
	Jubilee land laws	Jubilee land laws

Table 1. The ladder of abstraction for the jubilee land laws[13]

This is perhaps particularly true of principles concerned with equality and justice which can be expressed in many divergent ways. These problems are not insurmountable, but the fourth, especially, should encourage us always to check our thinking at every level against the paradigm and our hermeneutical reasoning.

Theories of legal reasoning note that the process of generalization cannot be value neutral. When we construct a set of principles we will select those that accord with our sense of justice. Of course, our sense of justice will be affected by the principles we find – there is a dialectical relationship between the two, and to the extent that we regard the source material as authoritative, we will be ready to suspect our sense of justice. But we cannot deny that our sense of justice plays a significant role in practice. One lesson from legal reasoning is that we should seek to understand by what principles the law was the right law at the time and in the circumstances. It is only at that level that we can then make the move to today. In seeking to build an appropriate coherent set of principles that are binding today we have two controls. First, we must be able to explain why the application of those principles in Israel's economic and social context should lead to the results it did. Secondly, we must show that the principles cohere with God's entire revelation of himself. Otherwise the set of principles we derive may be tainted by our subjective choice.

---

13. Source: adapted from Schluter & Clements (1990: 46).

In dealing with laws (not the only source for our ethical reflection) C. J. H. Wright (2004: 323) suggests a number of questions that might be asked in order to gain this understanding:

- What kind of situation was this law trying to promote or prevent?
- Whose interests was it trying to protect?
- Whose power was it trying to restrict, and how?
- What rights and responsibilities does it embody?
- What kind of behaviour does it encourage or discourage?
- What vision for society motivated this law?
- What motivation did it appeal to?
- What sanction or penalty was attached to this law, and what does this show regarding its relative seriousness or moral priority?

The commands of Scripture are audience-specific – though those audiences may in some cases be widely defined. The Ten Commandments were given to Israel after the exodus. The epistles were written to specific churches. As Rivers (2004) notes:

> Of course, we can very easily think of reasons for treating ourselves as in analogous situations, but once one draws analogies one has moved outside the circle of the addressees. And while we may be relevantly similar, we may also be relevantly different. To reason by analogy is always to exercise judgement oneself. Again, one suspects that we fail to take those judgments 'which obviously don't apply to us' with the seriousness they deserve, perhaps because taking them seriously is confused with treating ourselves as addressed by them. To take a judgement seriously is to seek to understand why it was right in the situation in which it was made. What was it about Corinth, women and hairstyles that mattered so much to Paul? Why, in the context of warfare in the Ancient Near East, might total destruction – if that was what it really was – have been legitimate? Biblical scholarship at its best fills in the cultural background enabling us to make sense of the texts, for it is only when we understand that we can begin to draw analogies.

It is this kind of reasoning that helps to determine which aspects of Israel's life should shape our framework for social reform. The reformers distinction between moral, civil and ceremonial law applies a filter that does not accurately reflect the nature of the texts.[14] Any one text may include any combination of these three purposes. Such filters may be helpful in guiding our reasoning, but they are the

---

14. See C. J. H. Wright (2004: 288) and Schluter & Clements (1990: 55) for a discussion of this.

outcome of our reflection and should not be the basis on which we select which texts to apply.

Dealing with culture

Culture change means a paradigm cannot simply be transferred to any culture at any time. It would be impossible to implement fully and immediately the ban on interest in today's global economy after 300 years of building institutions based on interest. Biblical teaching on the diffusion of power presumes a just society with limited need for corrective intervention. The biblical approach to government assumes that the law is God-given rather than man-made and does not provide a model for contemporary law-making government.

The lessons from both semiotics and jurisprudence described above provide guidance on the process of reasoning that can help us to derive principles for today from biblical texts. These texts come from a 'high context culture' where authors assume that their readers share a common culture and therefore do not need to convey much in the way of detail and exposition (Simkins 1994: 41–42). Burnside has argued that a semiotic approach 'helps to unlock the symbolic meaning of worlds of meaning that would simply have been assumed at the time the laws and narratives were written' and that 'style, grammar, narrative context, literary arrangement, choice of language, emphasis, inclusion and omission' are all relevant in uncovering these meanings (Burnside 2003: 28). A semiotic approach helps us to appreciate how the biblical culture (or cultures, for texts written over many centuries do not have a homogeneous cultural context) shapes the meaning of the text. It does not, of itself, tell us how those texts should be applied in another country or another era. However, it does support the paradigmatic approach of working by analogy and imitation, rather than a semantic, legislative approach.

William Webb has written on the hermeneutics of cultural analysis, arguing that the concept of a 'redemptive movement' helps to identify the merely 'cultural component' of a text and the 'transcultural components' that are timeless, universal and convey the values of the kingdom (Webb 2001: 24). Each isolated text is seen in the context of an ethical journey. When compared to, for example, the surrounding nations, the redemptive spirit of a law may be evident. But a literal application may well fall short of the 'ultimate ethic', characterized as the ideal intention of the law. In examining three dangers of his approach we may come closer to articulating the best way forward.

First, it is unhelpful to plot an ethical trajectory based on an inadequate ('static' in Webb's terms) interpretation of the text. Webb suggests an 'X$\Rightarrow$Y$\Rightarrow$Z' model; X represents the original culture, Y the Bible and Z an 'ultimate ethic' (Webb 2001: 38). In this model the 'Bible' is always seen as a redemptive improvement on the original culture but sometimes less than an 'ultimate ethic': so our culture may be worse than the 'Bible' or better. This raises some unnecessary concerns because Webb uses the word 'Bible' in his model to represent a limited literal interpretation of the text rather than a full understanding of what Scripture teaches.

The second danger is to confuse a movement that reflects changing expression of biblical values (recognizing that individual biblical texts may reflect culturally limited options) with some sort of ethical evolution through which a modern culture is presumed to be ethically superior to an ancient culture. Whilst recognizing that the application of values described by any text may be culturally constrained, we would not want to say that the biblical ethic, even in the context of difficult texts, was in some way deficient.

A third danger is that the concept of an 'ultimate ethic' raises the temptation of too easily dismissing as 'the less than fully redeemed cultural context' all that is alien or uncomfortable. Webb can perhaps be criticized for his treatment of the Old Testament 'slavery' texts, failing to see that they portray a very different structure to Roman or later Western slavery. The very word 'slavery' automatically prompts ethical suspicion today but a more accurate description of the Old Testament institution is 'bonded service'. 'Slaves' in early Israel were allowed to run away and most were set free every seventh year. As a mechanism for dealing with debt it compares favourably with, for example, Victorian debtor prisons.[15] Too ready a dismissal of the text may lead us to miss out on the challenging questions it raises about other areas of life.

We must be willing to be challenged by our reading of Scripture. There will always be some aspects of the social life of Israel that we find hard to understand or justify, as indeed the following chapters on the family indicate. Whatever one's view of Scripture, there is a case for giving such passages the benefit of the doubt in order not to short-cut the patient process of discerning the values and social and theological purposes behind these laws.

Conclusion

Our experience has been that this endeavour is worthwhile, even if not always easy. It is all too easy to dismiss difficult or culturally uncomfortable aspects of biblical law as primitive or lacking authority. But to forego the effort of teasing out the purpose and coherence of these passages is to miss out on valuable insights. The context of our study is important. If we read Scripture looking for the answer to specific problems (or, more dangerously, seeking confirmation of an answer already formulated) we may find what we seek but miss much that the

---

15. For a further discussion of 'slavery' in early Israel see the appendix to ch. 10.

Bible offers. In our work at the Jubilee Centre we have sought to avoid setting a research agenda purely by identifying modern 'strategic issues'. Rather we have taken the view that if there are subjects on which the Bible appears to have much to say then we should seek to understand it, whether or not it appears immediately relevant to contemporary debates. This has proved helpful in allowing the Bible to speak to its own agenda and not to be read solely in the light of ours. We must also be willing to accept that there are issues on which the Bible is largely silent. The Bible has much to say about health and wisdom, for example, but very little about the institutions through which healthcare and education are provided. Wider biblical principles may still guide our thinking but we should be cautious about seeking to concoct comprehensive sets of principles from the occasional passage of Scripture.

In the following chapters we have endeavoured to allow (as far as is humanly possible) the Bible to speak in its own terms. This means that we have included the awkward and uncomfortable texts and not simply those that might support a fashionable agenda. Space does not permit each chapter to offer a thorough theological reflection on each text. We have, where possible, suggested where more detailed biblical exegesis can be found. Each chapter then seeks to identify the key relationships addressed in this aspect of biblical teaching and the key principles governing the conduct of these relationships that emerge. Ultimately, we ask that you judge our approach, not just by its theological presuppositions, but also by its fruits. Does it open up the meaning and application of God's Word? Does it challenge our thinking and values? Does it help us to understand what it means to love God and neighbour in today's complex and varied situations? These are the critical tests.

We have argued that the people of God, called to be a priestly nation and a light to the Gentiles, can be seen as a paradigmatic model from which we can and should learn about the ordering of relationships in society. In Part 2 of this book, we explore key themes of this model in several important areas of public life, drawing principally but not exclusively from the example of early Israel. Many New Testament texts illuminate these key themes. We have not chosen the topics on the basis of contemporary importance and there are other topics important in social reform, such as health and education, for which a biblical perspective could be offered.[1] However, we now focus on those aspects of the paradigm about which the Bible seems to have most to say.

Chapter 6 considers the relational dynamic which should set both our personal and societal goals and which is often lacking in contemporary political values. This rather different mindset is an important context for understanding the approach to individual areas of public life in the following chapters. Chapter 7 considers what we should mean by 'nation', and the implications of this for our relationships. Chapter 8 then sets out a number of themes of political order and considers what it might mean for a constitutional order to express love between citizens. Chapter 14 broadens the perspective to consider relationships between nations.

Chapters 9 and 10 examine the role of the (extended) family and of welfare provision, and demonstrate the close connection between the two. In setting an agenda for social reform, it focuses more on the family as a social institution and how it is strengthened, than on providing ethical guidance for the conduct of intra-household relationships. Chapters 11 and 12 open up the radical scriptural teaching on economic life, with a long hard look at how divine wisdom on finance has been ignored. A key issue here is to explore how a concern to sustain relationships can effectively be built into the economic order. The restoration and nurturing of broken relationships is shown in chapter 13 to be at the heart of the Bible's teaching on justice, and how society may embrace an effective criminal justice system. All these relational themes are drawn together in chapter 15 which underlines the coherence of the biblical vision presented in Part 2.

---

1. Spencer (2004) offers a perspective on those issues which have consistently been rated as most important by the UK public in opinion polls.

6. The relational dynamic

John Ashcroft

Grasping the distinctive goals and values at the heart of the biblical social vision helps to clarify the rationale of approaches to individual issues. This chapter therefore introduces Part 2 by reflecting on the distinctive social dynamic of subsequent chapters. This dynamic is relational rather than materialistic. A person's individual goals are set in terms of knowing God – in the New Testament, knowing Christ (Phil. 3:7–10). At a social level, the individual's goals are defined in terms of character rather than wealth or profile, as the book of Proverbs reiterates. Character develops out of right relationships, and an ability to understand and reflect on the behaviour and relationships of others. Society, too, is to aspire to a strong relationship with God, and should contain strong relationships between neighbours.

How we define 'development' reveals much about the priorities that shape our society. Robert Kennedy eloquently expressed the dangers of an impoverished view:

> ... the Gross National Product does not allow for the health of our children, the quality of their education, or the joy of their play. It does not include the beauty of our poetry or the strength of our marriages ... it measures everything, in short, except that which make life worthwhile. (Kennedy 1968)

At the heart of biblical social ethics we see a group of values deeply concerned with the nature and quality of our relationships. Together they provide a rather different account of 'the good life' to that which is frequently evident today in policy goals and speeches, values surveys or in the choices and actions of individuals and organizations.

Relational values in the paradigm

Key elements of the biblical paradigm can be described in various ways. The Bible communicates relational values (an aspect of the good, and grounds for making choices) but does not offer a theoretical account of them. Rather it recounts the history of particular individuals and a particular nation making specific decisions and choices, and the values which (should) have guided them. These values are not cultural constructs: they are depicted as being rooted in the character of God and his concern for all creation. It should be no surprise that these values are rather different from those rooted in humanity's fallen aspirations.

Highlighting certain themes is always open to the criticism of subjective bias. In his quest for a truly Christian basis for political theology, O'Donovan notes the need for

> an architectonic hermeneutic which would locate political reflection on the Exodus with an undertaking that had its centre of gravity in the gospels ... Almost the whole vocabulary of salvation in the New Testament has a political pre-history of some kind: 'salvation' itself (*yeshuah*), 'justification' (*tsedequah*), 'peace' (*shalom*), 'faithfulness' (*hesed*), 'faith' (*emunah*), and above all the kingdom of God. Israel's knowledge of God's blessings was, from beginning to end, a political knowledge and it was out of that knowledge that the evangelists and apostles spoke about Jesus. (O'Donovan 1996: 22)

By exploring such terms we provide an important context for the following chapters. If we can understand the key concerns of the people of Israel as they reflected on the proper nature of their life together, and how these are taken up in the relationships of the kingdom of God, then we will be better able to engage with biblical teaching on how these values were to be sustained and realized in various areas of life.

The Bible is no stranger to greed, envy, fear, lust or malice. Biblical teaching represents ideals against which Israel, both individually and as a nation, consistently fell far short. This is true of such 'heroes' of the faith as Abraham and David as well as the more obvious 'anti-heroes' such as Ahab. To a certain extent the values that are highlighted are a response or antidote to the particular problems or social evils faced at any period of history. Peace is most valued when it is absent; justice in the face of injustice and oppression. However, while the priorities or focus of attention may vary, the values themselves are timeless. They are as resonant and relevant today. Those discussed below are necessarily illustrative rather than exhaustive. One striking feature of the values at the heart of the biblical social vision is that they are a closely knit family, frequently used in combination. For example:

All the ways of the LORD are loving and faithful.
(Ps. 25:10)

Love and faithfulness meet together,
    righteousness and peace kiss each other.
(Ps. 85:10)

Let love and faithfulness never leave you.
(Prov. 3:3)

'... I am the LORD who practises steadfast love,
    justice and righteousness in the earth,
    for in these things I delight.'
(Jer. 9:24)

    And what does the LORD require of you?
To act justly and to love mercy
    and to walk humbly with your God.
(Mic. 6:8)

'Administer true justice; show mercy and compassion to one another.'
(Zech. 7:9)

The theme of relationships is evident in all. Indeed, when compared to contemporary values, it is clear that they reflect a very different mindset. The more we understand this mindset – this passion for right relationships – the better we will be able to understand the logic and relevance of individual areas of biblical teaching and the challenge they present to us today.

Holiness

Holiness is, perhaps, the cardinal value. Being set apart and recognizing God's transcendent 'otherness' is the proper context for all valuing. Humanity's relative values are tested by the absolute demands of God's character – when it comes to holiness it is not possible to sit on the fence. The call to holiness was part of the call to the nation of Israel to be a kingdom of priests (Exod. 19:1–6). The command to be holy provides both the moral force behind a concern for values as well as shaping their content. God is holy (Lev. 19:2). Derivatively, places (Lev. 6:16), time (Lev. 25:10) and objects (Exod. 29:37) could be holy. Israel was called to be a holy nation (Lev. 19:6; Deut. 7:6) and Christians are called to live a holy life (1 Thess. 4:7). This has strong ethical implications, described to the Thessalonians in terms of 'living to please God'. O'Donovan links this to authentic possession of the law:

> The central accusation against the Pharisees is that they attempted to construct holiness from outside in. But the holiness acceptable to God was God's own new work, in which, as the prophets had predicted, he would write the law upon people's hearts. A constructed holiness could only be a futility. Appearances would, in the end, correspond to the life that generated them. (O'Donovan 1996: 102)

The biblical account of holiness is not some otherworldly asceticism. True holiness should invite relationship, not preclude it. Boundaries are as much points of connection as barriers. For Israel the purpose of being set apart was to be a light to the nations. The Holiness Code in Leviticus 17 – 26 is part of a 'bold', 'programmatic', 'even utopian' vision for society (Pleins 2001: 69–70). Jesus was not afraid of being tainted by contact with sinners and the 'unclean'. Indeed, the contrary image is that of salt preserving society. The desire to be holy provides the force behind a commitment to cleave to the good and eschew the evil whilst also displaying absolute compassion and commitment to those who are ensnared by evil.

An understanding of holiness protects us from idolatry and dishonouring God. Placing the wrong value on the wrong things can lead to putting things in the place of God. There is also the danger of dishonouring God through treating that which is sacred with contempt. Holiness also roots social values in the creative sovereignty of God rather than in people's choices and preferences. If our values are seen as reflecting something of God's character, then it is of great importance that we get our values right, not simply out of concern for the well-being of others, but because the Lord's name is at stake.

This gives rise to the concern for distinctive values. 'You must not live according to the customs of the nations I am going to drive out before you ... I am the LORD your God, who has set you apart from the nations' (Lev. 20:23–24). 'Do not conform any longer to the pattern of this world, but be transformed by the renewing of your mind' (Rom. 12:2). This does not mean that we should be dismayed when our values (at least sometimes) are shared by others. Rather, the concern for holiness serves as a reminder that our values should be shaped first and foremost by our faithful obedience to God rather than conforming to others.

Justice and righteousness

A biblical account of justice begins with the recognition that justice is a characteristic of God who establishes norms for our relationships.[1] The words 'justice' and 'righteousness' often appear together as a hendiadys (*mišpāṭ wĕṣĕdāqâ*). Weinfeld argues that together they are best interpreted as a concern for social justice which may be established by leaders who create the laws and are responsible for their execution. However, the application of justice is not limited to the field of legal jurisdiction (Weinfeld 2000). For O'Donovan (1996), judging justly lies at the heart of a political theology: it is God who judges, and, after the resurrection of Christ, all human judging is subject to his authority. Our concern for justice is, therefore, to be set in the context of witness to the Lord who now reigns and is the judge of all nations.

The term *mišpāṭ* on its own refers principally to judgments, and when those acts of judgment resolve a situation. It is an active concept: the image in Amos of justice rolling on like a river (5:24) means that 'the stream of juridical activity should not be allowed to dry up' (O'Donovan 1996: 39). *Ṣĕdāqâ*, according to Mays, is:

> the quality of life displayed by those who live up to the norms inherent in a given relationship and thereby do right by the other person or persons involved. The two most important spheres of righteousness were the relationships between Yahweh and Israel defined in the covenant and expressed in the cult, and the relationships of man in the social order of the folk ... In Amos' teaching *tsedeq* applies to the relational life of the social partners of the people of Israel. (Mays 1969, cited in Reimer 1997: 763)

Bruce Malchow also draws out this relational aspect of justice:

> *Tsdq*, thus, is the fulfilment of the demands of a relationship, with God or a person. There is no norm of righteousness outside of that personal involvement. When people fulfil the conditions imposed on them by relationships they are righteous. Every relationship has specific obligations. (Malchow 1996: 16)

Humanity seems to be hard-wired with a concern for justice – but *being* just is not something that comes naturally to fallen people. Just as young children quickly learn to cry 'That's not fair!' so all civilizations have wrestled with the question of how our relationships should be regulated. The biblical concept of justice is not an abstract legal norm to define what actions or outcomes may be

---

1. Ch. 13 gives a fuller account of the meaning of justice. Beaumont & Wotherspoon (2000) also provides a helpful overview as does C. J. H. Wright (2004: ch. 8).

considered just. It is rooted in a wide set of norms, the 'demands of a relationship', to which Malchow refers, but is characterized by its concrete expression in particular relationships.

Justice is set out as important for all people and all areas of life, often in the context of freedom from oppression. Chapter 10 shows how the biblical vision protects vulnerable groups without strengthening the role of the central state – recognizing that a highly centralized state with few checks and balances risked exposing people to less justice and greater political oppression. In dealing with crime (ch. 13) we see a vision for dynamic justice that seeks to right wrongs and restore the wide web of relationships that crime damages. Perhaps the most important feature of justice is that it focuses our concern on others. That is why the commands to love God and neighbour summarize the Law. A concern for justice does not set an agenda for our reasonable rights or entitlements, enforced through increasingly juridified relationships. Rather it sets an agenda of how we should treat other people – our duties and our responsibilities.

Shalom[2]

> The biblical understanding of peace points positively to things being as they should be; when things are not that way, no amount of security, no amount of peacekeeping in the sense of law and order and public tranquillity will make for peace ... Only a transformation of society so that things really are all right will make for biblical peace. (Yoder 1987: 22)

Shalom is the enjoyment of right relationships with God, others and nature. 'The peace which is shalom is not merely the absence of hostility, not merely being in right relationship. Shalom at its highest is enjoyment in one's relationships' (Wolterstorff 1983: 69). If justice defines and requires right relationships, peace is enjoying the relationship itself as well as the ability to enjoy its fruits. Its meaning is thus broader than an absence of conflict and includes a sense of material and physical 'okayness',[3] healthy relationships and the confidence of absence of guilt (Yoder 1987: ch. 1).

Shalom, while rooted in relationships, has physical and concrete expression. The apparent peace enjoyed by the wicked is understood in the material terms of physical health and prosperity (e.g. Job 21:7–13). This prosperity and abundance is promised to Israel (Jer. 33: 6, 9). Similarly in Psalm 37 the promise that the meek

---

2. This section draws on material from Jeremy Ive, prepared in the course of reflecting on the contribution of peace-building to social reform.

3. Yoder's term.

will 'enjoy great peace' (v. 11) is seen, at least in part, in terms of physical security and provision which were under threat from the 'wicked'. Right relationships have intrinsic value: they are properly 'ends' and not solely 'means'. Nevertheless the Bible is fully aware of the practical dividends of right relationships as well as the consequences of unjust relationships.

Shalom can apply to an individual and include a broad account of wholeness and well-being. It is also used to describe wider sets of relationships – a state enjoyed or desired by a community or a nation. The biblical vision is that all people should enjoy peace and that this should be reflected in domestic, national and international relationships.[4] We are commanded to 'turn from evil and do good; seek peace and pursue it' (Ps. 34:14), but we are also reminded that peace is a promise. The peace which in Isaiah characterizes the future glory of Zion (e.g. Isa. 60) is rooted in transformed relationships which are not yet fully realized. In articulating a social vision for today we need the balance of both the ideal vision as well as the realistic but challenging commands of how we should act.

The New Testament sees peace as rooted in love. The instruction to live (if possible) in peace with everyone (Rom. 12:18) comes in the context of the importance of love, seeking the welfare of others and overcoming evil with good. This is a reminder of the limits of any social vision. We can, and should, create the conditions for peace. But ultimately peace is God's gift. The peace of the Lord can be with us in the midst of trouble. Its physical expression is ultimately less important than the peace of heart and mind that comes from confidence in our right relationships with God and others. This links peace both to justice and forgiveness.

Restoration of right relationships is the only basis on which peace can be established. Peace, in turn, is the basis from which all other objectives can be achieved. In order to restore relationships, there needs to be a process of forgiveness, a relational process which involves a transaction between two or more parties (be they individuals, communities or national groups). Conflicts are destructive and divisive. They also distort community structures and inhibit the freedom essential for the healthy growth of all institutions – church, state, family and the range of voluntary associations and enterprises that collectively make up what is called 'civil society'.

Christians are called to seek peace with one another (Rom. 12:18), and, by implication, between their respective communities. This command to create a world filled with a holistic sense of peace (*shalom*) does not mean turning a blind eye to injustice, be it personal or structural. Indeed, the imperative of justice requires all people, as bearers of God's image, to work for the restoration of the

---

4. See ch. 14, below.

shattered and distorted social order in which we live. In the words of Isaiah, peace is the 'fruit of righteousness' (Isa. 32:17). The achievement of justice is a necessary prerequisite for the establishment of peace, but the justice to be worked for cannot be identified with the demands of any one class or party grouping – it must be truly impartial, without bias to the rich or the poor: 'Do not show partiality in judging: hear both small and great alike . . .' (Deut. 1:17).

Forgiveness is not the same thing as forgetting: wrongs and hurts need to be addressed and worked through. As Kierkegaard pointed out: 'When we say we *consign* something to oblivion, we suggest simultaneously that it is to be forgotten and yet also remembered' (Kierkegaard 1958: 118). Forgiveness is something that needs to be given concrete expression, and to show its fruit in the form of new patterns of relationship. Shriver identifies four major dynamics in the process. First, there is abandonment of revenge by the victims and abandonment of profession of innocence by the perpetrators. Secondly, there is the provision of the context of public hope for reconciliation as the basis for the uncovering of public truth about an evil past. The best example of this is the Truth and Reconciliation Commission established in South Africa in 1996. Thirdly, there is the finding of a new empathy between former enemies. Those who caricatured each other as somehow subhuman are brought together as fellow, feeling human beings. Finally, there is the move from apology to reparation. Material reparations cannot unmake wrongs, but they can be symbolic of restored relationships and new intent (Shriver 1995: 156–165).

Forgiveness is thus a public as well as a private act, which creates a new reality. As Peter Digeser puts it:

> As conceived of here, political forgiveness is what the philosopher J. L. Austin called an illocutionary speech act. Not only must the message of forgiveness be spoken (or somehow conveyed), but also what is said must have the effect of releasing the debtor or the transgressor from the debt. (Digeser 2000)

The grammar of forgiveness is derived from a larger story. For Christians, all things need to be seen in the light of the resurrection of Jesus, which is a concrete promise and guarantee of the reality to come. Because, for Christians, hope is finally to be understood as triumphant, the cycle of revenge and counter-revenge with its downward spiral to oblivion is replaced by the possibility of new life.

Loyalty

A satisfactory translation of ḥesed is difficult. It is used to describe steadfast love, kindness and mercy. Sakenfeld uses the term 'loyalty' and offers the following extended definition:

- Loyalty is to another person (or persons) in relationship with the one who acts loyally; loyalty is not to an idea or a cause.
- Loyalty is an attitude made manifest in concrete action.
- Loyalty is offered to a person in need by a person who has the ability to help; often only one person is in a position to fill the need. Narrative texts tend to focus on dramatic needs, but even the smallest need in the most everyday situation might become an occasion for showing loyalty, insofar as the fulfilling of the need is significant for the vitality of the relationship.
- The need places the potential recipient in a position of dependence on the one who might show loyalty.
- There are no societal legal sanctions for the failure to show loyalty; thus the doer is in a situation of free decision.
- Hence, loyalty is shown in a freely undertaken carrying through of an existing commitment to another person who is now in a situation of need. (Sakenfeld 1985: 131)

Hesed is something that is shown by God to people and is expected to be demonstrated between people. It is to be understood as conduct in accordance with a mutual relationship of rights and duties. Failure to keep the obligations of *hesed* is a great evil. Yahweh's *hesed* is often set within the context of his covenant love (e.g. Deut. 7:9–13). *Hesed* between people is often in the context of reciprocal favours: 'Now then please swear to me by Yahweh that you will show *hesed* to my family, because I have shown *hesed* to you' (Josh. 2:12). There is particular importance in extending *hesed* to the needy and vulnerable. As a value which underpins 'dutiful generosity', it was an important foundation for welfare provision (see ch. 10). *Hesed* is hard to sustain in an atomistic and fragmented society which lacks the rootedness and social ties to sustain reciprocity, commitment and generosity. However, it offers the prospect of a genuinely inclusive society.

Faithfulness

Faithfulness (*'ĕmûnâ*) is seen as an important attribute of God that we should display in our own relationships. Of the many moving descriptions of God's everlasting love, perhaps the greatest are to be found in Hosea and Jeremiah.

> Because of the LORD's great love we are not consumed,
> for his compassions never fail.
> They are new every morning;
> great is your faithfulness.
> (Lam. 3:22)

This faithful God, who keeps his covenant of love for a thousand generations (Deut. 7:9) strengthens and protects us (1 Cor. 1:9; 2 Thess. 3:3). Just as God's faithfulness to his covenant and promises is greatly prized, so too is human faithfulness. We are expected first to be faithful to God, so that the image of harlotry is frequently used to describe Israel's idolatry.

The value placed upon faithfulness has social implications. Psalm 85 links love, faithfulness, righteousness and peace. Without faithfulness there is no true love or righteousness. It lies behind the importance attached in the Bible to words and promises, and sets an expectation of the conduct of our family relationships. The modern reader finds it hard to comprehend the binding nature of a rash vow. We live in a culture that typically sees both political and personal promises as statements of intent, subject to revision in the light of new circumstances. Autonomy and freedom take precedence over faithfulness.

Faithfulness is an important aspect of trustworthiness and hence the foundation of the trust which is essential for efficient economic and political relationships. Indeed both *'ĕmet* and *'ĕmûnâ* are sometimes translated as faithfulness, sometimes as truth which is seen more as a reflection of character than the accuracy of a propositional statement. Thus, when the Lord says that 'truth has perished; it has vanished from their lips' (Jer. 7:28) in response to Israel's pursuit of 'the stubborn inclinations of their evil hearts' (v. 24), it is a broad indictment of the conduct of their relationships.

Values matter in societies with limited institutions, where there is a high degree of interdependence and enforcement mechanisms are weak. The development of complex institutions does not, however, make faithfulness redundant. Much has been written recently on the importance of trust and its corrosion.[5] As Bronk (1998: 228) argues: 'Trust is crucial to the success of economic relationships ... Where trust and honesty break down, society and individuals will have to spend a large part of their energy and resources in formulating detailed prescriptive rules and contracts, and then even more resources in enforcing them.' There is also widespread concern about the social and economic consequences of breakdown in family relationships. There can be no doubt about the continuing importance of faithfulness as a value that shapes our relationships.

Hope

Secular views of hope are easily confused with desires, longings, dreams and material expectations. Biblical teaching challenges our views of what is hoped for, and the basis of those hopes. This process will involve countering a culture of 'hopelessness' which may be characterized by cynicism, apathy and despair,

---

5. E.g. Fukuyama (1995), O. O'Neill (2002), Scholefield (2004).

with a positive vision for the future and a belief that God is at work to bring it about.

A message of hope enables the communication of a number of aspects of God's character. God's faithfulness underpins the certainty of a hope founded on him. The Lord declares 'there is hope for your future' (Jer. 31:17) in promising a return to the land. The certainty of God's promise is emphasized in Hebrews: 'we have this hope as an anchor for the soul, firm and secure' (Heb. 6:19). Related to this are God's love and belief in the value of all people, his power to change the most difficult situations, and his commitment to act to offer hope.

A Christian view of hope includes recognizing that hope is a gift and a promise, and that giving hope to others is an obligation. Seeing hope as a gift does not apply just to our future hope, the gift of God through his Son, but also our present hope. Hope is not rooted in our abilities or temperament but in the gift of opportunities and the capacity to take them. For the $g\bar{o}'\bar{e}l$ ('kinsman-redeemer') the giving of hope is an obligation. There are many ways of giving hope, including the gift of opportunity (e.g. a job), the gift of ability (e.g. training), the gift of encouragement (emotional and practical support both to cope and believe in the possibility of change) and the gift of healing and forgiveness (enabling hope in broken relationships).

As both a promise and a gift, hope is found in relationship with God and with other people. We therefore need to foster hope-giving relationships. This sets an agenda for social action. Hope should also be built into the structure of society. This sets an agenda for social reform. Examples of hope embedded in structures and policies include the jubilee land laws (see ch. 9) which promise the return of land and the restoration of economic fortune, and the sabbatical cancellation of debts and release of bonded servants (Deut. 15:1–8) which illustrates a commitment to ensure that no Israelite would be permanently without hope.

Love

All is summed up in love – the white light of which all other values are a refraction. It is love that motivates our faithfulness, compassion, mercy and commitment to justice for others. The command to love God and neighbour is the simple but challenging summary of the law and prophets. Love is the touchstone of the authentic Christian life. The sacrificial nature of biblical love, most fully demonstrated in Christ's love for us, means that any social vision that is to be called Christian must be characterized by a passionate concern for the well-being of others.

Of all the values discussed here it is love that most clearly exposes the limits of policy. Love can neither be presumed nor compelled. Jesus describes Moses' teaching on divorce as a response to the 'hardness of men's hearts' (Matt. 19:8). Policy can (and should) recognize that love can fail. Policy can create conditions which promote and encourage love and generosity. It does not remove the need for the transformation of individuals in order that a biblical social vision is fully realized. The beauty of the biblical paradigm is that it is thoroughly idealistic and thoroughly pragmatic. It is founded on the highest values that shape the whole tenor and direction of the social vision. It is also realistic about human nature and the potential for evil, offering practical guidance on how the goals of love can best be realized.

Contemporary political values

Contemporary values have generally lost the richness of their proper relational context. They are not wholly different from biblical values – for example, the concern for freedom and equality resonates strongly with biblical themes. But elevated to ultimate status, stripped of their relational context and applied outside a framework that enables their proper integration, they lead towards a distorted social vision. Of course, societies are not homogenous with regard to values. There are generational differences, and differences rooted in faiths and ideologies. Nevertheless, in the context of this diversity it is possible to summarize some influential and widely held values.

Liberty, freedom and choice

Both the exodus and jubilee traditions suggest that freedom from oppression is of great importance in biblical social ethics. Such freedom, however, is seen in very different terms to, for example, contemporary accounts of economic and existential freedom or moral libertarianism. In the Bible, freedom is a gift from God and a duty to others. So, for example, the memory of God's deliverance of Israel from slavery is used to commend the duty of concern for such vulnerable groups as widows, orphans and aliens (e.g. Deut. 10:19). The offensiveness of becoming enslaved is made clear in the complaint to Nehemiah: 'Although we are of the same flesh and blood as our countrymen and though our sons are as good as theirs, yet we have to subject our sons and daughters to slavery' (Neh. 5:5). The problem was rooted in debt, and Nehemiah's angry response was to ban the charging of interest (v. 10), which was undermining the free equality of the people of Israel. Because their freedom was seen as God's gift, denial of that gift to others cut to the heart of the covenantal relationship.

This was not absolute freedom: it was sustained in covenantal obedience. Paul's account of freedom in Christ does not lead to a licence to 'indulge the sinful nature' but rather to an instruction 'to serve one another in love' (Gal. 5:13). We know, of course, that absolute unconstrained freedom is unattainable. Life cannot be lived outside of relationships, and these unavoidably create constraints –

benign or otherwise. O'Donovan has reminded us that freedom is 'a social reality, a new disposition of society around its supreme Lord which sets it loose from its traditional lords'. This is contrasted to freedom 'conceived primarily as an assertion of individuality, whether positively, in terms of individual creativity and impulse, or negatively, in terms of "rights", which is to say immunities from harm' (O'Donovan 1996: 254). Freedom does not mean the absence of accountability; it means taking responsibility for the right ordering of our relationships. The desire for the individual freedom of self-realization – to be the author and director of our own lives – denies the relationships within which true purposive freedom is found. This is also true for organizations which can never be free from the demands of stakeholders, but may have a wide range of freedoms regarding the conduct of those relationships. The value of freedom, like money and, indeed, like life, is only found in spending it – by entering into the obligations of relationships. The freedom of unconstrained isolation is a prison.

If we cannot be free *from* all constraints, what kinds of freedom are sought? Common examples include freedom of speech, of choice (economic and political), of religion, of conscience, or freedom for our existential self-realization. Many of these are stated as rights, raising the question of who is the guarantor of our freedom. At a political level it is the state, although in some countries this occurs within a strong framework of constitutional law (see ch. 8). The promotion of free markets has become a dominant feature of Western economic and political theory during the last twenty years (but see ch. 12). Economic freedom is not an ultimate value – it serves other goals. The typical choice lies between growth or redistribution. The biblical model offers a balance of freedom, justice and obligation. Achieving an integrated balance today will require both a theological reassessment of how such values as freedom should be understood, as well as practical mechanisms for sustaining that balance.

Choice is the handmaiden of freedom and has triumphed over obligation. It is the consumer's value. As consumers we can choose our identity, our education, our healthcare, our careers, where we will seek to belong and to whom we will volunteer obligations. Our existential identity demands the right to choose. Our economic freedom expects it. Choice is the invisible hand that powers the market. As such our choices become a tool for performance management and resource allocation, with institutions structured to maximize and channel the power of these choices. Aggregated individual choices will not always lead to optimal outcomes, as recognized in the concept of market failure. Game theory reveals that the choices of other people may mean that protecting our interests leads to the impoverishment of all. If there are too many hawks it no longer pays to be a dove, even if a community of doves leads to the best possible outcome.

If freedom serves other goals, choice reflects them. Wise choosing is the essence of maturity. It is not, ultimately, the democratization of authority, giving to each a share in the vote to determine value. That authority rests with our Creator who pointedly reminded the people of Israel that there are only two choices: life or death (Deut. 30:11–20). The value we place upon choice today, as an expression of our freedom, raises the question of what values guide our choices. A social vision which elevates the process of valuing, whilst stripping it of any reference points to guide the content, is a recipe for market failure and social fragmentation. Choice needs the context of relationships of love and obligation. Idolizing choice and rebelling against anything that is obligated or regarded as a given risks destroying our social networks.

Individualized accounts of freedom and choice have become intertwined with tolerance. This is no longer seen in terms of respecting the right to disagree and make different choices, or upholding the moral accountability of the individual for her actions. The authoritarian-libertarian political axis is a continuing tension. Freedom to hunt, binge drink, or smoke is being curtailed. Concepts of 'conditionality' have been introduced to citizenship with, for example, suggestions that benefits might be cut if no action is taken to stop children playing truant. But while we may be willing to accept the authority of the state to regulate our relationships in order to limit antisocial behaviour or promote equality, we live in a society which is highly suspicious of any assertion of moral authority which might constrain the freedom of personal lifestyle choices.

Equality

The concern for equality dominates life today. This is not new. In his descriptions of nineteenth-century America, de Tocqueville commented that 'it has been said a hundred times that our contemporaries are far more ardently and tenaciously attached to equality than to freedom' (de Tocqueville 1972). This concern for equality tends to focus on groups of people, most frequently addressing issues of gender, race, sexuality and disability. Yet the values of choice and freedom are not easily reconciled with equality. In public services, for example, choice and diversity in provision may lead to improvements in quality but are no guarantee of equality. There is a tension between equality, ensured through central regulation, and the diffused power of local responsibility. The debate about whether to focus on equality of opportunity or outcome has a long history.

While it is clear that there is a strong theological concern for equality, rooted in the dignity of all persons and their shared relationship with their Creator, it is set in the context of sustaining relationships. Israel was concerned with the equality of 'brother' Israelites. This is seen in the concern to limit economic inequality (Deut. 15:1–3), preserve the independence of each household (Mic. 4:4) and limit the emergence of a political elite (Deut. 17:14–20; 1 Sam. 8:1–21). The ideal of a 'king' is of someone who does not acquire economic and military power and does not 'consider himself better than his brothers'. Jesus warns his disciples not to seek authority over one another, but to serve (Matt. 20:20–28).

Clearly a concern for equality is not inappropriate. But equality, *per se*, is not the primary biblical concern. The dignity of the person, unity among the people of God, and the quality of love in relationship are valued above equality.[6] That is the force of the epistles' teaching on the new relationships Christians have in Christ: we are one (Gal. 3:28). Inequality is, of course, impossible to sustain in this context, but it is a consequence, not the goal. We have wrongly substituted as a goal the equivalence of interchangeable individuals for an equality rooted in relationship.

Modern accounts of equality have, at times, been materially focused and lacking a transcendent dimension. No longer do we derive equality from the nature of our relationship with God, but from equality before the law; an equality of individualized status. The pursuit of this equality can be destructive of relationships, fostering division and resentment rather than reciprocity and justice. Indeed research on happiness leads us to question whether we really want equality (Layard 2002). Happiness is not found in keeping up with the Joneses, but in keeping *ahead*. That is why economic growth may lead to greater prosperity, but not to greater happiness. Contentment, like poverty, is relative. Here, too, we see that contemporary values need a deeper context. Rights can be asserted on thin foundations. Duties need a more robust rationale. We do not want to be unequal (at least not in the disadvantaged half of the equation), but we resist the love-inspired unity of relationship within which truly happy equality can be found. We want to distinguish ourselves as individuals, yet fear the diversity which threatens our account of equality.

Economic growth and prosperity

Concern for economic growth and prosperity drives our economic system and shapes much of our personal life. The 'growth fetish' has, in recent decades, been challenged from an environmental perspective and, more recently, by 'happiness economics'.[7] It is interesting, again, to note the prescience of de Tocqueville, who saw at an early stage in America the risk that democratic freedoms would lead to prosperity but at the risk of undermining the social relationships on which freedom and equality ultimately depend. He writes:

> As social conditions become more equal, the number of persons increases who, although they are neither rich nor powerful enough to exercise any great influence

---

6. Biblical social ethics are unfairly accused of not being egalitarian enough, especially in the realm of gender relations (see ch. 9).

7. See, e.g., Reeves (2003); Hamilton (2004) and Spencer (2003b).

over their fellows, have nevertheless acquired sufficient education and fortune to satisfy their own wants. They owe nothing to any man, they expect nothing from any man; they acquire the habit of always considering themselves as standing alone, and they are apt to imagine that their whole destiny is in their hands. Thus not only does democracy make every man forget his ancestors, but it hides his descendants and separates his contemporaries from him; it throws him back forever upon himself alone and threatens in the end to confine him entirely within the solitude of his own heart. (De Tocqueville 1972: 99)

He also warned of the dangers of materialism, 'a dangerous disease of the human mind':

> Democracy encourages a taste for physical gratification: this taste, if it become excessive, soon disposes men to believe that all is matter only; and materialism, in its turn, hurries them on with mad impatience to these same delights; such is the fatal circle within which democratic nations are driven round. It were well that they should see the danger and hold back. (De Tocqueville 1972: 145)

The concern for growth is, in part, a reflection of our personal desires, but is also, as chapter 11 argues, essential to maintain the stability of an interest-based financial system. It is not wholly inappropriate. Wealth is a blessing, albeit a dangerous one (Spencer 2003b). While growth does not automatically lead to happiness, economic decline is socially disruptive. We should not, however, make what should properly be the consequence of our right actions the goal of our life. Too often, social relationships are ordered merely to serve economic ends and are treated as without intrinsic value in the economic equation.

Security

Desire for personal and national security has come to dominate our concern for justice and profoundly shapes many of our relationships. In international relations, might is too often right. *Realpolitik* sees economic and military power as the source of security which, in the modern context, may need to be pre-emptively projected. As we shall see in chapter 14, the temptation for Israel was to seek security in alliances and to reject the call to trust in the Lord. Defeat and exile resulted. At a community level, fear of crime breeds a punitive culture, gated communities and preoccupation with 'stranger danger'. Responses to crime, itself rooted in relational failure, can further weaken the community relationships on which true safety depends. This is a far cry from the vision for criminal justice set out in chapter 13 which has at its heart a concern to uphold, protect and restore the relationships on which personal well-being rests.

In many ways, our social, economic and political institutions have developed to offer us far greater security than previous generations could expect. Following the introduction of the welfare state, the giants of want, disease, ignorance, squalor and idleness no longer loom so large over us. Yet a sense of physical, financial and emotional security remains elusive. The more our pursuit of security damages our relationships, the more alienated from the true source of security we become. Proverbs commends the prudence of the ant (6:6); the security that comes from thrift and hard work is not to be despised. Yet there is a point at which individual security is an illusion and a trap. We cannot insure and protect ourselves against every eventuality. Indeed, seeking to do so erodes the very relationships that might otherwise have constituted an alternative community of security. At a personal level we are called to find our security in faithful and loving relationships, and challenged to offer what security we can to others, rather than seek it for ourselves.

> If one falls down,
>   his friend can help him up.
> But pity the man who falls
>   and has no-one to help him up!
> (Eccl. 4:10)

The vision for welfare described in chapter 10 points in this direction.

Conclusion

Even from this very brief review of biblical and contemporary values it is clear that there are significant differences. *Really* valuing relationships, individually and collectively, sets different priorities. It should affect, for example, who we meet and how we spend our time, recognizing the needs of those who look to us for relationship as well as finding pleasure in the relationships of our choice. The danger is that we are so steeped in our own values that we have difficulty in fully understanding the mindset of the biblical social vision, particularly with regard to our individualistic assumptions. We should not regard our Western culture as a given, nor view it as necessarily superior or more 'developed'. Recent years have seen a significant shift in values with respect to the natural environment. A similar shift is needed in how we regard the social ecology. This is the context in which biblical teaching on social and economic issues needs to be heard.

7. Nationhood

Julian Rivers

The problem of nationhood

Against the popular orthodoxy that the nation-state and nationalism were products of the modern era, Adrian Hastings has recently argued that the Israelite model of nationhood portrayed in the Bible was decisive in forming the character of the English nation in the mediaeval period (Hastings 1997). He traces references and allusions from the Venerable Bede's *Ecclesiastical History of the English People* (730) to Foxe's *Book of Martyrs* (1570), and suggests that a model of nationhood created by centuries of assumption that England was like ancient Israel was in turn exported to continental Europe and then to the rest of the world. In similar vein, Joan Lockwood O'Donovan notes the impact of Israel on the Christian formation of nations (Lockwood O'Donovan 2004), a process which Richard Tuck observes had 'astonishing resilien[ce]' (Tuck 2003: 148).[1]

This Christian vision of nationhood became increasingly secularized. Scotland, which depended primarily on a version of the Calvinist conception taken up since the Reformation, is a case in point (Storrar 1990). Of course, the process of secularizing nationhood has not been smooth. Early twentieth-century Netherlands

---

1. According to Tuck, the only new kingdoms created in Europe between 950 and 1700 were those of Portugal and Sicily. See also, the discussion between Anthony Pagden and Oliver O'Donovan in the same volume.

provides a classic example of a late flowering of explicitly Calvinist thought. But the underlying trend is clear.

There is considerable academic disagreement about the causes and significance of the rise of nationhood, a disagreement mirrored in disputes about the meanings of 'nation', 'nationalism' and 'nation-state'. Confusion is compounded by uses of the word 'nation' where what is referred to is clearly not a matter of nations at all.[2] As regards the idea of the state, Max Weber's definition is largely accepted: a state is that organization enjoying a monopoly of legitimate force over people in a certain defined territory. It differs from a tribal organization of political power in that power-relations are defined primarily by reference to territory not to personal relationship. Nationalism is the view that each nation should have its own state, and that each state should be based on one nation: the nation-state is the ideal political form for the nationalist. But what is a nation?

One might think that whatever a nation is, it comes first, and that Nationalism is the demand that the nation take on a certain political form. One could envisage a nation without a nation-state. So it has been suggested that nations are 'imagined communities'. This is not to say that they are not real. Rather, they are cultural artefacts rooted in how we think and feel about others. It would seem that any shared group characteristic could be the basis for the formation of national identity and nationhood: it may or may not have ethnic, religious, linguistic or political components. But nations are not simply concerned with how we *think* about others beyond the family and locality. Though we rarely interact directly with our compatriots as such, we are subject to laws and conventions which presuppose a willingness to relate in certain ways and affect our actions towards them as well.

Ernest Gellner famously argued that nations are actually a product of Nationalism (Gellner 1983). His thesis was that growing industrialization through the nineteenth century required much higher levels of mobility and education than in predominantly agricultural societies. This provided the conditions under which people became aware of differences of prosperity and capable of responding collectively. Any feature of the people's history or culture could be adopted as a unifying device in creation of national consciousness and the demand for political autonomy. Thus was the nation invented, and by definition it needed a state to sustain it. As in Max Weber's account of Capitalism (Weber 1904–5), religion, particularly Protestant Christianity, might have a role in explaining

---

2. The United Nations, for example, would be better called the World Council of Governments, and international law, inter-statal law. See Walker Connor, 'A Nation is a Nation, is a State, is an Ethnic Group . . .' excerpted in John Hutchinson and Anthony D. Smith, *Nationalism* (Oxford: Oxford University Press, 1994, pp. 33–46).

the rise of industrialization and universal education. But it was not nation-forming as such.

In fact, Gellner accepted the argument associated with Kohn (Kohn 1985) and Plamenatz (Plamenatz 1973) that there are two main types of nation-forming process: 'Western' and 'Eastern'. According to this thesis, in Western Europe (primarily Germany, but also Italy) a common cultural heritage already existed in the nineteenth century, as indeed did a distant political heritage – so that the nationalistic unification movements later in the century were building on a pre-existing understanding of national identity. We can understand Hastings' recent work as an attempt to assert even more strongly, and at a much earlier stage of development, the priority of the cultural over the political in the Western model of nationhood. In Eastern Europe, however, nations were the product of processes of political reaction closer to Gellner's model. This is also the case in the two-thirds world, which has, ironically, reacted against Western colonial imperialism to adopt a political framework of nation-states also provided by the West, creating both nations and states in the process.

Whatever the processes by which the world has come to be divided up into nation-states, they now face a series of unprecedented challenges. Internally, politics seems to be increasingly stretched between an individualistic liberalism, whose cosmopolitanism holds out the ideal of a rootless individual enjoying universal human rights, owing allegiance only to common democratic institutions, and the movement towards multiculturalism, which senses that nationhood is too homogenizing, that it suppresses other relevant group identities (Kymlicka 1995). Multiculturalism seeks greater protection for minority rights, and often seeks to create and enhance the political rights of regional governments. Externally the pressures on nation-states are no less great: the economy and criminal activity, both of which need legal regulation, are increasingly global in organization, requiring international responses. The European Union represents an unprecedented attempt at integrating a large number of powerful nation-states for these purposes.

Thus even if one accepts Gellner's sociologically determinist account of the inevitability of the rise of nations, we are still left with questions and choices. David Miller (Miller 1995: 2–3) usefully identifies four groups of such questions: first, there are questions about boundaries. How big should states be? On what basis should they be constructed? Secondly, there are questions about sovereignty. Is it true that the governing body of a nation should be fully autonomous? What about lower levels of autonomy, such as present in federal arrangements and devolved regional government? What about membership in supra-state entities such as the European Union? Thirdly, there are internal questions, questions of immigration and citizenship policy, education and welfare rights. Finally, Miller asks ethical questions about the weight of the demands of nationality. Are the claims of a nation absolute? More prosaically, for example, how much should a state be spending on foreign aid as opposed to its own healthcare system? All of these questions are politically important, but they miss out on the prior relational questions: should there be a level of community beyond my own circles of family, work and local community, which is not simply the rest of humanity? If so, on what basis do the members of this community relate? And does that relating necessarily have the strong political and governmental components that the nationalist – and indeed Miller's questions – suggest? In short, what properly constitutes a nation?

This chapter cannot answer all these questions. However, it will attempt to begin to address them from a biblical foundation. It starts from the assumption that the nation of Israel as constituted, reconstituted, governed, described and criticized in the writings of the Old Testament is in some sense – quite how is admittedly not straightforward – normative. It was to be a 'light to the Gentiles' (Isa. 42:6). Important in understanding that 'light' is the relationship between Israel and the surrounding nations. But that light also has to be refracted through the prism of the New Testament, which in many different ways affects the political consequences of what it means to be the 'people of God', and hence the sphere of the social and political.

Israel as a nation

Out of the diversity of peoples, God called one people to be his nation. For Israel to be a nation, it needed to be commonly subject to Yahweh, and it is from that basic relationship that it took its shape. Michael Schluter and John Ashcroft (Schluter & Ashcroft 1988) identify six key components of Israelite national identity. First, there was shared ancestry. All looked back to Jacob, renamed Israel, the one who wrestled with God (Gen. 32:22–32), and were thus called the tribes of Israel, taking their names from the sons, or in the case of Ephraim and Manasseh, grandsons, of Jacob. Beyond Jacob and his father Isaac, their identity went back to Abraham, who had left Ur with the promise that he would be made a 'great nation' through whom all the 'families of the earth' would be blessed (Gen. 12:2–3).

Secondly, there was shared historical experience. The experience of exile and slavery in Egypt, the wanderings in the desert, and working together as life unfolded in Canaan built up bonds of unity between the tribes. Their relationship with God was expressed in historical terms: first those of the patriarchs: Abraham, Isaac and Jacob; and later those of the people as a whole. God is repeatedly identified as the one who brought the people out of Egyptian slavery (Exod. 19:4; Deut. 26:5–9; Josh. 24:2; Ezek. 20:5–26).

Thirdly, there was shared law. The common law code, or constitution, was known to every citizen and was central in creating national unity. Where the people fell away from this, it resulted in national decline. The key reform and movement for national renewal instituted by Josiah involved a reading of the Law, probably the book of Deuteronomy, rediscovered in the temple (2 Kgs 23:1–3; 2 Chr. 34:29–32).

Fourthly, there were shared regular cultural events. The three major national festivals – of Passover, Weeks and Tabernacles – were to be attended by every male adult every year. They made people from all parts of the country mix socially and reminded them of their common history. Some Old Testament scholars have suggested that the original form of the nation of Israel was an amphictyony (federation), centred on a common cult (Noth 1960), although this has been questioned as an adequate characterization (Mayes 1974). Certainly, a major point of contention after the division of the kingdoms was the attempt by Jeroboam to set up separate centres of worship in Bethel and Dan, independent of the temple in Jerusalem. The overthrow of the Northern Kingdom brought those remaining there back into the central cultus, and the book of Chronicles specifically describes how Josiah removed idolatry 'from all the territory that belonged to the people of Israel' (2 Chr. 34:33), followed by a re-unified celebration of the Passover in Jerusalem (2 Kgs 23:21–23; 2 Chr. 35:1–19).

Fifthly, 'social services' were not aligned ethnically. The Levites and priests, although themselves an ethnic group, had no special ethnic ties with any of the tribes of Israel. They lived in forty-eight towns scattered through the other tribes, including six cities of refuge for those fleeing their accusers.[3] Their role in health care, education and interpretation of the law made them a significant factor of national cohesion. The Levites were symbolically important as the tribe from which the priesthood came, and who had special duties within the temple. They preceded the monarchy as a focus of national unity and, together with the king, represented the presence of God among his people.

Finally – and with a certain degree of ambiguity – there was a common head of state. International relations require some central authority with overarching responsibility for maintaining links between polity and the external world. It was quite clear that the king expected to conduct negotiations with other powers, not only Egypt, but also Hiram of Tyre and the Queen of Sheba (1 Kgs 5 and 10). Where a purely tribal leader emerged, it was too narrow a base to represent the people as a whole. Even the judges were only able to call on ad hoc coalitions of tribes – seldom on the nation as a whole. While the tribes had no single person as head of state, there was a tendency to anarchy (Judg. 21:25). However, the role of

---

3. See Lev. 25:32–34; Num. 35:1–8; Josh. 21; 1 Chr. 6:39–66.

the king was heavily circumscribed by the law (Deut. 17:14–20; 1 Sam. 8), in order to limit his role to that of national figurehead, with a specific responsibility to care for the disadvantaged and to handle foreign relations. Although Samuel had queried on God's behalf the move towards a monarchy, it brought the benefits of a single and continuing authority of a central institution. However, it should be noted that scholars continue to dispute whether the weight of the biblical material lies on the side of cautious affirmation (O'Donovan 1996) or grudging acceptance (McConville 2002) of this element.

In short, Israelite nationhood consisted of a common faith, common language and literature, common religious practice and institutions, common laws, common political institutions and common history all located in a clearly defined territory. The biblical authors consistently conceive of Israelite nationhood in terms of a complete intertwining of all possible aspects of social identity. It has well been described as 'monolithic' (Hastings 1997: 18). Regardless of how this was actually experienced at any particular stage of history – and we know that the reality was often partial and conflictual – the *ideal* of a completely integrated community is regularly and clearly set out.

At the same time, certain elements of this integration receive special emphasis or are downplayed. In Joshua 22:19 the transjordan tribes were offered land within the inheritance of the other tribes, if that were necessary to preserve the unity of worship. The precise boundaries of the territory were only ever aspirational, and not absolutely critical. The gruesome events of Judges 19 – 21 display both the overriding need to preserve moral purity in Israel and the need to retain representatives of 'the twelve tribes'. Most striking of all is the downplaying of ethnic purity as a marker of national identity (Burnside 2001). Biblical law draws a distinction between different types of 'foreigner', ranging from those who were long-term residents across several generations and who wished to assimilate into Israelite culture, to 'strangers' or 'resident aliens' who might be only short-term visitors. The latter were to be treated fairly, but were not granted full civil rights. By contrast, Israel was remarkably open to foreigners wishing to assimilate. Biblical law specified that they should have the same legal rights and be subject to the same legal prohibitions as natives. They were to benefit from equal participation in the religious and political life of the nation; they were to have equal access to the cities of refuge and, most radically, at least one later text insists (perhaps only prophetically) that they were to have equal rural land rights in addition to property in the walled cities (Ezek. 47:22–23).

Furthermore, the effects of intermarriage could blur the racial boundaries. While there are several warnings against 'marrying foreign wives' (Exod. 34:16; 1 Kgs 11:1–3; Ezra 9 – 10; Neh. 13:23–27), of the four women mentioned by Matthew in the genealogy of Christ, two were Canaanite, one was Moabite and the fourth had married a Hittite. Moses married a Cushite (Num. 12:1). Apart from one case in which linguistic purity is threatened (Neh. 13:24), whenever intermarriage is prohibited, the reason is for the preservation of religious – not racial – purity. In other words, the first component of nationhood identified above is rendered subsidiary. The insignificance of ethnicity in the construction of Israelite nationhood is particularly interesting in the light of Adrian Hastings' distinction between French and German notions of citizenship. The former was historically rooted in territory – the *ius soli* – and has thus over time proved more amenable to social integration than the German, rooted as it is in the *ius sanguinis* (Hastings 1997: 13; Brubaker 1992).

While ethnic purity (and hence physical descent from Abraham) was down-played, the role of covenant in achieving national consciousness was emphasized. The solemn occasion at Sinai, when leaders of all the tribes pledged to follow Yahweh, was a key reference point for all the tribes to their common commitment to God and to one another. It was often recalled and renewed (e.g. Deut. 29:1), and was central to the way they understood themselves.

> A covenant creates a perpetual (or at least indefinitely continuing) bond between parties having independent but not necessarily equal status. That bond is based upon mutual obligations and a commitment to undertake joint action to achieve certain defined ends which may be limited or comprehensive, under conditions of mutual respect in such a way as to protect the fundamental integrity of all parties involved. A covenant is much more than a contract ... because it involves a pledge of loyalty beyond that demanded for mutual advantage, often involving the development of a certain kind of community among the partners to the covenant, and ultimately based upon a moral commitment. (Elazar & Cohen 1985: 8–10)

It has been argued that the book of Deuteronomy takes the form of the treaty with the Great King (Mendenhall 1955; Kline 1972). The centrality of this coven-ant to Israel's identity can be seen in the comment by the Deuteronomistic historian on Josiah: 'Neither before nor after Josiah was there a king like him who turned to the LORD as he did – with all his heart and with all his soul and with all his strength, in accordance with all the Law of Moses' (2 Kgs 23:25). It is significant that the good king is one who fosters justice and solidarity among the people.

The relation of God to his people is continually referred to as the basis of their identity and national structure. This underlying moral commitment of the parts to the whole orientates the body politic towards decision- and policy-making through negotiation and bargaining. It points towards federal arrangements which are by nature multi-centred and do not rely on the trend of centralized mechanisms associated with the modern nation-state (Logsdon 1991). A key component of national identity is a sense of horizontality – of people committed to each other, and owning their institutions and laws (Hastings 1997: 25). It was the covenant of Israel with God that above all else produced that sense of mutual commitment.

Israel among the nations

Israel was never a super-power, and yet it is clear from the Psalms and the messages of the prophets that whatever happened to them mattered supremely to God and, indeed, to the world. So what impact does the unique calling of Israel have on national identity more generally? The problem arises because the nations are defined in terms of their difference from Israel. Most importantly, they worship their own gods (Mic. 4:5). But they also speak their own languages, have their own laws and forms of government, and their own histories. Are they nations in the same sense as Israel?

Jonathan Sacks has recently argued that the covenant with Israel means that 'the Bible represents the great anti-Platonic narrative in Western civilization' (Sacks 2002: 51). In his view, the Old Testament affirms the value of national diversity unreservedly, even diversity in matters of faith and morality.[4] Further evidence for Sacks's radical thesis can be found in the value placed by biblical writers on cultural integration. Jeremiah's letter to the exiles exhorted them, in the light of their ensuing seventy-year absence, to 'build houses and settle down; plant gardens and eat what they produce. Marry and have sons and daughters . . . seek the peace and prosperity of the city to which I have carried you' (Jer. 29:5–7). Daniel and his friends received new names and became expert in Babylonian language and literature. Nehemiah was trusted enough to become cupbearer to the king, and Mordecai second in rank in the kingdom.

However, at one point assimilation was to be resisted: faith in the God who had revealed himself and saved his people was not negotiable.[5] Sacks fails to note that while cultural integration was good, it was subordinate to the preservation of religious truth.[6] This is key. For the judgment of nations is brought about by a God who has made his name known in a specific way to a specific people. He is Yahweh, not just any idea of God. And the nations must acknowledge that *this*

---

4. Sacks insists only on the 'natural law' limits implicit in the covenant with Noah.

5. Dan. 3:16–18; 6:10–11; it is likely that the refusal to eat the king's food was simply a marker of Daniel's refusal to accept total control over his whole life, rather than reflecting a concern for ritual purity (Baldwin 1978: 83).

6. This can give rise to tension when religion and culture are closely intertwined. See Ps. 137.

God is God. That, surely, is the point of Dagon's nosedive, Sennacherib's assassination and Darius's conversion (1 Sam. 5; 2 Kgs 19:20–37; Dan. 6:25–27).

For unlike the surrounding nations, the first affiliation to God by the patriarchs developed into a concept of the God of the nations, a theology well described as 'mono-Yahwism'. God is not a tribal deity like the others. Later still, through the period of exile, God was the one who exercises rule over all nations. Although this can be seen as a development, it was also implicit in the original promise to Abraham, 'in whom all the families of the earth would be blessed'. How else could Israel be 'a light to the Gentiles' except by bearing witness to this God as God? So to the extent that nations are nations because they serve different gods, the irruption into human affairs of the actions of *this* God raises a question about national identity. If the gods of the nations are not really gods at all, for only Yahweh is God, where then is nationhood?

In fact, the Bible contains a considerable amount of material about nations other than Israel. Karl Barth observed that in this respect the Bible opens on a note of ambiguity (Barth, *CD* III/4: 311–323). They are not part of the created order, which instead is based on the unitary nature of humanity derived from one set of parents. Rather, the nations are first of all (Gen. 10) a fulfilment of the creation mandate, renewed with Noah (Gen. 9:7), to fill the earth, and to do so in all diversity. This table is repeated in 1 Chronicles 1:1 – 2:2, where the nations of the world are listed in order from North, West, South and East with Israel at its centre. God gave the land of Canaan to Israel, but he assigned territory to other tribes as well (Deut. 2:5–9; Lorberbaum 2003: 25). This vision of the world is taken up again by the prophets (Isa. 66; Scott 1994). National and linguistic diversity is portrayed here in a positive light: a divine contribution to the richness of the cultural as well as the natural order. By contrast, the destruction of Babel in Genesis 11 sees linguistic diversity as a mark of God's judgment on human pride. It prevents the accumulation of power by a system of cultural checks and balances. It is a necessary evil rather than a positive good. This contrast is not equivocation on the part of Scripture. Rather it reflects a tension found throughout the biblical texts and in our own experience as well.

However, the matter is more complex than either Sacks's radical cultural diversity thesis, or Barth's moderate realism allows. One of the strongest markers of national identity is language. Quite apart from the Babel narrative the use of language as an index of national identity is common. To be dominated or surrounded by foreign languages is a threat.[7] The imperial decrees recited in Esther and Daniel are addressed to 'peoples, nations and languages' and elsewhere in the prophets national diversity is tied to linguistic diversity (Jer. 5:15; Ezek. 5:6;

---

7. See Deut. 28:49; Neh. 13:24; Ps. 114:1; Isa. 28:11–13.

Zech. 8:23). It is therefore striking to read passages that connect the eschatological vision of the realized rule of God to a common language. Isaiah 19:18 refers to five cities in Egypt speaking the language of Canaan, and Zephaniah 3:9 rather more ambiguously talks of the 'purification' of the speech of the peoples. Metaphorical or not, this is instructive because it gestures towards a future 'greater Israel' rather than national diversity under one God.

The book of Psalms is astonishingly full of such expansive visions of future blessing. The Lord, who loves the righteous, watches over aliens and sustains the fatherless and the widow, is the same God who rules over the nations (Ps. 82). All peoples will praise God for his just rule and salvation (Ps. 67); Rahab and Babylon, Philistia, Tyre and Ethiopia were born in Zion, the glorious city of God (Ps. 87), and will gather there to worship (Ps. 102:2).

In short, the prophetic vision of universal blessing arising from Israel can be conceived as many nations (gôyim) joined to become one people ('am), as in Zechariah 2:11. 'Nation' is here understood in a minimalistic tribal sense, so the vision is essentially unified, imperial and theocratic. Just as God had taken the tribes of Jacob and constituted them a people for himself, so he would do with the whole world. This understanding of the nature of Israel's future and idealized relationship to the nations is fully compatible with the remarkable openness to ethnic integration noted above. And the vision of divinely orchestrated empire is also consistent with the constant critique of human empire-building. It is God's prerogative to build a world empire, and he will do it (Dan. 2:44–45).

The conclusion one has to draw, from the Old Testament alone, is that nations are God-given groupings of people characterized to varying extents by different factors. We might envisage the Israelite nation as a series of concentric circles, with a common faith in, and law of, Yahweh at the heart, common language and history around it, centralized political institutions around that, and common ethnicity right at the periphery, even dropping out of the picture. The religious component means that while there are nations apart from Israel, no nation is quite like Israel. False worship at the heart of a nation does not destroy identity as a nation, so it is good to be a nation, but better still to be joined to Israel in its worship of Yahweh, whose loving intent is to bless all peoples through his people.

Nationhood transformed

The most important claim of the New Testament is that Jesus Christ represents the fulfilment of Israel's eschatological hope. The Gospels present the ministry of Jesus as radically inclusive in the face of organized religion's exclusivity. He himself experienced ethnic prejudice on account of his perceived origins in Nazareth (John 1:46), and he taught and healed in Samaritan and Gentile regions around Israel.[8] Of course, Jesus' inclusivity was not without limits, made apparent, for example, in John 4. While he broke social convention by speaking to a woman and a non-Jew, he neither compromised his ethical criticism of her serial polygamy (vv. 17–18) nor his belief in the superiority of the Jewish understanding of God (v. 22). Racial and cultural barriers are broken down, but doctrinal and ethical truth is reasserted. This distinction remains the hallmark of apostolic teaching, summed up by Paul in Galatians 5:6: 'neither circumcision nor uncircumcision has any value. The only thing that counts is faith expressing itself through love'.

The deep divisions between Jew and non-Jew in the early church led to an emphasis on cultural and ethnic issues in the epistles. Paul insists that a Christ-centred view of the world will mean equality of status for Christians whatever their racial or ethnic background. Christians are part of a single building, a holy temple in the Lord; they are fellow citizens in the context of the church, they are co-inheritors, co-members and co-partakers of the promise in Christ (Eph. 3:6). So the idea of foreigners as equal citizens in Israel is spiritualized and universalized by the apostles (Eph. 2:12, 19), as the prophets had foretold.[9] Imagery of the perfect heavenly city in which all believers have the privilege of citizenship is common-place.[10] Once the New Testament authors made the connection between the expansive Old Testament vision of the future blessings of Israel and the kingdom of God announced by Jesus, there might have been nothing more to say about social and political organization in the present. Whatever structures exist simply form the backdrop to the growth of the church, which is the new society seen prophetically. But there are ample reasons for doubting this.

First, national identity matters because it is part of the riches of the kingdom of God. It is precisely because the proper worship of God has been removed from the political sphere, that national diversity is – if anything – more valued in the New Testament than seen as problematic. So it is transformed, not removed. At Pentecost, each person heard God's salvation proclaimed in his own language, not in a new common tongue (Acts 2:6). Paul accommodated himself to the cultural diversity of his audiences, and the new Jerusalem is filled with the nations and the splendour of the kings of the earth. Here, there is diversity without division.[11]

---

8. Mark 7:21 – 8:21 is an extended account of Gentile inclusion in the kingdom of God.

9. See the way in which Heb. 8:11 translates Jer. 31:34.

10. E.g. Phil. 1:27; 3:20; Heb. 11:10, 16; 12:22; Rev. 3:12; 21:2, 14; 22:14, 19.

11. Rev. 7:9; 22:2. Whatever language it is that we will use to worship the Lamb together, it is better understood as a multiplicity of natural languages. In this respect there is development from the 'Zion-imperialism' of the later Old Testament.

However, the fact that cultural distinctions are insignificant does not mean that they are to be disregarded. Just as the Holy Spirit worked through different languages to reach the crowds at Pentecost, so Paul was willing to use cultural distinctives as a vehicle for the communication of the gospel (1 Cor. 9:19–23). Timothy was circumcised, Titus was not. What was wrong was the collective insistence on 'moral' or ritual requirements which only perpetuate division and give a spurious sense of moral purity (Gal. 5:2–3; Col. 2:16–22). When the early church formally considers whether all Christians should follow particular cultural norms, almost all are ruled out (Acts 15). Thus there is no attempt in the New Testament to obliterate national or cultural distinctives. It is equality of status and complete unity in the body of Christ, rather than cultural uniformity, which are the concerns of the apostles.

Secondly, national identity matters, because Israel still matters as a nation. In Romans 11:25, Paul argues that the rejection of 'Israel' is only temporary, part of the purposes of God to ensure the salvation of the Gentiles. In verse 12 he contrasts the 'riches' which their rejection of Christ has meant for the world, with the 'much greater riches' of their fullness in the future. Attempts to understand the whole of Romans 11 in terms of a spiritualized Israel (i.e. the church) make a nonsense of this argument. There is a corporate salvation by which God honours his promise to the patriarchs. 'All Israel' is the greater Israel of which the prophets spoke – both Jew and Gentile united in worship of God and the Son by which he has revealed himself (Moo 1996: 670–739).[12]

Finally, national identity matters because the cultural and the political have been divided. Oliver O'Donovan rightly observes a shift in the function of government from Old to New Testaments. In part, he locates this shift in a loss on the part of government of responsibility for the perpetuation of tradition. Its function is now solely the exercise of judgment, as stressed by Paul in Romans 13:1–7, a move, as it were, from culture to law (O'Donovan 1996: 146–147).[13] This means that, under Christ, political identity is less significant and provisional only. It also opens up the possibility of multiple identities: Paul is simultaneously a Jew of the tribe of Benjamin (Rom. 11:1; Phil. 3:5), a Roman citizen (Acts 21:39) and an apostle of Christ Jesus (Rom. 1:1, etc.). For our purposes, it suggests that we should draw a distinction between who we are in relation to government (our civic identity), who we are in relation to our nation (our cultural identity) and who we are in the church (our ecclesial identity). This of course means that we should be

---

12. This reading of Rom. 11 is, of course, controversial.

13. Chaplin (2002: 290–304) would want to argue that the New Testament assertion of justice ('judgment') as the central role of government is a recovery of a creational mandate, not a new act of God.

thinking in this area in terms of three distinct types of relationship: to fellow-citizens as political equals, to those with whom we share a national culture as cultural equals, and to fellow-members of the church as brothers and sisters in Christ.

To summarize, what we find in the Bible is, first of all, a balance in the claims of nationhood. It is good to be part of a nation, but national identity is not the most important feature of personal identity. Secondly, we find guidance as to the proper components of nationhood, a playing up of language and history, a playing down of ethnicity. Thirdly, and later, we also find a distinction between culture and government, which has become more narrowly legal. And finally there is the need for transformation, for national identity must be brought under the sovereignty of Christ and fulfilled in Christ.

Nationhood in the modern world

The Bible does not answer every question that arises in the context of a discussion of nationhood, but it does offer some pointers.

First of all, it is positive about nationhood and explicitly negative about empire-building for political and cultural purposes.

Secondly, it is impossible to square the biblical material with a romantic, or organic, conception of nationalism. Dominant in the late nineteenth and early twentieth centuries, this suggests that peoples have a natural national character best protected and expressed through a unified political order. It tends to pursue ethnic purity and idolize the collectivity. It reached its apogee in fascism, and was rightly resisted by the confessing church in Germany. How can Christians who accept equal status before God with those of other races in the spiritual state, then deny those same people equal political and economic status in the secular state? An earthly citizenship which is equally guaranteed to all is a better symbol of spiritual reality than any form of legal stratification or classification.

On the other hand, one cannot simply rest content with the civic conception of nationalism that has come to dominate since the Second World War. This presupposes that nations are simply societies of autonomous individuals coming together for convenience under a regime of universal law, or in the modern idiom, universal human rights. All they share is a commitment to democratic governmental institutions. This assumes too readily the accidental nature of national boundaries and treats human beings as non-cultural rational beings.

Thus, thirdly, we should be looking for a conception of nationhood that mediates between the organic and the civic (Miller 1995). Critiques of 'pure' notions of organic and civic nationalism are not uncommon. For example, the Scottish nationalist and constitutional theorist, Neil MacCormick acknowledges that nationalism is generally assumed to be incompatible with liberal political morality (MacCormick 1999). However, he argues for a middle ground between what he calls 'civic' and 'ethnic' nationalism, which depends on identifying aspects of 'cultural nationalism' rendered necessary by the requirements of respect for persons as 'contextual individuals'. In a move reminiscent of communitarian critiques of liberal individualism he argues that humans are necessarily socially constituted. National identity is in that sense natural. Of course, a nation may not map directly on to a state. Scotland retains a strong (and MacCormick implies, positive) cultural identity regardless of its political status. And of course, national self-determination is only one principle among many others, including non-discrimination and respect for human rights. But in principle – according to MacCormick – political and legal authority should map onto national identity. There is a connection between self-determination and respect for individuals as autonomous, but socially-constituted, agents. Most of the hostility to nationalism derives, he suggests, from notions of the absolutely sovereign nation-state, not from ideas of national identity *per se*. In short, his point is that a conception of nationalism that goes beyond a purely Kantian universal-individualistic civic nationalism is required by morally significant aspects of human nature and fully compatible with liberal principle.

The problem is knowing where to locate those non-threatening, but non-voluntary, components of national identity. Joan Lockwood O'Donovan argues that what is missing from the modern debate about nationhood is a Christian sense of the nation as a community of judgment. Picking up on the Christian tradition of political reflection, she writes:

> In the feudal conception of the judge (whether king or lesser magistrate) as one who 'found' the law rather than 'made' it, and in the respect paid to the commonly 'found' customs of communities, the close relationship between the law and the moral judgment of both the one and the many was affirmed. And therein was also affirmed the close relation between laws and the broader sentiments, tastes, manners and affections of communal life. Indeed it is just this relationship between a society's political-legal definition and its cultural-moral community that the concept of 'the nation' chiefly expressed in the theo-political tradition. (Lockwood O'Donovan 2004: 294)

While the centrality which Lockwood O'Donovan wants to give to common law in her conception of nationhood is initially attractive, and has obvious resonances with the centrality given to covenant in the Bible, one must note a major New Testament difficulty. Law today is not simply the concretized custom of a community but the pre-eminent tool of governmental power. So it follows that by rooting nationhood in law, one fails to capture the possibility of a conception of nationhood prior to, and independent of, government. The biblical idea of a nation seems to be culturally richer, but less politically implicated, than this.

The Bible affirms a conception of nationhood that is ethnically open, centred not finally on government, but on language, literature, history and faith. It is not the function of government to enforce religious orthodoxy (see ch. 8, below), but this does not mean that the nation is not blessed 'whose God is the LORD' (Pss. 33:12; 144:15). In what domain can this blessing be experienced if not in the transformation of culture? While deploring the legacy of oppression, Western Christians can rightly glory in the historic role of our faith and Bible in forming national character, language and literature.[14] We do well to trace the work of God over time, for as far as cultural integration is concerned, it has been pointed out that we do not each need to tell exactly the same story about our history, so long as the basic materials are held in common.[15] The widespread ignorance of English history and literature is a far greater threat to national identity than immigration or religious pluralism. This may suggest a better, if rather old-fashioned, remedy to cultural integration than citizenship studies, useful though they may be.[16] But this strong sense of national identity is acceptable only if it is also politically and legally tolerant. From a political and legal perspective, all citizens must be treated equally in respect of their religion or none. The danger of Lockwood O'Donovan's conception of nationhood as a community of judgment is that it would seem to result in a dilemma. Either one is committed to equal basic civil and political rights in law, which leads to a universal-individualistic liberal civic nationalism which fails to explain our richer sense of belonging, or one is prepared to abandon basic rights, which leads to an oppressive *Kulturstaat*. In short, by making 'law' the mediating component between organic and civic nationalism, she jeopardizes the limitation of government to which the Bible also bears witness.

Ultimately this means that from a biblical perspective we should be suspicious of too close an identity of nation with state. For we relate to our fellow-citizens on the basis of political equality – whatever their language, background and faith. But we relate to our compatriots on the basis of our common language, history and, hopefully, faith as well. A perfect distinction is not possible, or even desirable,

---

14. See Daniell (2003) for a recent and robust celebration of the massive cultural impact of early English translations of the Bible.

15. David Goodhart, *The Guardian*, 24 February 2004.

16. It is reported that Chinese schools are increasingly teaching the Bible in order to assist in understanding Western culture. At the same time widespread ignorance of the Bible at home makes the teaching of English literature an uphill struggle.

since the Rule of Law requires a certain basis of cultural homogeneity. Law can never be culturally pure. But in principle it would seem that we should be aiming for a sense of nationhood that is less political, and a politics that is less national. Moderating forms of political organization found in federal or regional systems such as Canada, Germany, Belgium or Switzerland – or even the UK after devolution – are likely better to achieve this.

8. Government

Julian Rivers

On reading the Bible politically

The use of the Bible to establish binding norms of political morality has to surmount several difficulties. Many of these are canvassed elsewhere in this book and need not be rehearsed here. However, two points in relation to this chapter's subject-matter should be emphasized. The first is that there is a long tradition of Christian political reflection on the Bible which is both an inspiration and a liability. The diversity of political arrangements which have been justified 'biblically' is about as broad as the diversity of political arrangements which have ever been defended and implemented within the Western world.[1] This suggests a certain degree of humility, if not downright scepticism, about the possibility of establishing a biblical framework for political order (Kraynak 2001).

To the modern reader many older political readings of the Bible appear unacceptably narrow. When Archbishop Cranmer compared Edward VI to King Josiah, this might have been pastorally appropriate at the time (if you are going to enforce religious reformation, you had better make sure you get it right!) but a consistent political theory built on the basis of the godly Old Testament monarch – as for example in Bossuet's *Politics Drawn from Holy Scripture* (pub. posth. 1709) – is not only oppressive; it neglects vast tracts of the source material. The same

---

1. See O'Donovan & Lockwood O'Donovan 1999, for an invaluable sourcebook in Christian political thought.

point can be made about one of the more powerful political theological movements of the twentieth century: liberation theology. This takes an important theme within the biblical witness and treats it as the whole. One of the strengths of Oliver O'Donovan's *The Desire of the Nations* (1996) is that it seeks faithfulness to the whole of Scripture. The relatively recent rediscovery within biblical studies of the political resonances of the New Testament (N. T. Wright 2002) has the potential to make all the more fruitful the enterprise of reading the Bible politically.[2] So one of the aims of this chapter is to set out themes within the whole Bible which are of particular political significance.

Indeed, we will undoubtedly want to organize our political theology around a biblical *leitmotif*. One might take (as O'Donovan does) 'the kingdom of God' as the key concept, seeking to reflect on the political consequences of what God has revealed about the nature of his kingdom and the role of human government in relation to that kingdom. Alternatively, one might point to the primary significance of 'covenant' structuring the relationships between God and human beings, spiritual and political (McConville 2002). The idea of the 'law of God' is another candidate for the same function with an honourable tradition.

Furthermore, the political themes we identify in the Bible will have to be sensitive to development and perspective. Our political thought must be located salvation-historically between Pentecost and the return of Christ, and that means not implicitly in Eden, on Sinai, in the earthly ministry of Christ or in the world to come. The biblical writers wrote incarnationally: to specific people in specific situations. The fact that the civil obedience of Romans 13 may need balancing by the anti-institutional polemic of Revelation 18 does not *necessarily* mean that there is an underlying ethical incompatibility. All this affects not only our sense of who and where we are, but also how we adapt and adopt what was normative for others in their context.

Supposing, then, that we can construct a biblical account of political order, we face a second major difficulty located in the translation process from 'then' to 'now'. Establishing a biblical ethic in matters of personal morality is *relatively* straightforward, since forms of human behaviour remain reasonably constant. However, our basic political concepts ('state', 'sovereignty', 'constitution', 'government', 'law') are themselves the cultural products of past political and ethical choices. Even the concept of 'the political' is culturally contingent, implying today a series of distinctions, for example, from commercial, religious, social and private spheres, which are not universally necessary. These concepts are not neutral conduits

---

2. Bauckham (1989) has provided us with nine wonderfully insightful political readings of the Bible, which are nevertheless not systematized.

by which biblical content can be brought to bear on the present.[3] They cannot function as a foundation, to be defined at the outset; rather they point merely to an area of thought and human endeavour in which we wish to think biblically.

In the light of these difficulties, it is tempting simply to trace the impact of the church on political order over time, and from that sociological-historical enterprise to derive normative lessons. But just as the Bible is not 'unaware' of its potential impact on the political sphere, so we in our turn are not released from the obligation to sketch a systematic political theology, however tentative. This chapter will first identify a number of interlocking ideas which establish the modern domain of political morality before identifying those biblical themes which seem to bear upon that domain. Inevitably, this will represent only an initial and programmatic orientation towards the material. But the chapter does also have the function of establishing the basis on which it is appropriate in subsequent chapters to look much more closely at specific Old Testament texts in relation to specific political issues, for it is only in the light of a whole-Bible perspective that these can be properly considered.

'State' and 'government', 'constitution' and 'law'

The dominant tradition within Western political thought from the late eighteenth century finds in the idea of a constitution a means of bringing the government of a state under law. Following Max Weber, a state has three basic components: an organization enjoying a monopoly of legitimate force, a people and a territory. The 'organization' can be termed 'government'; government for these purposes embracing not only 'the Government', or the policy-making and executive branch, but the entire process by which political authority is exercised. A constitution is a codified, legally binding statement of the fundamental principles of political order, entered into on the basis of a democratically grounded constituent act, and making provision for a separation and limitation of legislative, executive and judicial branches of government, representative democracy, the Rule of Law, the legal protection of individual civil and political rights and basic social welfare. This definition is closely associated with the idea of the nation-state, hence the common assumption that adopting a European constitution must symbolize the creation of a European nation-state. Sovereignty, which is the ultimate form of human authority, resides in the nation-state, and is to be expressed in and through a constitution as defined above.

---

3. It is fashionable to refer to these concepts as 'essentially contested' after Gallie
   (1964: 157–191).

In reality, there is considerable diversity about the use of these terms, a diversity which is not simply linguistic, but sometimes masks underlying value-judgments about proper political order. A number of relatively recent shifts in the nature of political order should be borne in mind.

First, there has been a shift in the nature of law from customary or common law to legislation. While law was still predominantly created out of a tradition of judicial decision-taking in individual cases, it was still possible to conceive of law as part of the natural social order. Thus in the eighteenth century there was a real practical sense in which general principles of the law and the constitution were identical. Government could be seen as just one part of that order, under law, fulfilling certain defined functions such as the administration of justice, defence and the preservation of public order. As the nineteenth century progressed, the volume of legislation increased exponentially, such that law became increasingly the law made by a system of government, in principle subject only to the will of the legislature, albeit a democratically legitimate one.

At the same time as the nature of law was changing, so also government was taking on in ever-increasing measure responsibility for the complete well-being of society. Thus the nature of the executive branch changed from 'execution' in the classical sense of carrying out the decisions of other institutions, such as the King in Council, Parliament and the courts, to being a complex administrative structure for the formulation and delivery of policy in every conceivable area of life. Controversy about the limits of 'the state' became a familiar feature of the twentienth century as a result.

Most recently of all, the nature of constitutions has been redefined in the light of these developments. After a brief early flowering in Cromwell's *Instrument of Government* (1653), the golden age of constitution-framing paralleled the rise of legislation and legal codification, stretching from the last quarter of the eighteenth century until today. The United Kingdom is almost unique in not having a codified constitution. Earlier constitutions were only intended to establish and regulate the principal organs of government, and more narrowly the executive branch of government. There is in this perspective an extremely close connection between the idea of a constitution and the separation of powers.[4] Such constitutions often emerged against a background of existing law and legal institutions which were as much presupposed as affected by the emerging constitution. So in a narrow sense constitutional law was simply the law of governmental institutions, distinct from (say) family law or criminal law, and merging imperceptibly into administrative

---

4. Article 16, 'Declaration of the Rights of Man and the Citizen' (1789): 'A society where rights are not secured or the separation of powers established has no constitution at all.'

law. Furthermore, many of the earlier 'constitutions' were not intended to be judicially enforceable; they were merely aspirational or conventional. For example, the French 'Declaration of the Rights of Man and the Citizen' (1789) was a purely political statement, incorporated by reference into the Constitution of the Fifth Republic of 1958, but only given legal significance from the early 1970s (Bell 1992: 29–33). It was a stroke of considerable political genius when in *Marbury v. Madison* (1803) the United States Supreme Court declared the Constitution to be fundamental law and thus judicially enforceable. Even today there are continuing debates about whether political goals, such as 'full employment' or 'universal literacy', should appear in constitutional texts, and whether conventional standards of political behaviour, such as governmental accountability to Parliament, should be judicially enforceable.

However, in recent years, largely as a result of an expanding constitutional rights jurisprudence, and in line with a significant 'juridification' of many aspects of society, the scope of constitutional law has expanded considerably until it embraces the fundamental principles of all areas of law.[5] Since in practice the constitution means what the constitutional judiciary say it means, there has been to some extent a return to a 'common law' position in which the fundamental legal order of a society is seen as customary, rooted in its particular political values, and applied in concrete cases by the judges. The key difference is that the judiciary increasingly dominate the legislative process, leading to an unstable tension, both in theory and practice, between constitutional rights and democratic law-making.

These developments mean that inevitably we approach the biblical material with a set of predetermined questions and problems: what is the meaning and scope of political action? What functions should be carried out by centralized executive institutions? What is the role of law, and the judiciary, in the political order? And while it is right to seek biblical answers to these questions, we must recognize that they are not questions the biblical writers consider directly.

Themes of political order

Government rests in the people under God

The Bible ultimately locates all authority, including political authority, in God. Once the trinitarian distinction of roles emerges, it is exercised on his behalf by Jesus Christ.[6] This means that all those who wield political authority do so on

---

5. See Alexy (2002: ch. 10) for a defence of the view that all law is constitutional.
6. Ps. 2; John 19:11; and Phil. 2:11 (in which the point is that Caesar is *not* Lord).

behalf of God and are accountable to God for the use they make of that authority. The right to exercise authority on God's behalf is given to humanity at creation (Gen. 1:28; 9:1–7) but is claimed and will be reclaimed by Christ at the end of time (Matt. 28:18; Rev. 11:15–19). So God is portrayed in the Bible as exercising his political authority both directly, through the providential rise and fall of nations, and indirectly, through human beings (Matt. 22:15–22; Rom. 13:1–7; 1 Pet. 2:13).

On the classical question of whether government should be by the one, the few or the many, the Bible is mostly silent. Anyone who fulfils the tasks of government has the authority of government (Rom. 13:1). This general point is strong enough to lead a considerable body of Christian political thought not to express any view on the proper location of human authority. At the same time, the Bible seems to express a preference for locating ultimate human political authority with 'the many'. In bringing the tribes (*gôyim*) of Israel out of Egypt, God not only formed them into a people ('*am*), but constituted them into a political assembly (*kol-'ēdâ yiśrā'ēl*) (Elazar & Cohen 1985: 11). It was this 'whole congregation of Israel' that was the covenant partner with God, involved in the making and renewal of the covenant and in the acclamation of kings.[7] The political act of constituting a disparate mass of human beings into a corporate entity receives its spiritual counterpart in the New Testament, in which to be 'a people' is similarly rich in connotation (Rom. 9:25–26; 1 Pet. 2:9–10). Thus it is best to conceive of political authority in the Bible as resting humanly in the People under God, even though others may legitimately exercise it on behalf of, or even in place of, the People.

The ultimate source of constitutional authority in the United Kingdom is obscure, and indeed deliberately was left obscure in the settlement following the Revolution of 1688. Although the doctrine of Parliamentary Sovereignty has been taken by some to be the 'ultimate political fact' (Wade 1955), which might indicate a location of authority in 'the People', in reality that doctrine is itself limited and limitable by the judiciary. Modern constitutions tend explicitly to locate ultimate authority in the People, and this is expressed by the processes by which such constitutions are adopted.

Locating ultimate human authority ('sovereignty') in the People is a constitutional commonplace; acknowledging that the People are under God is not. One might think that there is no real difference, but it is significant in three respects. First, it sets limits to political sovereignty. In fact, it means that there is no such thing as sovereignty, if that is understood in the Rousseauian sense to mean 'the right to set any content as law'. The People are obligated to God to do justice, because they are under God. But secondly, the limits set to the authority of the

---

7. See 1 Sam. 8:24; 1 Kgs 1:39; 2 Kgs 11:12; 23:1–3; Neh. 8.

People are not the limits set by natural morality. One of the biggest challenges of Western constitutional theory has been to explain the legitimacy of government on the basis of natural morality alone. This is a challenge because states claim the right to do things which no person could claim of another (to send conscripts to fight in a war, for example). Because governmental authority derives from God, it has a remit beyond that of natural morality. Finally, the fact that authority is located in the People under God explains why there can be ongoing responsibility to victims of state oppression even after radical personal and constitutional change.

These considerations seem to indicate that it is actually quite important that the constitution of a state acknowledge its obligation to God. Of course, at one level what matters is that the limits to political authority are secure, and this may be done without referring to the theological or philosophical justifications for those limits (Chaplin 2002: 289). On the other hand, the symbolic limitation to be found in the texts of preambles, legislative prayers, acts of coronation, and even certain types of Christian establishment may also play an important part.[8]

Government has a divine purpose

The function of government is to use force (Rom. 13:4) to ensure peace (1 Tim. 2:2), justice (Rom. 13:3; 1 Pet. 2:14) and liberty (1 Tim. 2:4; 1 Pet. 2:16). While Christians are to eschew violence in their personal relations, the maintenance of justice by force is the assumed social context of that self-denying ordinance. John the Baptist commanded repentant soldiers to be content with their wages and avoid oppression (Luke 3:14); two of the earliest believers were centurions in the Roman army (Matt. 8:5–13; Acts 10 – 11). It is never suggested that their new-found faith was incompatible with their existing role. For Paul, divinely mandated government bears the sword, and this is not just symbolic. The best way of reconciling all this material with Christ's injunction of non-violence (Matt. 5:39) is to accept that the existence of government is morally significant, that political and personal morality are distinct. Governments are allowed to do what as individuals we may not. Government is thus the collective practical expression of a certain sort of love of neighbour, which both justifies and sets limits to the use of force (Ramsey 1968). Put only slightly differently, the task of government is judgment: to render determinate and enforce the justice of God in human affairs.

A cursory reading of New Testament passages on government gives a picture of a minimalist, night-watchman state, concerned to establish defence and criminal justice, but leaving social welfare up to private enterprise. Many American

---

8. O'Donovan argues that a form of establishment may be justified on the basis that 'the church has to instruct [ruling power] in the ways of the humble state' (1996: 219).

Christian republicans end up being remarkably libertarian as a result. But it is important not to confuse the scope of the political sphere with the means of achieving desirable ends. It may well be that poverty is best addressed only through schemes of charity (although the evidence suggests not); the question is whether a concern with poverty is legitimately within the scope of politics. It is a striking feature of Old Testament law that it seeks simultaneously to achieve social welfare *and* limited government. This law is continuous with God's character. Psalm 146 is striking in its universal application of the key social features of Mosaic law: as is so common in the Psalms, a statement of God's universal authority over all creation is followed by a celebration of his character in ethical terms and its outworking in social terms. Nothing in the New Testament suggests that the values set out here are not equally and universally good, and legitimately within the scope of society and its political institutions today.

Government is limited

The mere fact that political authority is under God implies limitation. One of the clearest political principles to emerge from the New Testament is the fact that government has no authority over religious matters (Acts 4:19–20). With Christ the kingdom of God is no longer a political entity (John 18:36). As had already been foreshadowed in the Law's division of priestly and kingly roles, there is a fundamental distinction between church and government (Luke 20:25). This means that there can no longer be any easy parallelism between covenanting at Sinai and constituting a state. We take this so much for granted now, but from a world-wide and historical perspective it is revolutionary. The idea that one should refrain from using governmental power in the service of ultimate truth is barely intelligible, so it is hardly surprising that the church of the fourth century should fall for the temptations of political power. This belief, in the non-competence of the state to enforce matters of Christian truth (and *a fortiori* to enforce religious falsehood), is the power-house of the civil liberty we now enjoy. Oliver O'Donovan calls this idea, 'the doctrine of the Two' (O'Donovan 1996: ch. 6). Even at the height of mediaeval politics, the church was not the state and the state was not the church.

The problem is knowing how broadly to define the scope of the 'religious' over which government has no jurisdiction. Religion impacts on ethics and thereby on law. One way of proceeding is to generalize out from activity which is distinctively Christian. On this account, prayer, praise, reading, meeting, teaching, ceremonies, proselytism, and service to the poor, the sick and the oppressed are 'religious' activities, whatever their doctrinal basis and content. In these matters there is liberty, because they are not the law's business.

The problem of delimitation means that we may have to accept certain overlaps between the spheres of church and state, for example in education and welfare, in which each has to respect the responsibility of the other and cooperate to satisfy the needs of humanity. Just as law inevitably gets caught in a tension between nationhood and statehood (see ch. 7 above), so also it gets caught in the tension between church and state.

Government must act through law

Law is the opposite of sin (Rom. 7:7–8). There is some universal knowledge of this, which is consistent with the biblical witness to the unity of humanity and the universality of God's justice (Rom 2:14–15).[9] The idolatrous worship of economic prosperity, persecution of God's people, treaty-breaking, torture, slave-trading and desecration were all included by the prophet Amos in the causes of God's anger against nations (Amos 1:3 – 2:3). But law is also a special gift of God. To have his law is to have wisdom and to be blessed among the nations (Deut. 4:1–8). Just as political authority derives ultimately from God, so also law is the mode by which that authority is expressed. Government authority – whether kingly or secular – never escapes from the requirements of God's law (Deut. 17:14–20; 1 Sam. 10:25).

God does not simply project his law onto his creatures. He enters into relationship with his creation by way of covenant, and law constitutes the terms of that relationship. There is dispute over whether the concepts of covenant and contract are interchangeable in the biblical context. The difference between the concepts is that a covenant is a unilateral but potentially conditional expression of willingness to be bound; a contract is a bilateral arrangement whereby failure by one party releases the other from their obligations. The distinction turns on the source of the obligation; in the case of covenant it is self-motivated; in the case of contract it derives from submission to the will of the other. At any rate in the case of God it seems more appropriate to talk in terms of self-binding (covenant) rather than submission to human will (contract).

There are numerous injunctions in the Old Testament to internalize the law (e.g. 'bind them to your foreheads', Deut. 6:4–9), and Psalm 119 is an extended meditation upon it. Jesus' ethic is at root not a denial of law but the requirement to internalize taken to its limit. The great salvation promise was that 'the law' would be written on people's hearts, not on tablets of stone (Ezek. 36:24–28). Paul can even go as far as saying that the law is contrary to everything that is contrary to sound gospel teaching (1 Tim. 1:9–11). Modern accounts of the Rule of Law stress the need for official action to conform to stated rule, and the requirement to internalize law could be seen simply as a means to this end. But the culturally

---

9. Natural law argumentation is much more common in the Old Testament than is generally assumed (Barton 1998: 58–76).

contingent public/private distinction should not be read into this: a country lives under the Rule of Law when all people live by a common conception of justice rendered concrete in law. This in turn places limits of simplicity, clarity and stability on the law. Thus the requirement that law be internalizable, and hence liveable, which comes across so strongly in the Bible, can function as a single organizing idea behind the many aspects of the Rule of Law discussed in the current literature.

If law is to be internalized, it must be known. From a historical perspective, it is striking what a huge influence the Magna Carta (as close as England ever got to a constitution) had on popular legal consciousness (Hastings 1997: 50). The symbolism of the written word is remarkably powerful. At the same time, codified constitutions can seriously mislead. The United States Constitution actually gives very little help to the student of American government, and there are plenty of high-minded constitutions in tyrannical states not worth the paper they are printed on. But perhaps we should take more seriously in the United Kingdom the need to codify our constitution.

Above all, law must be practised. The Old Testament is full of injunctions to 'do' the law. The whole point of the law is to foster obedience.[10] 'Doing' the law applies to both the substance of what is right and the processes by which wrongdoing is managed. The two basic principles of natural justice within English common law (the duty to give each person a hearing, and judicial impartiality between parties) can already be found reflected in a number of biblical texts.[11]

The Rule of Law is the central element of constitutionalism. At root, it insists that authority should be exercised through law, rather than arbitrarily or disproportionately. The act whereby a People gives itself a constitution as higher law is the supreme expression of this commitment. Particular conceptions of the Rule of Law vary in their extent, from merely requiring lawful authority for all government action, through to a full-blooded commitment to an ideal political order. What is striking about the biblical conception of the Rule of Law is the way it insists on the need to ground law in daily experience. Law is above all about how to live, and it must be liveable. Even those modern-day conceptions of the Rule of Law which get closest to this seem more concerned to make laws effective as instruments of policy than expressive of how to live well.

Government must be based on equality

That constitutions can and should be democratic in nature is a foundation of modern constitutionalism. At the same time, there is a widespread popular sense

10. E.g. Deut. 28 – 30, esp. 30:11–18.
11. Gen. 3:13–18; Exod. 23:6–9; Deut. 19:15; Prov. 17:15.

that theological conceptions of government must tend towards aristocracies or even monarchy.[12] This is perhaps a legacy of the strongly hierarchical and overtly Christian nature of much mediaeval political thought. Both points are vastly overstated. The reality of democracy in large industrialized nations is quite different. In practice government is carried out by oligarchies (most of whom are unelected 'experts' in a broad sense) under a degree of popular oversight and control. Anything approaching the direct democracy of ancient Athens is simply inconceivable and would lead to consequences deeply distasteful to the majority of the population. In that sense, there is popular consent to a substantially undemocratic system of government. At the same time, there is no necessary connection between a theological conception of the constitution and monarchy. For democracy is closely related to political egalitarianism, to which the Bible contains a deep-rooted commitment displayed in numerous facets.

Equality is implicit in the creation of all humanity from one pair (Gen. 3:20),[13] in the universality of sin (Rom. 3:9ff.) and in the collapsing of implicitly hierarchical distinctions within the church (Gal. 3:28). The ministry of Jesus was radically inclusive in the face of organized religion's exclusivity, a fact the church has struggled to emulate but never completely lost sight of.

A comparison of the Old Testament law codes with equivalent documents of the Ancient Near East reveals a remarkable absence of class-based punishments. Each person counts as one, and punishment depends on the seriousness of the offence, not the relative status of victim and perpetrator (Barton 1998: 98–102). Local decision-taking was carried out by the 'elders', who were at least representative of all families, clans and tribes, even if they did not include every free male.[14] Furthermore, it is striking how often in the history of Israel, the less obvious person is appointed to exercise the authority of God on earth. The first-born is regularly passed over; the one chosen by God excels in character, not outward appearance (1 Sam. 16:7). Judges were chosen by Moses for their moral qualities (Exod. 18:21), and a similar set of qualities appears in the qualifications for office in the church (Acts 6:3; 1 Tim. 3:1–13). God gives gifts of leadership, and the human task is to recognize those gifts – which may, from a human perspective, seem almost random – and allocate authority accordingly. This in turn means that anyone *could* be a future office holder, which is effectively an assertion of universal human dignity.

---

12. Kraynak (2001) has also recently criticized the egalitarianism in the 'new consensus in Christian politics'.

13. 'When Adam delved and Eve span, who was then the gentleman?'

14. The precise constitution of 'the elders' is a matter of scholarly dispute (Umhau Wolf 1947; McKenzie 1959).

Attention has already been drawn in the previous chapter to the remarkable degree of ethnic inclusiveness in Israel. The division of the land and the jubilee laws were designed to ensure broad economic equality as well. The prophets are full of denunciations of those who heap up wealth and estates (e.g. Amos 6:1–7). And it would appear that the Nazirite – anyone, male or female, could become a Nazirite – enjoyed a 'holiness' status in Israel during the period of his or her vow comparable to, or even higher than, that of the high priest (Jenson 1992: 50–51).

In the church, all are now equal citizens.[15] Bruce Winter has argued that Paul's injunctions to the Thessalonians to work and not be idle (1 Thess. 4:11–12; 2 Thess. 3:6–13) are to be understood as rejecting the parasitic patron-client relationship of the Graeco-Roman world with its flattery and dependence on handouts, promoting instead a model of independent citizenship capable of doing 'good works' or making benefactions to the city as a whole. If that is how Christians should seek to act in a hostile environment, the environment should be structured to foster that, if at all possible.

Thus the commitment of the biblical writers to equality is much stronger than we might expect. This equality is neither a formal equality 'before the law', nor an amoral equality of beliefs and lifestyles, but an experienced equality which extends to the social and economic realm as well as the civil and political (Forrester 2001: 77–106). It implies horizontal relationships of mutual concern and respect between diverse people. What is more, the biblical grounding of equality may still have a role to play, as attempts to ground it in secular reason alone are found inadequate. For example, Jeremy Waldron has recently argued that Locke's Second Treatise, in which he sets out his justification for the liberal state, is far more indebted to his biblically informed egalitarianism than his secular progeny care to admit (Waldron 2002).

Government must be divided and diffuse

The division of political authority is a staple of the Christian political tradition, whether in the form of neo-Calvinist sphere-sovereignty theory (Heslam 1998) or – in more muted form – in Catholic doctrines of subsidiarity (McIlroy 2003).[16] Barry Logsdon has suggested that the Old Testament lends support to a six-point multipolar constitutionalism involving the individual, the family, the locality, regional government, the professions and central government (Logsdon 1991). Three aspects of the division of authority are particularly apparent.

First, there is a strong strand throughout the Bible in favour of national diversity and against imperialistic concentrations of political power (Johnston 1977: 83). This

---

15. See Eph. 2:19; Phil. 1:27; 3:20; Heb. 11:10–16; 12:22; Rev. 3:12; 21:2, 14; 22:14, 19.
16. See ch. 3, above.

has already been alluded to above in the chapter on nationhood, and will be considered again in the context of international relations. The anti-imperialist critique might be thought a natural response of a small and weak nation in a disturbingly strategic geopolitical context. But at the same time, and secondly, the organization of Israel also shows a careful concern to disperse political, economic and military power. There was no central executive as originally envisaged (1 Sam. 8). Military arrangements were defensive, with obligations of mutual defence, economic production was localized, and law enforcement was principally local, although Moses seems to have arranged a hierarchy of courts in the interests of justice (Deut. 1:9–18).

Finally, three domains, or functions, emerge through the Old Testament, and are increasingly strictly separated: *keter kĕhunnâ*, priesthood; *keter tôrâ*, prophetic office; *keter malkût*, governorship or kingship (Elazar & Cohen 1985: 60). Although the patriarchs exercised all functions, the priesthood came increasingly to be separate, a distinction which even the emergence of a single king could not undermine (1 Sam. 13:8–14). It is significant that when the Solomonic temple is built, bringing the priesthood substantially under the political control of the king, the prophets come into their own as the check on political power (2 Sam. 12:1–15). Scholars disagree over how substantial or sustained the Old Testament's critique of monarchy is. Whatever the right answer, it is clear that conceptions of monarchy were far removed from sixteenth- to eighteenth-century European absolutism. Deuteronomy 17, closely followed in 1 Samuel 8, is concerned to limit the power of the king, and above all to secure his subjection to the law. And the overriding message of the books of Kings which follow is that God blesses monarchical obedience and judges monarchical illegality. In the New Testament these functions are unified in Christ (prophet, priest and king), but re-expressed through the diversity of gifts and offices in the church (1 Cor. 12:27–31).

The idea that the good constitution is based upon a separation of powers has been a staple of Western constitutional thought since the seventeenth century. The justification for dividing power tends to be negative: power tends to corrupt, so a system of 'checks and balances' is the most appropriate means of limiting its corrupting tendencies. Modern conceptions focus on a horizontal dimension, whereby different persons fulfil legislative, executive and judicial functions, and a vertical dimension, distinguishing between local, regional, national and inter-national (and perhaps European) levels of government. At the same time, many constitutions contain substantial links between executive and legislative branches, to ensure that the policy-making branch of government has adequate access to the legislative means to implement its policies. Furthermore, there is a strong tendency to unify judicial power in a single hierarchical structure. Thus the picture that tends to emerge in practice is of an independent judiciary horizontally with strong internal vertical connections, and independent executive/legislative bodies vertically, acting within defined fields of competence, with strong horizontal connections. Historical accounts (Locke, Montesquieu) have yet another way of distinguishing between the functions of government that need separating. Clearly there is considerable potential for disagreement about the degrees of connection and independence between the various elements.

From a biblical perspective the modern state seems to display dangers of centralization in both the horizontal and vertical dimensions. It is vitally important that the government should not control the church or the media (which can be seen very loosely as priestly and prophetic respectively). At the same time the last three decades have seen a major reduction in local autonomy of government and other types of lower-level community. A reconsideration of the status and functions of local and regional governments would seem necessary.

Government must be accountable
Apart from the possibility of loss of office, accountability consists of a requirement publicly to justify action and a 'forum' within which that public justification takes place. The one accountable is required to give reasons in a process of communication with others.

Political rulers do not have uncontrolled power but are accountable to God for the use of their power. There is a judgment of each person for what they have done with the opportunities – political, social or personal – God has given them (Matt. 25:31–46; Rom. 14:10–12). The Bible interprets the rise and fall of kings and emperors as an indication of God's direct judgment for sins committed. Pharaoh, Nebuchadnezzar and Herod are all brought down by God in their turn (Exod. 9:13–19; Dan. 4:28–32; Acts 12:21–23). This principle of accountability also requires institutionalizing politically. If, as we have seen, the Bible tends to favour political equality and participation, one might expect the people to play a part in ensuring the accountability of their political leaders. In 1 Samuel 12:2–3 the prophet gives an account of his life and work to the people. C. Umhau Wolf suggests that there was a principle of kingly accountability to the people, which might go some way to explaining the fear Saul had of David (Umhau Wolf 1947: 105). We see this principle in operation in the need King Josiah had to involve the people when he sought to renew the covenant (2 Kgs 23:1–3). Indeed, one can see the same attitude in Paul's defence of his life before the Ephesian church (Acts 20:18–35), and possibly even in Jesus' rhetorical question in John 8:46, 'which of you can accuse me of any wrongdoing?'

An ongoing form of accountability, perhaps more akin to that provided by the media today, could be seen in the role of the prophets. As Moses was to Pharaoh, so Samuel was to Saul (1 Sam. 15:10–23), Nathan to David (2 Sam. 11:27b – 12:15), Elijah to Ahab (1 Kgs 17 – 21), and Jeremiah to Zedekiah (e.g. Jer. 32). The incident of Micaiah and the false prophets (1 Kgs 22:1–28) warns against institutionalizing the critique, which might at times succeed in silencing it.

The most critical judge of the quality of reasoning is the person most affected by a decision. It is far harder to take an unjust decision in the presence of the victim. At a more mundane level, hints of the significance of directness can be found in Israelite judicial practice, most notably the requirements that the judge should be present during punishment (Deut. 25:2) and the rule that witnesses to a capital offence should be the first to cast stones.[17] And of course, regular public business was transacted in the presence of the 'elders' at the city gate, who function both as a forum for accountability and as witnesses of transactions (Deut. 25:5–10; Ruth 4:1–2).

Conclusion: relational government?

We would not, perhaps, think immediately about government in terms of relationships, although of course the social contract tradition has long seen it as the consequence of a mythical bargaining relationship between autonomous individuals. Still less might we think of government in terms of love. Nevertheless, the themes identified above are to be seen as the political outworking of Christ's command that we love God wholeheartedly and our neighbour as ourselves. The important point is that the political expression of that command means neither that love can in some simplistic way be enforced by governments, nor that constitutional arrangements merely provide a framework in which love may be chosen or rejected at will – this assumes an unbiblical opposition between justice and love. Rather, the best constitutional order expresses a love between citizens. We saw in the previous chapter the need to distinguish civil/political relationships from national/cultural and churchly relationships. Christian politicians or judges show their 'civic love' for non-Christians not by abusing their office but by preserving the civic space within which the church can evangelize. So too *as citizens* we are committed to preserving order, and *as Christians* to using it to extend Christ's kingdom.

What is the nature of this civic love? It is a love that secures to each citizen the goods of material well-being allocated according to an agreed scheme of justice. The continuing constitutional authority of the People under God means that there can be no such thing as constitutional revolution in the sense of a complete break in the legal chain of continuity. Societies may at times experience radical shifts in the way in which authority is exercised and in their conceptions of justice,

---

17. See ch. 13, below.

and it is not wrong to call these 'revolutions'. But at root there is constitutional continuity. We are unavoidably identified with our political communities, and share collective responsibility for their actions, because we are always a people under God. Civic love is inescapable.

As we have seen, the elements of the Rule of Law which find greatest expression in the Bible are the equal subjection of all to law, a radical insistence on the need to internalize the commitment to law such that it becomes part of one's life, and a stress on those features of law which make this possible: clarity, simplicity and publicity. Law is thus one of the principal means by which a polity is united – and, given the New Testament's separation of the religious and the political, it becomes the principal means of unity. It is the ultimate source of civic commonality. Civic love requires us actively to promote lawfulness among all around us. As we have also seen, a very strong case can be made that the Bible contains the wellsprings of political equality and democracy. From a relational perspective (see ch. 15 for further discussion of the dimensions of relational proximity), this means that citizens experience parity in their civic relationships. Civic love requires us to treat all individuals (including those with whom one disagrees politically and religiously) as equals.

It is tempting to understand the biblical material on the separation of powers as rooted ultimately in a negative: the human potential for sin and desire for mastery over others. The founding fathers of the US Constitution may have been strongly influenced by doctrines of total depravity in designing the strict separation which characterizes that instrument. While this is undoubtedly present, it is important not to overlook the positive benefit to be gained by the division of power. It is a necessary consequence that people act in different capacities towards each other, as they relate in different ways. In relational terms, there is multiplexity in civic relationships. On a personal level this results in the need to be aware of one's role in the polity, even if that is simply as engaged citizen. Civic love requires us to honour and respect those with distinctive political roles.

Finally, all the elements of accountability can be summed up in the idea of directness. The well-ordered polity is one in which there is as much directness as possible between power-holders and those influenced by their decisions. So civic love requires participation, and the steady refusal to accept the distancing from public life that both materialistic self-fulfilment and post-Christianization conspire to force on us.

These pointers should remind us that to love as a citizen is not easy; it is not some watered-down version of full Christian love. In many ways it is much easier to love family and those we come into direct contact with each day. But if secular government is to be brought under the government of Christ, no less is required of us.

9. Family

Michael Schluter

Foundations of Family Policy[1]

Family law and family policy in any society must rest on strongly normative foundations if they are to have coherence. The way family is defined and the supporting institutional structures depend on presuppositions about what constitutes 'right relationships'. Thus, family policy requires clear articulation of the theological or philosophical foundations on which it is built as well as discussion of societal goals.

In Christian teaching, the theological basis for families is found in the central importance of relationships for persons made in the image of God, who is himself in relationship (see chs. 2 and 3). So in Genesis 1, humankind is made male and female: one gender on its own would not have expressed the relational nature of the Godhead. After the creation of Adam, God says, 'it is not good for the man to be alone' (Gen. 2:18). Relationships are essential for human well-being, and thus Eve is created as a companion. Family law and policy in biblical teaching rest on the theological foundation that individuals need to live in the context of close personal relationships to reflect the image of the God who made them.

Having set humankind in a relational context, the next question is what constitutes 'right relationships'. Again, it is the character of God which guides the

---

1. The author is especially indebted to Jonathan Burnside for his advice in exploring the biblical material in this chapter.

values which are to undergird family relationships. Holiness, faithfulness, justice, love, kindness and harmony (*shalom*), set out in chapter 6, lie at the root of the definitions of family and the roles family members are expected to fulfil. Most obviously, the permanence of the marriage covenant reflects the loyalty and faithfulness which are characteristic of relations in the Godhead.

In this chapter, we shall explore what biblical law has to say on three issues: the purpose of family law and policy, the structure and composition of the family, and the role of property ownership and 'roots' in supporting family structure.

The purpose of family law and policy

The purpose of family law and policy comes back to the purpose of families. The biblical account suggests there are three main roles which the family is intended to perform:

1. To provide the individual with context, and a sense of identity

As noted above, God gives as his reason for creating Eve that 'it is not good for the man to be alone' (Gen. 2:18). The psalmist also comments, 'God sets the lonely in families' (Ps. 68:6). Similarly, the book of Proverbs comments on the many benefits a man receives from a good wife (e.g. Prov. 18:22; 19:14; 31:11–23) and thus on the advantages of marriage over singleness. Early Israel could claim to be as 'family-focused' as any society that has ever existed, because of the elaborate system of laws which gave the family social responsibilities and defended it from encroachment by centralized power. Like many societies at that time, the nation of Israel was clear that its origins lay in the life of one specific married couple. Through tribal and clan names every Israelite could trace his or her ancestry back, at least in theory, to Abraham and Sarah.

Family was the main source of the individual's identity. Whereas today people in the West primarily identify themselves by their profession or place of work, an Israelite would primarily be identified by his or her lineage. Although several words described 'family' in early Israel, there was no term for the nuclear or conjugal family. The smallest unit recognized in the language was the three- or four-generation family (Hebrew, *bayît*). 'Households in ancient Israel were multigenerational and consisted of two or three families, related by kinship and marriage, who lived in a residential complex of two or three houses connected together' (Perdue 1997: 163–222). Larger kinship units were the territorial clan (*mišpāḥâ*) and the tribe (*šēbeṭ*). A clan was a group of families with bonds of kinship and marriage, often living together in the same village. Clans would have been held together by 'language, economic co-operation, shared traditions of law and custom, ancestral stories and a common religion' (ibid. 177). Clan elders would sort out disputes between households in the clan, and would judge disputes among family members within a household (e.g. Deut. 21:13–17). As the clan was a territorial unit, like the tribe, the village or town, it would often have a name that was interchangeable with the clan or subclan (Anderson 1970).

The narratives in Numbers and Joshua describe the division of the land into tribal territorial units according to the sharply differing sizes of the tribes. The overlap of regional and ethnic identity was important in strengthening and maintaining that identity over long periods of time. However, the tribes as differentiated ethnic groups were always at risk of political rivalry, as is clear from Joshua's instructions when the land is divided up (Josh. 18:5).

An individual's name generally referred to each of these levels of family-social organization (see, for example, the way Saul is identified in 1 Sam. 9:1). The name listed the most important facts about his or her social and political affiliations and thus established their status in society (Anderson 1970). It also reminded the individual of the importance of family-related institutions as the foundation of his or her identity. Exceptionally, a person's name may incorporate key events in that person's life, such as the renaming of Jacob as Israel (Gen. 32:28), or the shaming of the unwilling *levir* (Deut. 25:10, see below). Both Matthew and Luke devote considerable space in their accounts to Jesus' ancestry, so that he is located within the tribes and clans of Israel, in the history and personalities encapsulated by that lineage.

The levirate marriage law (Deut. 25:5–10) provided for a man to marry his deceased brother's widow. Its purpose is to prevent the dead brother's name from being blotted out from Israel (Deut. 25:6). The key issues seem to have been the allocation of the land within the clan, and the continuation of the dead man's name within the clan; on both counts issues of lineage are the key to understanding why this obligation existed.[2]

Given the importance attached to family as the primary means of locating the individual within Israelite society, it is not surprising to find so much attention being paid to lineage throughout Israel's history. In the same vein, great importance is attached to procreation and the nurturing of children. For Israel as a society, fertility was one of the blessings which followed obedience to the law, and a curse on 'the fruit of your womb' was one of the consequences of disobedience (Deut. 28:4, 18). Psalm 127:3 sums up the Old Testament attitude towards children:

Sons are a heritage from the LORD,
　　children a reward from him.

---

2. The welfare aspects of this law will be considered in the next chapter.

In biblical thinking, tracing the lineage of an individual was not to establish privilege but to root identity in past relationships. The emphasis given to lineage throughout the Old Testament, as well as in locating Jesus as a historical person, suggests this is an issue with permanent significance in the social order. In the Old Testament, it is only the prophets who are not identified in terms of their lineage; perhaps this is precisely because their message is conditioned not primarily by their genetic code, or by the personalities or relationships of their forebears, but is 'a word from the Lord'.

Some might argue that Paul does not care an iota about his lineage; it is not an issue for him (Phil. 3:4b–11). He emphasizes how important, *compared with* his Jewish background and lineage, it is for him to know Christ. For membership of the kingdom of God, human lineage is of no significance whatever. However, Paul never claims that lineage is unimportant for social structure, and nowhere does he address the social foundations necessary to sustain family life in society at large. His message is for Christians regarding their identity in the kingdom of God, not for the social policy of the state. This is but one example of where there are different criteria for membership in the kingdom and membership in the state.

In the West, we are so used to identifying ourselves as individuals that we find it strange to think of ourselves as part of a larger family tree, where our forebears clearly have an influence on who we are and how we behave. To speak of lineage smacks of nepotism, and challenges our notions of meritocracy. There are risks, of course, in a familial basis of identity, not least when ethnic loyalties lead to rivalry and even violence. However, the alternative of focusing exclusively on professional skills as the basis of individual identity also has disadvantages, not least the marginalizing of less skilled individuals and the loss of social connectedness in the way people think about themselves.

2. To ensure cultural continuity

A key role of the family in the Old Testament was the transmission of traditions and values from one generation to the next. This played a vital role in God's plan of salvation because religious and cultural values, as in all societies, were intertwined. It was essential that Jewish law and culture was still sufficiently strong when Jesus came to provide the explanatory context for his teaching and sacrificial death. Right from Abraham himself God was teaching his people the crucial importance of family for passing on cultural traditions, and in particular knowledge about God.

The importance of the household, or three-generational family, is perhaps best illustrated by the traditions associated with the Passover meal. This great annual celebration, which reminded the nation of its historical traditions and identity, was always to be eaten in the household, acting as a primary focus for transmission of national cultural tradition (e.g. Exod. 12:24–28). The original intention was for all households to have their Passover meals at 'the place [the LORD your God] will choose' (Deut. 16:5–6), to reinforce further the national cultural significance of the Passover tradition.[3]

Teaching is the most frequently cited duty of the parent, both mother and father, instilling in the child his or her identity as a member of the community of God's people, and the responsibility to obey the commandments which God had given to his people for their good (Deut. 4:9–10; 6:4–8; 11:19). These passages require first that parents obey the God-given laws, so that they have the moral authority to teach them to their children. Jesus puts the same emphasis on his disciples practising God's law themselves as well as teaching it to others (Matt 5:19). Parents, especially fathers, have the duty of passing on to their children the cultural traditions of Israel, and especially to recount God's saving acts in Israel's history (Exod. 12:26–27; Deut. 4:9; 6:7; Josh. 4:21–24).

Likewise there are instructions throughout the book of Proverbs to teach children the law of the Lord, together with the requirement to discipline children. As Kidner comments, 'law ... basically means direction and its aim here is to foster wise habits of thought and action which will help a child find his way through life with sureness and honour' (Kidner 1964: 51). Occasionally, discipline has to be hard because 'folly is bound up in the heart of a child' (Prov. 22:15); it will take more than words to dislodge it. The teaching of children is seen as important not just for the good of the child as an individual, but for the long-term public good (Deut. 32:46–47). To fail to teach a child was a failure of responsibility to God, the child and your neighbour.

An obvious question which arises in the context of this emphasis on cultural tradition is whether this was only relevant to the Jews in the Old Testament period due to their particular role in salvation history. Several points can be made against this view. All nations, tribes and languages, and hence also their cultures, are of some significance in God's eternal purpose, for each plays a part in the final glorification of Christ on his throne (Rev. 7:9). Also, it seems unlikely that God would lay down for Israel a pattern for children's education and place in the family which was fundamentally inappropriate for other societies to follow.

Of course, under the new covenant, the primary institution of cultural transmission is the church. So Paul encourages Timothy to entrust what he has learnt from him 'to reliable men who will also be qualified to teach others' (2 Tim. 2:2). However, Paul also regards it as significant that Timothy's grandmother and mother had shared the 'sincere faith' which now lives in Timothy (2 Tim. 1:5). Although faith in Christ depends not on inherited beliefs but on the personal

---

3. This place is simply where God 'chooses' to set his name as the tabernacle travels around the country, stopping at Shiloh and elsewhere (Niehaus 1992).

commitment of each person in his own right, it seems certain that Timothy's mother and grandmother had taught Timothy this faith, and thus 'passed it on' to him.

3. Economic and welfare roles

In the original mandate given to humankind in Genesis 1, the command to 'subdue the earth' is given to both man and woman, thus to husband and wife together, of course not precluding the activity of single people. This 'subduing' (i.e. agrarian, economic and technological activity) is a primary context for gender co-operation. Given the property distribution system, described below, the primary economic unit for both income generation and welfare purposes was the family, and it seems the intention of many laws, such as the ban on interest discussed in chapter 11, was to keep it that way as society became wealthier and more complex.

A major threat to this expansive role for the family in any society is the activity of national government. Through the tax system, and the demands of central administration for skilled and educated personnel, a national government can easily rob the (extended) family of the human and financial resources it requires to flourish. In Old Testament Israel, the prophet Samuel warns the people of this danger in a long and impassioned speech when the people ask for a king (1 Sam. 8:4–18). The way this warning was fulfilled in Israel's history is described with particular clarity in the story of King Ahab expropriating the vineyard of Naboth, a peasant farmer in Jezreel in the ninth century BC. The same tension between the functions and powers of central government, and the role and cohesion of families, exists today.

These themes are explored further below, and in the next chapter.

The structure and composition of family relations

The extended family is the key social institution in the biblical paradigm

As noted above, there is no word in Hebrew for the 'nuclear family', and even in the New Testament the word used to describe parents and children living together is 'household', rather than 'family'. The smallest unit for which there is a Hebrew word is the three-generational family (Hebrew, *bayît*), as discussed above. It is the three-generational (3-G) family which meets together to celebrate the Passover, and for other cultural events. Smaller than extended family or clan, the 3-G family is a substantially larger group of people than the nuclear family or household. For example, if one assumed a couple with three (surviving) named children, each with three (unmarried) children, the 3-G family would consist of seventeen individuals (of whom eight would be adults) living in four closely connected households on the same site. The extended family, or clan, would be a much larger group again, colocated in the same village.

The structure of households and 3-G families, set within extended family networks, is integral to the organization of society in the biblical social vision. This is particularly clear from the way land was to be distributed in tribal and clan blocks when Israel first entered the Promised Land, rather than arbitrarily to individuals without regard to location of kin. God intended that this initial distribution be maintained over subsequent centuries through the jubilee legislation; which would have ensured that the arrangement of kin-neighbours would remain in place. In addition, each Israelite had a personal obligation to prevent neighbours being forced to move away from kin through poverty or distress. The welfare, judicial and other responsibilities of kin-neighbours for one another were substantial, as set out in the next chapter. This principle of obligation to the extended family, and especially to immediate relatives, is endorsed both by Christ and Paul in the first century AD, at a time when these relationships were obviously under pressure (Mark 7:9–13; 1 Tim. 5:3–8).

Within (extended) families, the marriage relationship takes precedence

The centrality of the marriage relationship within the family structure is discernible from the earliest chapters of Genesis. Jesus himself quotes it: 'A man shall leave his father and mother and be united to his wife, and they will become one flesh' (Gen. 2:24; Matt. 19:5–6). This is especially remarkable in requiring marriage to take precedence over ethnic and clan loyalties which even today often trump marriage commitment. Jesus emphasizes that a oneness is achieved in marriage unmatched in any other human relationship. A crucial implication of this 'unity' is that the primary emotional attachment of parents should be to one another rather than to anyone else, even their children. This sets Israelite and Christian teaching apart from many contemporary national cultures where the primary emotional bond is between brothers, or between mother and child, rather than between husband and wife.

A man's primary loyalty is to be to his wife rather than any other member of his three-generational or extended family. While for most of the Israelite period a man's marriage may not have involved a geographic separation from the rest of his family (it would have been the wife who left her home to live on her husband's family land), the leaving of parents involved a psychological distancing from them (and surely from other relatives). The 'one flesh' idea finds practical expression in the co-authority that parents exercise over children, their joint responsibility for 'teaching' children religious history and values (Deut. 4 and 6), and their acting as one legal unit in many cases involving the honour or stability of the family.[4]

---

4. E.g. Deut. 21:18–21. There are also occasions when the father alone appears to be singled out to accept responsibility (e.g. Deut. 22:21).

There are blunt commandments against committing adultery and coveting one's neighbour's wife in the most weighty summary of Mosaic law (Exod. 20). In the Torah, adultery was subject to criminal rather than civil proceedings, indeed the death penalty. However, Proverbs 6:32–35 seems to presuppose a background of negotiation between the parties that could take the form of civil proceedings. In a pre-DNA-detection society, adultery had the added serious consequence of creating doubt about the paternity, and thus the paternal lineage, of any child the woman might deliver. Exactly the same problems of paternity are created by promiscuity during the period of betrothal, which is why in early Israel sexual intercourse with a third party during betrothal was regarded as seriously as adultery, even though the betrothed couple had not yet experienced sexual union;[5] the relational rootlessness of any resulting child would have been a most serious matter given the emphasis of family and lineage as the primary source of an individual's identity and material support.

If marriage was regarded as central and inviolable, why was legal provision made for divorce (Deut. 24:1–4)? Jesus himself provides an answer to this question when asked by the Pharisees: 'Moses permitted you to divorce your wives because your hearts were hard' (Matt. 19:8). For our purposes, the main points to note from Deuteronomy are that the reason given for divorce is 'something indecent', implying inappropriate sexual behaviour, immodesty or indecency not amounting to adultery (Westbrook 1986), and that divorce is regarded as an internal family matter rather than one in which the community should involve itself on a formal legal basis.

This biblical understanding of family structure is very different from that which prevails in Western societies today, or in Africa or Asia. Three-generational and extended family responsibilities challenge the nuclear family model of Britain and the US. The priority of the marriage relationship over parent-child relationships challenges the mother-son emphasis of many Asian cultures and the primacy of clan loyalties in Arab cultures. Equally, the priority of nuclear over extended family challenges the pattern in most African societies. In Britain, Christians are presented with a major challenge to reform public policy to reflect this centrality of the marriage relationship – both for the stability of families and for the nurturing of children. It will require a monumental shift of mindset in government and the media.

The position of women

Many feminists take the view that women were treated harshly, and on a basis that was far from equal, in the Mosaic law. Indeed, some scholars have argued

---

5. See the discussion of Deut. 22:13–21 in Burnside (2003: 137–155).

that wives were treated as no more than the property of their husbands. A number of points can be made in answer to this charge; most fundamentally we have to start with biblical categories rather than a modern Western notion of gender identity and equality.

In biblical teaching, there seems to be no objective of treating men and women on a basis of precise equality. While all are to be treated with respect and dignity, there are situations where men and women are treated differently: for example, in rules for women regarding sacrificial requirements (child-bearing/uncleanness), access to the tabernacle (men only) and of the value of sacrifices (male animals more valuable than female). There was elaborate provision for the jealous husband to test his suspicions against his wife (the *Sotah* of Num. 5:11–31), but no mention of a test for the jealous wife to conduct on her suspected husband. The explanation in this latter case is probably that there can be no dispute at birth as to who is the mother of a child in the way that it is possible to dispute who the father is (Burnside 2003: 137–155).

It is fundamental to the Torah that women are to be treated with respect, and not as an instrument for male use, service or pleasure. Leon Kass has argued that God spent a long period educating 'Father Abraham' about the true nature of the marriage relationship before granting him the gift of Isaac. Abraham had to understand that 'woman as wife means not "one's missing flesh", nor even a beloved because beautiful adornment to one's self-esteem, but one's chosen and equal partner in generation and transmission'. At the same time, God institutes a long period of barrenness before allowing Sarah and Abraham to have a child, 'so that the woman (and her husband) will realise that a child is not the woman's creation and possession, but an unmerited gift' (Kass 1994: 19).

The concern to treat women with dignity and respect is particularly striking in the Ten Commandments. The fourth commandment reads, 'On it (the sabbath) you shall not do any work, neither you, nor your son or daughter, nor your manservant or maidservant, nor your animals ...' (Exod. 20:10). Unless one suggests that God allows wives to work when all else in the family (including animals) must rest, then the 'you' in this commandments must be addressed equally to men and women. Children are commanded to 'honour' fathers and mothers without distinction (Exod. 20:12–15). A mother's teaching, in Proverbs, is put alongside that of the father, so for example a child is encouraged thus, 'Listen to your father, who gave you life, and do not despise your mother when she is old' (Prov. 23:22). Men and women both suffer the same penalty if caught in adultery (Lev. 20:10).

The approach of biblical social teaching is not to concentrate on individual rights (although some laws have the effect of protecting some rights): rather, the aim is to create a social structure and culture characterized by strong, supportive, mixed-gender relationships both inside and outside the home which provide a platform for true gender co-operation.[6] The heart of biblical teaching is not a search for gender equality, whatever that might mean, or gender uniformity, but rather to seek to ensure a mutually satisfying relationship in the context of local community participation, which provides both women and men with opportunities for connectedness, security and friendship, making issues of strict 'equality' of lesser importance. This community participation is achieved by such features of the social paradigm as the land-holding system discussed below, the decentralization of political and economic power (see chs. 8 and 12), and the high levels of participation expected in the criminal justice system (see ch. 13).

Patriarchy and gender interdependence

The term patriarchy means rule by the father, or a system of family government where the father is the head. However, it has come to be associated with male power and oppression so that, understandably, for many women it has become a term of abuse. Patriarchy in this chapter is used primarily as a lineage term, describing in particular a pattern of land inheritance, which resulted in social outcomes we shall explore below.

In an agricultural society, land has to follow either the male line or the female line if plots are not to become hopelessly fragmented. If all the children, male and female, inherit the land and they all marry, the land will much more quickly be subdivided into small uneconomic parcels. The cultivator households then spend much of their time travelling from one tiny plot to another, and face additional problems in regard to those plots which are furthest from their homes such as preventing theft, carrying out weeding and arranging marketing of the produce. To keep land as consolidated as possible, inheritance needs to pass through either the male or the female line, which then requires that the non-inheriting partner moves to the home-place of their spouse. In Israelite society, inheritance generally passed through the male line. This had many implications for the way gender relations operated in practice.

Lineage also had to follow either the male or female line for family and clan solidarity, and to make it possible for family and clan to have the kind of legal and welfare functions described in the next chapter. Whichever was chosen was bound to have far-reaching social implications. Biblical teaching assumes that lineage will follow the male line, which seems to go right back to the earliest chapters of Genesis where Adam is created first, and it is only the sons of Adam and Eve who are recorded. If lineage is considered important, and if lineage passes

---

6. For development of this argument, see Michael and Auriel Schluter, 'Gender Co-operation: some implications of God's design for society', *Cambridge Papers*, Vol. 12, No. 2, June 2003.

through the male line, this means special social importance will attach to the birth of sons, just as if lineage was to pass through the female line, special social importance would attach to the birth of daughters.

The story of Zelophehad's daughters in Numbers 27 and 36 makes it clear that the issue of male inheritance is about land consolidation in addition to lineage issues. When Zelophehad dies with no sons, God decrees that the land should pass to his six daughters rather than to his brothers. There was no problem in principle with women inheriting the land. However, when Zelophehad's daughters want to marry, they have to do so within the clan, or – we may assume from the context – lose title to the land. The text makes it clear that the issue at stake is maintaining consolidated blocks of land in the tribes and clans according to the original allocation, rather than the incapacity of these women to manage the land effectively. However, the fact that it is men who inherit land in almost all cases inevitably increases their responsibilities and influence in the affairs of the clan, even though they are bound by the law as to who will inherit the land from them (Deut. 21:15–17).

Many of the responsibilities of men within the community are implicit rather than explicit in Mosaic law. For example, it seems to be assumed that the older men would represent the interests of the household in the community (i.e. 'sit in the gate' where legal cases would be heard and political matters discussed). Women are nowhere precluded from this, and some obviously did play a highly significant political role (e.g. Deborah). Under certain circumstances women could initiate cases 'at the city gate', for example when seeking to shame a man for refusing to fulfil his obligations to her (Deut. 25:5–10); however, the boundaries of such initiatives are reasserted in the case directly following (vv. 11–12).[7] In cases of apostasy, all are to be held equally accountable, but it is men who are responsible for seeing that such people are rooted out of Israel (Deut. 13:6–15). That this responsibility is gender-specific may be due to the violent nature of punishment if guilt is established.

There is one case where it is explicit that men have the 'final say' within a marriage relationship, and which also makes clear a man's responsibility for his *words*. This relates to the question of vows made by women living in a household (Num. 30), which may well be one of those laws that in dealing with specific circumstances is designed to provide guidelines for a much wider range of issues (Burnside 2003: 137–155). If a married woman living at home makes a vow to God, her husband can overrule her vow or pledge as long as he does so as soon as he hears about it. On the one hand, the wife's decision to make the vow is respected, for the husband cannot nullify it at will at any time. On the other, the

---

7. For a detailed discussion of these cases, see Jonathan Burnside (2003: 111).

husband is given the final say in this household affair. Rash vows were clearly a significant source of trouble in Israel. Men have no way out of the consequences of ill-considered words they speak on the spur of the moment.[8]

The formal roles of men in lineage definition, land ownership and household representation in the community may lead to false conclusions about the way households were meant to operate on a daily basis. As argued elsewhere, the emphasis of Scripture is on interdependence rather than hierarchy.[9] That interdependence can be traced back to both women and men being made in the image of God; God made humanity asymmetrical such that their fulfilment would depend on co-operative mutual support. The tasks of procreation and stewardship of resources belong to them jointly (Gen. 1:28). While Paul argues that male responsibility in marriage is derived from man being given authority in his relationship with women in the Genesis narrative (1 Tim. 2:12–15), he also argues elsewhere that a man's responsibility is to love his wife sacrificially, as Christ loved the church (Eph. 5:25–28). Woman's role as 'helper' to the man does not carry an implication of subordination, any more than God's role as 'helper' of Israel carries such a message.[10] However, within the mandate jointly to 'fill the earth', women have specific responsibilities in bearing children despite the physical and emotional pain this involves. A woman's extensive role in household affairs in the biblical social vision is spelt out in the description of the activities of the noble wife in Proverbs 31, clearly illustrating the expectation that household management involves shared responsibilities.

Boundaries and flexibility in family structure

It is helpful to consider where there is, and is not, flexibility in the biblical understanding of the family. Above, we have set out some fixed boundary markers: within these there was much flexibility, for example in regard to forms of dress or dance, or gender roles in financial or administrative oversight of the household. It is vital to distinguish between what is prescribed, and what is left culturally indeterminate, in the biblical pattern for the family.

Land and family rootedness

'Family policy' includes issues which on the surface seem to impact on family life only tangentially, but which on closer examination affect profoundly its

---

8. E.g. Jephthah's vow in Judg. 11 and Saul's in 1 Sam. 14:24.
9. Michael and Auriel Schluter, 'Gender Co-operation'.
10. E.g. Exod. 18:4; Deut. 33:7.

cohesiveness and functioning. Such issues today include education, housing and childcare provision. In Israel, a primary purpose of the elaborate laws governing the distribution of land, and subsequent property transactions, appears to have been to protect the geographic proximity of the extended family and clan, as this was regarded as the essential foundation of family cohesion. The colocation and rootedness of the extended family is so fundamental to the long-term role and strength of the family that a more detailed look at the biblical understanding of land and property is necessary.

The starting point for the Israelites' view of land and property was that the earth was not neutral, homogeneous space. They believed in a creator God who is distinct from what he has created but who intervenes in his creation on behalf of his people. In Genesis 2, we read that 'the LORD God had planted a garden in the east, in Eden; and there he put the man he had formed' (v. 8). Here is a planting followed by a planting; hence the importance of the physical realm for developing relationships (cf. Acts 17:26). That is why so many places have special spiritual significance. The Promised Land is explicitly identified as the place where God dwells, since the dwelling of God with his people was the greatest blessing of the old covenant, and his departure its greatest curse. There are many texts that bring out this truth.[11]

Land as place is to do with individual security and belonging, and the foundation of strong communities; the people were not to ignore the social, psychological and religious value of land and treat it merely as an object to be used and discarded. An Israelite farmer who was threatened with losing his land did not see the issue in terms of being deprived of an economic asset but felt he was being removed from a place where he lived and belonged, given to him by God.[12] The daughters of Zelophehad (see above) were right to be concerned that they should receive property among their father's relatives, so that their father's name should not disappear from his clan; God himself validates their claim (Num. 27:1–11). God is seen as the creator of all land (Ps. 24); all things belong in an ultimate sense to him, so the position of humanity is that of stewards. For the Israelites, human 'ownership' of the land carried with it obligations and responsibilities (Lev. 25:23).

Just as land was a gift to humanity, passed from one generation to the next, so land was to be passed from one generation to the next within families. This was the major bulwark against the growth of individualism on the one hand, and the centralized power of the state on the other. Within the Old Testament, land ideally was to be owned in perpetuity within families. This is implicit in the concept of the jubilee, described below (Lev. 25:8–11). Land was held collectively

---

11. E.g. Num. 35:34; Ezekiel chs. 1, 10, 11.
12. E.g. 1 Kgs 21:1–3.

by the family, within the context of the clan and tribe. This relates also to the underlying vision of the purpose and role of the family as a small collective. Contrary to the prevailing values and mindset of Western individualism, biblical thinking is much closer to the ideological outlook of the archetypal peasantry: 'Exclusive, individual ownership with the possibility of disposing of the rights in an object was absent. This explains to a very considerable extent the identification of farm and family; the household was the basic unit of ownership' (Macfarlane 1978: 21). Within this social understanding, no person had individual or exclusive property rights, and no-one could sell off their share of the family property. In societies where women cultivated the land, this also provided protection of their property interests. In addition, the recognition that land is an inheritance to be passed on had environmental implications; it was an incentive to responsible ownership and use.

The primary significance of land and property for colocation of relatives is made transparent by the distinctions made between rural and urban land in the Mosaic law (e.g. Lev. 25:29–31). Rural land could provide a base for a family over succeeding generations as there was space to provide new housing nearby, enabling the family to remain in close proximity and be a source of mutual support and welfare. In the urban context, property does not provide an inheritance in the same way; generally all but one child is compelled to move away in search of housing. So in Israel's law urban land could be sold in perpetuity; it was not protected for future family use in the same way as rural land through the jubilee provisions (see below). Only in the special cities reserved exclusively for Levites is urban land subject to the jubilee provisions (Lev. 25:32–34).

Property ownership was not to be the exclusive privilege of the wealthier sections of society; *all* families were to own land. The books of Numbers and Joshua explain how the land was allocated first at the level of the tribes, and then subdivided further at the level of the clans. Every family received a parcel of land as far as we can tell. The only tribe not to receive an allocation was the Levites; the Lord was to be their inheritance. Instead of rural land, forty 'cities' throughout the land were given to them, together with an area around each where they could graze their flocks and herds. Within these 'cities', which we would describe today more as large villages, each Levite household would own its own home. These arrangements should have ensured there were no landless Israelites; only foreigners and resident aliens would have been without land. That every family would own a piece of land seems to have been fundamental to Israelite thinking, for it recurs as a description of the social ideal at later points in Israel's history (Mic. 4:4; Zech. 3:10).

To ensure for each household a long-term stake in the land and to preserve the proximity of the wider family in the locality, the Mosaic code contains the now-famous jubilee laws, which were unique in the Ancient Near East. In brief, the jubilee provided that there could be no freehold sale of land in Israel: sales could only be leasehold and the lease would expire automatically every fiftieth year. The land would then revert free-of-charge to the family which originally owned it (Lev. 25). In the case of Levite families in the towns, the same provision applied to their properties. The specific command to each Israelite in the law is that in the fiftieth year 'each one of you is to return to his family property and each to his own clan' (Lev. 25:10). The purpose is evidently to maintain a long-term commitment to the wider family and to the specific place where the clan was originally located. As further reinforcement of this obligation to remain committed to the wider family, the people are commanded to do all in their power to prevent their neighbour-relatives from having to move away due to poverty (Lev. 25:35).

Some might argue that the jubilee legislation was never implemented and therefore it is of doubtful relevance for a discussion of Israel's family or social policy. This is a fallacious argument; human failure to comply does not empty divine norms of their force. For example, the Israelites are held accountable by God for failing to observe the seven-year rest for the land over a period of nearly 500 years (2 Chr. 36:21). In addition, Israelite society continued to regard land titles as providing a source of permanent rootedness for the wider family, as is illustrated in the incident of Naboth's vineyard (1 Kgs 21). A high degree of manipulation was required by the royal family, at a time when power was already becoming centralized, before the king was finally able to gain access to the land of a local elder in a provincial town. After Ahab and Jezebel had appropriated the physical base of Naboth's household and wider family, as well as murdering its most senior member, their own family was wiped out; the punishment fitted the crime (1 Kgs 21:17–22).

The main point to grasp from this land system is the proximity and perman-ence of extended family ties. The household was not an isolated two-, three-, or even four-generation unit. There would have been a wider supporting context of relatives. Some might think that such a system would be claustrophobic. Small village life often is. However, the three trips to 'the place which the LORD your God will choose' required each year for the festivals (Deut. 16) would have expanded the horizons of the individual and provided the opportunity to meet people from other parts of the country. The advantage of close long-term ties in the local community is the support of vulnerable individuals such as the physically disabled and psychologically troubled, and an effective informal system of welfare (see ch. 10).

It is impossible, of course, literally to transpose this framework of land distribution and rootedness into modern Western societies. We are not suggesting that every family should be rooted in a single piece of land now. However, we are suggesting there are important relational benefits when individuals have long-term roots in a particular locality. The footloose individual or nuclear family has less security; it is vulnerable without the relational solidarity of the wider family and community. Equally, the footloose person is less likely to be conscious of the long-term environmental consequences of public policy decisions, so will not be committed to the long-term ecological viability of the locality. In terms of care for children, the elderly and those with physical or mental disability, there are substantial advantages in the colocation of relatives who can share the work involved in care and provide each other with mutual support.

Some implications of biblical norms for policy today

Method of application of the biblical text

To apply these principles to society today is not without difficulties. The culture of contemporary Britain bears little resemblance to that of biblical times. For example, there were no single women in early Israel who could be described as having independent means and 'pursuing a career'. The state played a minimal role, so it was the family that was responsible for welfare. Society was predominantly rural and agricultural, whereas today in Britain it is highly urbanized and post-industrial. However, as argued above, the nature of humanity and of human flourishing has not changed over the centuries, and neither, in broad terms, have the ways in which people relate to each other. Technology and accompanying opportunities have to be adapted to people, rather than the other way round. The biblical authors assure us repeatedly that the ways of God as recorded in their writings have eternal significance as a source of wisdom and direction (e.g. Deut. 4:5–8; Ps. 119; 1 Tim. 3:16). So we are on solid ground in seeking applications for life today.

As spelt out in chapter 5, our approach to application today is to consider contemporary society from the perspective of the major normative themes from the biblical social framework and then discuss how society today might be made to conform more closely to those norms. The approach is not unlike the traditional approach of seeking biblical principles from the text and then applying them today. The main differences are:

- rather than relying on one or two proof texts, or arguing from a single verse, we look at major themes emerging from many parts of Scripture;
- themes are not considered in isolation, but in the context of the framework as a whole;
- in terms of the 'ladder of abstraction' discussed in chapter 4, the themes are derived at a relatively high level of generality and thus are less subject to the dangers of cultural bias in interpretation.

So in the context provided by Part 1, and using this approach, what conclusions can we draw for today?

Giving a greater role to the family

Families and households should be recognized as the institutions which most shape our culture and economy, not merely the passive recipients of state initiatives. In Western societies, many of the traditional roles of the family have been taken over either by government (national and local) or by corporate business. For families to play the role which God intends, they need to be re-empowered and reactivated so that they can play a greater role in every area of political, economic and social life. To achieve these outcomes requires that some way is found to formalize the structure and activity of extended families. A family grouping needs to be able to interact formally with other public and private sector institutions. In the Lebanon, this has been achieved through institutions known as 'Family Associations'.[13] These can comprise as many as 50,000 people. From a relational perspective, these groups are too large to provide the communication and interaction benefits being sought in the context of welfare provision, although such a large kin-based institution could provide an alternative source of low-cost finance to help young people meet housing and education costs.

The concept of 'savings syndicates' has been developed in Britain as one way to create a formal structure for groups of relatives (Crook 1996). Giving families a sense of purpose is crucial to building relationships among their members. This is true even in the context of marriage. As early as 1951, the eminent sociologist George Homans wrote,

> Today, the jobs that a married couple carry out together are much fewer. The partners choose one another on grounds of romantic love, because the social system offers nothing else to guide their choice, but when the dream of romantic love has faded, as fade it must, they have to rely upon sexual relations and mere companionship to form the foundation of their marriage. Yet sexual relations are a weak basis for an enduring bond ... If the man and the woman are to be companions, they must find activities to be companions in. In the old-fashioned family, the activities did not have to be contrived; they were given. (Homans 1951: 277)

---

13. Khalaf (1971: 235–250).

The importance of shared purpose or goals has been shown to be crucial to relationship-building in many sections of public and private life, and is part of a new psychometric tool to assess the health of relationships within and between organizations.[14] In the context of family today, this purpose potentially could lie in the spheres of insurance, investment, housing, education, healthcare, business, pensions or care for an elderly person. In Western societies, one of the most difficult constraints on bringing this about is the difficulty many couples will have in deciding whether this larger family activity should be undertaken with the husband's 'clan', or the wife's.

Colocation and rootedness

To enable extended families to play a greater role in economic and social life it is important to encourage close colocation of relatives and a sense of rootedness.[15] A significant problem posed by urbanization is the difficulty it creates for members of the extended family to find housing near to one another. At the same time, high levels of mobility among individuals and nuclear families make it difficult to create a sense of community in any locality: without a sense of obligation towards neighbours, it becomes difficult to give local communities responsibility over issues such as crime prevention and education. As many as one household in nine moved house in the twelve months to April 2001 in Britain.[16] Although some of these households move only a short distance, for many the move has a profound influence on relationships with friends as well as relatives. So what can be done to encourage colocation and greater rootedness?

Little exploration of these questions has taken place in current policy debate, because the relational and economic benefits of rootedness and kin colocation have not yet been recognized. Thus, the policy prescriptions here are necessarily tentative. Options to consider might include a financial incentive for relatives to colocate by allowing joint taxation of larger family groups if they live within the same local authority, as this could reasonably be expected to lower demands on, and thus costs of, public services, especially for care of older people. Mobility of executives for career reasons could be reduced, at least in the public sector, by changes in training arrangements in the NHS, greater financial incentives for teachers to stay at least five years in a school, and lower requirements for mobility among defence forces personnel. Higher education is another

---

14. For details of 'Relational Health Audits', visit the Relationships Foundation website at: <http://www.relationshipsfoundation.org>.

15. For a more detailed discussion of the important theme of roots, see Spencer (2002b).

16. Office for National Statistics, Census 2001, 'Focus on People and Migration', see: <http://www.statistics.gov.uk/focuson/migration>.

major cause of high mobility because British students, unlike their counter-parts in France and Australia, go away from home to university; and there is little or no effort by British universities to encourage parents to take an active interest in the students' university education until it concludes on graduation day. Relatively few students in Britain return to live in their pre-university home-town.

The relational benefits of rootedness also provide fresh rationale for regional economic policy which acts to reduce inter-regional migration. The absence in Britain of a 'Community Reinvestment Act' (CRA) of the kind enacted in the US in 1971[17] means that there are no constraints on capital being sucked out of depressed areas, and levels of inter-regional and inter-community mobility are high. To increase people's permanence in communities will also require greater attention to both physical and social infrastructure.

As the discussion of land ownership also suggests, the need to seek to ensure every family has the opportunity to *own* property, which in some low-income countries would require massive land redistribution, needs to be high on the Christian agenda for social reform.

Support for marriage and lineage

If marriage is regarded as the key to the strength and stability of extended families, much greater government resources should be focused on their encouragement and support. There is now compelling new evidence from a study of over 100 US cities that a public policy in support of marriage can significantly lower divorce rates.[18] Also studies of the best relationship education programmes suggest divorce rates can be reduced substantially amongst couples getting married.[19] Married couples should be treated as a legal entity, to reflect the theological reality of them being one flesh, and thus taxed as an entity rather than as two unrelated individuals. A further issue is the organization of working hours to ensure that married couples can have at least one shared day off each week, as provided traditionally in Britain through the Sunday trading legislation.

Names could also acquire greater significance, as an emphasis on lineage can contextualize an individual's self-understanding and show them why sustaining family solidarity matters. Support for the idea of lineage would mean that in

---

17. For information about the Community Reinvestment Act, see <http://www.occ.treas.gov>.

18. P. J. Birch, S. E. Weed & J. A. Olsen, 'Assessing the Impact of Community Marriage Policies on US County Divorce Rates'.

19. J. Carroll & W. Doherty, 'Evaluating the effectiveness of pre-marital prevention programs: A meta-analytic review of research'.

Britain the father's name would be on birth certificates where it is known. This requirement was abolished in 1987 in Britain for unmarried parents, and has wider implications for parental responsibility and child support. Governments could also facilitate personal lineage research in ways pioneered by the Mormons. Note also that the reason for women changing their name at marriage originally was to ensure lineage clarity.

Children as a priority in national life

If families are of key importance in defining cultural identity, for transmission of cultural values and for economic growth and welfare functions, there is need for greater attention to procreation, and the nurturing and protection of children. If 'family' is truly central in God's design for social well-being, it is important for married couples, in general, to prioritize the bearing and nurturing of children over professional career goals. The difficulties of doing this when little family support is available have to be recognized, and point back to the earlier discussion of the need to promote colocation of relatives. In Britain questions must be raised about the Government's promotion of childcare as a means of encouraging women's participation in the labour market, because a child's relationship with a carer is inevitably more limited and short-term than with parents; the adult:child ratio is, after all, almost always highest in the home. Similarly, an obvious need is to limit the length of the working week if parents are to have the time they need properly to nurture their children (Storkey 2004).[20]

Gender relations

What can we learn from such a distant example, both in historical and techno-logical terms, for gender and family relationships in Britain today? Among many possible lessons, here are three to consider. First, rather than a rights-based approach seeking gender equality, the biblical paradigm proposes an emphasis on interdependence in a context of interconnectedness. So every step towards greater mobility, towards individuals and nuclear families becoming autonomous, and towards distancing work from home and community life, is likely to increase pressure on relations between men and women. There is less to share, less to participate in together, less to discuss, and less opportunity for secure, long-term relationships to be established. Secondly, gender co-operation depends on both men and women recognizing the unique contribution of the other gender in the

---

20. For further discussion of time pressure on parent-employees, visit the Keep Time for Children website at: <http://www.keeptimeforchildren.org.uk>.

rearing of children, and thus that both men and women have distinct and crucial roles in parenting. Thirdly, locating places of work close to people's homes is likely to facilitate the kind of flexible working arrangements which are so important if both women and men are to be able to fulfil domestic relational responsibilities, while at the same time using their training and their gifts to contribute to economic, political and social relations outside the home.

Conclusion

Biblical teaching on family and household relationships discussed in this chapter represents divine wisdom for the ordering of a society in which the majority do not know God, and are not under the controlling motivation of the Holy Spirit. We live in an imperfect world, and family life today is far from the ideal of stable marriages and strong, proximate, extended family networks. Divorce is commonplace and millions of children live with step-parents. All this, however, does not lessen the need for a relational template against which to set contemporary laws and family practice. Without a set of norms, Christians have no framework to guide their efforts to reform family policy, or to assess proposals coming from other sources. Biblical teaching provides such a relational template and thus a basis for critique of many aspects of family structure and governance, not just in Britain but for societies in all parts of the world.

10. Welfare

Michael Schluter

Welfare then and now[1]

One of the major issues facing any society is how to meet responsibly the needs of vulnerable individuals or groups. The problem is faced at two levels. At a personal level decisions are required as to who should be entitled to receive welfare, how much they should receive, and what should motivate other individuals to provide it. Secondly, the same questions need to be asked at the level of the community, or society as a whole, where issues become more complex. They now include social structures and legal mechanisms that *prevent* the individual falling into severe need. In addition, societies need to decide on mechanisms and procedures to deliver help to those who need it without undermining incentives for the self-sufficient to remain so. These fundamental questions about whether and how to help disadvantaged individuals or families were as relevant in Israel a thousand years before Christ as they are in Britain today.

Both the Old Testament and the New Testament have much to say about entitlement to support and donor/lender motivation. However, whereas the New Testament envisages a context of multicultural societies and suggests church structures to provide welfare for needy individuals and groups who call themselves Christians, the Old Testament focuses largely on the social structures

---

1. The author is especially indebted to Jonathan Burnside for his advice in exploring the biblical material in this chapter.

and mechanisms appropriate to the nation of Israel as a whole. A special concern in both testaments, as we shall see, was how the community could provide welfare support without undermining the family structures that were meant to take responsibility for it. Both Old and New Testaments assume an underlying understanding of the support guaranteed by God to his people as an act of grace, which should prompt a response of generosity by God's people towards all those they encounter in need. We shall consider four major themes of the biblical texts:

- eligibility criteria for welfare support
- right goals for a welfare system
- emphasis on prevention
- whose duty of care?

We shall then consider briefly the application of these themes to the contemporary welfare debate in Britain.

Eligibility criteria: those with no close family to help

General provisions
Biblical teaching has a less materialistic understanding of poverty and deprivation than contemporary societies. Lack of *relational* support – the absence of those to whom you can turn for emotional encouragement – is as critical as lack of financial resources. Of course, financial and relational deprivation are closely linked. Then, as now, the financially deprived find it hard to maintain friendships and family links (Prov. 19: 4), often because they lack the funds with which to entertain, give gifts and play a role in community affairs. Equally, we know today that those lacking emotional support often suffer greater stress and ill-health, psychiatric disorders, have lower educational achievement and are more likely to commit crime. The probable result of this combination is financial deprivation (O'Neill 2002). Biblical teaching recognizes that support from the extended family is likely to be less than a person might reasonably expect from the nuclear family. Thus, in both the Old and the New Testament there are three specific categories of people who are mentioned repeatedly as being in need. These are the orphan (or fatherless), the widow and the immigrant, each of whom lacks the socially supportive structures of a nuclear family to help them cope with their economic and social distress.

Concern for these groups is expressed in a number of ways. Sometimes it is in the form of negative commands: for example 'Do not take advantage of a widow or an orphan' (Exod. 22:22), and sometimes radically positive ones: for example, 'The alien living with you must be treated as one of your native-born. Love him as yourself, for you were aliens in Egypt. I am the LORD your God' (Lev. 19:34). In the latter example, the divine character of Yahweh is directly linked to the way his people should treat aliens, who are often oppressed.[2] The alien, in this verse, has no automatic right to be loved by the Israelite, nor does the Israelite have an obligation directly to the alien to love him. However, for Israel, there is an obligation to love the alien which is an obligation to Yahweh, because of what Yahweh has done for the Israelite in liberating him from Egypt. He is expected to reflect on Yahweh's behaviour, and in the light of that relationship work out what is appropriate in his relationship with the alien. Most solemn of the motive clauses is the ritual curse of Deuteronomy 27:19: 'Cursed is the man who withholds justice from the alien, the fatherless or the widow.' Imitating the just character of God in dealing with the poor is imperative. In the New Testament widows and orphans are eligible for welfare (e.g. 1 Tim. 5:3–8; Jas 1:27), highlighting the ethical continuity of the covenants.

The special case of immigrants and refugees[3]
There are two key words in Hebrew used to describe the foreigner. The first, *nokrî*, refers to the person who lives outside the borders of Israel, and serves other gods. The second, *gēr*, is usually translated 'resident alien' or 'sojourner', but is probably best translated as 'immigrant'. This is because *gēr* refers to someone from a different ethnic background who has nevertheless taken up long-term residence in Israel. In the Mosaic law, the immigrant is associated with the landless labourer, or 'hired man', the poor, the widow and the orphan. He or she lacks the social protection and economic advantages of the native population (Burnside 2001: 14).

Unlike today, immigrants in Israel did not live together in large urban settlements, but were either individually adopted by households (e.g. Exod. 20:10), or lived self-sufficiently at the margins of society (e.g. Deut. 24:19–22). They were not perceived as a group, but as individuals trying to cope with the problems of living in a foreign culture without the protection of central or local government. Israelites were under an obligation to show them hospitality as guests in the land.

These immigrants (*gērîm*), perhaps refugees, fell into two main categories depending on whether they had chosen to assimilate (i.e. put their trust in Yahweh). Assimilating immigrants had many of the same privileges as other low-income Israelites. In particular, they were able to eat the Passover along with the native Israelites as long as males of their family were circumcised. The non-assimilating *gērîm* were outside the community and not allowed to take part unless they converted to Judaism. Participation in other cultic events such as the Day of Atonement was also limited to assimilating immigrants, and similarly

---

2. Similar injunctions to treat aliens well are found in Exod. 22:21; 23:9 and Deut. 10:19.
3. Drawn largely from Burnside (2001).

participation in the covenant ratification ceremony and the reading of the law. The ability to offer sacrifices is another privilege almost certainly reserved for those who assimilated (Burnside 2001: 31–32).

However, all *gērîm*, whether they had assimilated or not, seem to have had the benefits of charity made available to the most vulnerable members of society. They were included in the rejoicing and free agricultural produce associated with the offering of the first-fruits (Deut. 26:11) and were beneficiaries of the handouts from the triennial tithes (Deut. 14:28–29; 26:12–3). They were also able to join with other low-income groups, including widows and orphans, in having the opportunity to gather the gleanings after the harvest (Lev. 19:9–10; 23:22; Deut. 24:19–22). The Israelites were answerable to God as to whether they had ensured immigrants had their own small grain, olive and grape harvest.

All immigrants also enjoyed a wide range of protective privileges not available to those categorized as 'foreigners'. The year of debt-release and the ban on interest did not apply to foreigners, but it seems by implication that they did apply to immigrants. The benefits of social bonding arising from this legislation were important in giving immigrants a sense of belonging to the community. The immigrant also enjoyed the full benefits of the weekly day of rest (Exod. 20:8–11), and was covered by other laws which brought benefits to employees, such as the requirement on employers not to withhold daily wages (Deut. 24:14–15).

In summary, to a remarkable degree, the immigrant was to be treated before the law in exactly the same way as an Israelite. He was to receive the same punishment for breaking the law advertently or inadvertently (Num. 15:29). He had exactly the same rights before the law as the native Israelite. If he chose to assimilate, he could take part in all the religious festivals and had the same access to welfare benefits as an Israelite. It is only those who do not choose to assimilate, and those from a small number of ethnic groups with a history of hostility to Israel, who are excluded from membership of the community, from political rights (Deut. 23:3–8) and from the possibility of being king (Deut. 17:15). However, those non-assimilating immigrants still enjoyed almost all the same economic benefits as those who assimilated. The difference it made for an immigrant to assimilate into Israelite culture was primarily religious and political, not economic.

Biblical goals for a welfare system

Maintaining household self-reliance

The ownership of property plays a major role in ensuring self-reliance for the household and the individual in any society. This is especially the case in agricultural societies where land does not just provide a home, but also income for the household. The land-holding system that God gave Israel has as its objective that every three-generational family, as part of a larger clan, should own a piece of land in perpetuity (see previous chapter). Circumstantial evidence that this was initially realized in early Israel is strong. There is no mention of landless Israelites until the late monarchy, nor is there any provision in the law for land purchase by landless families. The narrative in Joshua strongly suggests that every family was allocated a piece of land at the time of the entry into Canaan, although later it seems that Arameans (Syrians) and Philistines displaced some Israelite households.[4] The constant repetition of the Levites' landlessness (they were to own only urban property) again suggests that everybody else did own some land. (Israelite society was not based on any fixed hierarchy except perhaps one of age.) At later points in Israel's history the social ideal of universal family land-holding recurs (Mic. 4:4; Zech. 3:10).

It seems probable that there was a degree of equity between families in the distribution of land. Certainly God intended as much between ancestral tribes, as he says through Moses: 'Distribute the land by lot, according to your clans. To a larger group give a larger inheritance, and to a smaller group a smaller one. Whatever falls to them by lot will be theirs. Distribute it according to your ancestral tribes' (Num. 33:54).

From a welfare perspective, it was not just the near-universal ownership of land that was so crucial, but the jubilee legislation which was designed to ensure that families under no circumstances lost ownership of their land-holding (Lev. 25:8–17). To provide some flexibility, land could be leased out until the next jubilee year. This allowed people in grave financial distress some way out of their difficulty, without permitting outright sale. After limiting leases in this way, to be doubly certain, every forty-ninth year the land had to be restored to its original owner free of charge.

Maintaining personal dignity

Many aspects of Israel's welfare system had the effect of maintaining the dignity of those who were not able to provide for themselves. Most obviously, the community was obliged to provide opportunities for employment, whether this was leaving the corners of the field to be gleaned by the immigrants, orphans and widows (Deut. 24:19–22), or taking on the responsibility of providing board and lodging for bonded labourers. Gleaning would have been hard work for relatively little return, as indicated in the book of Ruth; so no-one could feel that this welfare benefit was a 'soft option'.

Equally, the practice of giving those on low incomes loans, rather than grants, would have helped recipients retain a sense of self-reliance (see next chapter). The

---

4. Josh. 13 – 19.

provision that these debts would be written off in the next year of debt release (every seventh year, Deut. 15:1–6) would have prevented these debts from becoming millstones dragging the recipients ever more deeply into poverty. The requirement that creditors could not enter the homes of debtors in pursuit of collateral, nor keep clothes required for warmth over night, are further evidence of the intention of the law to preserve the dignity and ensure the well-being of the most vulnerable (Deut. 24:10–13).

Emphasis on prevention

Many aspects of the welfare system described in both the Old and the New Testament were designed to ensure that households did not become financially dependent on the community. The most radical and far-reaching of these provisions related to the jubilee legislation. The obligation of relatives to prevent a household selling its land and moving away,[5] and the right of relatives or the owner himself to redeem land at any time before the next jubilee year,[6] reinforced the commitment to maintain the self-reliance of the household.

The way loans and debt were handled – notably the ban on interest – similarly points towards a determination to prevent households falling into destitution (see also the next chapter). The ban on interest is closely related to the requirement that all debts should be cancelled every seven years (Deut. 15:1–11). Not only are the interest ban and year of debt remission given in the same legal form – apodictic (direct, universal) rather than casuistic (conditional) – but both allow the same striking exception, which is that loans to the immigrant/refugee are not subject to these provisions.[7] The interest ban and year of debt remission apply only to loans between Israelites.

The exception points to the underlying rationale of these laws, which comprehends the impact of lending on the social structure. The effect of both an interest ban and the year of debt remission is to discourage those with surplus resources from lending outside the circle of those with whom they already have close relationships. There is no economic motivation for lending without a return on the capital, and with the risk of losing the capital completely every seventh year. Lending to foreigners (i.e. those living outside Israel's borders) would generally be a high-risk option given the absence of legal means to enforce debt contracts beyond national boundaries. Therefore, the individual with surplus resources is likely to turn to his or her kin, or to friends outside the kin network, to find ways to use those resources productively. Even if the resources do not yield a direct financial return,

---

5. Lev. 25:35–38.

6. Lev. 25:25–27.

7. Compare Deut. 23:19–20 with 15:1–6.

they create a network of obligations that ensures a return of some sort at a later date. By the same token, absence of sources of capital outside the kin-group and friendship networks would prevent the financial interdependence of the kin-group from being undermined by non-kin capital. Those in need, or requiring capital for production, have little alternative but to seek the resources within the kinship system, or from friendship networks, as nobody else would be willing to lend.

A further reason for the ban on interest and the year of debt remission may well have been to prevent the jubilee legislation being undermined. If a person was deeply in debt without any year of debt remission, the only way he could pay off the loan would be to sell his land again after recovering it in the jubilee year. This would then defeat the point of the jubilee. The farmer would start the next fifty years with less than full restitution of his land, thanks to the debt hanging over him from the previous fifty years.

The attempts to restrain lending in early Israel were important as a mechanism to protect the three-generational family from the downward spiral of debt. The classic way in which a peasant family or kin-group today is broken up and loses its identity is:

- debt is incurred – either through adverse circumstances as in a period of drought or low product prices, or more often through heavy drinking or other excessive expenditure;
- following a bad harvest or some other catastrophe, the land is sold to pay off the debt;
- the two-generational family, now landless, migrates to the city in search of work and becomes physically separated from the wider kinship group.

In early Israel, lenders were discouraged from lending, so this process would be stopped at its root. It is often the desire of those with extra resources to increase their wealth through lending at interest outside the kinship structure, which frequently results in the destruction of other families.[8]

Whose duty of care?

The individual
Throughout the Bible, and especially in the New Testament, an important strand of teaching is that the individual has a duty of care for the person in need. The

---

8. For a more detailed and technical discussion of the ban on interest and its implications, see chapter 11.

Israelite is commanded not to be 'hard-hearted' or 'tight-fisted' towards a poor fellow-Israelite, but to lend freely, regardless of any family or clan affiliation (Deut. 15:7–11). In the New Testament, Jesus makes it clear that the criterion on which the individual will be judged 'when the Son of Man comes in his glory' will be on the basis of generosity to the person in need (Matt. 25:31–46).

The extended family

Under biblical law, the responsibility of the local community to provide protection, revenge and economic support is concentrated in one person, the *gō'ēl* ('kinsman-redeemer') – although the identity of the *gō'ēl* could change, or be vested in multiple persons. The *gō'ēl* would normally, by default, be the closest male relative. However, more than one person may have potential responsibility for redemption. What probably happened in practice was that the extended family nominated someone from within their ranks to the job (with substitutes in case the nominee was unavailable), naturally choosing the person best suited to the particular tasks. If a person fails to perform his role of *gō'ēl* adequately, the responsibility may devolve to other male relatives (Ruth 3:12–13). God himself is described as *gō'ēl*, most famously in Job 19:25, 'I know that my redeemer lives.' In Isaiah 44:24, God is 'Your *gō'ēl*, who formed you in the womb.' Just as God himself redeemed Israel from slavery in Egypt (Mic. 6:4; see also Ps. 103:4; Isa. 4:14; 43:1; 44:6, 22; 48:20), the *gō'ēl* must redeem an Israelite from enslavement to an immigrant family (Lev. 25:48–49; Deut. 7:7–9).

As *gō'ēl haddām*, the 'avenger of blood', the kinsman-redeemer became responsible to avenge relatives that are killed (Num. 35:19). This is the case whether or not the killing was deliberate: even in cases deemed to be manslaughter, if the accused goes outside a city of refuge, 'the avenger of blood may kill the accused without being guilty of murder' (Num. 35:27). The possibility of an extreme desire for vengeance is noted: ' . . . the avenger of blood might pursue him in a rage' (Deut. 19:6).

The second responsibility of the *gō'ēl* is the provision of economic security – saving relatives from losing their land, and from debt and slavery. This is spelled out in Leviticus 25:25: 'If one of your countrymen becomes poor and sells some of his property, his nearest relative [the *gō'ēl*] is to come and redeem what his countryman has sold.' This redemption may be pre-emptive (avoiding the necessity of selling the land), or it may consist of buying the land back at an agreed price determined by the number of years until the next jubilee.[9] As noted above, blood relatives are also responsible for the redemption of Israelites sold

---

9. Lev. 25:14–17: no other basis for calculating agricultural land values is possible as the land has to be returned in the next jubilee year.

into slavery to aliens (Lev. 25:48–49). The *gō'ēl* also has specific responsibility to prevent the family having to leave the village and go in search of work elsewhere if at all possible. His aim must be that the neighbour-relative 'may continue to live among you' (Lev. 25:35–37).

A third, subsidiary responsibility of the *gō'ēl*, described in Ruth, was to act as a levirate substitute in cases where no living brother was available (see previous chapter). Boaz plays a double function for Ruth; he is the redeemer of the land, but he also acts as *levir* to Ruth. The two functions are coupled together because it is necessary 'to maintain the name of the dead with his property' (Ruth 4:5). Of course, it is also important to care for the widow in her old age.

The *gō'ēl* need not even be involved in active redemption. In Ruth 4:14–15, the newly born child Obed is described as Naomi's *gō'ēl*: 'Praise be to the LORD, who this day has not left you without a *gō'ēl* . . . He will renew your life and sustain you in your old age. For your daughter-in-law . . . has given him birth.' Obed is *gō'ēl* now, because in the future he will be responsible to provide economic security for Naomi.

The personalizing of the extended family's responsibilities in the person of the *gō'ēl* provides a relational framework in which obligation is felt keenly by one person, but choice is not removed entirely. There is no legal framework for compliance, other than the shame of being 'unsandalled' (Ruth 4:7–8). Also, by laying the responsibility on several people in order of closeness of blood relationship, the provision of support is well defined. This makes for clarity of responsibility, and support from multiple sources is available should one prove unable or unwilling.

The responsibilities laid on the extended family in welfare, especially in regard to elderly parents, are not confined to the Old Testament. Jesus makes it clear that the command to honour father and mother includes financial provision, and that he regards it as binding for all time (Mark 7:9–13). Paul, too, states in the strongest possible terms the obligation of Christians to provide for their relatives, and especially their immediate family. In a culture where Christians were setting aside these obligations, he reaffirms responsibility and says that for children and grandchildren to 'repay' their parents and grandparents is pleasing to God (1 Tim. 5:3–8; see also Mark 7:9–13).

The local community

Several Israelite institutions guaranteed the poor and oppressed freedom from complete destitution. The first of these is the gleaning legislation: 'When you are harvesting in your field and you overlook a sheaf, do not go back to get it. Leave it for the alien, the fatherless and the widow' (Deut. 24:19–21). 'Leave it for the alien . . .' is not an accurate translation: the exact Hebrew wording is 'to the alien, it shall be . . .', implying a divinely ordained right of the poor to the gleanings of the harvest (Wright 1996: 261). The poor must thus work for their food, and the leftovers of the harvest are hard work (Lev. 19:9–10). However, they are guaranteed it by legislation, and by participating in the harvest they are co-opted into the enjoyment of the land that symbolizes God's relationship with his people.

The taking of tithes for the poor also offers them economic support. Tithes must ordinarily be collected every year, and are then either directly eaten at the temple, or sold for silver which is then spent on feasting to the glory of God, at the temple. However, every third year, the tithe must be stored in the towns 'so that the Levites . . . the aliens, the fatherless and the widows . . . may come and eat and be satisfied' (Deut. 14:29; repeated at 26:12). Additionally, both at the Feast of Weeks and at the Feast of Tabernacles, the aliens, the fatherless and the widows who live in the towns may participate even though they can bring nothing of their own (Deut. 16:9–14). They are not to be excluded from religious and national celebrations on account of their poverty. It is important that 'they may eat it in your towns' (Deut. 26:12); the emphasis of 'towns' reinforces the fact that the poor are incorporated into the very heart of the covenant community.

In addition to gleanings and tithes, Deuteronomy 15:7–8 insists: 'If there is a poor man among your brothers in any of the towns of the land that the LORD your God is giving you, do not be hard-hearted or tight-fisted towards your poor brother. Rather be open-handed and freely lend him whatever he needs.' The emphasis here is on *loans* rather than *grants*. However, of course, in the year of debt remission all these loans would be cancelled, in effect making each loan into a grant or gift unless it had already been repaid. Indeed, the writer of Deuteronomy anticipates the objection that people may refuse to give loans close to the seventh year because there was so little chance that the loan would be repaid (v. 9). However, the emphasis is on generosity, with a promise that this will result in blessing upon 'all your work', and on 'everything you put your hand to' (vv. 10–11). It is hard to imagine a promise of more comprehensive blessing.

The motivation for treating the poor generously is threefold. First, shared experience and imaginative empathy: ' . . . rejoice before the LORD, you, your sons and daughters . . . the aliens, the fatherless and the widows. Remember that you were slaves in Egypt, and follow carefully these decrees' (Deut. 16:11–12). The same justification is given in regard to keeping the Sabbath (Deut. 5:15). Secondly, out of expectation of divine blessing: 'so that the Levites . . . the aliens, the fatherless and the widows . . . may come and eat and be satisfied, and so that the LORD your God may bless you in all the work of your hands' (Deut. 14:29). Thirdly, it is direct obedience to God's commands: 'I have removed the sacred portion and have given it to the alien, the fatherless and the widow . . . I have obeyed the LORD my God: I have done everything you commanded me' (Deut. 26:13).

By contrast, communities that mistreat the vulnerable are condemned throughout the prophetic writings; exploitation of the poor is one of the most frequent sins decried by God's messengers (after idolatry) and seen as symptomatic of the complete moral degeneration of the nation. It is attacked by Job:

> 'They drive away the orphan's donkey,
>   and take the widow's ox in pledge'
> (24:3);

by Isaiah:

> They do not defend the cause of the fatherless;
>   the widow's case does not come before them
> (1:23);

by Jeremiah:

> 'This is what the LORD says . . . Rescue from the hand of his oppressor the one who has been robbed. Do no wrong or violence to the alien, the fatherless or the widow, and do not shed innocent blood in this place.'
> (22:3);

and by Amos:

> 'They trample on the heads of the poor
>   as upon the dust of the ground
>   and deny justice to the oppressed.'
> (2:7)

Clearly the God of Israel wants the local community to be concerned about social justice and look after those who are vulnerable.

The laws governing the welfare system, including categories of recipients and forms of provision, were set nationally. However, much of the legislation would have been administered by the elders in the local community, often sitting at the city gate to administer judicial as well as welfare decisions. It was via the local community that the poor could gain access to glean land after the harvest. The elders of the local community were responsible for gathering in and distributing the triennial tithes and ensuring that all who needed it would benefit from the handouts made available at the three great annual feasts. No doubt they would also have been responsible for ensuring that debts were cancelled every seventh year, that no interest was charged on loans and that bondservant contracts were adhered to by both sides.

The advantages of this local responsibility are numerous. It helps to maintain a sense of local solidarity and community self-belief, and avoids the tendency towards dependence on a centralized state. It helps to ensure limited resources are allocated to those with greatest claim to them. Above all, local administration of welfare through compassionate and informed oversight is crucial to avoiding 'the poverty trap', where nationally set rules mean that a person loses huge amounts of welfare benefits if they go back to work. At the same time, rules set nationally avoid the possible stigma associated with local charity and give to those on low incomes, and especially the relationally deprived, entitlement to welfare benefits.

The king?

One of the most striking aspects of the biblical material we have examined is the absence of any role envisaged for the king, or what today we would call national government. How should we understand this silence? In biblical times, was dependence on the government for welfare provision just not an option because the financial and administrative resources necessary to organize a national welfare system were not available, or was there some moral or even theological objection to the state taking on this role? Coming to the same question from another angle, was there relational benefit in ensuring the wider family and local community took on this responsibility?

The biblical teaching on the nature of kingship appears implicitly to oppose a centralized role in welfare provision. The king was not to accumulate wealth, which would have been necessary for him to play a major role in welfare provision (Deut. 17:14–20). There is evidence that Israelite kings, or 'the state' such as it existed at that time, did on occasion give handouts to the people (2 Sam. 6:19), and provide paid employment on a large scale (2 Kgs 9:15). However, such actions are nowhere commended. The role of the king seems to have been to seek to ensure justice, including social justice, intervening perhaps as much through existing institutions as by direct action.[10] The one exception to this general rule is that the king appears to play the role of *gōʾēl* for those with no male protection, such as widows and orphans. That is why the prostitutes came before Solomon for a decision (1 Kgs 3:16–28). Wealth is not always required for the provision of justice to the marginalized.

There is also evidence from the law codes of surrounding nations, such as the code of Hammurabi in Babylon, that the king was envisaged as playing a much greater role in welfare than in Israel.[11] However, how much the Babylonian king

---

10. A key passage is Ps. 72:1–14 which does not make clear how exactly the king might intervene.
11. A translation of the law code of Hammurabi can be found at:
    <http://www.yale.edu/lawweb/avalon/medieval/hamframe.htm>.

did in practice (as opposed to what is proclaimed on a national monument) to promote welfare is open to question.[12]

New Testament teaching on the state follows the same priorities as the Old Testament material. Jesus' cryptic comment, 'Give to Caesar what is Caesar's' (Matt. 22:21) does not shed light on the parameters, moral or functional, within which the state ought to operate. There is, in fact, a hint that the state may make demands outside its proper remit (Townsend 2002: 3). The primary text on the role of the state in the New Testament, Romans 13, focuses on its responsibility in the areas of law, order and defence. Other texts speak of the state 'commending those who do good', encouraging and promoting social responsibility by the affluent (e.g. 1 Pet. 2:13–14). However, this falls far short of a social vision where the state is a major, or even a significant, provider of welfare.

Application of these themes to Britain today

Eligibility criteria

In the Bible, the fact of poverty does not automatically entitle a person to a call on resources from the community. The Old Testament certainly urges all citizens to lend to those in distress who seek help. But legislated provisions mentioned above, such as gleaning access to fields and vineyards and the distribution of tithes, were reserved for specific categories of persons who could not draw on family support. Others in desperate need, for whatever reason, have to sell their labour 'in advance' to realize the capital needed to pay off debt (i.e. to become a bonded labourer and rely on their new masters to house and feed them).[13] In the New Testament, widows who have children and grandchildren are not to look to the community for support, but are told to rely on their relatives. Only those 'really in need' are recognized as being eligible for welfare (1 Tim. 5:3–4).

However, note that in both Old and New Testaments the categories of 'deserving' and 'undeserving' poor did not depend on an assessment of character or moral rectitude by the community, or even an assessment of physical and emotional ability to work. The criteria for receipt of special community treatment was the absence of relatives who could provide the necessary material support. Relatives were expected to play their part in supporting those in need, and were

12. Archaeologists are unsure of the exact implementation of the codes. The kings could have been exaggerating their benevolence in the inscriptions on these public monuments to bring themselves honour.

13. See the appendix on Bonded Labour on pp. 193–195.

under a powerful moral constraint to do so. Indeed, Paul goes so far as to say that any Christian who fails to provide for a relative in need 'has denied the faith and is worse than an unbeliever' (1 Tim. 5:8).

This points to the need for fresh efforts today to involve relatives more in the provision of welfare support for those unable to care for themselves. This is obviously not an argument for totally abandoning state welfare schemes. However, it does suggest that there is a high degree of 'moral hazard' in the state taking over welfare roles which should rightly be performed by family members, and that recovery of family values in a society may wait upon family members becoming once more financially interdependent.

Goals of the welfare system: promoting household self-reliance and personal dignity

Despite the present UK Government's efforts to encourage single mothers back to work, and commendable efforts to tackle unemployment, there is no consistent strategy to promote household self-reliance as a goal. There is no public commitment, as in Sweden, to ensure every adult who wants to work can have a job. There is no longer any strong commitment to increasing levels of home ownership. It is generally impossible for welfare recipients to take part-time work as a route back to full-time employment. If they take such work, they automatically lose *all* their benefits, and it may take a number of months to regain them if they then lose their employment. Whilst there is a loan element – the Social Fund – within the UK welfare system, the vast majority of benefits take the form of grants: this cultivates dependence on the welfare system and the need for strong inducements to be given to seek work. The lesson of the Old Testament welfare model is that the opposite should be the case, with loans administered locally (e.g. to finance training or business start-up) forming an integral element of the welfare system to encourage local interdependence and signal faith in the recipients' willingness to repay.

In terms of preserving the dignity of those on low incomes, historically there has been concern to avoid means-tested benefits lest it result in stigma for the recipient. However, there are virtually no legal constraints on the actions which debt collectors may take to recover outstanding debts. Where government grants to those on low incomes have been replaced by loans, there is no seventh year of debt remission, so such loans often reinforce poverty and indebtedness.

Emphasis on prevention

The biblical focus on prevention finds little resonance in British society. Despite the enormous amount of state funds being pumped each year into deprived communities, virtually no funds are available for 'capacity building', to enable the community to tackle its own problems more effectively in the future, and funds for preventative strategies are pathetically small! There was a painful lack of economic planning and preparation at a civic level in Britain's northern cities as traditional industries such as coal, steel and ship-building shed large amounts of labour in the 1980s; there was simply not a mindset of poverty prevention. So, too, when laws governing consumer credit were abolished with the 'big bang' in the City of London in 1986–87, little work was done with the public, or in schools, to educate people in the dangers of indebtedness. As a result, tens of thousands of households fell into severe debt with disastrous consequences for relationships between spouses, and between parents and children (Lang 1988).

In many low-income countries today, there is equally little care taken to prevent people falling into destitution. A key factor is laws governing land ownership and transfer. If there are no constraints on individuals selling their traditional land-holding, or losing land rights due to the modern equivalent of an enclosure movement, many individuals and households are likely to sell their farms to pay debts following a bad harvest or personal difficulties. They then become landless and drift into marginal existence in urban areas (Lipton 1977).

Whose duty of care?

In Western societies especially, there has been little attempt to sustain the extended family so that it can play a supportive role, and little expectation that it should do so. The assumption that no obligation is inherent in extended family relationships has encouraged individuals to pursue mobility; we often live too far away to give much practical help and support to relatives in need. The extended family has become scattered, leaving many nuclear families isolated and thus vulnerable. The support of an outside party is increasingly important in ensuring justice is done following a crime, in supporting marriages in difficulty, ensuring patients are given proper medical care in hospitals, and helping teenagers take advantage of education and employment opportunities. This is in addition to direct financial support in periods of (nuclear) family difficulty due to unemployment, old age, illness or catastrophe.

Another major reason for the withdrawal of extended family support is the expectation that it is the duty of the state, not relatives, to provide economic support, even though levels of government support for matters such as education are being steadily eroded.[14] These factors feed back into each other. It also means that little thought is given to minimizing costs to the community. If a full welfare package is available for unemployment, housing, disability allowance and medical

---

14. Individuals protect themselves collectively through a National Insurance system, to which most contribute via taxation.

care from the state, why should relatives take time and make effort to reduce the associated expenditure? This 'dependency mindset', where the majority look to the government, has done much to undermine the aspiration of (extended) family and household self-sufficiency which seems to be at the heart of biblical teaching. The ultimate goal of the biblical vision for society is for every man (and his household) to live in peace 'under his own vine and under his own fig-tree' (Mic. 4:4) without interference from the state or from hostile parties, free from bureaucratic hassle or fear of the power of centralized government.

In contemporary societies, where there is often need to transfer resources across regions from relatively wealthy communities to the deprived, there has to be some role for central government in collecting and transferring revenue. However, some societies (the UK included) have unnecessarily reduced the role of local government in the welfare system. The result is to diminish the sense of community responsibility felt locally for disadvantaged households.

From a relational perspective there are several reasons why we might expect a family/community-based system of welfare to be preferable to a state-based approach. Although there are many notable exceptions, state-provided welfare is likely to be less effective in providing relational or emotional support. Relationships between the state-funded welfare officer and the 'client' are often short-term and involve little knowledge of the client's wider personal circumstances. Such relationships, whether between a job-centre adviser and an unemployed person, or between a nurse and an old person in a home for the elderly, are more likely to be functional rather than take on the wider dimensions of friendship. There is likely to be greater relational distance. A consequence of this is that the state will find it difficult to distinguish between the deserving and undeserving poor, a concern of Paul's in his discussion of welfare provision by the early church (1 Tim. 5:9–16).

A counter-argument might be that 'professional' caring relationships allow more effective delivery of care because emotions such as anger and guilt are less likely to be present. However, not only does this overlook the positive emotions and qualities associated with close relationships, such as appreciation, compassion, commitment, but also there is little evidence of the 'professional help' approach producing greater happiness. If it is the case that in situations of great need family relationships fail to deliver much emotional support, this is hardly surprising in a society where such relationships have not been nurtured over a lifetime because they were unnecessary for economic survival or essential welfare provision. Meanwhile, the financial burden of welfare provision is threatening to overwhelm the budgets of Western governments.

There is, therefore, a powerful pragmatic argument for recognizing relatives as primary welfare providers, especially for older people. Public sector bodies alone simply will not be able to cope. Based on care costs in 2000, the economic value of the contribution made by over 6 million carers in the UK was estimated at £57.4 billion.[15] A social worker or home help is typically responsible for forty people, and a district nurse around 120 people, so none can give more than about forty minutes a week to any individual. The cost of full-time care is such that it can be available to only a small minority of those who might want it. Inevitably, with an ageing population it is relatives and friends who will play the key supportive roles. As a study by Peter Wilmott concluded in the late 1980s, 'although the central position of kinship in care and support has been confirmed, the research also suggests that friends have some distinctive contributions to make' (Wilmott 1987: 65). The main burden of care is generally borne by relatives, often at immense personal cost to the primary carer, and too often taken for granted by the community and other relatives; it is vital that such carers are given greater support.

The relational arguments against the state-based welfare system also concern its impact on the institutions of family and community which play such an important role in the welfare of children. While family and community obligations in some sense limit the freedom of the 'strong', they generally increase the freedom of the 'weak' (the mentally ill, physically disabled, the elderly, children). The case most conclusively demonstrated in recent years is that children growing up with both natural parents in a stable home do better in terms of mental and physical health, educational attainment and employment outcomes than those without this household context (R. O'Neill 2002). If provision of state welfare weakens family and community as institutions, the relational cost to children – not least in terms of the love and support of parents – is high indeed.

Other arguments against state welfare provision are perhaps less tangible, but are nonetheless real. The financial resources required for state provision involve levels of taxation that are likely to be increasingly difficult to raise in a global economy. The concentration of political power required to impose high levels of taxation may in times of crisis threaten democratic freedom. At a personal level, the consequent loss of personal responsibility in a household context may contribute to a culture of narcissism and self-absorption. For the state-welfare recipient, there is equally the moral danger (perhaps exaggerated by the Right in the interests of lowering taxation) of that person ceasing to have a sense of obligation to contribute to the community. Setting the institution of the state between welfare provider and recipient may perhaps reduce stigma for the recipient, but also reduces the possibility of love and emotional support being added to the financial transfer.

---

15. *Without us . . . ? Calculating the value of carers' support* (2002) [Internet], published by
    Carers UK, available at: <http://www.carersonline.org.uk>.

Conclusion

The arguments above against state welfare provision are especially relevant for middle-income countries where wealth is increasing rapidly so that state provision to replace family and community becomes an option. The experience in the West should act as a warning that once those family and community networks have been undermined by state services as a right, it is difficult to find a way back. The West's experience also demonstrates that the knock-on effects of removing family and community welfare roles on the values of society more generally are immense. For high-income countries, there needs to be a gradual transition back towards greater emphasis on the role of family and local community support. This will only be possible if ways are found to give incentives to families to become more rooted in communities and to facilitate families to colocate and develop shared financial arrangements over their lifetime as discussed in chapter 9. In the meantime special care and attention will need to be given to those increasing numbers who find themselves without any family and community support, especially in old age.

For the moment, the welfare system in highly urbanized societies, where the extended family inevitably has become geographically dispersed, must involve contributions from a widely diverse group of individuals and agencies including family members, friends, neighbours, health sector agencies, private companies and public sector service providers. In such a complex welfare environment, some agency needs to provide a degree of co-ordination and regulation. Rather than relying on the relationally distant departments and agencies of central government, local or even neighbourhood government arguably would be better placed to ensure that so far as possible families are encouraged and resourced to provide the support required by needy individuals, perhaps within a national framework of minimum standards, in line with biblical norms for welfare provision.

Appendix to Chapter 10
Bonded labour: the ultimate safety net in early Israel[16]

Arguably, the word translated 'slavery' in the English version of the Old Testament should be translated 'bonded labour'. 'Slavery' conjures up images of the Greek or Roman institution where the unfortunate individual had virtually no rights, and little chance of obtaining freedom from one generation to the next. Israelite 'bonded labour' was very different. As we shall see, these bonded servants had significant rights, not least – for the Israelite among them – the right to release after six years of labour or in the jubilee year and the right to run away. Bonded labourers in early Israel could not be passed on from one generation to the next, unlike foreign 'slaves', nor could the labourer be considered the property of the employer. Such a set of rights makes it inappropriate to use the term 'slavery' as a description of the institution. This is not to suggest that life was always comfortable for the Israelite bonded labourer, or to sanitize the brutality of some employers of this labour, but it is to make a sharp distinction between categories of domestic contract.

There are several sections of the Torah which set down the rules to govern the employment and welfare of bonded labour. In reading these passages, it is important to distinguish categories which each have different rights and privileges:

- The Israelite man working as a bonded labourer for an Israelite employer (the main passages dealing with this case are Exod. 21:2–6; Lev. 25:39–43; Deut. 15:12–18)
- The Israelite woman, sold as a wife or concubine to an Israelite man (Exod. 21:7–11)
- The Israelite man sold to an immigrant (alien) employer (Lev. 25:47–54)
- The immigrant or foreigner, sold to or captured by an Israelite (Lev. 25:44–46; Deut. 21:10–14)

The right for a bonded labourer to run away (Deut. 23:15) appears to apply to all of these categories. In the short space available here, it is not possible to explore all the issues involved for each of these categories, so we will look briefly only at the laws governing the first group.

---

16. Further research on the slavery contract is in progress at the Jubilee Centre. Publication is likely to be late in 2005.

The important point to consider is how welfare can best be provided for the destitute in a society that has neither the trained personnel nor the financial resources to provide a comprehensive government welfare system. At the same time, what forms of punishment are appropriate in a relational society like early Israel which does not want to use imprisonment because it isolates the prisoner from the community, and requires taxation of poor households to finance it? Early Israel solved both these problems by a privatized form of welfare provision, under which a citizen in effect volunteered to provide work, and meet the basic needs of a destitute person, under a bonded-labour contract lasting up to six years in total (longer, if the destitute person chose to stay). The role of the local community was only to ensure that the terms of this contract were adhered to on both sides, in particular making sure that the bonded labourer was not abused in any way.

How did people get into the situation of becoming bonded labourers? As discussed in chapter 10, the first step was often to sell use of the family land to pay debts. This would leave the family as landless labourers who would then have to depend on the goodwill of neighbours for work outside the peak periods when labour was needed for land preparation, sowing and harvest. Once an individual or family was in debt, and without land, the only way to raise capital to pay off the debt was to sell labour in advance for a period of years, until the next year of debt release comes around (see chapter 11). Hence the bonded-labour contract. Exodus 22:2b also envisages a situation where a thief is required to pay restitution but has nothing to sell. The only way he can raise the capital needed to pay restitution is through the bonded-labour contract.

Much attention is given in Mosaic law to the relationship between the employer and the bonded labourer. The employer had a number of rights under this contract of employment. After paying a lump sum to the labourer or his creditor at the beginning of the contract, the employer was entitled to the work or product of the bonded labourer in return for providing no further remuneration beyond simple board and lodging. He (or she) had the right to discipline the bonded labourer, or servant, including use of corporal punishment, but within limits (Exod. 21:11).[17] While such rights to discipline an unruly servant will seem harsh today, it is necessary to consider why any employer in that society would agree to rescue the destitute person without the ability to administer such penalties if they should find it necessary to do so. There would, of course, have been good employers and bad ones as in any society; the law here as elsewhere is taking into account 'the hardness of the human heart' (Matt. 19:8).

---

17. The typical limits to the use of force would have given little comfort to the bonded labourer, and would have been an important disincentive to getting into debt (Jackson 2000).

The rights of the bonded labourer in this contract were many. He was guaranteed one day off a week, the Sabbath (Exod. 20:8–11). He would be released at the end of six years of service, and indeed the employer is urged to be generous at the time he lets him go (Deut. 15:12–15). Of course, many such bonded labourers would have had nowhere to go if they had sold their land, so they would have had to make another contract with an employer immediately. This contingency is covered in the law by allowing the bonded labourer to make a much longer commitment, to be publicly acknowledged by the servant having his or her ear impaled on a doorpost (Deut. 15:16–17). In the jubilee year, which might come in the middle of the six year contract, the bonded labourer could go back to 'his own land and the property of his forefathers', with his family, which he would receive back without having to make a payment, and could then resume farming in his own right (Lev. 25:41).

Other rights of the bonded servant included the right to be redeemed by a relative at any time, even if sold to a non-Israelite (Lev. 25:47–53), and the right not to be treated harshly or 'ruthlessly', presumably a requirement to be enforced by the local community. The appeal to the employers and to the wider community to observe this command goes back to their own experience of bondage in Egypt (Lev. 25:42–43). In addition, if a bonded labourer was treated really badly, and the local community refused to do anything about it, in desperation he had the right to flee to any other part of the country and seek refuge there. His employer was not permitted to force him back. Even the possibility of this happening may have acted as some restraint on the harsh employer.

Is there any potential application of the bonded-labour contract in society today? Let us focus just on those facing a prison term. In the same way that the bonded-labour contract with a local farmer in early Israel was an alternative to prison, could private sector employers today provide jobs for those who would otherwise go to prison (costing the taxpayer around £20,000 a year) and in effect supervise community service orders (CSOs) over a defined period of time? In the same way that potential employers in early Israel needed to be given incentives in order to take on the destitute, so today private sector or local government employers would also need some incentive. If offenders were to be made to work for nothing for local employers while they fulfilled their CSO, there would be legitimate concerns from Trade Unions about the effects on jobs displacement of other low-income employees. Much would probably depend on whether sufficient manual jobs could be identified which were worth doing at close to a zero wage-rate to provide work for up to, say, an extra 50,000 people each year without impacting negatively on local labour markets. The potential benefits to both the offender and to society as a whole of keeping the offender in the community, and having them in a genuine working situation during the CSO period, make such a scheme worthy of closer examination.

11. Finance

Paul Mills

Introduction

The 'Jubilee 2000' and 'Drop the Debt' campaigns demonstrate that Christians believe that biblical models of finance have applicability today. The Old Testament concepts of the jubilee and the cancellation of debts have been deployed with some effect to the case of the international debts of lower income countries. While welcome in itself, this rediscovery of what the Bible has to say about finance was limited by the failure to articulate and apply the whole of the biblical model as it addresses financial relationships. As a result, Christians campaign against international debt, a symptom of financial relationships going awry, but fail to grasp the underlying malaise that afflicts the financial system.

This myopia is not unusual. Until the 1980s, it was rare to find an economist who thought that finance 'mattered' in any significant way. Amazing as it sounds, economic theories were written in which financial relationships and money had no impact on the 'real' world, just on the level of prices. Finance was seen as merely a 'veil' that could be stripped away to reveal the real economy of producing and consuming. Fortunately, economists have begun to realize that finance does have important effects on the real world and that relationships and the sharing of information are at the heart of understanding those effects.

By definition, whatever we understand as 'finance' entails a relationship in the sense that it entails the need for future contact. The two parties to a bargain arrange an initial transfer of value (usually money) from one to the other in exchange for the prospect of the future return of that value. There are, of course, numerous complications and variants on that simple model, be they the form of the contract (loan, shares, rent, etc.), the length of time involved, the likelihood of the return and the granting of security. But ultimately finance boils down to a relationship between two parties, usually mediated through money, over time.

It is not surprising, therefore, that economists have turned to 'game theory' to gain a greater understanding of what is going on in a financial relationship, as if the two parties were seeking to maximize their pay-outs from a game. Hence, contract terms are the outcomes of 'strategies' and security on a loan becomes a 'hostage' taken by one side to ensure the good behaviour of the other. Whilst this approach runs the danger of over-simplifying the motives of the parties involved, it does shed light on the prerequisites for long-lasting healthy financial relationships, such as trust, reputation and repeated interactions.

Healthy financial relationships are integral to the Old Testament paradigm: what it says about their governance is central to the promotion of prosperity and economic fairness. After four hundred years of the West largely ignoring scriptural teaching on finance, with hindsight we can now discern the wisdom of the Old Testament law. Before enunciating its model, this chapter will provide the theological foundation to understanding the biblical view of wealth and finance. Following an examination of the key Old Testament passages, the chapter will turn to what goes wrong in our contemporary financial system because we have ignored their teaching and how we might put healthy relationships back at its heart.

Theological foundations of the biblical financial model

The wider context for the specific biblical teaching on the conduct of financial relationships is that we are to express our love for God and neighbour through our use of money.

Financial wealth is a rival deity vying for our worship

We must never forget that financial wealth is merely a means to higher ends, not an end in itself. We frequently disregard Jesus' analysis of Money ('Mammon') as an idol competing with the true God for our worship: 'No-one can serve two masters. Either he will hate the one and love the other, or he will be devoted to the one and despise the other. You cannot serve both God and Money' (Matt. 6:24). Consequently, when thinking about the management of financial assets, we must be mindful that wealth is not spiritually 'neutral' in interacting with our fallen human natures – it is apt to tempt us to evil (1 Tim. 6:10). In addition, finance does not operate autonomously under a set of moral rules that fall outside God's dominion. As with other false gods, claims are made that the financial sphere is 'outside' the scope of obedience to biblical revelation. Yet it too will come under God's judgment.

Ultimate security cannot be found in financial wealth

One of the traits of the worship of Mammon is to regard it as the source of security in one's life. Precautionary saving, insurance and holding onto wealth are motivated by the instinctive human desire for material security and certainty about the future. Yet true security is to be found only in God's provision.[1] As with other idols, financial wealth ultimately fails to deliver. Despite being christened with such reassuring epithets as 'security', 'bond', 'index-linked' and 'guaranteed', every financial asset involves some degree of risk – inflation erodes, debtors default, markets crash, governments renege, thieves steal, companies collapse, currencies devalue, assets depreciate, taxes rise, wars ravage, disasters strike, crooks defraud and banks fold.[2] There is no such thing as a totally safe asset. Risk is ubiquitous, as holders of 'guaranteed' annuities from some insurance companies have discovered.

Financial wealth is a bad long-term investment

From the biblical perspective wealth is fleeting; death robs everyone eventually (Eccl. 5:15; Zeph. 1:18; 1 Tim. 6:7, 19). 'Life assurance' is something of a misnomer; financial wealth makes no difference beyond the grave:

> Our life is but an empty show, naked we come and naked go;
> Both for the humble and the proud, there are no pockets in a shroud.[3]

But perhaps the most surprising element of the Bible's denigration of wealth is that it is couched in self-interested terms. In the spiritual scheme of things, the long-run return on worldly savings is non-existent. Jesus is sure that a new age is dawning in which this world's wealth will be worthless (Matt. 6:19–21; Luke 12:33–34) – sterling futures of that maturity trade at zero (see Jas 5:1–3). Consequently, the smarter investor patronizes the *Banque Celestiale* by choosing savings media that will survive the looming financial crisis: the asset with the requisite durability is the good done to others. Hence, Jesus' cryptic advice: 'I tell you, use worldly wealth to gain friends for yourselves, so that when it is gone, you will be welcomed into eternal dwellings' (Luke 16:9; cf. 12:33; 1 Tim. 6:18–19).

---

1. E.g. Ps. 62:8–10; Prov. 3:5–6; Matt. 6:25–34; Luke 12:22–31.
2. See Prov. 23:5; Matt. 6:20; 1 Tim. 6:17.
3. Attributed to James Hill by B. C. Forbes, *Forbes Epigrams* (1922).

Accumulating financial wealth should be subordinate to cultivating relationships
Given that the good done to others is the only medium for the transfer of savings into the life to come, Scripture is unequivocal in preaching the subjugation of accumulating wealth to the cultivation of loving relationships. Added to Jesus' urging to use this world's wealth to develop friendships is the ever-present duty to support one's dependants and wider family members (Lev. 25:25; Mark 7:9–13; 1 Tim. 5:3–8). Saving and investing are never seen as self-justifying ends but always means to the service one can offer to others. Hence, the investment method itself should not breach the principle of service to others.

Similarly, we should not use the abundance of wealth as a means of economizing on working on our relationships. Some church payrolls have an unnerving tendency to expand with posts that would be redundant if church members were engaging with one another.

One is accountable before God in the use of financial wealth
The most widely quoted principle of biblical teaching for the practical issues of saving and investment is that of stewardship. The creation narrative teaches that, whilst God is the source of all material resources, he has condescended to entrust their preservation and development to humanity (Gen. 1:26–30; 2:15). In a number of parables, Jesus develops this theme by picturing his disciples as servants given charge of property. Their performance in its use will be assessed at the consummation of the kingdom.[4]

These parables apply to our use of all resources, spiritual and material, entrusted by God to his servants until the coming of the kingdom. The servants' performance is assessed purely on the basis of financial return. Praise is reserved for those servants who have achieved a healthy profit through business ventures. The lazy servant is condemned for not even attempting to make a return. A literal reading makes the sole priority the maximization of financial return.

But this would be a misguided interpretation. First, the 'return' spoken of is wider than just the pecuniary and includes the total good done to others. Secondly, the means by which profit is obtained also matters to God. The Old Testament law accepts the legitimacy of trade for profit *per se*, since trade is presupposed and profit is unregulated. However, any wealth that results from dishonesty, theft, monopoly or exploitation of the poor is legislated against[5] and denounced by the prophets.[6] Consequently, the righteousness of any monetary return is conditional on the absence of the exploitation of customers, workers,

---

4. Matt. 25:14–30; Luke 19:11–27; cf. Matt. 24:45–51; Luke 12:42–47; 16:1–12.

5. E.g. Lev. 19:13, 35–36; Deut. 19:14; 24:15; 25:13–15; 27:17.

6. See Isa. 10:2; Jer. 17:11; 22:13; Ezek. 18:12–13; 22:12–13; Amos 2:6–8.

creditors and suppliers. The ethic of stewardship applies not only to how productively we deploy God's resources, but also to what righteous purposes we deploy them.

Knowing exactly who is using your savings and for what purpose is a prerequisite for this. Not only do the close ties between saver and investor ensure a ready flow of information about how money is used and how business is going, but investing in this manner may help to cement further the relationship between them. By contrast, the trend of modern financial investment has been away from saving with people that you know to channelling savings through anonymous intermediaries in order to reduce risk and save cost.

The immediate problem this poses for most Westerners is that we have relinquished the stewardship of our savings to fund managers and banks. In most cases, we have no idea of the activities and methods used to derive a return on our money. It is contradictory to bemoan economic exploitation of low-income countries and yet fail to realize that our interest and pensions are being secured by the same exploitation perpetrated in the name of shareholders and bondholders.

Financial returns must come from somewhere – they do not spring automatically from the action of impersonal 'market forces'. Investment affects the distribution of assets, the products and services supplied and their relative prices. It has an inherent moral dimension. In practice, there are few morally flawless forms of investment. We have to choose the least of numerous evils. However, the absence of a first best option does not mean that we are absolved from the responsibility of making such a choice.

The need to avoid presuming on the future

Humanity is tempted to believe that the future is knowable – or at least predictable. We extrapolate from past experience and plan on the basis that the future will be within that compass (2 Pet. 3:4). Yet only God knows the future with certainty (Prov. 27:1). Consequently, the wise are those who are humble in their attitude towards the future, whereas the foolish presume upon future profits.[7]

Investment decisions are largely guided by expectations of the future. Although there is no contradiction between believing in God's providential care and simultaneously making plans to meet financial needs, to believe that one can know the future, and to incur financial obligations on that basis, is to claim an attribute of God for oneself.

The need for humility towards the future leads to circumspection when borrowing, especially when speculating on the movements of asset prices. This

---

7. It is those 'without knowledge' who claim that 'tomorrow will be like today, or even far better' (Isa. 56:11–12; Luke 12:16–21; Jas 4:13–17).

insight also points towards the wisdom of financial relationships and contracts that acknowledge the future is uncertain and explicitly take account of risk. This is in contradistinction to our widespread reliance on interest-bearing debts that are contracted on the basis that the borrower will be able to repay in the future.

Destination: wealth is to be used as an expression of our service to God and others
Given its prominence in Jesus' teaching, perhaps our greatest temptation is to place the pursuit of wealth ahead of our worship of God. As we shall see in the next chapter, the Old Testament economic framework does not spurn the prospect of economic well-being and security, but it is to come from seeking to be faithful stewards and promoting equity rather than pursuing wealth for its own sake. When a personal or societal choice is to be made, material concerns (beyond those of survival) are to be subordinate to the promotion of healthy relationships. Hence, rather than being a law unto itself, finance is a tool whose use is to express our obedience to God and service to others.

The financial framework of jubilee economics

Within a decentralized market economy with in-built checks on the concentration of economic power (see ch. 12, 'Economy'), Old Testament law adds very specific rules about the forms of contract through which financial relationships were to be conducted, and how any financial return was to be structured. Finance is never allowed to be autonomous; rather, it should be subordinate to personal relationships and structured in a way that reinforces them. What to contemporary ears sounds illogical then becomes an expression of the use of money for the purpose of relationship-building.

The dangers of debt (Deut. 15:1–18)
Borrowing was, and is, integral to needy people receiving support (see ch. 10, 'Welfare'). The Old Testament law exhorts those who have wealth to lend readily to those in need of financial assistance (Lev. 25:35; Deut. 15:7–9). Indeed God's ultimate ownership of one's wealth requires open-handedness when lending (cf. Luke 6:35). The Psalms attest to the righteousness of someone who lends readily to the poor (37:26; 112:5). In relational terms, loans are often more fulfilling than gifts because the exchange is between relatively equal parties (in that the borrower is expected to repay), the lender places trust in the borrower's willingness to repay and repayment takes place over time, increasing the number of interactions between the parties. Giving is often vital to relieve short-term suffering but can easily lead to dependency and subordination (Sacks 2002: 120), whereas a loan expresses confidence in the prospects and integrity of the borrower.

Despite exhorting lending to the needy, the law gave ample protection to lenders seeking their money back. Security on a debt could be taken (Deut. 24:10–13), whilst debt servitude in a limited form was sanctioned (Lev. 25:39, 47; Deut. 15:12). These laws underlined the strong obligation on the borrower to repay – failure to do so was tantamount to theft (Ps. 37:21).

The emphasis on repayment obligations is consistent with the tenor of the Wisdom literature – that is, borrowing involves the undertaking of such a serious commitment and loss of financial freedom that it should be embarked upon only when absolutely necessary. The borrower is automatically at the weaker end of a power relationship:

> The rich rule over the poor,
>> and the borrower is servant of the lender.
> (Prov. 22:7)

Since the obligation to repay was taken so seriously, indebtedness could easily become debt servitude (Lev. 25:39) – the Old Testament form of indentured labour. Left unchecked, debt obligations and servitude can become a perpetual burden that, even today in some parts of the world, is transmitted to the third and fourth generation. To combat the perpetuation of debt and its role in immiserating poorer borrowers, the command to lend freely is closely associated with the injunction to cancel all debts, except those of foreigners, every seventh year (Deut. 15:1–3) and to release debt servants (15:12–18). The combination of an ample supply of loans for poverty relief, the periodic cancellation of debts and the non-existence of interest (see below) would have prevented the development of a commercial loan-market and ensured that poverty through misfortune was only temporary. It is no coincidence that the promise that there would be 'no poor in the land' if the law code was followed is given in the context of the injunctions to lend freely and cancel debts (Deut. 15:4–5). In addition, the cancellation of debt would have ensured that the outright level of borrowing would have been kept low and directed at vital poverty relief, whilst offering the prospect of freedom and a clean slate to even the most financially impecunious. The association of debt cancellation with freedom is the analogy that Jesus uses when describing the forgiveness associated with entry into the kingdom of God.[8]

The emphasis of the Old Testament law is that lending is encouraged to promote the welfare of the borrower, that debts should be honoured wherever possible but that repayment should not entail the degradation of the borrower, be it through seizure of collateral vital to their welfare (e.g. Deut. 24:17) or perpetual debt.

---

8. E.g. Matt. 18:23–35; cf. 6:12.

The prohibition of interest (Deut. 23:19–20)

The prohibition of interest occurs three times within Old Testament law.[9] This repetition signifies particular emphasis. On two of these occasions, the prohibition is placed specifically in the context of lending to the poor (Exod. 22:25; Lev. 25:36–37). The third reference, however, stresses the universal nature of the prohibition when lending to fellow Israelites: 'Do not charge your brother interest, whether on money or food or anything else that may earn interest' (Deut. 23:19). The deliberately all-embracing terminology of this verse rules out the possibility that the proscription applied only to dealings with the poor. The only exception to the ban was interest taken from foreigners (v. 20). The importance of obedience to the prohibition is emphasized by a uniquely comprehensive promise of blessing that will result from observance. However, no penalties are prescribed for non-compliance.

The subsequent references to interest in the Old Testament in no way weaken the prohibition – neither do they introduce any distinction amongst types of interest, be it charged to the poor or on a 'commercial' loan or at 'excessive' rates. Rather the moral gravity of lending at interest is underlined by placing it in the context of other blatantly sinful acts. David says that the righteous will shun interest as well as slander and bribery (Ps. 15:3, 5). Ezekiel lists lending at interest, in conjunction with theft and idolatry, as acts of the person destined for destruction (18:13) and as one of the gross sins of Jerusalem (22:11–12). Proverbs juxtaposes the moneylender with the man who is kind to the poor (28:8), whilst Nehemiah reimposes the interest prohibition centuries after its initial conception (5:1–13) in a post-exilic urban context. The Old Testament's judgment of interest is, therefore, clear: it is contrary to God's law, is avoided by the righteous and prohibited on all loans to borrowers regarded as 'brothers'.

It is sometimes claimed that Jesus' teaching has overturned the Old Testament prohibition of interest. In particular, the Parables of the Talents (Matt. 25:14–30) and the Ten Minas (Luke 19:11–27) are cited as examples of Jesus implicitly sanctioning the receipt of interest by Christians, as the lazy servant is condemned for not putting his master's money out at interest. A contrary reading of the texts

---

9. Two Hebrew words are translated as 'interest': *nešek*, meaning a 'bite', and *tarbît*, meaning an 'increase'. No consensus exists as to whether a distinction between the two terms was made. *Nešek* may have referred to a loan where the interest was already discounted and *tarbît* to interest that was added to the loan upon repayment (Stein 1953). However, there is no basis in the Hebrew for the modern distinction between reasonable and exploitative rates of interest, between interest and 'usury'. All forms of return on a loan were prohibited.

is more natural, however, given the Old Testament background. The lazy servant is 'judged by his own words'. He should have attempted to invest the money in business opportunities. If he *had* truly believed that his master was a 'hard man', as he claimed, then he should have put the money on deposit at interest, for this is what a 'hard man' would expect. The receipt of interest is effectively 'reaping where one has not sown' (Luke 19:22–23).

This interpretation is supported by Jesus' other teachings on lending. Rather than softening the Old Testament injunctions to lend interest-free to 'brothers', Jesus makes them even more radical by advocating lending to anyone who wants to borrow (Matt. 5:42) and lending to anyone, including enemies, without expectation of anything in return (Luke 6:34–35). Although the idiom used is somewhat ambiguous, the latter text means that either Jesus' disciples are to lend to anyone, in the full realization that repayment may not be forthcoming, or that they should lend having no concern for 'a return' either in the form of the recovery of the principal or future reciprocal loans, let alone interest (I. M. Marshall 1978: 271–273). Jesus takes as read the Old Testament prohibition of interest and radicalizes the instruction to his disciples to lend in an even more liberal manner.

A relational rationale for the prohibition of interest

Whilst Christians have often seen the need for a maximum limit on interest rates to protect poorer borrowers, many have been unable to agree with or observe the Old Testament prohibition. After all, the debtor voluntarily enters into the arrangement and so interest is not theft, and without it loans would be less readily available. Why should the Old Testament be so doctrinaire on this issue?

Apart from pragmatic observation as to what goes wrong when interest-bearing debt finance is given free rein in an economy (see below), interest transforms a loan – which is rich in relationship-reinforcing potential – into something that is inherently 'commercial', where self-interest appears to be the motivating factor. If the lender is charging interest, there is no reason to believe that the motivation is charitable or that, if the borrower finds difficulty in repaying, the lender will countenance debt forgiveness. This transformation can be grasped quickly by considering a loan between neighbours of the proverbial 'cup of sugar'. Repayment terms are not specified and the loan will be made good either in kind or in the form of reciprocal favours. However, if the lender specifies when the sugar is due to be returned and how much more sugar the borrower is to return for the privilege, then the loan is transformed into something that 'neighbours' do not engage in. Shakespeare illustrated the point in *The Merchant of Venice*. The first act of the play contrasts the attitude of the financier who shares in the risks of the ventures that he is backing (Antonio) with that of the moneylender who would extract interest (Shylock):

'If thou wilt lend this money, lend it not
As to thy friends – for when did friendship take
A breed of barren metal of his friend? –
But lend it rather to thine enemy;
Who if he break, thou mayst with better face
Exact the penalty.'[10]

This distinction reflects that of Deuteronomy 23:20, between the ban on interest on loans between 'brother' Israelites and the permissibility of interest on loans to 'foreigners'. The rationale for this dichotomy has often exercised Jewish and Christian commentators. The same distinction also applies to the periodic cancellation of debts (Deut. 15:3) and comes within the context of a mark of blessing on Israel being that they will 'lend to many nations but will borrow from none' (15:6; 28:12). Consequently the 'brother/foreigner' distinction is probably best understood as a way of reinforcing a sense of 'economic brotherhood' within the community of Old Testament Israel and ensuring reciprocal treatment in cross-border loan agreements.[11] For his disciples, Jesus then universalized the prohibition of interest and went further in advocating a radical approach to lending. Certainly, to charge interest to a borrower indicates that the lender does not regard that person as part of their relational community.

Alternatives to debt contracts
The corollary of this critique of interest is that financial contracts that explicitly share risk, through partnerships or equity shares, are positively sanctioned. No specific biblical warrant exists for such contracts and so their legitimacy must be inferred from the support given to reasonable commercial profit fairly obtained, the legitimacy of rental contracts (see below) and the support given to trade and risk-taking.[12] However, two of the previously established principles point to the validity of such profit-sharing contracts. First, they explicitly acknowledge that profit is uncertain and is not presumed upon. Secondly, a profit-share contract is more risky for the provider of finance as they retain ownership. This necessitates greater information flow between the user and supplier of capital, so reinforcing their relationship.

---

10. Antonio to Shylock, *Merchant of Venice*, Act 1, Scene 3, 133–137; the 'breed of barren metal' is the interest on a loan of gold or silver coins and alludes to a description of interest by Aristotle.

11. Jerome first proposed the Christian 'universalisation' of the interest prohibition on the grounds of universal 'brotherhood' (Nelson 1969).

12. E.g. Prov. 31:10–31; Eccl. 11:1–6.

In addition to profit-share arrangements, a return from property can be derived from rental contracts and leases. Exodus 22:14–15 describes a rental contract where hire charges act as compensation for the owner as they retain the risk of the objects rented out. Leasehold contracts on land are also envisaged as part of the jubilee legislation (Lev. 25:14–16, 29–31).

Why has such a distinction been made between interest on monetary loans and a return from profit-sharing investment or rentals? The answer lies in the allocation of risk within the various forms of contract. In a loan, the ownership of the principal and its associated risks are transferred to the borrower, whereas in a profit-share partnership or rental contract, ownership and ultimate risk remains with the original supplier of finance or owner of the property. A return on financial investment is justified only if legal ownership is retained, with the concomitant risk of loss. In contrast to Marx's 'labour theory of value', the Old Testament distinction rests on a 'risk theory of capital' – financial capital must 'earn' its return by directly bearing the risks of ownership. It lies behind the distinction in the Parable of the Talents between 'putting one's money to work' and placing it on deposit at interest ('reaping where one has not sown'). In addition, by acknowledging risks at the outset, partnership and rental arrangements do not presume upon future outcomes, whereas interest-bearing loans embody the assumption that the venture will be profitable or that the borrower will be in a position to repay.

The Old Testament financial system

Putting these elements together within the context of the wider framework of Old Testament economic law allows us to discern how the envisaged financial system would have operated. First, borrowing was permitted and even encouraged as an integral part of the welfare system to help members of the community over times of temporary difficulty. Its repayment was taken so seriously that collateral could be taken and enforced servitude might be required to discharge unpaid debts. Secondly, though, the absence of interest and the preset cancellation of debt meant that someone could not be indebted for ever, nor could their children be enslaved permanently. Debt and compounding interest could not be used to oppress one's 'brother'. The interaction with the jubilee legislation also meant that moneylenders could not use debt foreclosure on farmers to accumulate large tracts of land (cf. Isa. 5:8), so preserving the initial tribal allocation of land. Thirdly, the absence of interest (and periodic debt cancellation) would have ensured that lending was done either for charitable purposes or for mutual favours between family, neighbours or business partners. There would be no incentive to develop an anonymous debt market. Fourthly, investment finance would have been channelled into alternative, risk-sharing and rental contracts rather than commercial loans. Again, this would have entailed a closer relationship between business partners than is necessary between creditor and debtor. Within such a system one can envisage that financial intermediaries – investment funds or banks that pool savings from a number of sources into a limited number of projects – could arise. However, the return to savers would need to be linked directly to the profitability of the investments made rather than fixed and guaranteed upfront in the form of a 'deposit' or 'bond'. Overall, finance in the Old Testament model acts as an adhesive that strengthens family and community relationships. Unfortunately, too often in the contemporary economy, finance acts as a solvent.

What goes wrong when Old Testament principles are ignored?

The Old Testament financial model comes as something of a shock to the modern economist grown accustomed to the universality of interest and debt. After all, if interest were so iniquitous or inefficient, why does it persist? By economizing on the need for information flows between borrower and lender, interest makes financial agreements much less costly to reach and monitor (so raising the return on savings or lowering the cost of capital to borrowers). Also, by creating a return for the use of money over time that is not tied to its use, it offers a way for very short-term loans (even overnight ones) to generate a 'return'. Borrowers (such as governments and consumers) willing to pay to access finance merely pay for current consumption at the expense of higher costs in the future. One often hears commentators, even the Governor of the Bank of England, say that debt is 'a good thing'. Nevertheless, a number of our economic ills can be ascribed to our economic system being reliant upon long-standing interest-based debts rather than non-interest financial arrangements.

The unjust and destabilizing allocation of returns between the users and suppliers of finance
There is no necessary link between a commercial borrower's profitability when using interest-based finance and the return to the lender. This leads to obvious injustices. When a borrower's profits are rising, the lender receives no extra reward in excess of the basic rate of interest for having the foresight to lend to a successful business. Yet when a borrower's profits are falling, small or non-existent, the responsibility to pay interest at the going rate remains. The lender does not suffer within the contractual terms for financing an unsuccessful business, and may foreclose on a business that could continue to survive if it need not service the debt. In this way lenders deepen recessions by bankrupting some firms unnecessarily. We forget that the banks are acting in this way on our behalf as bank depositors.

This same aspect of interest tends to amplify the economic cycle. On the upswing, businesses that borrow heavily retain a greater proportion of their profits, and will be encouraged to borrow and invest even more. On the downswing, these businesses will find themselves burdened by high interest costs when profits are low or negative. Most will reduce their investment and production – many will be bankrupted. If businesses used forms of finance that shared profits (or losses), and spread these widely to savers, the financial system would amplify the economic cycle far less.

A propensity to finance speculation in assets and property

Debt finance facilitates and exaggerates speculative booms and busts in asset markets (such as property and shares). When the price of an asset in relatively fixed supply begins to rise, buyers borrow to purchase more of it, so as to maximize their capital gain. Lenders acquiesce because the value of their collateral is rising and they face little risk of loss even if the borrower defaults. The process spirals upwards with more lending causing higher prices, which encourages even more lending. However, when the 'bubble' bursts (often due to sharply increased interest rates or a sudden loss of confidence) and asset values begin to fall, speculators are forced to sell their assets on a falling market in order to pay their debts, and lenders are reluctant to finance the purchase of depreciating assets. These factors depress prices even further, leaving many borrowers with debts greater than the worth of their assets (as in the UK housing market in the early 1990s).

Throughout their history, interest-based debt markets have displayed a remarkable penchant for financing speculative booms, and exaggerating the ensuing slumps. Financial arrangements whereby risk and speculative return, if any, were shared between borrowers and lenders would make both more cautious when asset values were rising, and force fewer 'fire sales' when they were falling.

An inherently unstable banking system

It is all very well to say that it would be better if lenders bore more risk, but wouldn't this make banks vulnerable to collapse? The fact is, however, that conventional banks are unstable by their very nature in offering nominally fixed value deposits that can be withdrawn at short notice. These render the bank vulnerable to bankruptcy if it sustains losses in excess of its reserves and capital; or it could suffer a 'run' where depositors demand immediate repayment, and be unable to satisfy them.[13]

---

13. The 1990s witnessed a number of banking-system collapses from Savings and Loans in the US, to Scandinavia, Russia and East Asia. The latest occurred in Argentina in 2002. The Japanese banking system has been close to collapse since the mid-1990s and is only just recovering following substantial bail-outs and state support.

Only the first of these threats is definitely the result of operating on an interest-basis. By guaranteeing the value of its depositors' funds, the bank gives the impression of keeping them safe and secure whilst risk is being taken with that money. That banks have largely succeeded with this *legerdemain* is due partly to their ability to diversify their lending, and partly to the guarantees that central banks and governments have been forced to give them to protect them from losses of confidence by the public. No other private sector operation enjoys such generous support from government, with the effect that larger banks often take excessive risks knowing that they are 'too big to be allowed to fail'. Interest-based banking systems have survived thus far because taxpayers have underwritten the costs they impose on the wider economy.

These three factors together mean that an interest-based financial system exaggerates the economic cycle. Use of financial contracts whereby the suppliers of finance retained the risk of its use would curb speculative bubbles and borrowing on the upswing and share the burden of falling profits and asset values more widely on the downswing.

The necessity of rising prices for economic growth

With debts generally fixed in nominal terms in an interest-based economy, unexpected inflation benefits borrowers at the expense of lenders. But borrowing companies, governments and consumers are usually the main sources of growth in demand in large economies. When they get into trouble servicing their debts due to rising interest rates or falling profits and asset prices, consumption and investment are quickly reduced and unemployment rises. If prices begin to fall in a heavily indebted country, such as contemporary Japan, demand quickly stagnates. Hence the necessity in such countries for the authorities to ensure that the price level does not begin to fall and the ubiquity amongst central banks to target a low and stable *rate* of inflation rather than a stable price level.[14] This need to protect debtors is ultimately why the UK retail price level has been allowed to rise by a factor of 52 times (5200%) since 1910.

The entrenching of differentials between rich and poor

In the first instance, loans are granted more readily and on more favourable terms to those who have security to offer; so those who do not have assets are either

---

14. Economists also argue for some inflation to permit changes in relative real wages and prices to occur without the need to cut wages and prices in nominal terms (which is often resisted). However, one of the reasons for the resistance to nominal wage and price cuts is because debts are fixed in nominal terms. Widespread indebtedness entrenches the constituency in favour of inflation.

excluded from access to finance or face significantly higher interest rates. This belies the claim of economics textbooks that a free-loan market will allocate finance to its most productive users. Rather, loans are granted most readily to those with collateral, not those with the most productive prospective projects or those most in need of finance. Secondly, by enabling a relatively risk-free rate of return to be achieved on financial capital, interest-based savings enable wealth to compound upon itself, so entrenching pre-existing differentials unless inflation or bank collapses intervene. Thirdly, those who borrow at interest and fail to service their debts can be penalized heavily. They may be forced into bankruptcy and have their assets seized, or into financial stringency for an indefinite period, and still be unable to extricate themselves from the debt trap due to their outstanding debts growing at a compound rate. By allocating risk so unevenly, interest ensures that the rich can largely protect themselves from the vicissitudes of economic life, whilst the poor can be legally subjected to financial servitude.

Perhaps the most obvious example in which the interest-based financial system has manifested most of these undesirable traits is that of lower-income country (LIC) debt. Christian opinion in rich and poor countries alike has condemned the injustice of billions of dollars being paid by the poorest countries to the richest without recognizing that this is how an interest-based financial system typically operates.

The results of the heavy indebtedness of the poorest countries have included the degradation of the world's environment (to produce more cash crops for export); the net transfer of resources from poor to rich countries (despite aid, further loans and numerous initiatives to relieve existing ones); and cuts in the living standards of the world's poorest populaces, to pay for loans from which they have derived little benefit. Millions of lives have been lost as a direct result.

Responsibility for this tragedy must be shared between the originating banks, the borrowing governments and donor countries who now own most of the debt and who have been tardy in its relief. If the relational distinction between interest-free lending for charitable purposes and the provision of risk-bearing finance for commercial enterprise continues to be blurred, then international debt will continue to enslave poorer countries and entrench differentials in income.

The need for, and consequences of, limited liability companies

The prevalence of debt to finance commercial enterprise, encouraged by its privileged tax position (see below), has necessitated the creation of limited liability – that is, capping company shareholders' liability to pay the outstanding debts of the company to their share in the company's capital. This legal device was created in the nineteenth century to enable companies to raise large amounts of shareholder capital and has since been the foundation of most large-scale commercial investment. It prevents a limited company's creditors from pursuing its share-holders if an insolvent company is wound-up leaving unpaid debts.

Limited liability results in a number of traits that tend to work against close financial relationships.[15] First, it means that the shareholders do not need to know each other since their stake at risk in the company is not dependent on the wealth of others. Secondly, shareholders do not need to know too much about how the company is managed – indeed, limited liability means that shares can be traded anonymously on a stock exchange with investors ignorant of the underlying business of the firm they are investing in. Thirdly, limited liability permits companies to leverage themselves (i.e. borrow heavily) so that their debts are multiples of their shareholder capital, thus enabling a large increase in the scale of a company's operations. Indeed, even if company debt was not tax advantaged, it is in the interests of existing shareholders to raise additional finance through debt rather than equity as they receive the full marginal benefit of profitable investments (net of interest costs) but have their downside capped by the limited liability provision. Fourthly, this increase in corporate scale means that shareholders need to appoint professional managers to manage the company for them. However, these managers are unlikely to have purely the interests of shareholders at heart (as company shares will not comprise all their wealth). Although numerous attempts have been made to find ways of re-aligning managers' and shareholder incentives, the recent wave of corporate accounting scandals demonstrates that this is a recurrent problem in a limited liability company. Fifthly, these problems mean that bad management may need to be disciplined by contested takeover bids to protect shareholder interests, but the outcomes of such bids are often decided without reference to the interests of the other stakeholders in the firm (employees, customers and creditors). Finally, in the case of corporate insolvency, once shareholder capital and company assets have been exhausted, there is no-one liable to pay the remaining creditors who may include suppliers, customers, employees and the company pension fund. It is ironic that anti-globalization campaigners decry the activities of multinational companies because of their scale, their dissociation from local communities and the frequent excesses of executive pay. These are the inexorable results of the principle of limited liability, but rarely does one hear the correct diagnosis of the underlying problem.

A rapid flow of financial capital across regions and countries
It is of the nature of debt contracts that they economize on the information necessary for funds to be transferred from saver to borrower. Only the rate of interest and the quality of the collateral need be known for a transaction to occur.

---

15. For a more comprehensive discussion see Schluter 2000b.

With profit-related or rental contracts, however, because investors are incurring greater risk, they need more information before committing their capital (e.g. on the trustworthiness of the borrower or the exact amount of profit being made with their funds). Such information is most readily available at the local or regional level.[16] Consequently, interest (and limited liability) permits financial flows to occur on a far greater scale than would otherwise occur. Economic theory may assert that this will improve the efficiency of investment, but it contributes to the erosion of community and regional cohesion as jobs tend to follow flows of financial capital. There are benefits to financial intermediaries spreading risks to savers across a number of regions and countries, as well as channelling finance to where opportunities are numerous but capital is in short supply (such as middle- and low-income countries). But debt markets tend to channel cheaper funds to already stable areas where collateral is available and asset prices are rising.

Summary
Northern Europe and the US have now experienced four centuries of a financial system in which the Old Testament's relational precepts have been largely ignored. The above discussion has shown that the resulting financial system tends to exaggerate the economic cycle; is inherently unstable, necessitating either taxpayer bailouts or inflation; concentrates economic power in large companies; promotes anonymity of finance (so that savers and investors do not, or do not need to, know how their money is being invested); and acts to entrench inequalities of wealth within and between countries. A more relationally rich model inspired by Old Testament law would not rapidly solve all these ills but, when embedded within the wider economic framework of the following chapter, would serve to alleviate some of the problems encountered by Western economies.

Practical steps towards making healthy financial relationships paramount at all levels

International and development finance
Whilst the Old Testament model endorses the role that lending can play in poverty relief, the sorry tale of low-income countries' debt in the 1980s and the

---

16. Banking relationships work best when contacts are close, long-standing, cover a wide range of services, on a roughly equal basis between financier and customer and are reinforced by personal contacts (Holland 1994).

later hesitant attempts at debt relief indicate that we are still a long way from understanding international development finance. The confusion comes from blurring the distinction between lending for poverty relief – which should always be interest-free and capable of forgiveness if the borrowers are incapable of repaying – and commercial finance to support economic development.

The latter goal has led to the establishment of multilateral agencies (such as the IMF and World Bank) to channel loan finance to middle- and low-income countries on quasi-commercial terms.[17] However, these agency balance sheets need to be run on a solvent and prudent basis; their constitutions prevent *ad hoc* loan write-offs in response to borrower repayment difficulties. There is greater scope for bilateral loans (those from one government to another) to be written-off, but here domestic politicians need to demonstrate that they *are* imposing conditions on borrowers (to justify debt forgiveness to taxpayers), and show that other rich lenders are not benefiting from their country's charity in relieving debts. Hence, whether the debt is to multilateral agencies or bilaterally between countries, our current reliance on interest-based lending for development always has the potential to reinvent the international debt crisis, no matter how many current debts are relieved.

If wealthier governments wish to provide true development finance to low-income countries, they should do so through equity participation in commercial projects whereby profits and losses are shared (such as equity partnerships in power generation or toll-charging transport projects). That way, governments would be more circumspect about the projects they choose to finance in the first place and, if a project proves to be uncommercial, the borrowing economy is not saddled with an ever-growing debt burden. Otherwise the net transfer of resources from poor to rich countries will continue.

One way for richer countries to participate more fully in development at a local level in low-income countries would be to provide equity capital for microcredit lending organizations, such as the Grameen Bank in Bangladesh. Although operating on an interest-basis, it provides small loans on tight margins to poorer households to finance small start-up enterprises. Nevertheless, it has a default rate (c. 5%) lower than comparable commercial banks because it lends predominantly to women and emphasizes the need for repayment in order to enable the bank to lend to new borrowers. Such an approach facilitates local development without recourse to moneylenders whilst emphasizing the need for neighbourly solidarity in preserving access to finance for others.

---

17. Only loans from the International Development Agency (part of the World Bank) can be made interest-free.

The domestic financial system

Fundamentally, the economy can be made more stable, and households and firms more secure, by being weaned off reliance on debt finance. For instance, in the UK, although the personal incentive to borrow through mortgage tax relief has finally been removed, companies still have an incentive to borrow heavily, rather than use equity finance, because debt interest is counted as a cost before corporation tax is levied, whereas dividends (and capital gains) on shares are not. Hence, company debt finance is positively favoured by the UK tax system, whereas the foregoing discussion on risk to the economy should indicate the reverse. A first step would be to disallow interest as a cost before the levying of corporation tax so as to level the playing field with equity finance.[18] Household indebtedness could be reduced by encouraging alternative means of house purchase that do not entail mortgage debt but rather rely on part-buy/part-rent schemes whereby the occupier gradually acquires the property, renting from the financier as they go.

The stability of the banking system could be enhanced by splitting deposits into either transactions accounts that are nominally fixed but offer no rate of return, and savings accounts that participate in the profitability (or otherwise) of the bank's operations similarly to a share in an investment trust. Such a division would shift much of the risk of poorly performing assets from banks to savers, making it very difficult for a bank to go bankrupt. Also, a safe payments system would mean that governments would not have implicitly to underwrite the banking system (which currently encourages banks to take even greater risks).

Local and personal finances

As we have seen, finance can be used as a glue to strengthen ties between lender and borrower. This can be implemented at a local, church and community level through establishing financial institutions that place financial return lower than the use of money for relational purposes. For instance, a mechanism now exists whereby a local, interest-free bond can be issued in a locality with the foregone interest being used to finance local job creation and regeneration schemes.[19] Financial ties within a community and church congregation can be strengthened through the establishment of a credit union. Alternatively, an interest-free loan fund can be an alternative to outright charitable gifts within a church congregation,

---

18. The 2003 Bush administration measure to relieve income tax on dividends is a step in this direction, although it favours companies which pay out dividends rather than retain earnings and invest.

19. City*life* has issued bonds for Sheffield, Newcastle and the East End of London, raising millions of pounds and creating hundreds of jobs in these localities (see ch. 17).

enabling members to overcome temporary cash-flow difficulties or families to afford necessary durable purchases. To some degree, mutual financial institutions (building societies, provident societies and credit unions) place greater emphasis on the bond that their members share through their pooling of finance for their mutual benefit. Whether such institutions provide better returns than the profit-driven competition is irrelevant. Rather, membership embodies the principle that money should be used to bolster relationships rather than be used to their detriment.

On a personal basis, the main lesson of relational finance is that we should know what our money is being used for, and try to ensure that our money is used in a way that contributes to the economic benefit of others rather than financially enslaving them. This notion runs totally against the grain of conventional financial practice that relies on financial intermediaries (such as banks and fund managers) who can reduce costs and diversify risk. Unfortunately, this means that most of our money is being lent and invested in ways we have no knowledge of. However, there are banks that are committed to 'ethical' lending practices and advisory services that provide information on the activities of companies so that one can invest in ways consistent with relational principles if one is prepared to put in some effort (Mills 2000a).

Not only can we choose whether to know how our money is used when we save but we can often also choose whether to 'save' for our old age via our offspring and wider families or through pensions, property and savings. At the margin, we may decide that we cannot afford to have additional children because of the need to save for our old age. Yet such thinking is to place the quest for material security above the cultivation of intergenerational dependence and mutual support.

Conclusion

For three quarters of its existence, the church understood that money and finance should be subordinate to the health of the relationships between borrower and lender. Alas, we forgot Jesus' warning that Money craves worship and to be treated as if it has a life of its own. Despite the detailed and delicate financial teachings of the Old Testament model, debt finance was let out of its confinement and we have suffered the consequences ever since in booms and busts, unstable banking systems, inflation, international debt and the growth of the mega-corporation. Whenever the system wreaks havoc on the host economy, the doctors treat the symptoms but never excise the parasite because they cannot conceive that the patient could survive without its presence. We mock the Old Testament financial prescription as the concoction of an eccentric apothecary but, as we have seen elsewhere, we are only just beginning to grasp the breadth of wisdom embodied in the paradigm.

12. The economy

Paul Mills

'Leviticus Chapter 25 is a passage that makes *Das Kapital* look tame ... it is no longer Morris, Keynes and Beveridge who inspire and change the world – it's Leviticus' (Hutton 1999).

Introduction

The ancient land laws of the Bible have joined the vocabulary of international finance. The jubilee concepts of a periodic cancellation of debt, release of debt slaves and return of family property have become a powerful paradigm for the advocates of debt forgiveness.

Yet 'Jubilee 2000' and the wider Christian contribution to the globalization debate are typical of how the economic ideas of the biblical law have been used in Christian political discussion throughout the church's history. In the main, convenient precedents or analogies in Old Testament law, the Prophets, the Sermon on the Mount or the parables have been used to bolster existing positions. Rarely have the laws of the Pentateuch been studied as an integrated whole in order to provide the outlines of a biblical model of how to order economic relationships.

From considering biblical law as a whole, an integrated model for economic relationships emerges that satisfies the prerequisites for both fairness and efficiency, and leads to fewer wasteful and damaging side-effects than the current Western economic prescription. We will then combine the model with that of finance from the preceding chapter to outline how an economic and financial system established on relational lines would work.

The state we're in

Misguided ends

The goal of a Western government's economic policy is usually framed in terms of a high level of income or wealth generation combined with widely dispersed access to that wealth through employment or redistribution. Low inflation is seen as a means to that end.

Notwithstanding the well-known shortcomings of the measures of national income used to assess the level of prosperity,[1] the biblical assessment of human personality indicates that this is the wrong objective. By making wealth our goal, we have succumbed to the idolatry of Mammon about which Jesus warned so strongly (Matt. 6:24). Rather, the ultimate goal of economic policy ought to be enriching the quality of relationships within a society. Too often these are sacrificed to the pursuit of short-term economic efficiency. Economic wealth may be a helpful means to the end of a relationally healthy society but should not become the goal.

This assertion of priorities does not solely rest upon the personal responsibility to love God and one's neighbour that is at the heart of Old and New Testament ethics and which permeates the other chapters of this book. Remarkably, it can also be seen as chiming with the utilitarian premise of economics that the maximization of human 'satisfaction' or happiness is the ultimate goal for organizing society. In the past, this has almost invariably been translated into the objective of maximizing consumption or choice. However, when studies are made of what leads to personal 'happiness', it is *not* ineluctably linked to ever-greater consumption. The richest countries are usually amongst those whose populations claim to be most satisfied, but once a minimum standard of living is reached, happiness is increased by the quality and closeness of personal relationships, the enjoyment of physical health and the position one occupies within society. In some of these studies, the people of the Philippines claim to be as 'happy' as those of Austria or Japan. A consistent finding from survey evidence is that Westerners' declared level of happiness has not risen in the post-war era

---

1. The statistical measure of Gross Domestic Product throws up a number of anomalies from a commonsense perspective. For instance, GDP rises if two families pay each other for their childcare, whereas there is no 'production' if each looks after their own children.

despite economic growth: 'People in the West have got no happier in the last 50 years. They have become richer, they work much less, they have longer holidays, they travel more, they live longer, and they are healthier. But they are not happier' (Layard 2003: 14).

This unease is manifest in a number of ways. The prevalence of clinical depression has increased significantly since 1945 – possibly sevenfold in the US (Layard 2003: 20). Rates of suicide are positively correlated with income per head amongst the richest countries, possibly because singleness and divorce rates, significant triggers for suicide, are also positively linked to average income (Oswald 1997). Survey evidence on well-being finds that the event with the largest detrimental impact on happiness is marriage separation, followed by ill-health and unemployment, which dwarf the impact of large drops in income (Layard 2003: 3). In addition, people are much happier if they feel that they live in a friendly and harmonious society in which people can be trusted. Unfortunately, US and UK surveys have shown a halving in the proportion of people who agree that 'most people can be trusted' since the late 1950s, with a consequent decline in well-being (Putnam 2000). Hence, even if we accept the premise that maximizing human satisfaction should be society's overarching goal, this now results in the need to place the quality relationships at the heart of economic policy.[2] As a recent Government Strategy Unit policy paper concluded, 'Social relationships have a much larger impact on life satisfaction than financial income, at least within wealthy nations such as the UK' (Donovan & Halpern 2002).

Neither should the biblical emphasis on the quality of relationships be equated to one that despises material prosperity or increasing productivity. The initial creation mandate (Gen. 1:28) has inspired the Judaeo-Christian belief in the need to husband and develop the material world in obedience to God and for the benefit of future generations. As long as the acquisition of wealth is justly achieved and kept as a means to a higher end rather than an end in itself, the biblical attitude supports mankind's progressive stewardship of creation and envisages some of its products being woven into the matrix of the new creation (Rev. 21:24–26). Indeed, whilst the following analysis rests on the premise that the quality of relationships should trump short-term economic prosperity as the ultimate driver of economic policy, in reality this is a false dichotomy. By placing primacy upon healthy economic and social relationships, prosperity should follow – as the Old Testament law envisaged (e.g. Deut. 28:1–14). Looked at purely from a pragmatic perspective, the debate is over the means that should be employed to achieve a similar goal.

---

2. Of course, a number of other factors have been found to be positively correlated with a person's happiness, including belief in God and time spent in prayer.

Misguided means

With the demise of Soviet-style central planning and dilution of Thatcherite *laissez-faire* policies, Western societies have accepted a compromise between relatively free trade and markets on the one hand and a sizeable role for the state in the form of redistributive welfare and regulation on the other. Bureaucracies still control the expenditure of 40–50% of national income in Europe, but for the remainder, companies and individuals decide what is produced and valued through market processes.

Besides the political apathy it engenders, this diluted form of Capitalism has a number of worrying features that are undermining its long-term viability. Companies tend towards monopolies that subvert competition unless checked by regulation or technological change. The workings of the market system tend to commercialize every relationship and erode family and community structures by emphasizing rootlessness, mobility and the 24-hour society. The pre-eminence of consumer choice and absence of commitment to long-term employment arrangements reduces incentives to foster trust and long-standing reputation. Indeed, the Western market system has an inbuilt contradiction: it works only if people observe 'the rules of the game', trust each other and do not exploit every small advantage to the limit and yet, by undermining the social environment (such as rootedness) conducive to such behaviour, the market system undermines its own foundation.

In addition, the free market system's legitimacy relies on its marriage to a complex system of taxation, state redistribution and welfare. The shortcomings of this process are well-known: taxation distorts people's behaviour in a number of deleterious ways, from reducing work incentives (through high marginal rates of income tax) to penalizing employment (through National Insurance charges); then, a multitude of tax officials, accountants and lawyers do battle to apply the tax code; finally, the welfare system distorts recipients' behaviour in a number of ways, from penalizing saving for old age to facilitating the creation of one-parent households. We have lived with these costs and distortions for some time. But the increasing global mobility of companies, savings and workers is likely to mean that governments will be unable to maintain taxes at a sufficiently high level to continue the current degree of redistribution particularly to the dependent population that, in turn, gives the system its legitimacy.

Essentially, we need to retain the disciplines and efficiencies of a market system but devise another mechanism that promotes fairness in the allocation of wealth and opportunities and that does not require a burdensome tax and welfare system. Rather than a system of taxation and redistribution after the process of wealth creation, the *initial* allocation of wealth needs to be roughly equitable and maintained over people's lifetimes. Such a system would then combine the efficiency benefits of competitive market processes with a concern for fairness for those with lower incomes. It is the premise of the following discussion that, by emphasizing the pre-eminence of parity in economic relationships and limits to the scope of pure 'market forces', the Old Testament economic model achieves a better balance between efficiency and fairness that we have spurned to our detriment.

Economic relationships and institutions

Before embarking on a description of the Old Testament model, it is worth outlining the panoply of relationships within an economy to establish the frame of reference. First, and foundational to all others, is the interaction of people with their *natural environment*, be it through hunting, food production, mining or construction. As previously mentioned, the biblical vision is one of stewardship for the natural creation with mankind sanctioned and encouraged to develop and cultivate the natural world, remembering that ultimate ownership rests with God.

Once the allocation of land has been established, whilst purely self-sufficient existence is possible within agrarian societies, the near-universal observation is that families specialize in the production of a narrower range of goods and services and exchange them with others who have specialized in other areas. Indeed, such specialization and exchange is crucial to increasing the efficiency of production and supporting a higher population. These economic relationships between *producers and consumers* are usually intermediated through markets via a price-setting mechanism, facilitated by a monetary medium that enjoys widespread trust in its value and acceptability, or through collective allocation mechanisms (village elders, commune hierarchies) that decide on the distribution of produce. When the most productive technologies entail investment or land usage beyond the means of individual producers, they require finance from *suppliers of capital*, be they investors or lenders; and when these technologies necessitate additional labour, this entails the employment of *outside workers* and the payment of wages (either in money or in kind). Provision of collective services (such as defence) to the society then necessitates *joint decision-making* and a mechanism for financing such services, usually via taxes. Embodied within any economic decision to invest, use land or collectively borrow is then an expression of the relationship between, and priority given to, *current and future generations*. Hence, the functioning of any economic activity beyond the purely self-sufficient requires a network of relationships.

Only relatively recently have economists understood that how these relationships are structured – the economic institutions of a society – is crucial in explaining socio-economic success or failure. For instance, the enforceability of property rights, the honesty of tax and customs officials, the credibility of the currency and the promotion of competition rather than state monopolies all help to reduce transaction costs and further the gains in productivity that come from specialization. These costs are lowered even more when there is a widespread expectation that third parties will honour and uphold these institutions without the need for burdensome enforcement actions (such as legal action). What makes a society prosperous is not, ultimately, its natural resources or geographical endowments but its economic institutions and laws that either incentivize or penalize risk-taking and specialization (North 1990).[3] The network of property rights, predictable and honest bureaucracy and openness to competition establish the framework within which investment and innovation can be undertaken profitably.

The pillars of the jubilee economic model

The economic model put forward in the Old Testament law is embedded with the legal code of Israel set out in the books from Exodus to Deuteronomy. These are then worked out and illustrated through Israelite history under the judges, kings, exile and restoration. The laws are principally concerned with the preoccupations of a tribal, agrarian society, although trade (both internally and internationally) is envisaged and mentioned.

'Universal' property ownership (Lev. 25)

Perhaps the pivotal institution that shapes the economic institutions envisaged in Old Testament law is that concerned with the ownership of land, as governed by the jubilee. When the Israelites first entered Canaan, the land was divided up on a relatively even *per capita* basis. It was allocated at random by tribe and then by clan and family (Josh. 13 – 21). This much is unremarkable. The critical element comes with the inheritance and jubilee land laws then working together to ensure that the roughly equal allocation of land between families, and their geographical rootedness, was preserved.

Leviticus 25 describes in detail the ways in which a leasehold market for agricultural land was to operate (vv. 14–16, 27), so enabling a family access to the

---

3. A notable example of the importance of institutions is the difference in impact that large natural endowments (such as oil) have on the wealth of an economy. Japan has virtually no natural resources, yet maintains one of the highest incomes per head, in contrast to Russia. Oil reserves have been judiciously husbanded in Norway but have, if anything, served to make Nigeria poorer by acting as a focus for corruption and state redistribution.

capital value of their asset if they were in need and without relatives to provide financial support, with the future rents from the land until the next jubilee acting as the limit to one's ability to consume now. However, a freehold land market was explicitly proscribed because God was the ultimate owner of the land (v. 23).[4] Every fifty years, and coinciding with the release of bonded servants (vv. 40–41, 54–55), the sounding of a trumpet throughout the land signified that the land was reverting back to its original familial owners who were to return to occupy their holdings (vv. 10, 13). The explicit intentions of the jubilee legislation were to prevent the development of a freehold land market whilst enabling those in hardship to gain access to the leasehold value of their asset; to place the onus on extended family members for the welfare of their relatives and the integrity of the familial property; and to cement close extended family ties to a particular locale by requiring the periodic relocation of families back to their tribal territory. Indeed, one can perhaps detect a faint echo of the jubilee principle in the Christmas story with the return of Joseph to his original clan town of Bethlehem (Luke 2:4).

It is debated to what extent the jubilee was observed in practice. The year of release is referred to in the context of other laws (Lev. 27:23–24; Num. 36:4) and the duty of kinsmen to redeem a family's land is described in practice (Ruth 4:4; Jer. 32:7). However, no reference is made in the Old Testament historical narratives to the subsequent adherence to the institution, and the non-observance of the Sabbath year for the land (2 Chr. 36:21) suggests that a jubilee year may also not have been observed, at least in the monarchic period. Nevertheless, the extreme significance to an Israelite family of its 'inheritance' in a specific piece of land lies behind the heinous nature of Ahab's crime in dispossessing and murdering Naboth (1 Kgs 21). The future kingdom of God is portrayed as a state where the jubilee is declared (Isa. 61:2), applies (Ezek. 46:17) and results in universal property ownership (Mic. 4:4).

How the jubilee fits into the wider Old Testament economic model will be described below. Suffice it to say at this stage, there were a number of clear economic purposes behind the institution. First, the jubilee worked to preserve in the long run the initial, relatively equitable, distribution between families of the main means of production (agricultural land) at the time. The ideal that all, rather than none, should have access to property and capital is the very antithesis of Marxism (R. North 1954: 159). Secondly, in line with the sabbatical cancellation of debts and release of bonded servants (Deut. 15:1–18), the jubilee ensured that the economic slate was wiped clean at least once in somebody's lifetime. A family

---

4. A careful distinction is made between agricultural land, urban property that could be sold freehold (vv. 29–31) and the holdings of the Levites (vv. 32–34).

should not have been totally without means of independent support for more than a generation. Thirdly, the onus for poverty relief was placed upon the extended family network as an obligation under the law, rather than charity from strangers or the state (e.g. Lev. 25:25, 35, 47–49). Only if this support could not be provided was a family to resort to selling the leasehold of their land or their labour to others. Fourthly, the ability of the extended family to provide such support was reinforced by the requirement of each family that had leased their land to return to it at the jubilee (Lev. 25:10), so entrenching the association of an extended family network with the original allocation of land and resetting each family back within their kinship support network every fifty years.

There would also have been a number of other side-effects from the jubilee land laws. Some freehold property could be traded in perpetuity within cities (Lev. 25:29–30), thus enabling those without an initial allocation of agricultural land some access to property ownership. But the fact that many towns were surrounded by an allocation of land to the Levites that could not be sold permanently (vv. 32–34) would have prevented the sprawl of large cities and encouraged a dispersed pattern of urban settlement.

The constrained monarchy (Deut. 17:14–20)

Although cast in negative terms, the role envisaged in the law for the central state, embodied by the monarchy, is as important a backdrop to the Old Testament economic model as the jubilee. There is deep ambivalence about the institution of an Israelite monarchy given that Israel's true King was only ever God himself. Nevertheless, Deuteronomy contains provision for the appointment of a monarch, albeit in terms more reminiscent of a modern constitutional monarchy than the absolutist rule invariably enjoyed by Israel's neighbours at the time. There was to be no large-scale standing army, the royal entourage was not to be large and nor were the king's coffers (Deut. 17:16–17). Indeed, great play is made of the need for the king to be 'under the law' and to know and apply it (vv. 18–20) rather than make it. What is remarkable is what the law does *not* make material provision for the king. There is no independent tax-raising power, no ability to command the labour or wealth of his subjects and no means by which the king can promulgate new laws. Rather his task is to apply those already revealed. As such, the king was to have been a fellow subject of God under the law and able to relate to any other member of society on a comparable basis.

This conception of the monarchy contrasts sharply with that described by Samuel when warning the people how a king would act in practice (1 Sam. 8). Whilst a monarchy should ensure clarity over the succession (v. 5) and provide a figurehead and military leadership (v. 20), a king would also conscript the population into a standing army, central food production or weapons production (v. 11). A king would confiscate property, food and livestock for his own use or to allocate to his entourage and begin to enslave the populace (v. 17). By taking a tithe of the land's produce and the best of the livestock, the king would usurp God's rightful position at the pinnacle of the social hierarchy. In the record of Israel's monarchy, it did not take long for these traits to manifest themselves. Saul's first act of disobedience was to eliminate the distinction between the monarchy and the priesthood (1 Sam. 13); David committed murder through wielding his power as supreme commander (2 Sam. 11) and conducted a misguided census to assess the strength of his army (2 Sam. 24). But it was under Solomon that Samuel's warnings were fulfilled most clearly with his accumulation of a large chariot force (1 Kgs 4:26; 10:26), an enormous harem (11:3) and a substantial workforce (9:20–23). This expense may initially have been met from Solomon's empire but the monarchy was soon requiring forced labour to meet its expenditure requirements (1 Kgs 12).

Whilst Deuteronomy made provision for a limited monarchy operating under the law, as soon as a king was anointed, the boundaries of state power established in the law were breached and the monarchy became the primary source of economic power. No longer was the king a fellow citizen who could relate easily with his compatriots, but a ruler over them.

A non-inflationary monetary system

Closely associated with the constraints on the central state is the absence of any central control over the money supply or price level. While direct biblical teaching on monetary systems is limited, it offers some useful pointers.

Precious metals were used as the monetary base

Money originally acted as an aid to trade through avoiding the need for direct barter by substituting a portable, inherently valuable commodity for one side of each bargain. Initially, precious metals were used for the purpose. The first instance of metals being used in this way in the Bible is of Abraham paying 400 shekels of silver for Sarah's burial site (Gen. 23). Gold and silver were chosen because of their scarcity, malleability and decorative qualities. But desire for their ownership runs deep in human nature and gives them a widely recognized intrinsic value.

There is no positive teaching on the form of money to be employed in Old Testament Israel. Rather, the value and use of precious metals in fixed weights seems to have been assumed and legislated for (e.g. Deut. 22:19, 29). A metallic monetary base generally provides a long-term anchor for the price level without the need for central state intervention. Unless there is a large-scale discovery of the metal or a technological discovery that alters underlying demand, approximate price stability is maintained through fluctuations in the amount of the metal mined or taken out of circulation. If the relative price of gold or silver rises (i.e. the price of goods falls), gold can purchase more, is more profitable to mine and is taken out of hoards (e.g. jewellery) and put into circulation. Conversely, when the price of gold falls relative to other goods (i.e. there is inflation), less is mined and more is stored. Hence, the supply of commodity money tends to move to match demand, so roughly stabilizing the price level. As an example, the price of people and land stayed roughly constant over several centuries in Israel. For instance, Jesus was betrayed by Judas for thirty silver coins (Matt. 26:15). This was approximately the value of a slave in the Mosaic period (Exod. 21:32; cf. Gen. 37:28). The same sum was used by the chief priests to procure a field in Jerusalem (Matt. 27:7–10); Jeremiah had bought a field in Jerusalem for seventeen silver shekels centuries earlier in a depressed land market (Jer. 32:9).[5]

A long-term anchor for the price level is important for both moral and economic reasons. Modern economies seem endemically prone to rising price levels and inflation due to their reliance on debt contracts to finance consumption and investment.[6] This is an immoral aspect of modern economic life. Unless perfectly anticipated, inflation redistributes real wealth between creditors and debtors, savers and borrowers and those on fixed and inflation-linked incomes. Inflation, especially when unexpected, is an arbitrary transfer of purchasing power from one group (who cannot protect themselves) to another. It also erodes the incentives for long-term saving, investment and risk-taking (by making real returns more unpredictable) and confuses relative price signals within an economy as people confuse real price increases for the effects of general inflation. This leads to inefficient decision-making (King 2002).

Political sovereignty is closely tied to issuing currency
The next major monetary development, first recorded in Lydia around 700 BC, was to mint coins from precious metals of set weights so that a coin was known to have a certain intrinsic value. Unfortunately, minted coins were vulnerable to debasement with inferior metals, leading to inflation. State-controlled mints were established to attest to the inherent value of the coin whilst their designs and inscriptions attested to the reliability of the issuer. But cash-strapped states soon realized that they could procure easy revenue by debasing their coinage themselves and passing it off for its face value. The implicit tax that a state receives through increasing money in circulation in excess of its production costs or intrinsic value is known as 'seignorage'. The process continued with governments printing paper

---

5. A similar degree of price stability was enjoyed in Britain from the end of the seventeenth century to the beginning of the First World War. Subsequently, the retail price level has risen approximately fifty times.

6. See preceding chapter.

money eventually unbacked by gold or silver. This is a lucrative source of revenue even today.

While an absolutely fixed link of a currency to a precious metallic base is maintained, the monetary system remains 'automatic' and apolitical. However, the possibility of debasement and seignorage makes money creation an inherently political process. On the one hand, states saw it as a mark of their trustworthiness and reliability that their currency circulated widely and was exchanged for its face value. On the other, if debasement was occurring, it was important for a state to be able to force the use of its currency on the populace to maximize seignorage.

This connection between political control and the issuing of currency informs Jesus' answer to the vexed question, 'Is it right to pay taxes to Caesar?' Requesting a Roman coin, Jesus asks whose inscription and portrait were on it. He then gave his famous reply, 'Give to Caesar what is Caesar's and to God what is God's' (Matt. 22:15–22). This teaching makes clear that the state has legitimate but limited claims upon the resources and loyalty of Jesus' disciples. But the inference drawn by Jesus is groundless unless the use of a government's coinage by its citizens legitimates its tax-raising claims; if the Jews are to enjoy the economic benefits of the *Pax Romana*, as exemplified by their use of Roman currency, they should not resist the taxation required to maintain it, however idolatrous that empire.

This close connection between political authority and issue of currency has been remarkably firm throughout history once debasement and seignorage became possibilities. Almost invariably, non-metallic currencies are issued by the government of the state in which they circulate, although state control over the money supply in circulation (including bank deposits) is now exercised through setting short-term interest rates. Modern banking systems can effectively lend into existence as much credit as is demanded at the prevailing interest rate so most governments opt to control the amount of credit in their economy by setting the price for short-term credit to the banking system via the central bank.[7]

Some commentators have sought to interpret the use of precious metals as money in the Old Testament economy as an affirmation of commodity money (such as the gold standard). The absence of a specific injunction in the law defining the monetary medium argues against asserting that commodity money is the only legitimate biblical system. However, contemporary non-commodity monetary systems rely on the backing of debts (either of governments or banks) rather than real assets. The Old Testament periodic cancellation of debts and prohibition of

---

7. In the UK, as of March 2004, the vast proportion of the money supply (around £1,000 billion) comprises bank and building society deposits (96%) relative to notes and coins (4%).

interest would make such systems inoperable. Also, the general lessons to be learned from the breakdown of commodity standards are that if central state authorities can profit from increasing the money supply and price level through seignorage or inflating away their debts, they invariably will – be they democracies or dictatorships. Heavily indebted sectors of an economy find it hard to survive if the price level is stable or falling – hence Britain's ultimate exit from the gold standard in 1931 and the strenuous efforts of Japan since the late 1990s to restrain falling prices whatever the cost. These lessons strongly suggest that control of monetary conditions should be taken out of the hands of the central state (either through independent central banks or currency regimes that cannot be manipulated for political ends) and that high levels of borrowing in an economy will ultimately endanger either economic prosperity or the price level because it leaves important sectors vulnerable to unexpected changes in circumstance. Whilst the Old Testament model is not absolutely prescriptive about the form of monetary system, it did embody the ingredients necessary for a stable long-term price level.

These three institutions (the jubilee, the constrained monarchy, the non-inflationary monetary system) provide the framework around which the two main strands of biblical economic insight are woven to provide the Old Testament economic model. On the one hand, the infrastructure for a 'market' economy was envisaged with a limited role for government, property laws and a stable price level. On the other hand, economic justice and equity were to be preserved by restrictions on the markets for land, capital and labour that were instituted without the state needing to redistribute wealth or income.

The framework for a market economy

The biblical model contains a number of features that, with the economic hindsight of three thousand years, should have promoted economic growth and efficiency.

A general acceptance of liberal product markets

Apart from the ceremonial food laws and the observance of the Sabbath, the only constraints on trade in biblical law are the exhortations to merchants to maintain fair weights and eschew adulteration (Lev. 19:35–36; Deut. 25:13–16). These statutes recognize the need for a basic degree of confidence by consumers in what they are buying. There is no notion that trading for profit is inherently 'wrong' (although profit from an artificial monopoly was condemned – e.g. Prov. 11:26). There is also ample evidence that trade was relatively commonplace and Israel participated in the international trading networks of the time (Deut. 28:12; 1 Kgs 10:14;

Neh. 13:16; Ezek. 27:17). We can thus infer both the acceptance of competitive markets and the presumption that the 'just price' for a good is that which results from fair competition – rather than either the value of labour it embodies or 'whatever the market will bear'.

A capped and proportional rate of income tax

A centralized state system of taxation on income, wealth or expenditure was unnecessary in Israel due to the limited nature of the apparatus of central government. Instead, the criminal justice system and military were structured in such a way that did not require a police force, prisons or a standing army. Tithes of 10% on income were directed to local poverty relief, the support of the local priests and Levites or to religious celebrations (Townsend 2001), although the number of tithes in any single year remains uncertain (Lev. 27:30; Deut. 14:28). The limited role of the state apparatus also reduced the potential for arbitrary confiscation by the state – an all too familiar feature of monarchies at the time (1 Sam. 8). There was no redistribution mechanism for portable wealth. Hence, there were few marginal disincentives to work or save, whereas many Western tax and benefit systems still face the richest or poorest with marginal tax rates of over 50% of everything extra they earn.

A stable monetary system and price level

As we have seen above, the approximate long-term stability of the price level that arose from a monetary system outside centralized control should have encouraged saving and trade by providing a stable store of value and clear price signals.

A well-defined legal code

Biblical law establishes property rights and makes provision for debt collection deriving from the commandment against theft. Whilst property rights over land were restricted and debts periodically cancelled, there was nevertheless a well-defined code of property law and debt collection, including means for enforcement such as fines for theft and bonded labour for the repayment of debts. As is clear from the limited success in the development of some former Communist economies, the absence of a predictable property code deters investment and promotes hoarding. Economists are also only just realizing how crucial the clear definition of property rights is to enable the rural and urban poor to develop their land or raise capital. Indeed, it is the absence of property rights for the poor, particularly over land, that is now blamed for the observation that Capitalism does not seem to work in many societies that follow its prescriptions (de Soto 2000). Such property 'rights' in the Old Testament model were, of course, tempered by obligations to others (see below), but the law embodied the negative that property certainly was *not* theft.

A limited role for the state

As we have seen, the intended structure of Israelite society did not include a privileged class to be supported through the labour of others. Nor did it envisage a princely 'court' or aristocracy. This deliberate restraint on the scope and power of the monarchy was unique for the time. The absence of a rigid hierarchy meant that there were no incentives to forsake economic activity in favour of seeking concessions from the ruling class. Bribery and the corruption of the judicial process were strongly condemned.

The combination of low taxes, a small state infrastructure, a stable price level and predictable property rights would have encouraged economic growth by maintaining incentives to work, save and invest. Given the right preconditions, market-based economies have generally proved to be better than bureaucrats at processing information about the desired types of production and the most efficient technologies. These factors promoting prosperity would have been reinforced by free trade of produced surpluses both locally and internationally. The biblical legal model contains what are now recognized as the prerequisites for a successful market-based economy.

The limits to laissez-faire

The problems with a purely free market approach are the tendency towards inequalities both of wealth and income, and monopolies that subvert the very market forces that brought them about. It is in its treatment of the markets for the factors of production (land, labour and financial capital) that the biblical model addresses these undesirable and self-destructive aspects of free-market Capitalism.

Land transfer

Ownership claims over a family's particular piece of land were established at the initial division of the land and then reinforced by repeated prescriptions against the movement of boundary markers (e.g. Deut. 19:14; 27:17). As we have seen, the jubilee would then have operated to ensure that the roughly equal initial allocation of land between families was preserved whilst permitting a leasehold market, so families in dire economic straits had access to the market value of their assets until the next jubilee year. This also allowed the temporary transfer of land to those best able to use it. Although subverted in practice, the jubilee should have prevented a central state from accumulating land (e.g. 1 Kgs 9:17–19, and see 1 Sam. 8:14).

Implications of this novel economic institution are numerous. The jubilee would have ensured that the initial extended family structure was preserved and rooted in an ancestral locality. It prevented the accumulation of large estates by the wealthier families or by foreclosing moneylenders and so stood as a bulwark against the development of permanently landless poor or the nationalization of land to be used for the benefit of the central state or its officials.

Restrictions on the labour market

Whilst a relatively unrestricted wage labour market could have developed, the welfare provisions of biblical law should have kept wage levels above subsistence levels. The requirement for employers to pay wages punctually (Deut. 24:15) and to be responsible for their workers' safety (e.g. Exod. 21:28–29; Deut. 22:8) shows the detail of the thinking behind the law in the protection of the waged labourer. Sabbath restrictions on work also underlined the importance of placing relationships to God and family ahead of material provision and reduced the pressures on vulnerable workers. The welfare institutions of the tithe (that periodically went to the poor), gleaning and interest-free lending would have provided further protection for those with the lowest incomes.

The prohibition of interest

As described in the preceding chapter, the Old Testament law contains a number of complex financial arrangements. As well as detailing sophisticated leasehold arrangements, it describes a rental contract and careful rules for the treatment of different forms of security for a loan, including bonded servitude in the case of default. It also envisages a vital role for interest-free lending between family and community members as a means of poverty relief. Yet the model expressly prohibits all loans at interest, for both commercial and consumption purposes, at least within the Israelite community. As a result, there was no place for a commercial loan market – a conclusion reinforced by the laws which prescribed the cancellation of all debts (and debt servitude) every seven years. Although the text is not explicit as to why interest is prohibited, the problems associated with a debt-based financial system are numerous, and we are only now fully appreciating their extent. Low-income country debt is but one aspect. In the context of the wider economic model, perhaps the most important implications of the prohibition of interest were that it encouraged both non-interest charitable lending and risk-sharing business finance (so distributing the profits or losses from commercial ventures more widely). Financial power could not be accumulated without sharing in the risks of enterprise, while no-one could be permanently enslaved in debt without prospect of release.

Hence the biblical model has a strong underlying current of concern for the poor and the wide dispersion of economic power. Yet its approach to the distribution of wealth and income is radically different from the familiar approach of redistributive taxes and welfare benefits. Instead, the biblical model does not concern itself with differences in portable wealth or consumption. Indeed, the acquisition of wealth was often seen as a blessing from God and provided incentives to work hard. Rather, its aim was to ensure that everyone, even the poorest, was able to gain access at some time in his or her life to the means of production (in this case, land); that no-one was in debt or debt bondage for more than seven years; that the primary responsibility for care of the poor was the extended family and local community; and that no-one could entrench their wealth through simply lending money at interest without risk. Immigrants were able to procure urban property.

The result should have been a relatively egalitarian society without the intervention of intrusive tax bureaucracies and welfare states. Biblical law achieved this by eliminating the existence of three forms of contract – the freehold sale of agricultural land, permanent debt (including the slavery that often goes with it) and the interest-bearing loan. Portable wealth was not redistributed by forcible means – rather the conditions necessary to give economic independence to the poor and to place a brake on the accumulation of the economic power of the rich or corrupt officials were built into the fabric of society's finances and organization.

Evaluation

With the benefit of hindsight, we can recognize that the Old Testament ethical and legal framework embodies the necessary prerequisites that we now under-stand are instrumental in fostering economic development. The limited role for the state, an ostensibly honest judiciary and the preservation of the initial allocation of land limited the scope for incentives to exert effort and take risks to be skewed by confiscation, taxation or bribery. The enshrining of property rights, and mechanisms for even the poorest to raise temporary capital from the leasing of their land, should have ensured that families had the incentive and some ability to invest in productive enterprises; whilst a market system set within a context of a stable price level, honest weights and measures and frequent interactions within the local community should have reduced transactions costs. Such a benign context for free market exchange was viable *because* of the protections of the poor and unfortunate that were built into the land, labour and capital markets.

Possible contemporary applications

Numerous applications to the economic questions of our day suggest themselves; those applicable to finance were explored in the preceding chapter. Perhaps the key insight of the Old Testament model is for governments not to interfere in product markets via state ownership of the means of production, or rely on taxes to achieve wider goals of wealth redistribution. If one is to have incentives to encourage effort and risk-taking, then inequalities in portable wealth and income must automatically arise – indeed, they are intrinsic to the maintenance of those incentives. Rather, the emphasis should be upon preserving the institutional architecture that permits a market-based economy to flourish and achieve the goals of protecting the most vulnerable through safeguards in the factor markets of land, labour and capital. Land reform, to ensure that enforceable property rights exist for a significant proportion of the population (as opposed to just aristocracies, collectives, central bureaucracies or wealthy families), is the fundamental step to the creation of a decentralized entrepreneurial society (as witnessed in contemporary Chile and Taiwan). Two further possible applications are:

A national investment fund

The key to an 'equitable' economic society is not for the state to confiscate the results of people's labour and pass it to those it deems deserving of assistance, but to ensure that everyone has access to the means of production and support. A safety net will always be necessary to assist those in temporary difficulty, but Western welfare systems confuse the provision of this safety net with the means of rectifying the tendency for wealth and income to concentrate. Rather, the issue should be tackled earlier by ensuring that a wider distribution of assets is preserved. For instance, the goal of the jubilee of giving every family access to an income-generating asset could be emulated. Assets act as a form of insurance against temporary falls in income, they allow people to invest in their own income-generating capacity (through education or business) and have been found to have a positive psychological impact (IPPR/CASE 2003). Instead of a share in agricultural land, a national investment fund could be established, an equal share of which would be bestowed upon every citizen when reaching voting age and relinquished at death. A non-political board of trustees would oversee investment policy and a profit-related dividend would be paid each year linked to the returns enjoyed by the investments in the fund. If the fund was large enough, this dividend could provide a basic minimum income. Citizens could borrow against their dividends for, say, ten or twenty years (to finance education, training, house purchase or a business start-up). Crucially, however, citizens would not be able permanently sell their shares to any third party. It is this jubilee principle that distinguishes the idea from other suggestions for a universal capital endowment (Brittan 2000). At some time in the not-too-distant future, everyone would receive back title to their share in the fund.

Such a fund would provide everyone with an income top-up or a way to raise initial capital, contribute to the sense of citizenship in society and reinforce incentives to ensure the wider success of the economy. The UK has already passed up two chances to establish an initial fund (in the form of the receipts from North Sea oil and the privatization of nationalized industries). However, the Children's

Trust Fund, whereby the government provides an endowment to every child at birth that can be topped up by family members to provide a lump sum at the age of eighteen, is proceeding. Although the Fund endowments need to be appreciably larger to have any significant impact on the distribution of wealth, and need to pay out an income rather than the capital sum, this is the first step towards a contemporary jubilee that seeks to universalize access to wealth (Brittan 2003).

A rediscovery of rootedness

The jubilee was structured to preserve the universal ownership of property and to return an extended family to its ancestral lands at least once every fifty years. This not only recognized the contribution of widespread property ownership to economic freedom, but it underlined the importance of rootedness and a sense of place. It is only through the physical and prolonged proximity of extended family members and neighbours that society can deliver care of dependants without ever-greater reliance on the state or on purchased 'care' (Schluter 2000a: 81–91). Mobility also has undesirable social effects:

> ... if people are highly mobile, they feel less bonded to the people among whom they live and crime is more common. The evidence shows that crime is lower when people trust each other, and that people trust each other more if fewer people are moving house and the community is more homogenous (Layard 2003: 7).

Yet current economic thinking encourages workers to be as geographically mobile as possible (HM Treasury 2004), with no cognisance of the damaging relational side-effects and economic costs when families are uprooted from their kinship and community networks. As well as recognizing the external benefits that rootedness brings, government policy could be more explicitly geared to encouraging regional rootedness and identity. For example, as in Scotland, students could be encouraged to study at local universities through preferential loan terms.

Conclusion

The subtlety of the economic model set out in the Old Testament law is a further sign of God's providence and inspiration of Scripture. Two hundred and fifty years of Western political economy have not got close to emulating the law's economic wisdom for the state of development of its day. As ever, great care is needed when translating the economic model of the Old Testament into a jubilee manifesto for today. Nevertheless, there are sufficiently tangible and realistic ideas for economic policy to make a valuable and practical contribution to developing the relational society.

13. Criminal justice

Jonathan Burnside

Introduction

It should be said at once that there is something odd about using 'criminal justice' as a chapter heading in a book about biblical perspectives. The term 'criminal justice' reflects the fact that, in a modern legal system, criminal proceedings are a unique category of legal actions because they have as their object the punishment of a public offence. 'Criminal justice', however, is not a relevant category in biblical law. This does not mean, of course, that biblical law did not make distinctions of its own[1] or assign certain types of cases to particular jurisdictions.[2] It is simply that the term 'criminal justice', as applied to biblical law, is an anachronism. This is not a novel insight but it is important nonetheless. We should not expect the taxonomy of a pre-modern society such as ancient Israel to have the same content or even form of modern classifications.[3]

---

1. For example, the numerous gradings and dimensions of the priestly world-view, e.g. holy/profane/clean/unclean etc. (Jenson 1992).
2. Some decisions were referred to tribal judges (Deut. 16:18–20), others to the Levitical priests (Deut. 17:8–12) or the king (1 Kgs 3:16–28).
3. See, for example, the close links between biblical laws and the narrative in which they are embedded, together with the use of particular styles of literary presentation, including binary oppositions and chiasmus (mirror-image) (Jackson 2000: 187–230).

Yet although taxonomies differ, punishment is universal – as is the need to justify it (Walker 1991). It is not surprising to find that biblical law has a great deal to say about justice and punishment and, specifically, about how to dispense punishment with justice. This remains a matter of the utmost political importance. In fact, the leading newspaper item today, as I write, is a statement by the most senior public servant responsible for criminal proceedings in England and Wales condemning the 'grotesquely' high jail population. Since crime and punishment is hardly a subject on which we can say we need no further instruction, we may as well listen in on what the Bible has to say and see what lessons can be learned.

We will begin with a general account of justice and punishment in the Bible before going on to isolate some of its principal themes. We will then consider its relevance in a contemporary setting and conclude by noting some of the reform possibilities to which it points. In doing so it should be made clear at the outset that biblical law has far more to say on the subject of criminal justice than can adequately be surveyed in one short chapter. There is more relevant material on this issue than perhaps any other subject in this book. Given this embarrassment of riches we will not attempt a comprehensive picture but rather supply the main contours of biblical thought. Readers seeking a discussion on single issues (such as capital or corporal punishment) must look elsewhere.[4]

A brief account of justice and punishment in the Bible

Justice is a characteristic of God

Perhaps the best starting-point is the biblical proclamation that 'justice' is a characteristic of the God of Israel and that he is the source of it all:

> ... the Rock, his work is perfect,
> and all his ways are just.
> A faithful God who does no wrong,
> upright and just is he.
> (Deut. 32:4; cf. Isa. 30:18)

Unlike the Western liberal legal tradition, justice is not an abstract conception. We cannot expect justice to be completely expressed in a form of words. Knowledge of justice is relational, not propositional (Knox 1982).

If justice is a characteristic of God himself, it follows that justice is something

---

4. For example, Cohn (1970), Kaufman (1979), Hallard (2000) and C. Marshall (2001).

about which God is passionate. God delights in justice because it reflects his character. Through the prophet Jeremiah God declares,

> '... I am the LORD, who exercises kindness,
>   justice and righteousness on earth,
>   for *in these I delight*,'
>   declares the LORD.
> (Jer. 9:24, emphasis added)[5]

The association of justice with God, and therefore with what is 'good' (including love and righteousness) means that true justice takes sides when it comes to 'good' and 'evil'. Justice is partial in the sense that it always upholds what God defines as 'good' and is opposed to what God defines as 'evil'. Justice is a vigorous virtue. The usual term for justice (*mišpāṭ*) can bear a variety of meanings, including 'judgment'. Justice is vigorous in this sense as well because it is subject to God's intention to produce it by means of acts of judgment.[6]

Of course, this picture of vigorous justice is not at the expense of procedural wrongdoing. God's justice takes sides on the matter of right and wrong, but it is impartial so far as the identities of the parties are concerned. This is seen in Moses' exhortation to the children of Israel, 'For the LORD your God is God of gods and Lord of lords, the great God, mighty and awesome, who shows no partiality and accepts no bribes. He defends the cause of the fatherless and the widow, and loves the alien, giving him food and clothing' (Deut. 10:17–18). Justice in Israelite society was to take no account of the status of the parties, whether small or great (Deut. 1:17), native or outsider (Deut. 1:16). Indeed, one of the basic requirements for appointing judges in ancient Israel was that they should be 'trustworthy and ... hate a bribe' (Exod. 18:21). These criteria governed the appointment of judges under both Moses (Deut. 1:16–17; 16:19) and Jehoshaphat (2 Chr. 19:7).

Our responsibility to seek justice
Yet although God is the source of justice, 'doing justice' is not an exclusively divine activity. The early chapters of Genesis (Gen. 1 – 9) suggest that the descendants of Noah (that is, all humanity) have a part to play in bringing divine

---

5. There is no tension between God's steadfast love, his justice and his righteousness. On the contrary, as we shall see, true justice needs to be understood in the light of these other characteristics.
6. I am grateful to Gordon McConville (personal communication) for this observation.

justice on earth (Steinmetz 1994). It is a divine-human partnership.[7] We cannot expect justice if we are not willing to play our part. The Bible advises us to seek justice and that demands effort. Moses' valedictory address to Israel exhorted: 'Follow justice and justice alone, so that you may live and possess the land the LORD your God is giving you' (Deut. 16:20). 'Follow' is a rather weak translation of the verb *rādap*, which is often used of someone giving chase at top speed.[8] Justice requires 'hot pursuit'. It cannot be achieved by sitting back and leaving it to God. It is a matter of national priority that takes precedence over other things that are worthy in themselves. Jesus condemned the Pharisees not for tithing herbs *per se*, but for doing so at the expense of 'the more important matters of the law – justice, mercy and faithfulness' (Matt. 23:23).

So how do we, as human persons, lay hold of justice? According to the Bible it is something that we learn to do as we grow in wisdom and character. Because God is the source of justice, a right relationship with God was the prime quality required of an Israelite judge. Israel's judges were to be 'able men . . . such as fear God' (Exod. 18:21). The reference to the fear of God is significant because

> The fear of the LORD is *the beginning of wisdom*,
>   and the knowledge of the Holy One is understanding.
> (Prov. 9:10, emphasis added)

Israel's judges were to be 'wise men' in the sense that they know God, which is a relational and not a purely intellectual matter. Thus the content and application of biblical law, that is, its substantive and procedural aspects, have much in common with wisdom. Knowing whether a biblical norm is relevant and, if so, how it should apply to the case in hand requires wisdom, especially when the case in hand seems far removed from the 'paradigm' case[9] (e.g. Paul's application of Deut. 25:4 in 1 Cor. 9:9–10).[10] Consequently, true justice can be pursued only in the context of a close relationship with God. As the book of Proverbs says:

---

7. A common theme elsewhere in Scripture. Cf. Paul's description of himself and others as 'fellow workers' with God in 1 Cor. 3:9 and 2 Cor. 6:1.
8. For example, it describes Pharaoh's pursuit of the Israelites in Exod. 14:4.
9. For a discussion of the meaning of 'paradigm cases' in biblical law see Jackson 2000, Burnside 2003 and ch. 5, above.
10. 'For it is written in the Law of Moses, "Do not muzzle an ox while it is treading out the grain." Is it about oxen that God is concerned? Surely he says this for us, doesn't he? Yes, this was written for us, because when the ploughman ploughs and the thresher threshes, they ought to do so in the hope of sharing in the harvest' (1 Cor. 9:9–10).

> Evil men do not understand justice,
>> but those who seek the LORD understand it fully.
> (Prov. 28:5)

Two sides to justice and punishment

If true justice upholds good and opposes evil, it follows that there are two sides to justice in the Bible. On the one hand, justice brings down the oppressor and on the other hand it liberates the oppressed. Accordingly, a single act of justice can be experienced differently and have different outcomes depending on whether one is the oppressor or the oppressed. For one person, justice is cause for pain, for another, justice is cause for celebration. Psalm 146 is a psalm of praise to 'The LORD'

> ... who upholds the cause of the oppressed
>> and gives food to the hungry.
> The LORD sets prisoners free,
>> the LORD gives sight to the blind,
> the LORD lifts up those who are bowed down,
>> the LORD loves the righteous.
> The LORD watches over the alien,
>> and sustains the fatherless and the widow,
>> but he frustrates the ways of the wicked.
> (Ps. 146:7–9; cf. Ps. 103:6)[11]

The same act of justice brings down oppressors and 'lifts up those who are bowed down'. The oppressed are typified as the hungry, the blind, those in bondage and those who have no male protector to act on their behalf in a patriarchal society (viz. aliens, widows and the fatherless). All are archetypes of vulnerability and beneficiaries of justice in the Bible.

God's just acts

i. The exodus

It follows from this that the greatest example of God's justice in the Old Testament (judging oppressors, liberating the weak) is the exodus. God destabilized the totalitarian rule of Pharaoh in order to deliver the descendants of Abraham from slavery. The climactic moment occurs when God parts the waters of the Sea of Reeds, Pharaoh's armies are destroyed and the Israelites are set free:

---

11. Note again the partial nature of justice ('the LORD loves the righteous') as well as its vigorous virtues.

Then Moses and the Israelites sang this song to the LORD:

'I will sing to the LORD,
  for he is highly exalted.
The horse and its rider
  he has hurled into the sea.
The LORD is my strength and my song;
  he has become my salvation.'
(Exod. 15:1–2)

In this paradigmatic act of God, justice, punishment, freedom and salvation are inseparable (cf. Isa. 63:7–14).

ii. The cross

Likewise, the greatest example of God's justice in the New Testament is the crucifixion of Jesus;[12] an event that is expressly characterized as the 'new exodus'. Luke's Gospel describes the exchange between Jesus, Moses and Elijah on the Mount of Transfiguration, in which they 'spoke of his [Jesus'] departure, which he was to accomplish at Jerusalem' (Luke 9:31). Jesus' 'departure' refers, of course, to his looming crucifixion, and the Greek word is literally 'exodus'. Elsewhere, the death of Jesus and baptism in the name of Jesus are likened to the slaughter of the Passover lamb and the crossing of the Sea of Reeds, respectively (1 Cor. 5:7; 10:2).

The cross is a new and better exodus because it overthrows a greater oppressor than Pharaoh and liberates a greater number of people (see Heb. 3 – 4). For Jesus, the real oppressor of Israel was not the Romans but the Accuser, Satan (N. T. Wright 1996, 2003). Consequently, those who stood in need of liberation were not the inhabitants of occupied Israel alone but all those who were enslaved to Satan's power. The victory of Israel's Messiah took place on the cross (Col. 2:13–15) and it was on the cross that the Messiah was enthroned (Mark 10:37–40; cf. 15:27). Paul describes this greatest act of salvation as a manifestation of God's justice: 'He did this [the crucifixion] to demonstrate his justice, because in his forbearance he had left the sins committed beforehand unpunished – he did it to demonstrate his justice at the present time, so as to be just and the one who justifies those who have faith in Jesus' (Rom. 3:25–26). The cross is the ultimate act of God's justice in the Bible because it overthrows the ultimate oppressor and bestows the ultimate freedom from tyranny (Heb. 2:14–15; Rom. 8:14–17). The cross itself should never

---

12. As many have noted, this is ironic, because Jesus' execution is the result of human injustice.

be separated from Jesus' resurrection and ascension which together amount to God's 'vindication' of his people and his purposes. Vindication is itself a moment of, and the completion of, God's redemptive justice.[13]

In both the 'old' exodus and the 'new' exodus, doing justice means acting on behalf of those in need. As David sang,

> I know that the LORD secures justice for the poor
> and upholds the cause of the needy.
> (Ps. 140:12)

In practical terms, doing justice means putting other people's interests before our own. In this respect, there is again no tension between justice and love; there is perfect harmony (Ps. 85:10–11).

iii. The last judgment

The last judgment is an act of divine justice that finally brings the victory of Israel's Messiah on the cross to bear eternally upon the whole of creation. There is eternal retribution and eternal restoration. There is judgment upon evil (the 'lake of fire': Rev. 19:20–21; 20:10, 14–15) which paves the way for healing, transformation and restored relationships, in the closest possible sense: 'I saw the holy city, the new Jerusalem, coming down out of heaven from God, prepared as a bride beautifully dressed for her husband' (Rev. 21:2). Everything that oppresses God's creation is overthrown and everything that seeks freedom from bondage is fully liberated.

Again, the justice embodied is relational in the sense that it is God's final 'underlining and ratification of the relationship towards him that we have chosen in this life' (Travis 1986: 54). This is because heaven and hell are not a reward or a punishment for the kind of life that we have lived but the logical outcome of our relationship to God in this life. 'Heaven is not a reward for being a Christian any more than marriage is a reward for being engaged' (Travis 1986: 54, n. 76). Nor is hell best seen as a punishment for spurning Christ. It is simply, logically, frighteningly, where the road ends. 'If we have fellowship with God now, we shall enter into a fuller experience of his presence then. If we do not know him now, we shall not know him then' (Travis 1986: 54).

The prospect of perfect punishment

It is clear from these examples of God's just acts that punishment can have a role to play in securing justice (overthrowing the oppressor and liberating the oppressed). Of course, the practice of punishment can be unjust, but it is not

---

13. I owe this observation to Jonathan Chaplin.

inherently unjust.[14] God does not take pleasure in inflicting pain, in contrast to some today who take malicious satisfaction in seeing offenders suffer: 'I take no pleasure in the death of the wicked, but rather that they turn from their ways and live. Turn! Turn from your evil ways! Why will you die, O house of Israel?' (Ezek. 33:11). Punishment in the Bible takes place against the baseline of God's readiness to forgive. As the psalmist declares, in praise of God's holiness,

'O LORD our God,
You answered them [Moses and Aaron];
You were a forgiving God for them,
but You exacted retribution for their misdeeds.'
(Ps. 99:8, Jewish Publication Society)

In Romans 13:3–4 and 2 Peter 2:4–7 the New Testament affirms the value of pain in just punishment (see O'Donovan 1996). However, the fact that punishment is not just about punishing the oppressor but liberating the oppressed reminds us that we should look beyond retribution to consider its relational and restorative potential.

Consider the purpose of the two great acts of justice in the Old Testament (the exodus) and the New Testament (the cross). The goal of the exodus is stated by Moses and Aaron to Pharaoh in the following terms: 'This is what the LORD, the God of Israel, says: "Let my people go, *so that they may hold a festival to me in the desert*"' (Exod. 5:1, my italics). That is why the book of Exodus ends with the Presence of God coming to dwell among his people (Exod. 40:34). The goal of justice is relational. Likewise, the achievement of the cross is described in relational terms. The cross is the place where God creates for himself a new family (e.g. Heb. 2:11–13). And as with the exodus, the goal is the worship of God on the new 'holy mountain' (Rev. 14:1).

Justice is transformative

For all these reasons, therefore, true justice is transformative, a saving action by God that puts things right, and this is reflected in biblical images of justice. Amos declared:

'. . . let justice roll on like a river,
    righteousness like a never-failing stream.'
(Amos 5:24)

---

14. *Contra* some exponents of restorative justice who have attacked the entire social practice of judicial punishment. For a brief summary, see Johnstone (2002: 88–92).

Justice is here seen as a mighty, surging river, like the Jordan in full flood. This picture teaches us that justice is not a static state (like a set of scales) but an intervening power: it strikes and changes, restores and heals. It brings life to a parched land. Amos's picture of justice is very similar to Ezekiel's vision of a river that flows east out of the temple in Jerusalem, through the countryside, becoming so wide and so deep that no-one can cross it. Eventually this river empties into the Dead Sea and its effect is to make even this place of death a source of life. 'Swarms of living creatures will live', we are told, 'wherever the river flows' (Ezek. 47:9).

So much, then, for this brief overview. Clearly, the Bible presents us with inspiring pictures of soteriological justice. But how were these qualities supposed to be translated into everyday life and practice?

Justice with its boots on: aspects of punishment in biblical law

Putting things right

We have seen that justice in the Bible is not simply a matter of punishing people but of putting things right. There is a variety of examples of this in biblical law. Exodus 21:18-19 imposes a duty on the perpetrator of a physical assault to see that his victim is 'thoroughly healed'. Rather than simply paying a fine or damages, he is to see that the victim is restored to her original position, so far as possible. The goal is not (as in our modern 'compensation culture') to give money but to restore the situation. So, for example, if the victim was a farmhand and unable to work, the natural thing would be for the offender to send his son to farm the land, or else to send someone to look after him. There would be no calculation of 'damages' because the obligation is one of restoration not compensation.

Moving from personal injury to theft, Exodus 22:1-4 prescribes restitution for animal stealing. The sanctions vary according to whether the stolen goods have already been slaughtered or sold and hence unrecoverable (Exod. 22:1) or still in the thief's possession (the paradigm, perhaps, of being 'caught in the act') (Exod. 22:4). The advantage of multiple restitution is that it not only puts the victim back in the position she was before the crime (insofar as that is materially possible) but also places her in a financially better position. Crime pays – for the victim! At the same time, the offender is made to suffer the original loss, which means he now knows what it is like to stand in the victim's shoes. Multiple restitution may then provide a strong disincentive to theft.[15]

---

15. Although this assumes, perhaps unrealistically, that offenders weigh up the costs and benefits of committing crime in advance, as *per* modern 'rational choice theory' (Newman et al. 1997).

It is also worth noting that in Exodus 22:5 (concerning agricultural delicts), restitution is simply made 'from the best in his own field and in his own vineyard'. There is no guarantee that it will fully compensate for the loss. However, any disparity must be offset by the advantage of resolving the matter quickly and allowing the parties to get on with their lives. We cannot always expect perfectly calibrated justice in this life and there are times when the quest for it is detrimental (e.g. long delays in reaching resolution). Human justice can sometimes express divine justice, but often it is only approximate. Outstanding injustice must be left, ultimately, with God.

Desert without degradation

The punishment of individuals in the Hebrew Bible is bounded by a deep respect for personhood. This follows from the idea that punishment takes place in the context of God's love and forgiveness. Just punishment confers dignity upon offenders, because it treats offenders as responsible. It affirms that offenders are persons of moral worth, with the power of choice and who deserve to be held to be accountable for their actions. This is part of what it means to be made in the image of God. Deuteronomy 25:1–2 suggests that offenders deserve to be punished in proportion to their offence: 'When men have a dispute, they are to take it to court and the judges will decide the case, acquitting the innocent and condemning the guilty. If the guilty man deserves to be beaten, the judge shall make him lie down and have him flogged in his presence with the number of lashes his crime deserves.' Significantly, there are limits upon desert: '... he must not give him more than forty lashes. If he is flogged more than that, your brother will be degraded in your eyes' (Deut. 25:3). No offender deserves to be degraded.

Respect for personhood is relevant when we are considering utilitarian justifications for punishment. From a utilitarian perspective, punishment is justified only if it can be proven to benefit society by reducing future crime, usually by means of incapacitation or deterrence. However, giving an offender a sentence that is either more or less than what he deserves on the grounds of a predicted effect, which may or may not be accurate, treats the offender simply as a means to an end. He is not treated as an autonomous person who is accountable for his moral choices but as a manipulable variable in a social equation. It is sometimes said that biblical law approves a utilitarian (deterrent) approach (e.g. Phillips 1973: 96), quoting the formula 'Then all Israel will hear [of this punishment] and be afraid, and no-one among you will do such an evil thing again' (Deut. 13:11). However, in my view this formula simply recognizes a possible, and beneficial, side-effect of punishment ('justice' works its own 'deterrent'). It is not in itself a complete justification.

Diverse penal registers

Specific forms of punishment in the Hebrew Bible (including forms of capital punishment) are generally 'of their time'. What is informative is the way in which the form of the punishment has a particular symbolic and educative function. For example, the punishment of 'burning' for a priest's daughter for 'playing the harlot' (Lev. 21:9) signifies that she has 'profaned' her status and that the resulting 'pollution' must be cleansed by 'purgative' punishment (Burnside 2003: 126–133). Punishment in the Hebrew Bible is a morally communicative act. It is an aspect of the didactic nature of biblical law. This takes the opportunity, when punishing an offender, to express something of the nature of the offence, thereby facilitating the communication and inculcation of moral values.[16] Punishment teaches everyone a lesson, not just the offender.

Many examples could be given but one of the most symbolic is the 'red heifer' ritual performed in response to an unsolved murder (Deut. 21:1–9). First, an arbitrary rule (geographical distance) ensures that the local community takes corporate responsibility for the death, regardless of whether any of their number was involved. The case was so serious that it could not simply 'lie on the file'. Secondly, the symbolic purity and physical value of both the sacrifice (an unworked heifer) and the location (unworked land) responds to the crisis of an unsolved murder, and its assault on the divine image, by powerfully expressing the sanctity of human life.

Another example is the shaming sanction in Deuteronomy 25:5–10. This is a legally symbolic act that visually expresses the seriousness of the brother-in-law's offence (Burnside 2003: 105–119). The removal of the sandal (which signifies property) enacts what the brother has done (he has taken his dead brother's share of the property instead of raising up an heir who will succeed to the title). The resulting image of 'going barefoot', associated with shame, vulnerability and defencelessness, signifies that the brother-in-law belongs to the 'lowest of the low'. Spitting in his face lowers him in esteem, especially when, in a dramatic reversal of gender power-relations, it is performed by a woman. Finally, the renaming of the brother-in-law is a form of talionic 'name-punishment'; the brother-in-law who has no concern for his brother's 'name' finds himself the object of excessive concern about his own 'name'. And so on.

It is because punishment is used as part of a sophisticated communicative enterprise (Burnside 2003: ix–xi, 233–238) that biblical law uses a diverse range of penal registers for different offences. The toolkit includes: capital punishment; kōrēt ('cutting off'); social exclusion; shame (Bechtel 1991, 1994); curses; childlessness; physical mutilation and restitution. Each of these could take different forms

---

16. Biblical law was seen as a source of wisdom, to be mulled over and talked about (see, for example, Deut. 6:6–7).

depending on the circumstances. Sometimes there is a range of options for the same offence. Adultery, for example, could be dealt with by means of capital punishment, social exclusion, familial wrath, damage to reputation, ransom, public disgrace and humiliation. Despite this range of options there is, significantly, no equivalent to the modern practice of mass imprisonment (although capital punishment in the Bible certainly serves an incapacitative purpose).

Due process

Biblical justice and punishment were supposed to operate against a background of regard for due process. Ensuring that sentencers were of sound moral character was one aspect of this (noted above); rules of evidence was another. According to Numbers 35:30 a single witness was inadequate. Deuteronomy 17:6 (= Deut. 19:15) uses the formula 'only on the evidence of two witnesses, or of three witnesses' – an intensifying rhetorical device that emphasizes the need for as many witnesses as possible; the greater the number, the safer the conviction.[17] To underscore this, it is preceded by this injunction: 'you must investigate it thoroughly. If it is true and it has been proved that this detestable thing has been done in Israel, take the man or woman who has done this evil deed to your city gates' (Deut. 17:4–5). The formula could never be reduced to a numbers game, especially if the witnesses themselves were of doubtful character.[18] A ban on false testimony (Exod. 20:16) appears near the head of the Covenant Code and the false witness bore the punishment that would have fallen on the offender (Deut. 19:16–21).

Informal social control

Biblical law lacks a special, professionalized legal language. It was addressed to all the people (Exod. 24:3, 7; Deut. 1:1) and subsequently given wide publicity (Deut. 27:1–3; 31:9–11). It was also capable of being applied by everyone. A number of texts attest to the use of 'rules of thumb' that obviate the need for third parties or experts to settle disputes (Jackson 2000: 82–87). Examples include 'walking abroad with a staff' (Exod. 21:19); the slaves' survival (Exod. 21:21); damages for agricultural delicts (Exod. 22:5) and the loss of an ox (Exod. 21:35). This mixture of 'civil' and 'criminal' cases recalls the caveat regarding 'criminal justice' at the

---

17. For a similar formula see 'a day or two days' (Exod. 21:20–21). This could mean two days, a week or several years.

18. It is wrong to regard 1 Kgs 21:1–15 (the Naboth incident) as demonstrating the weakness of biblical rules of evidence. Accepting the testimony of 'two base fellows' (vv. 10–13) was itself an outrage and at odds with the purpose of Deut. 19:15. The author makes it clear that not only Jezebel and the false witnesses were guilty of the death of Naboth but also 'the elders and the nobles' for accepting such testimony.

start of this chapter. The use of 'rules of thumb' may reflect the relational value of victims and offenders settling their own disputes (Prov. 25:7–10). But it may also reflect, more prosaically, the need for a quick resolution, especially in an agricultural community where this was sometimes necessary for physical survival.

Biblical law frequently assumes a background of negotiation between the parties, even in cases that we would today identify as 'criminal'. For example, the law relating to damages for a homicidal ox states: 'If a ransom is laid on [the owner of the ox], then he shall give for the redemption of his life whatever is laid upon him' (Exod. 21:30). 'Whatever' is not to be taken literally; it is a matter of negotiation between the family of the deceased and the owner of the ox. More generally, the *lex talionis* ('eye for an eye' formula) may also have been a matter for negotiation. In the phrase, the word 'for' (*tahat*) can mean 'in the place of', that is to say, one thing being given in the place of another. Thus 'life for life' (e.g. Exod. 21:23) may mean compensation, in other words, the return of a living creature for a dead one, rather than another dead one. Thus *talion* may have provided guidance as to the appropriate level of compensation and not just the permissible level of retaliation. In fact, this is implicit in the classic statement of the *lex talionis* in Leviticus 24:13–23 (Milgrom 2001: 2128–2133). Verse 18 states: 'Anyone who takes the life of someone's animal *must make restitution* – life for life' (my italics). This is mirrored in verse 21a; 'Whoever kills an animal *must make restitution*'. 'Making restitution' is more consistent with compensation than retaliation and so it was likely that the *lex talionis* was a matter for negotiation. The ban on ransom (Num. 35:31–32) suggests that negotiating a punishment for homicide (intentional or accidental) was at one time possible between the parties. But there were other limits to negotiation. Proverbs warns that the offender cannot always presume on the victim's willingness to negotiate, for example, in a case of adultery:

> for jealousy arouses a husband's fury,
>   and he will show no mercy when he takes revenge.
> He will not accept any compensation;
>   he will refuse the bribe, however great it is.
> (Prov. 6:34–35)

Victim involvement

Victims had ownership of their disputes and were expected to take the initiative in reporting and prosecuting their cause (e.g. Deut. 25:7 where the victim goes up 'to the gate to the elders' to state her complaint). This is akin to the 'litigant in person' in modern civil law. Access to justice was local, except for certain categories of cases which were dealt with centrally (e.g. Exod. 18:26; Deut. 17:8–9; 2 Chr. 19:10–11). Legally significant sites in ancient Israel (as in the Ancient Near East generally) included everyday locations such as the city gate (e.g. Deut. 21:19), the threshing floor (e.g. 1 Kgs 22:10), or the threshold of a relevant parties' house (e.g. Exod. 21:6; Deut. 22:21; Judg. 19:27; Matthews 1987). Victim participation is sometimes presented as a radically empowering experience. A dramatic example is Deuteronomy 25:9–10, where the behaviour of the woman is a radical subversion of traditional gender norms.[19] The ethos is one of self-help within permissible limits. Examples of regulated self-help include the *lex talionis* ('eye for an eye') formula which is best understood as setting limits to retaliation ('no more than an eye'), in contrast to the disproportionate ('seventy times seven') response typified by Lamech (Gen. 4:23–24). Compensation was made directly by the offender to the victim (e.g. restitution cases, Exod. 22:1–5; Num. 5:6–7).

Community involvement

All the people were supposed to be involved in securing justice. The person who is told about the existence of an idolater in their community is expected to 'inquire diligently' (Deut. 17:4). The Israelite was not to turn a deaf ear, or a blind eye if he was a witness to an offence. Leviticus 5:1 suggests that a curse be pronounced against the witness who withheld testimony. In biblical law, witnesses do not simply give evidence or report facts; they take responsibility. This responsibility is signified in the most powerful way possible when the witness 'casts the first stone'. Deuteronomy 17:7 states; 'The hands of the witnesses must be the first in putting him to death, and then the hands of all the people.' It is notable that the whole community (or representatives thereof) take direct and personal responsibility for punishing the offender. Punishment is carried out in their sight and in their midst.

Proactive witnesses and communities were necessary given the relative lack of 'professionals'. The judges appointed in Deuteronomy 16:18–20 may have been intended to be relatively specialist although subordinate to the judge at the central sanctuary (Deut. 17:8–9). Apart from these, the only 'professionals' apparently involved in ancient Israel were 'semi-professionals' whose role in the judicial process derived from some other social status, for example, the king (1 Kgs 3:16–28), the high ranking 'civil servant' or high priest (2 Chr. 19:11) and the Levitical priesthood (Deut. 17:8–9). Even the social role of the avenger of blood (*gōʾēl haddām*), who punishes the man-slayer appears to be carried out by a close relative, rather than someone who is specially appointed to the task.[20]

---

19. Just how radical is underlined by Deut. 25:11–12. These verses immediately reassert the traditional boundaries of female initiative after the extraordinary events of vv. 5–10.

20. See ch. 10, above.

Sentencer accountability

Sentencers were held accountable for their sentences. They are obliged to 'judge the people fairly' (Deut. 16:18) which means no perversion of justice, favouritism, or taking bribes (Deut. 16:19; 2 Chr. 19:7). Since judges are understood to hand down divine penalties ('judgment belongs to God', Deut. 1:17; '[the LORD] is with you whenever you give a verdict', 2 Chr. 19:6), it follows that their primary accountability is to God. A more subtle and psychological form of accountability is found in Deuteronomy 25:1–3. Where the sentence takes the form of corporal punishment, the judge must witness the administration of the punishment at first-hand. The sentencer is immediately confronted with the consequence of his sentence, whether responsible or irresponsible.

A compass for criminal justice

A biblical vision of justice might inspire a number of policies. The danger lies in isolating one element of an inseparable whole to the exclusion of others. The temptation is to stress, for example, retribution without any thought of restoration (the claim that 'prison works') or restoration without retribution (the belief that retribution is morally unacceptable, see Richards 1998). Either element, on its own, quickly becomes idolatrous and leads to injustice. Moreover, the implications of a biblical approach for a given criminal justice process at a given point in time depends on current practices and previous penal history. For this reason Christians in different countries have campaigned at different times to redress quite different balances. The penal context of Texas is very different to that of Romania or Brazil. So are the reform possibilities for those who wish to edge their penal practice closer to a biblical approach. What we cannot do is pretend that the biblical vision has no relevance whatever. Some of the features outlined above are eminently transferable. What follows, therefore, is not an attempt to provide a comprehensive agenda or a culturally specific manifesto but a compass from which we can take our bearings.[21]

---

21. One approach to the reform of the criminal justice process that has its roots in the biblical approach to justice is Relational Justice, as developed by the Relationships Foundation, Cambridge. Back issues of the *Relational Justice Bulletin* are available from the Relationships Foundation, 3 Hooper Street, Cambridge, England. Issues 2 and onwards are available to download online from the Relationships Foundation website, <http://www.relationshipsfoundation.org>.

Justice, not control, should be our national priority

The Bible urges us to 'seek justice' and to make this a national priority. But in many parts of the world, social, economic and political forces tend to push the quest for divine justice down the national agenda. Garland argues that the social organization of Western societies (notably the US and Britain) has moved away from a more inclusionary 'solidaristic' culture to a more exclusionary and controlling one (Garland 2001). Institutions of crime control and criminal justice have adapted accordingly and the result has been a shift from 'penal-welfarism' (the prevention of crime, individual correction and social reform) towards a 'culture of control'. The latter approach identifies an underclass as the source of the problem and suggests progressively punitive ways of excluding and controlling it. Garland argues that this change is not entirely due to rising crime, linking it to a civic culture that has become increasingly less tolerant, less inclusive and less capable of trust: 'The risky, insecure character of today's social and economic relations is the social surface that gives rise to our ... concern with control and to the urgency with which we segregate, fortify and exclude' (Garland 2001: 194). The result is that 'crime control and criminal justice have come to be disconnected from the broader themes of social justice and social reconstruction' (Garland 2001: 199). It is time to reconnect them. Sherman illustrates the counter-productive nature of police interventions when criminal justice is not interleaved with social justice (Sherman 1992). In the UK, the present government deserves credit for its efforts to embed informal social controls and to develop policies that will enhance social inclusion.[22] Unfortunately, these positive developments are undermined by some contradictory policies that, sooner or later, will have to be resolved (Faulkner 2003b).

Justice that is transformative

One of the best-attested findings in criminology is that most offenders tend to grow out of crime (Maruna 2001). Punishment should assist in this process of maturation and personal development, yet all too often this is not the case. Prisons, especially, seem almost designed to induce a state of 'arrested development' and to hinder personal growth and responsibility (Pryor 2001). This is a serious issue for the growing proportion of prisoners in the US and UK who are serving sentences of ten years or longer. One of the most crushing verdicts on imprisonment in modern times comes from Hans Toch who claims that most prisoners face a 'regime of eventlessness and a life that is redundant, monotonous and stultifying ... programmes that offer an opportunity to contribute to the

---

22. See the work of the Social Exclusion Unit:
    <http://www.socialexclusionunit.gov.uk/>.

world are virtually non-existent' (Toch 2000: 2). It is a far cry from the biblical vision of justice that heals and transforms at every level.

The system of justice that condemns a man should follow him into his cell. We should make every effort to ensure that prisons are places where people can, if they choose, address their offending behaviour and develop responsibility, rather than have responsibility taken away from them (Pryor 2001). If we do not, we have no moral authority for keeping them there. Sanctions and penal institutions should foster 'generativity' (that is, benefit to others). Examples of generative communities include mutual-help societies, volunteering, community service, restitution projects and active engagement in parenting (Maruna et al. 2002). We should place a strengths-based approach at the heart of the correctional enterprise. This is one that asks not simply: 'what a person's deficits are, but rather what positive contribution the offender can make. How can their lives become useful and purposeful?' (Maruna and LeBel, 2002: 167). Governors should be required to include prisoner work and vocational opportunities in their business plans (Ramsbotham 1999; Coyle 2001).

Punishment should reach beyond the offender and the executive and effect some repair of the social fabric. It certainly should not make the damage worse. To this end, there is value in courts adopting a problem-solving approach. In the West, this may take the form of greater specialism – drug courts, community courts, mental health courts and domestic violence courts (Kaye 2003). Employing more relational processes that lead to more relational outcomes challenge the cultural hegemony of managerialism. The economic language of 'best value' and 'cost-benefit' makes it difficult to experiment, limits discretion, is less likely to give individuated sentences and focuses on performance indicators that are unlikely to favour relational values.

Desert without degradation

Biblical justice suggests that punishment has a positive role to play in confronting wrongdoing. Taking a steer from Deuteronomy 25:1–3, we may say that punishment should be proportional to the seriousness of the offence, 'seriousness' being understood in terms of harm and culpability. Culpability is not always easy to judge, but nevertheless the notion of proportionality is a perfectly sound basis for a responsible sentence. It is both difficult and dangerous to move too far away from this (e.g. mandatory, indeterminate or exemplary sentences). Proportional punishment takes the person and their choices seriously. It is one way of affirming the moral value and dignity of persons.

However, precisely because the moral basis of punishment is related to the dignity of persons, care must also be taken to avoid degrading the offender. Punishment may lower an offender in the eyes of others but not to the extent that he loses dignity as a human person. This means that there are limits to proportionality and that proportionality is not an absolute principle. This is important given the increasing reliance upon imprisonment around the world (see below). Indeed, the institution of mass imprisonment 'depend[s] upon our refusal to comprehend the human beings we so completely condemn' (Garland 2001: 185). The human consequences can be degrading in the extreme. For example, one million people are imprisoned in Russia where the state lacks the physical infrastructure to deal with them. In 1995 the Head of the Russian General Penitentiary Department confessed that Russian prisoners died 'from overcrowding, lack of oxygen and poor prison conditions' (Coyle 2001: 2).

Degradation acts as a 'cap' on proportionality because no-one deserves to be degraded. We should remember that punishment is not something we to do to 'others'; '[it is something we do] to ourselves as full, if imperfect, citizens' (Rex 2001: 4–5). Offenders are citizens too and their degradation is our degradation. We have no moral right to treat offenders as though they are somehow less than human or icons of evil. Nor are we justified in using them in a utilitarian fashion as a means to some other (conscious or unconscious) end, for example, as a way of soothing middle-class fears or cultural anxieties (Garland 2001: 167–205).

Diversify penal registers

The last twenty years have seen a massive expansion in the use of imprisonment across the world. This increase is found regardless of whether the nation is democratic or totalitarian, rich or poor, north or south, east or west. In England and Wales, the prison population has grown from 36,000 in 1991 to 74,543,[23] an increase of 107% (Hough et al. 2003). This reflects an upward trend in sentencing. Ten years ago there was an average of 129 persons in prison at any one time for shoplifting; in 2004 the figure is now more than 1,400.[24] The 'reinvented' prison (exclusionary and eliminative in function rather than rehabilitative) is 'a ready-made penal solution to a new problem of social and economic exclusion' (Garland 2001: 199). Mass imprisonment is also popular with 'rapid-response' governments because it is immediate, easy to implement and can be said to work in some respects, even though it spectacularly fails in others (Garland 2001: 200).

This reductionism is as limiting as the golfer who plays a round of golf with only one club. There is an urgent need to minimize reliance upon imprisonment as the primary form of punishment and to diversify the range of penal registers. More imaginative processes and sanctions should be developed to make sentencing an effective form of moral communication. Particular emphasis should be given to the *meanings* of particular modes of punishment. What do they say to

---

23. As of 17 February 2004; 'Prison population hits record high', *The Guardian*, 18 February 2004.

24. 'Arrested development', *The Guardian*, *Society* supplement, 10 March 2004, p. 6.

and about offenders and how do they portray offenders' relationships to the political community and to the law (Duff 2001: 145)?

Seek due process

The blindfolded statue atop the Central Criminal Court in London, holding aloft the scales and the sword of justice, has much to commend it. She symbolizes the importance of impartiality, the thoroughness of a fair trial and the sureness of punishment. Seeking the highest standards of procedural justice will differ depending on the nature of the community where the trial is conducted. Questions such as the admissibility of reported evidence ('hearsay'), the status of forensic evidence, the availability of preparatory hearings to ensure that serious cases as well as complex ones can be properly prepared, the role of the jury in lengthy and complex trials, and what to do when they are at risk of intimidation are more pronounced in some circumstances than others. But regardless of whether the trial takes place in the mega-community of international criminal jurisdiction or the micro-community of a clan of Trobiand islanders, there is a need to ensure that the case focuses on the relevant issues and that the parties to the trial should hear all the evidence that fairly bears on the defendant's guilt or innocence.

Informal social control

There is a need to preserve the local accessibility and accountability of the criminal justice process (e.g. courts, affiliated services and local prisons) despite increasing pressure for rationalization and economic efficiency. Devolving responsibility to citizens and communities is a major challenge, given the huge presence that is nowadays assumed for the state in criminal justice and which grows continually. Government needs to recognize its inadequacy and the need to draw on the strengths of local communities. There needs to be a formal recognition that the criminal justice process can by itself have only a limited effect on the general level of crime, and action is needed by communities and between individuals as citizens that is beyond the scope and capacity of the statutory criminal justice agencies (Faulkner 2002).

Victim involvement

There has been a 'victimological turn' in criminal justice polices in many jurisdictions since about 1960 with the advent of such initiatives as Victim Impact Statements, Victim Support and so on (Bottoms 2003: 103–104). '[A]s the offender's perceived worth tends towards zero, victim's interests expand to fill the gap' (Garland 2001: 181). Moreover, victims serve a useful function in a pluralistic moral order where we do not agree on right and wrong. 'Collective moral outrage more easily proceeds from an individualised basis than from a public one' (Garland 2001: 200). In addition, victim suffering suits mass-media news values, powers punitive policies and sustains the 'war on crime'. For these reasons and more, the increased public profile of victims does not necessarily mean that victims are being treated properly within the system. Seeking justice for the oppressed means ensuring that the criminal justice process and, as far as possible, its outcomes take sufficient account of the needs and interests of victims of crime. This may mean giving greater scope for contact or negotiations between victims and offenders (e.g. Family Group Conferences and Community Group Conferences) where this is both possible and desirable (Pennell & Burford 1998). It may also involve giving a much greater role for (imaginative) forms of reparation and (multiple) restitution.

Community involvement

Garland contends that 'the criminologies of everyday life … offer an approach to social order that is, for the most part, amoral and technological' (Garland 2001: 183). Social order is seen to emerge, not from 'moral discipline and obedience to authority … [but] smart arrangements that minimise the opportunities to disruption and deviance' (Garland 2001: 183). We need to develop more relational strategies. We need to see crime, as Durkheim suggested, not just as a crisis but also as an opportunity – and as an opportunity to rebuild relationships and informal social controls (Lukes & Scull 1983). Everyone affected by crime has an interest in the outcome and so there is a need to take account of the needs of the wider community in which the offence occurred. The wider community may mean the school, workplace, housing estate, faith group, ethnic group or whatever other context(s) the victim or the defendant operates within. Some of these communities may be in conflict with others.

Communities also need to have more realistic expectations of the criminal justice process and must be prepared to take more responsibility. In some democratic countries, expectations of the ability of the state to deal with every social problem need to be scaled down, with agencies working *with* rather than *at* troublesome communities (Bowes 2002). Crime prevention flows from engaging people and communities in finding solutions to problems of alienation and dysfunction. In Western urban settings, community reparation schemes involve local communities in the rehabilitation of young offenders (White 2004). In Rwanda, community-style *gacaca* (or 'lawn') courts show the value of community involvement even in the extreme circumstances of genocide (Bishop 1999: 3).

In biblical justice, punishment is carried out by the community, in their sight and in their midst. Communities need to be better informed about criminal justice (e.g. levels of actual crime and the effectiveness of different kinds of penalties). They also need to know what sentencing options are currently available and what they mean (e.g. mistaken assumptions that modern 'community penalties' means 'planting borders'). Nor should prisons be 'invisible institutions'. What is done in them is done in our name: 'The central principle should be that prisons are part of society and not set apart from it; that they exist for the benefit of society as a whole and should contribute actively to its health and well-being; that prisoners deserve its compassion and staff should receive its respect' (Faulkner 2002: 2). Citizens need to feel some sense of ownership for their prisons and some sense of responsibility for their prisoners, as they often do for their schools and hospitals, rather than a means by which that responsibility can be avoided (Faulkner 2003a).

Executive accountability

We hear a lot about the need for offenders to be held accountable for their offences, but why shouldn't sentencers be held accountable for their sentences? There is a need for accountability on the part of policy-makers and sentencers with regard to penal policy. There is also a need for greater harmonization of aims (e.g. the numbers of prisoners and people under probation should be broadly consistent with the capacity of the penal system). Policy-makers and sentencers should recognize the built-in hunger of the incarceration industry, especially where new prison places are provided by private enterprise. This is particularly urgent where, as in England and Wales, it appears that people are being sent to prison for crimes that would not have attracted a prison sentence ten years ago and where there are large disparities in the ratio of custodial to community penalties in different parts of the country. Individual sentencers should know the consequences of their sentences – for example, in the form of court digests (Curtis 2002) – and, as the Lord Chief Justice Lord Woolf suggested, judges should occasionally visit those whom they sentence to custody.

Conclusion

There are two aspects to divine justice in the Bible. It overthrows the oppressor and it liberates the oppressed. For this reason, the greatest example of God's justice in the Old Testament is the exodus and the greatest example in the New Testament is the crucifixion and vindication of Christ. Punishment has a constructive role to play in securing justice. Although it can be unjust, its practice is not inherently so. Just punishment involves retribution but leaves open the possibility of restored relationships for the repentant offender. Punishment in biblical law serves multiple functions and has a pedagogic purpose. Relationships are central to punishing with justice. Biblical law is in the hands of the people, there is a high degree of community involvement, victims often take the initiative, negotiation between the parties has a high social value and there is accountability for sentencers. This picture helps us to see the strengths and weaknesses of our modern ideas of justice and punishment. It also provides a compass from which any criminal justice process can take its bearings.

14. International relations and defence

Jeremy Ive

The new global context

Nations are linked together by a number of factors: geography, trade, immigration, cultural influences and the exchange of ideas. The increased scale, nature and speed of these links is a feature of globalization. The revolution in modern communications means that events in other countries are immediately relayed across the world through satellite or the Internet. The digital revolution, for all the uncertainties that it has engendered, is changing the structure of the world's community, speeding up transactions and shortening lines of communication. This has both negative and positive consequences. On the one hand, there is openness to democratic ideas and the protection of human rights. On the other hand, there is also the less easily quantifiable process of the spread of consumerist values and the domination of culture by materialistic ideas. The structure of society is changing from one dominated by the mass mobilization of labour and the predetermined production of goods, to one oriented towards the diverse demands of a fragmented, yet closely interconnected market.

The fact of this much greater interdependency and vulnerability gives added poignancy and force to Cain's plea, 'Am I my brother's keeper?' (Gen. 4:9). Our responsibility to our neighbour needs also to be seen through the lens of Jesus' teaching, notably in the Parable of the Good Samaritan (Luke 10:25–37; Matt. 22:24–40; Mark 12:28–31). Being a neighbour can mean many different things: not only spatial proximity, but also an awareness despite distance, through a variety of different media and connections. These give us a responsibility for the other, no matter how physically distant or culturally dissimilar they are. The difficulty is that such an absolute injunction is impossible to fulfil globally and cannot be the basis for our setting of practical priorities. Furthermore, the sheer disproportion in the world's distribution of wealth and technical or economic power makes it difficult to judge how we should dispose of our resources.

Questions about the proper goals of a nation and how they should be pursued are at the heart of the issues of international relations and defence. Typically national goals might be articulated in terms of economic growth, national security and political or cultural influence. The means of achieving these are through military power, economic strength, political negotiation and recourse to international law and supra-national bodies. These means are interrelated with economic strength – a significant factor in sustaining both military power and political influence. The previous chapters, particularly those on nationhood, government, finance and economics, have a significant bearing on these issues.

In this chapter we start by looking at the universality of God's law as a basis for international relations. We then consider the importance of honouring past commitments and building peace. Where this fails we then consider the case for just and limited war, and the structure and political control of defence forces. The norms that govern international conduct are not easy to extrapolate from Scripture. The situation of either Israel in the Old Testament or that of the small Christian communities within the Roman Empire do not provide us with a direct model for the conduct of international affairs. However, within the wider perspective of the growth and development of the kingdom of God, principles can be identified. We need to take account of the transformations for good or bad (it is not always straightforward to discern which is which) in the structure of the Israelite polity. We also need to take into account today's changed situation with the opening out of the covenantal boundaries in the establishment of the Christian church, and the changed perspective occasioned by the destruction of Jerusalem in AD 70. Nevertheless, common themes can be traced, and models suggested.

God's law provides a universal basis for international relations

In the ancient world, national identity was inseparably bound to religion. The gods were regarded as the embodiment of national power and, in turn, the well-being of nations was tied to the status of their particular gods. Relations with a national god were considered as a transaction: local arrangements were made applicable to a particular nation or group, but not necessarily to others, except if they were conquered – in which case the gods of the defeated nation were made to abase themselves before the deity of the conquering power alongside their defeated worshippers (Gnuse 1997: 153–154). In such circumstances, law could not be other than localized and culturally relative.

In Genesis, the first book of the Old Testament, God promised Abraham that in his descendants all the nations of the world would be blessed.[1] It was on this basis that he travelled with his household to the Promised Land, leaving the urban stability of Ur. After the sojourn in Egypt and the return to the Promised Land, the emergent Israelite nation was different from the surrounding nations. Israel did not see the God she worshipped as one confined to her and capable of co-existing with the gods of the surrounding nations, but as one who had exclusive claims first on them as a nation. Gottwald, following T. C. Vriezen, calls this 'mono-Yahwism': 'Yahweh, in appearing to demand much more than the Canaanite gods, actually gave back to his worshippers the benefits and potentialities of productive human life which a small Canaanite minority had arrogated to itself under the symbolic approval of hierarchic polytheism' (Gottwald 1979: 616).

With the unfolding story of Israel in Palestine came the progressive revelation of God's sovereignty over all nations, not just Israel. In the course of time and the experience of exile, God was understood as standing above all nations and calling them without exception to obedience to his rule. No nation could see itself as totally self-sufficient, or closed off from its neighbours. 'Old Testament ethics are *universal*, embracing the same standard of righteousness for all the nations of the earth as it does for Israel. Never did the biblical writers conceive of justice, righteousness, or the good as the special corner of truth reserved for Israel alone' (Kaiser 1991: 11–12).

The demands of Deuteronomy are potentially applicable to all the nations. In chapter 28, the blessings and curses are set in terms of outcomes which apply to all nations, of whom the faithful Israel will be made the head. At the heart of communications sent by messenger or ambassador to foreign nations was God's standard of righteousness, as in Jeremiah 27:3 and 51:61 (Kaiser 1991: 11). The seventy bulls found in Numbers 29:13–39 correspond to the symbolic number in Genesis 10 of seventy nations on the earth (Sutton 1987: 46). In Isaiah 2 and 60, and in Micah 4, there is a vision of Jerusalem being raised up as a representative focus for God's rule over all nations. Israel was created 'for the sake of all nations, as an example and a light, and was God's redemptive response to human failure to live by the values and ordinances of creation' (C. J. H. Wright 1995: 176). In the context of the New Testament revelation, Oliver O'Donovan makes a similar point: 'Through this unique political entity God made known his purposes in the world . . . the governing principle is the kingly rule of God, expressed in Israel's corporate

---

1. See ch. 7, 'Nationhood'.

existence and brought to effect in the life, death and resurrection of Jesus' (O'Donovan 1996: 27).

The idea that surrounding countries should be envious of the laws of Israel implies that they would do well to copy them. The prophetic vision of universal blessing extends to a unified place of worship. Isaiah closes with a majestic vision of all the nations of the earth being gathered to God's holy mountain in Jerusalem. The vision from Isaiah 5:1–8 was of Zion providing a beacon for the nations. By Isaiah 66 we have a vision of Israel going out to all the nations to bring them God's law (Bauckham 2003: 63–65). The picture presented in both the 'apocalyptic' literature of the exilic and post-exilic period, and in the New Testament book of Revelation (which draws heavily on Old Testament 'apocalyptic' concepts and language) is of a God who calls all nations to account for their actions and relationships, and who alone is the final judge.[2]

The prophets also proclaimed that God does not make exceptions for any individuals or peoples when calling them to account for unjust action. Amos's denunciation of the nations comes to Judah and Israel after dealing with their immediate neighbours – making it clear that they, too, were to be judged for their injustice (Amos 1 and 2). His critique of the Northern Kingdom at its time of prosperity (eighth century BC) makes it clear that Israel comes under the norms of all the other nations. Both Isaiah (2:3) and Micah (4:2) proclaim the rule of God extending out from Zion to the whole world. Isaiah charts the rise and fall of nations according to their obedience to God (see especially Isa. 13 – 14). This is also true of Jeremiah, notably in his oracles against the nations in 46 – 51, as well as Obadiah, Nahum, Jonah, Joel, Ezekiel 25 – 32, Daniel 2 and 7 and Zechariah. The first fall of Jerusalem in 587BC, followed by the exile and then the return of the survivors underlined God's sovereignty over the whole world.

With the final destruction of the Jerusalem temple in AD70 a geographical focus for the kingdom was removed. The vast company in Revelation 7:9 are drawn from all nations, all equally praising God. This has two implications. First, those who are there can be seen as representative of the nations from which they are drawn. If (to draw a diplomatic analogy) the representatives are all accorded equal accreditation, the intention is that ultimately all are to have an equal and secure place in the kingdom of God (Rev. 21:24–36; 22:2). Secondly, this then makes

---

2. 'Apocalyptic' is applied to literature which sees the events of the world simply as the playing out of the heavenly drama. This understanding places the human participants as passive spectators in a cosmic theatre. In the Bible, even those parts that are often called 'apocalyptic' are properly to be understood as prophetic: while history is seen as resting in God's hands, at the same time we are fully participating in this great story.

universal the call for just dealings. It does not simply apply to those nations that directly acknowledge God (Rom. 1:20). The national quest for wealth and security, legitimate in itself, needs to be achieved through right dealings. All nations are called, as bearers of a common task, to act with concern for the shared environment and the well-being and welfare of all.

Universalized biblical law, as an ideal, looks forward to the time when all nations will be at peace with one another under the common rule of Christ. The norms of international relations, seen in microcosm in Old Testament Israel, are now seen in the macrocosm of the new order. All nations are to be made subject to the just and gentle rule of the Lamb of God. He is the Messiah, in whom the desire of the nations is being and will be fulfilled. Matthew picks this up with his account of the visit of the Magi to Jesus (Matt. 2:1–18). It is also a strong theme throughout Luke's Gospel, for example 2:29–32, where Simeon talks of light that will reveal Jesus to the nations. The structure of Acts, which sees the mission of Jesus' apostles, not least Paul, as reaching out to all the Gentiles ('non-Jews', literally 'nations'), also points towards the work of God in the entire world (Scott 1994). All peoples and all territories are encompassed in God's great plan of salvation through Jesus.

The universality of the law does not mean the ending of all national authority in favour of a supra-national or world government. Amos, Isaiah, Jeremiah, Daniel and Ezekiel all condemned political imperialism, with its accompanying ambition, pride and aggression. Just as Assyria was humbled for her sins, so too would Egypt and Babylon be (Ezek. 31; Jer. 50:17–18). Psalm 2, Isaiah (especially Isa. 13 – 27) and Daniel taught that God would repeatedly bring down every oppressive human empire through human agency until he eventually establishes his 'King on Zion' (Motyer 1993: 131–134). Only God can establish what arrogant humanity repeatedly fails to achieve. As Oliver O'Donovan comments, 'The theological impulse behind the conception of international law is altogether superior to the theology of empire. It acknowledges the claim of Christ to be the sole ruler of the nations, and avoids erecting the icon of world government in his place; yet his rule is not left as an empty ideal, but is given a clear institutional witness' (O'Donovan 1996: 267–268).

Such an account of the universality of law provides a basis for international law. International law cannot be applied as straightforwardly as domestic law. Unlike the domestic context, there is no automatic mechanism of enforcement, or clearly laid-down rules of procedure. Any course of action to uphold the requirements of international law can be decided only in the light of agreement between those concerned, and should not be imposed without a full and comprehensive consideration of their interests and historical antecedents. Laws cannot simply be imposed in the abstract: they need to be grafted into the life of the country concerned, and on this basis to receive the requisite acceptance and implementation. The focus is always on the future, not on the continuation of past vendettas, which have a life of their own.

Unjust regimes forfeit their legitimacy by their actions against their own people and against other nations, but this does not give an unrestricted right to other nations to intervene without due process and consultation with all concerned. Tyranny in a neighbouring state cannot, and should not, therefore, be ignored. There is a considerable body of literature demonstrating that power concentrated in a small number of hands within a state influences its relations with neighbours, as there are fewer checks and balances on the regime's external policy, and more temptations to engage in foreign adventures – particularly if profit can be siphoned into the personal accounts of the government and officials.[3]

There is a need to interlock formal diplomacy with the informal building of common understanding. Without a transcendent vision, all diplomacy becomes at best jockeying for position and immediate advantage, or at worst the aggressive pursuit of domination or vengeance, with its downward spiral of threat and counter-threat and collapse into endemic violence. Those who oppose an international course of action (be it in the United Nations or in another forum) may be motivated by unjust motives just as much as those who propose such a course. There is no alternative to states themselves taking their full responsibility in keeping to the norms of international relations, and positively working to create an international environment, both in the world at large and in their regions, where commonly recognized codes of law and good conduct are developed.

Past commitments and relationships need to be honoured and nurtured

History creates a set of obligations that need to be honoured: first, because the course of international events is not a random series but a working out of God's purposes; secondly, because interpersonal trust and good faith needs to be replicated in the international sphere.

That said all nations have secret services, and have always had them. The need to ensure secrecy, if necessary by deception, in peacetime as well as in war, cannot be avoided. Diplomacy also often unavoidably requires secrecy, even deception, when vital national interests are at stake. Deception and acts of violence are not necessarily condemned. The assassinations of Eglon by Ehud (Judg. 3:12–30), and Sisera by Jael (Judg. 4:15–21; 5:24–27), both preceded by elaborate deceptions, are both celebrated. Joshua also used deception and espionage when occupying Israel; for example, sending spies into Jericho prior to its capture and destruction

---

3. See MacIntyre (2003) for a review of the literature.

(Josh. 2). Modern instances, such as deceptions for the hiding of Jews from the Nazis during the Second World War, can be found. Particularly poignant is the case of the German Resistance against Hitler, who included among their number the distinguished theologian Dietrich Bonhoeffer, arrested in 1943 and hanged in 1945. In a letter dated 5 December 1943, Bonhoeffer wrote:

> 'Speaking the truth' ... means in my opinion, saying how something really is – that is, showing respect for secrecy, intimacy, and concealment. 'Betrayal' for example, is not truth, any more than are flippancy, cynicism, etc. What is secret may be revealed only in confession, i.e. in the presence of God. (Bonhoeffer 1971: 158–159)

However, when treaties are made, the expectation is that they need to be respected. Jacob condemned Simeon and Levi for their violence in contravention of an agreement with Shechem (Gen. 49:5–7, cf. Gen. 24). The terms of the agreement with the Gibeonites (Josh. 9) were honoured despite being obtained by deception (though the Gibeonites were reduced to servitude and cursed). When, later, Saul dishonoured the treaty by slaughtering them, David avenged them, at their request, by the execution and punitive exposure of seven of Saul's descendants (2 Sam. 21:1–10). Hezekiah, a good king of Judah, was wrongly persuaded by the Egyptian envoys to break his oath to Assyria and rebel, despite strong warnings against this by Isaiah. He entered into relations with the envoys of the king of the rising power of Babylon, also against Isaiah's advice (2 Kgs 20:12–31; Isa. 30 – 31). The case of Josiah, another good king of Judah, going out against the Egyptians and suffering so tragically seems to indicate the folly of unnecessarily seeking an international confrontation (2 Kgs 23:29–30; 2 Chr. 35:20–25). Jeremiah's warnings against the rebellion of the king and people of Judah against their submission to Babylon is the most pertinent example of this, because it led to the destruction of the city and temple of Jerusalem.

Trust-keeping and fidelity between states binds the international community of nation-states. Where this is adhered to, as in the case of individuals, the harmony so achieved is to the best benefit of all. States can function as economic entities only in limited respects, but they can provide the circumstances for the advancement or undermining of trade or economic activity. Their specific role is the juridical one: that of the exercise of justice, both within their own territories but also in relation to their neighbours. Relations between nations need to be built up over time, with recognition of elements of common concern, and through mutual understanding of their respective national cultures. Common faith should not create a uniform culture; cultural differences need to be affirmed and nurtured, which requires careful engagement. As with individuals, the relations between nations need to reflect the need for directness (or the availability of communication), continuity (extending over time), multiplexity (extending over a range of different areas, cultural as well as economic), parity (based on mutuality, if not direct equality) and commonality (based on areas of common ground) (Schluter & Lee 1993).

Aid from wealthy to lower-income countries is an important way of showing international solidarity. However, the effects of indiscriminate aid on local economies, not least through the undermining of local agriculture, need to be taken into account. Flooding of goods, or the excessive advancing of credit, can have effects as negative as exploitation or direct colonial intervention (while the latter can be positive; witness the introduction of railways to India under the British 'Raj'). Aid is also distorted when it is used as a tool to promote the donor countries' own industrial base, commercial enterprises or financial interests. Strings can be attached so that what is portrayed as a gift can in fact quickly be an imposed obligation. Even with the best of intentions (and these cannot be assured), there is no guarantee that these negative consequences can be averted. Between the Scylla of 'colonialist' or 'neo-colonialist' intervention, and the Carybdis of indiscriminate 'kindness that kills', there is the middle-ground of sound co-operation and fair trade, combined with well-targeted assistance.

We need to move to a much broader and more flexible understanding of what makes for good international relations, beyond the direct relations between governments and their formal institutions. Informal diplomacy can be guided by faith, which looks beyond the strict demands of the law and formal procedures (which may not provide any resolution), and allows the building up of a common ethos to shape the coming into being of an order of peace where the issues of international injustice and conflict are addressed and resolved (Johnson & Sampson 1994).

The nations of the world are actively to work together for the creation of peace and to seek forgiveness for wrongs

The future vision of the Bible is of international peace, when the earth shall be full of the glory of God as the waters cover the sea (Isa. 11:9; Hab. 2:14). In the Old Testament, especially in Isaiah, this is focused on Zion: the nations will come to Jerusalem. The reign of Solomon was remembered as a time of prosperity, but there were serious defects in its religious basis, under the patronage of the Pharaoh of Egypt. The future vision is based on the nations coming to know God at the end of all things as they are consummated with the return of Christ (the parousia). The delay of the parousia is not an invention by the early church to explain their disappointment at the lack of Jesus' return within their generation (as Rudolph Bultmann and his school postulated), but a tension which runs across the centuries of Christian experience from the Apostolic age until now. Our situation in this respect is no different from that of the first believers.

Conflicts throughout the world are inimical to the growth of a truly God-centred society. Not only are they destructive and divisive in themselves, but they also result in the distortion of community structures and inhibit the freedom that is essential for the healthy growth of all institutions – church, state, family and the range of voluntary associations and enterprises – which collectively make up 'civil society'. The culture of peace that permits the harmonious growth of relationships and makes possible human flourishing in all its aspects cannot coexist with a culture of war, whose climate of fear and suspicion engenders hatred and the centralization of control.

Christians are called to seek peace with one another (Rom. 12:18) and, by implication, between their respective communities. This command to create a world filled with a holistic sense of šālôm does not mean turning a blind eye to injustice, be it personal or structural. Indeed, another imperative, that of mišpāṭ ('justice') requires all people, as bearers of God's image, to work for the restoration of the shattered and distorted social order in which we live. The achievement of justice is a necessary prerequisite for the establishment of peace, but the justice to be worked for cannot simply be identified with the demands of any one class or party grouping – it must be truly impartial, without bias to the rich or the poor: 'Do not show partiality in judging: hear both small and great alike' (Deut. 1:17).

There is, however, a practical tension between 'peace-making' and 'prophetic' roles. The peacemaker's objective is to facilitate harmony between conflicting parties while the prophet directly confronts injustice and those responsible for it. If we focus exclusively on the peace-making role there is the danger that injustice and inequality will be underplayed in the attempt to encourage discussion and conciliation. In the prophetic role, the risk is of alienating one or both of the parties that should be brought together. The tension can be sustained creatively only by keeping in view the wider perspective. A biblical Weltanschauung is based on the concept of covenant. While the covenant refers primarily to God's relationship with humanity, if we approach Scripture to see what it says about a whole range of relationships, we will find that it provides us with a critique of present injustices and also gives us an outline of what a transformed social order should look like. This vision can then be applied to a conflict situation in an informed and carefully considered way.

Christian peacemakers are thus called to seek reconciliation in situations of conflict, without softening their opposition to the injustices that exist. And although they are to be motivated by their Christian faith and the biblical vision for society, this does not mean that they cannot work with those from different faiths or none at all. As all humanity is created in the image of God we can expect to share common points of ethical concern with those from different faith-communities. Moreover, in the Christian understanding of God as Trinity, the relational call to humanity which Jesus, as the 'person for others', embodies in himself is set within the context of his call and authorization by his Father, and within the empowering and transforming dynamic given to him by the Holy Spirit. As we respond to Jesus' call and shape our action and understanding of society by his example, our relationships with others are also transformed by the work of the Holy Spirit. This stance not only provides motivation for peace-making but also provides the basis for constructive action in the world created, redeemed and being moved to its final glory by the triune God.

This raises new questions about the view that we as Christians should take on defence and security. On what basis and with what means may (or should) wars be fought? What shape should the organization of defence and security take? What should be the nature of the relationship between the defence and security structure and the representative political authorities of a nation? Answers to these three questions can be traced through the biblical account.

Warfare needs to be limited and in a just cause

The most difficult international relations issue in the Bible is, arguably, the *ḥerem* ('ban') by which the Israelites were required by God to exterminate the Canaanite peoples.[4] Found in its fullest form in Deuteronomy 7, the *ḥerem* is not to be understood as a form of ethnic cleansing, but a prohibition that ensured the full destruction, without private profiteering, of the old order and its undergirding idolatry. It is about placing a ban on the culture and does not necessarily imply total physical annihilation (Jenson 2002). It is not a precedent for policy today, for it goes back to the specific degradation of Canaanite culture and points forward to the final judgment of God. The Israelites were told to show the Canaanites no mercy (Deut. 2:34; 7:3; 20:17–18). A case in point is Saul's later refusal to execute Agag according to the demands of the *ḥerem*. He was consequently denounced by Samuel and his dynasty deposed (1 Sam. 15). Whether or not the *ḥerem* is reinterpreted in this way, arguments about the question of war tend to be mediated by forms of 'just war' theory.

'Just war' theory argues that it is important that the cause for going to war as well as the methods should be just.[5] Jephthath may have doubted the justice of his cause and resorted to a deal with God in order to prop up his sense of security. Perhaps this explains the severity of the judgment against him (Judg. 11:14–40): his

---

4. C. J. H. Wright (2004) includes an appendix which addresses the concerns frequently raised in response to this.
5. For further reading on this see Jenson (2002) and O'Donovan (2003).

unintended sacrifice of his daughter. On several occasions kings of Israel are at pains to spell out the righteousness of their cause and methods when going to war. In 2 Chronicles 13:4–12, Abijah pleads the justice of his cause on the basis of God's covenant with David, against which Jeroboam has rebelled; Jeroboam is subsequently routed (13:13–20). Asa defeats Zerah the Cushite on the same basis (2 Chr. 14), as does Jehoshaphat, fighting Moab and Ammon (20:1–30). By contrast, in 2 Chronicles 18, the wrong-headed alliance between Jehoshaphat and Ahab against the Arameans leads to the latter's death.

The Old Testament set rules for treatment of war prisoners (Deut. 21:10–14). Proper treatment of civilians was also ensured. The Israelites were to offer peace to a city if they attacked it, and to protect all the inhabitants if they surrendered on those conditions. Even if a siege were necessary, the women and children were not to be killed (Deut. 20:10–15). Ammonite slaughter of pregnant women in the course of military conquest was condemned by the prophets (Amos 1:13). The overall offensive aim was not the annihilation of populations, but the destruction of oppressive power structures and their idolatrous cultures. There was room for the adoption of strangers and assimilation of conquered peoples under common subjection to the law of God. To see the taking of the Promised Land simply as a war of liberation would be reductive; from the time of Abraham there had existed a covenantal justification for the occupation. Once installed, however, the Israelites engaged mostly in defensive military action to safeguard the Israelite polity, not seeking to dominate other peoples.

There are guidelines laid down for the treatment of the environment when fighting war. A distinction is made between the fruit trees, which must be left, and other trees that can be cut down strictly for the purpose of constructing siege works. This puts a limit to ecological devastation (Deut. 20:19–21). The case where the Israelites strewed stones on the fields of the Moabites, stopped up the springs and cut down the good trees contravened the prohibition on destruction of the environment (2 Kgs 3:25). Their action was in accordance with the prophecy of Elisha (3:19) and, much later, Jeremiah, dealing with a different situation, prophesies that salt will be put in the Moabite fields (Jer. 47:9). Despite Elisha's prophecy, the action implicitly brought them into God's disfavour (2 Kgs 3:27); this is a complex example, but it seems that what is foreseen is not necessarily approved.

There are several Christian traditions regarding the involvement of believers in war. The pacifist tradition interprets the teaching of Jesus and the early church as calling for complete abstinence from any military or war-making activity. Pacifism was the stance of Tertullian (c. 160–c. 225)[6] and Origen (c. 185–c. 254)[7] – although

---

6. *Apology*, 30–35; *On Idolatry*, 19; *The Chaplet*, 6, 11, 12.

7. *Against Celsus*, 3.7; 8.73–75.

it may be argued that neither was necessarily representative of the mainstream. For the early church, pacifism was related to the rejection of emperor worship, usually involved in army service.[8] With the Christianizing of the empire under Constantine, this barrier was removed,[9] and indeed the defence of the now Christian empire became a Christian duty. The view of warfare as a Christian duty was tempered, however, by the doctrine of the 'just war', developed notably by Ambrose[10] and then Augustine,[11] and considerably elaborated in the Middle Ages and afterwards by Thomas Aquinas and the later Scholastics. Elements of what would constitute a just cause for war, and its just prosecution, were defined and tabulated. The continuing difficulty is to match this with the vagaries of international statecraft, the rise of internal conflicts within states, and indeed with new factors, such as the use of weapons with destructive powers undreamed of in previous eras.

Regardless of whether one adopts a pacifist or a 'just war' approach, the vision in Isaiah 2:4 and Micah 4:3 of swords being turned into ploughshares provides Christians today with a motivation to work for justice in international dealings. The calculation of national interest cannot be the sole criterion of defence policy. The paradox is that making national self-interest a relative rather than an absolute criterion may eventually be in the best interests of all concerned, since it avoids undue confrontations between powers on a zero-sum basis.

Continuing conflict between and within states, with their complexities now much closer to the surface, is setting back attempts to build an international order on sound relational principles. The temptation is to resort to the application of force without engaging fully with the underlying issues, the relational factors involved in culturally and geographically diverse regions. Nor can the sheer application of financial/economic levers, conceived of and described in mechanical and impersonal terms, be a satisfactory means of achieving international harmony and prosperity. Enforced compliance and external control will undermine the sense of human dignity that is the basis of all sound relationships; a cage with golden bars is no compensation for the lack of true partnership and mutual

---

8. Whether or not this was the decisive factor is a matter of considerable debate between the two basic traditions. There are important exceptions, notably the case of St Maurice who, according to the fifth century probably semi-historical *Passio Agaunensium Martyrum* commanded a Christian legion during the time of the persecuting emperor, Diocletian (reigned 286–305), and suffered martyrdom with his soldiers for refusing to sacrifice to the emperor.

9. Again, the nature of this modification is a matter of much debate.

10. *De officiis ministrorum*, 1.27.129.

11. *Reply to Faustus the Manichean*, Book 22, Sections 73–78.

respect. This challenge calls for new and innovative approaches to deal with both the structural and proximate causes of conflicts whilst transforming over time the relationships and systems embedded in the conflict.

The control and deployment of military and security forces need to be shared and balanced between the centre and the localities

The Israelite army was composed of tribal levies. The basic unit was the 'elep (literally 'thousand'), which corresponded to the main tribal sub-division, the mišpāḥâ. The size of the Israelite nation at the time of the exodus is a matter of some discussion. Key to this is the interpretation of the census in Numbers 1, but the number of men under arms was probably nearer 6,000 than the 600,000 totalled by the editor in Numbers 1:46. If the original meaning of the word translated 'thousand' ('elep) is taken as a unit rather than a precise number, then the forces total 598 'ălāpîm (or 598 'allûpîm – unit leaders), roughly 5,550 men (Mendenhall 1958: 52–66; Wenham 1981: 62–66).

When the people demanded a monarchy, Samuel warned against the danger of kings taking the sons of the Israelite families for his personal retinue and the imposition of taxes and corvée on both sons and daughters (Deut. 17:14–20; 1 Sam. 8; 11:1–18). Both Saul and David came to power at the head of Hebrew retinues: this is clearest with David who went into the service of the Philistine King Achish of Gath when he was out of Saul's favour. Both kings had lists of 'mighty men', their personal champions (2 Sam. 23:8–39). The development of kings' personal retinues supplemented the tribal levies which existed from the time of the conquest, based on the elephim supplied by each mišpāḥâ. This can be seen clearly in the episode where the young David is sent to supply his brothers who have been called up as the 'elep. Each mišpāḥâ had to supply their 'elep with provisions, which David does, taking ten cheeses to the 'elep commander for the supply of the unit as a whole, together with flour and ten loaves of bread, which, it seems, were to go to the brothers directly. In return, David was to receive the token, 'ărubbâ, the certificate that the delivery had been made (1 Sam. 17:17–22). In this way, links with the family support-unit were maintained, and there was a restraint on where the 'ălāpîm could be deployed. The song of Deborah shows that prior to the monarchy the response to a call to arms was at the discretion of each tribe. There was no physical sanction against those who refused to fight, but it could be seen as a refusal to help Yahweh and his people and a breach of the covenantal commitment. There is some question about whether Meroz, mentioned in the song, was actually an Israelite town, but it was cursed for its refusal to join the forces of Israel in the time of need (Judg. 5:23).

For some operations (e.g. the taking of Jerusalem) David seems to have depended on specific groups of soldiers rather than on the Israelites generally. Putting the whole nation on a war footing by mustering the *'ălāpîm* was an extraordinary act which required a special sacrificial payment (Exod. 30:12–16). The Israelites as a whole were mustered only in the case of emergency, and David's attempt to keep them mustered in peacetime (and, it seems, without giving the required sacrifice) was disastrous (2 Sam. 24:1–17). In peacetime, the nation reverted to a decentralized structure. In the debate between Ahithophel and Hushai, Hushai's plan for the mustering of all Israel in support of Absalom's insurrection proved finally fatal to the latter's cause (2 Sam. 16:15 – 17:29). The tribal levies were not suitable for that purpose. On the other hand, they proved highly effective against external threats. Asa achieved considerable success with tribal levies (2 Chr. 14:8–15), as did his son Jehoshaphat (2 Chr. 17:18–19). Other kings of Judah, such as Amaziah (2 Chr. 25:5) and Uzziah (2 Chr. 26:12), organized their forces in the same way and were commended for it.

The extension of participation to the population as a whole creates political balance. Standing armies provide the conditions necessary for military intervention because they can establish themselves as a state within a state, potentially in opposition to any government, or, equally insidiously, as instruments of tyrannical power. In the English Civil War, Parliament on 3 July 1644 passed 'the Act for putting the Associated Counties ... into a posture of Defence' which provided for the direct provision of horse, dragoons and foot by property holders in counties in the East of England where Parliament was in the ascendant. This provided the basis for the defence of England, preceding the much better known establishment of the New Model Army in 1645, and provided most of the forces for Oliver Cromwell's defeat of Charles II and the Scottish invasion forces at the Battle of Worcester in 1651. As Cromwell wrote to William Lenthall, the Speaker of Parliament, 'Your new-raised forces did perform singular good service; as also for their willingness thereunto, – forasmuch as the same hath added so much to the reputation of your affairs. They are all despatched home again ... It is for aught I know a crowning mercy' (Carlisle 1888: 295).

This is an early example of what Bobbitt describes in a wider context as a shift from the 'kingly state' to the 'territorial state' (Bobbitt 2003: ch. 7), but there was the deeper principle here of the need to involve the whole population in defence in a representative and ordered way. Even after the Restoration of Charles II, the forces for the defence of England were predominantly local ones (still under Parliamentary control). Since 1689, the raising of armed forces in England (and subsequently the United Kingdom generally) has been done on a 'temporary' basis: Parliament is required annually to renew the Mutiny (now Army) Act, ensuring continuous Parliamentary control over the armed forces. This issue had originally precipitated the English Civil War in 1642.

In the Thirteen Colonies of what became the United States of America, the use of regular forces against the revolutionaries later impelled the Second Amendment (adopted 1791) to the US Constitution, which affirms the 'right of the people to keep and bear arms' – not, it must be pointed out, on an individualistic basis but within the context of 'a well regulated Militia' (Pritchett 1971: 133).[12] One of the constitutional thinkers of the time, Noah Webster put it in graphic terms: '[t]he supreme power in America cannot enforce unjust laws by the sword; because the whole body of the people are armed, and constitute a force superior to any band of regular troops that can be, on any pretence, raised in the United States' (Webster 1787). In *The Federalist Paper*, No. 46, first published in the *New York Packet* on 29 January 1788, James Madison contended: 'the ultimate authority resides in the people alone'. To a regular army of the US government 'would be opposed a militia amounting to near half a million citizens with arms in their hands'.

The Swiss model of universal[13] participation in defence of the country has advantages in relational terms. It means that all the population (both those called up and their families), rather than a remote élite, have to engage with military issues and call both the military and the defence establishment to account. One of the implications of having a militia-based defence force is that it makes going to war very difficult because a government must have real democratic support. In the emergent 'market-state' of the twenty-first century, the equivalent to the biblical model is the involvement of all householders in the organized defence and security of their localities under local control combined with small, highly mobile and specialist quick-reaction forces controlled by the centre. These latter would need to be kept strictly under central regulation (according to a clear and universally accepted code), as the danger of their misuse either by the central political authorities or indeed against them (or against any political institution) would need to be guarded against. With respect to policing, there is a similar need to develop organs of specialist response (to terrorism, international crime in general and drug-dealing in particular) alongside the much greater involvement of citizens in the security and policing of their own localities. This must of course be on a fully representative (rather than sectional) basis, with centrally provided training and regulation. Similarly, the leadership of both would need to be representative of the communities as well as professionally trained, selected and employed.

---

12. In the light of prior developments in seventeenth-century England that decisively shaped developments on both sides of the Atlantic (Ive 1986).

13. In this case male, but in some countries, female as well.

Military intervention in politics needs to be hedged against

The danger of abuse was taken very seriously in biblical Israel: there are limits on the military in terms of funding and power. We have seen this already in the case of the militia, which provided the primary hedge against overweening centralist power. Building up a chariot force, the most advanced military technology of the ancient world, was frowned on. Chariots could be used by a king to centralize power, robbing the regions of their decision-making abilities (Deut. 17:16). They made it possible for kings to go to war without the consent of the tribes, because decision-making was moved from the tribal authorities to the royal court. Chariot forces also sucked smaller nations into superpower confrontations, such as that between Egypt and the Hittites. Solomon's build up of his chariot forces took place largely in the strategic valley of Jezreel, around Megiddo (1 Kgs 9:15–19). After the division of the kingdoms, this chariot force was largely inherited by the Northern Kingdom, and then expanded. This led to a heavy centralization of the Northern monarchy, its size and ostentation located in the new city of Samaria – fiercely condemned by the prophets (Amos 2:6–16) and finally destroyed by the Assyrians.

It is noteworthy that pretenders to the throne made sure that they were seen in chariots (Absalom in 2 Sam. 15:1 and Adonijah in 1 Kgs 1:5) and that from Rhehoboam on, kings are described as going to war in their chariots, often to die in them (1 Kgs 22:29–40; 2 Kgs 9:14–29; 2 Chr. 35:24). The chariot force was used first by Zimri (1 Kgs 16:9–20) for his seizure of power; and later by Jehu for a bloody coup against the corrupt and brutal Omriid dynasty (2 Kgs 9 – 10).

Chariots become overt symbols of idolatry, worshipped instead of God (2 Kgs 23:11), and they sucked Solomon and his successors into the international arms-trade. In the Psalms there are warnings about trusting in chariots and horses, and in the size of armies (Pss. 20:7; 33:17): instead the people are called back to trusting in God. This is not so much a pious exhortation to individual spirituality (although that is involved as well), as it is a call for king and people alike to return to the covenantal basis for their defence. A dramatic instance of this occurred during the attack on Judah by the Assyrian army under Sennacherib, where God once again affirmed the Davidic covenant with Hezekiah. Consequently, the Assyrian army was laid waste by plague and Sennacherib was murdered by his own sons (2 Kgs 18:17–37; 19; 2 Chr. 32:1–23; Isa. 36 – 37).

There are many passages about the dangers of civil war, the most notable being that of Absalom's rebellion against David, where both the rebellion itself and the brutality with which it was put down, against David's wishes, inflicted deep wounds on the Israelite state. After the division of the kingdoms (itself a profoundly harmful development), the Northern Kingdom, with its insecure monarchy, was continually riven by internal conflict that contributed directly to its eventual fall. In the Northern Kingdom, both the chariot corps (by Zimri and later Jehu, as we have seen) and the standing army (in the case of Omri) were used as power-bases to overthrow kings. Excessive force was employed even by Jehu, the pretender anointed by Elisha to depose the house of Omri (2 Kgs 9:1–13), and so he was condemned (2 Kgs 10:31; note Hos. 1:4–5). Jehu's treatment of the Omriid dynasty contrasted with David's merciful treatment of Saul's family (2 Sam. 9).

From the history of ancient Israel it is clear that there are limitations that need to be placed on the security apparatus, not least because of the danger of its personal abuse, as the cases of David and Uriah (1 Kgs 11 and 12), and of Ahab and Naboth (1 Kgs 21) demonstrate. Today, in many parts of the world, the question must be asked, how can the army be kept out of politics? It can too easily become the instrument of oppression or the promoter of sectional interests. Even when it intervenes with a genuinely high-minded intent, the very fact of its intervention undermines the integrity of the political process in fledgling democracies, and goes against the fundamental requirement that all political acts be subject to the constitution and due process of law (Koonings & Kruijt 2002).[14] Moreover, there is the danger of politics being dominated by the need for military funding, in close alliance with the international arms-trade.

The question remains, however, of to what extent the army should be doing what it is told by its political masters, and to what extent it should be exercising conscience. Is it simply an instrument of its political masters regardless of the justice of what it is ordered to do? There are no easy answers to this, but two safeguards can be built in. One is to follow the biblical injunction to reflect continually upon the law. Legal process is vulnerable in the midst of conflict which may brutalize participants and cause the suspension or limited availability of peace-time processes. At such times deeply ingrained values (in both individuals and organizations) are the surest protection. Secondly, a militia system that depends on a high degree of democratic consent can introduce accountability in the values that govern actions, as can the promise of legal review when hostilities have ceased. The biblical record of Israel's experience highlights the role of prophets in providing a critique of military action, but does not give clear examples of individuals disobeying orders on moral grounds. It is, however, clear from the biblical record that all are responsible for their actions; the structure of the army as well as the call on each individual to bear that responsibility points to the need for each to act before God.

---

14. For a frightening case-study, see Luckham (1971) on the Nigerian military.

Conclusion

Sound international relations are not an optional extra. In the light of the biblical vision, all nations are called to live together harmoniously in anticipation of the time when all will enjoy the fullness of God's rule, when the 'wolf will lie down with the lamb' (Isa. 65:25). We have identified three elements as key to the creation of a sound international order: the recognition of a universal framework of law for international affairs based on the sovereignty of God over all nations; the importance of keeping trust; and the need actively to promote peace and forgiveness. In each of these areas, Christians can play either a direct part in their individual capacities, or corporately support the promotion of these aims.

The possibility of influencing international policy to promote the ideal of universal just dealings is increased in democratic situations where, through the electoral process or through lobbying, Christians can exert decisive influence on the shape and course of international affairs. This places great responsibility on Christians not just to bring pressure to bear, but to do so in a properly informed way. Informal networks, enabled by the new communication possibilities, can supplement and correct information available through the public or commercial media. In this way, through their partnerships, Christians can reflect and make actual the vision of just international dealings. However, until the *parousia* these partnerships will not be without pain, since they will be confronted with, and indeed carry within themselves, the inherited and incipient injustices that characterize international dealings.

Old Testament Israel was bound by the need to ensure that wars were fought on a just basis, drawing not only on a small professional army but also on the population as a whole, to whom it was responsible. It was a normative expectation that defence be structured as close to local communities as possible. The basic military unit from the time of the exodus, the *'elep*, was supplied directly by the *mišpāḥâ*, the sub-tribal family group. Even when Saul and David drew on the support of the extra-tribal, landless Hebrews, these were defined in terms of their direct personal relationship to their patron, and seen as supplementary to the tribal levies, which can be supplied only in time of war or crisis. The building up of extensive centralized (e.g. chariot) forces is regarded with disfavour by God, and certainly had negative consequences for the unity of the Israelites. It sucked later kings, both of Israel and Judah, into unnecessary confrontations with their neighbours and into super-power politics. The relationship between the king and the political order is implicated in the danger that a central army holds for political stability, as demonstrated in the history of the Northern Kingdom.

Defence and security were based on a close link to the family structure that held together the early Israelite state. Loyalty to God and obedience to his laws were the cornerstone of any arrangement upon which the whole edifice stood or fell. All was open to the movement of the Spirit of God, as he took Israel continually beyond the old order, often through difficult, painful or confusing detours into ever new anticipations of his final purposes when all wars are ended and perfect justice established under the rule of Christ, God's true warrior and victor over the last and ultimate enemies – sin and death.

15. A relational and coherent vision

Michael Schluter

In chapters 6 – 14, the agenda for Christian social reform has been explored by examining biblical teaching for a number of areas of public life, from family policy through to international relations. This analysis has been based primarily on the laws governing early Israel's political, economic and social life, but has taken into account how these institutions were modified in the light of the coming of Christ and the universalizing of the kingdom of God. The question considered in this brief chapter is how these various laws are connected with each other, apart from under the general theme of 'Love for God and love for neighbour', as articulated by Christ himself (Matt 22:34–40). It is this coherence of God's intentions for society, as chapter 5 has argued, that is an essential aspect of what it means for Israel to serve as a paradigm for the social order.

Goals of the system

As spelled out in chapter 2, Christianity is a 'relational religion'. God's character is expressed through his love for human-beings, and he desires, and requires, that human beings show love for him and love for one another as the only appropriate response to his extraordinary, unmerited love to us, his fallen and rebellious subjects. So the focus of God's interest is the quality of human relationships. In chapter 6, the various attributes of the person that are needed were explored; these included holiness, righteousness, justice, mercy, peace, loyalty and love. These are to apply to one-to-one relationships as well as inter-group, inter-organizational and international relationships.

This perspective on the overall goal of God's laws for society, however, raises a question. As we have gone through chapters 7 – 14 discussing biblical teaching on many different areas of activity there has been little mention of the word 'love'. If it is explicitly mentioned so infrequently, how can Jesus claim that it is the great overall theme of the law and the prophets? The answer lies in how we understand the word 'love'. Clearly, Jesus was not referring to romantic attachment. Broughton Knox has suggested 'other-person-centredness' as a definition (Knox 1988: 131). Love is certainly the antithesis of selfishness, as this definition suggests. However, surely 'love' must also include some element of emotional engagement which is expressed in words like care, comfort and compassion.

A necessary first step to loving someone is knowing them, so people knowing God and one another are major themes in the Bible.[1] Knowing overcomes indifference. Hence, the point of the story of the Good Samaritan arises precisely because the Samaritan did not know the Jew he was helping, and, due to the disastrous relations which existed between the two groups, was expected to have anything but love for this stranger he encountered.

What does it mean for one person to 'know' another? The word 'know' in the English language can refer to anything from casual acquaintance to intimate friendship. Five preconditions have been identified (originally from reflection on the Mosaic Law in the light of Jesus' summary in Matt. 22:34–40) as being necessary in a relationship if one person is to know another well:[2]

- directness of communication
- continuity in the relationship over time
- breadth of knowledge of the person's personal, family and work situations
- parity
- shared values and goals

Fulfilment of these conditions leads to what we have called 'relational proximity'. This refers not to whether people *like* each other, but whether they *know* each other. They are fulfilled perfectly in the Trinity.

Each of these five preconditions of one person knowing another point towards different facets of God's relationships with each of us. Taking *directness* first, we might reflect on the fact that empathy and compassion are best expressed directly. God so loved the world that he sent his Son, not just another prophet (Heb. 1:1–2). Jesus opens up a direct relationship with God. With respect to *continuity*, love

---

1. E.g. Ps. 9:10; Eph. 1:17; Phil. 3:7–10; 1 John 2:4, etc.
2. These were first articulated in ch. 3 of Schluter & Lee (1993). See ch. 17 for further discussion of relational proximity.

sticks with it through the long haul, through thick and thin. We might reflect on the faithfulness of God: God is faithful (1 Cor. 10:13). Regarding *multiplexity*, love is interested in the whole person. God knows us fully and is interested in every aspect of our lives (e.g. Ps. 139:1–12). With respect to *parity*, love empowers and does not dominate; it is courteous and respectful. So we find Jesus washing his disciples' feet (John 13:1–5), and his life is always characterized by humility (e.g. Phil. 2:5–11). Regarding *commonality*, love involves the sharing of dreams, information and objectives. So God graciously invites human beings to become his friends, to share his Father's goals, to know everything the Father has revealed to him (John 15:15). It is these characteristics of God's relationship with us that he longs to see in our relationships with other people.

We argue in this book that many of the laws given to Old Testament Israel, and other teaching on social ethics in the Bible, have the effect of ensuring or augmenting the preconditions of close relationship, so that love can flourish. This focus on protecting, developing and maintaining 'relational proximity', whether in a person's relationships with God, family or community, leads us to identify five sub-goals of the social, political and economic framework that have emerged repeatedly in the previous chapters. These are the sustaining of the five key relationships in any society:

- the society's relationship with God
- relationships between citizens as individuals
- family relationships
- community relationships
- inter-regional and inter-group relationships at a national level

The laws of a society cannot in themselves create love. All that laws and social institutions can hope to achieve is to create a set of preconditions for social relations that maximize the likelihood that on the one hand love will be expressed, and on the other that exploitation, oppression, social exclusion and social isolation will be minimized. People are less likely to exploit or ignore those they know well, and correspondingly more likely to help, support and encourage them. And it is in situations where individuals or communities know each other well that those characteristics described in chapter 6 of righteousness, peace, truth, and so on, are most likely to find expression.

Sectors of activity

These five sub-goals are expressed across all the different sectors of activity which we have discussed in the last eight chapters. Many of these sound similar to those of any Western society today, such as religious organizations, political structure, defence, welfare, justice, land and property, capital (finance) and international relations. In a modern economy, of course, the definitions are wider, and the issues more complex. Missing are some sectors which today make up major government departments, such as education and health. Although the meaning and content of education and health are widely considered in Israel's law and wisdom literature, little attention is given to the institutional mechanisms by which these services are delivered to the public. Other sectors of activity we have not discussed in previous chapters are the environment and employment conditions, where relatively few laws address the issue directly. It may be that they were felt to be 'residual issues' in the sense that if other relationships in society were practised in the way prescribed by God, then these issues would sort themselves out. Indeed, the flourishing of the environment is promised specifically if the people are obedient to God's law, and equally there will be a curse on the environment as a consequence of disobedience (Deut. 28).

Also missing from the last eight chapters is any discussion of how economic growth would have been stimulated. This is because in the Torah economic growth and prosperity are promised if there is obedience to specific laws, such as the ban on interest (Deut. 23:19–20), and, as with the environment, to biblical laws in general (see Deut. 28:1–14). There are no particular laws which are designed directly and obviously to bring about economic growth.

Some might wish to argue that in early Israel there was in effect no political decision-making, so it is inappropriate to include discussion of political structures. It might seem as if political decisions were precluded by the detailed nature of God's laws on such a wide range of issues. However, one could imagine a range of decisions that would need to be made locally from year to year within the framework provided by the laws of Exodus, Leviticus, Numbers and Deuteronomy. Such decisions might have included the allocation of tithes between needy groups and individuals, housing of immigrants, joint projects with neighbouring villages or regions and the setting up of synagogues or schools. Conceptually, such decisions seem to be little different from the way a national legislature passes laws within the constraints set by a national constitution today.

The interconnection of goals and sectors

Table 2 illustrates the coherence of Israel's social, political and economic institutions. Following Douglass North (1990), institutions are defined as the rules which govern the behaviour of organizations and individuals. So each square in the table contains one or more examples of laws or rules which illustrate how the goal represented by a particular row is furthered in the sector of activity

Sectors of public life / Goals: sustaining key relationships	Religious life	Family policy	Political structures	Administration of justice
Society's relationship with God	Levites role to teach the law (7)	Role of family to teach the law and pass on tradition (9)	God's ultimate political authority recognized (8)	God regarded as the source of all justice (13)
Relationships between citizens as individuals	Equality of all citizens before God (8)	Role of the family redeemer (gō'ēl) (10)	Rights of all citizens to protection and participation (8)	Protection of dignity of offender (13)
Extended and 3-generational family relationships	The Sabbath and Passover (9)	Honouring of parents (9)	Role of family elders in community affairs (9)	Relational concept of seriousness of crime (13)
Local community relationships	Tithes collected locally and redistributed in the community (10)	Overlap of kinship and community networks (9)	Constraints on king's centralizing power (8)	Major role for community courts (13)
National, inter-regional and inter-group relationships	The sacrificial system and 3 annual festivals (7)	All families gather in Jerusalem for national festivals (9)	National law, national culture and role of the king (7)	Role of 'court of appeal' and the king in justice issues (13)

Table 2. A relational and coherent vision: early Israel's social, political and economic institutions*

*Following Douglass North (1990), institutions are defined as the rules – formal and informal – which govern the behaviour of organizations and individuals.

Sectors of public life / Goals: sustaining key relationships	Land and property	Capital utilization	Welfare provision	International relations and defence
Society's relationship with God	God's ultimate ownership of the land acknowledged (9)	Accountability to God for use of wealth (11)	God has special concern for the widow, the orphan and the immigrant (10)	God's law a universal basis for international relations (14)
Relationships between citizens as individuals	Enforceable property rights (9)	Year of debt remission (11)	Laws protecting the dignity of the vulnerable individual (10)	Protection of prisoners of war and asylum seekers (14)
Extended and 3-generational family relationships	Jubilee laws ensure family roots and colocation (9)	Ban on interest (11)	Family required to be primary welfare provider (10)	Exemption from conscription for newly weds (Deut. 24:5)
Local community relationships	Jubilee laws help preserve community relationships in the long term (9)	Ban on interest (11)	Local community 'duty of care' for the vulnerable (10)	Community-based army units and laws against king having chariots (14)
National, inter-regional and inter-group relationships	A national basis of equitable regional allocation (9)	National currency and free trade (12)	Welfare laws apply across Israel (10)	The king's role in foreign policy (7)

Source: chs. 6–14. Figures in brackets indicate the chapter where the issue is discussed. The laws and social norms cited in each square are only examples.

represented by a particular column. For example, looking at Table 1 (on p. 97), the goal of protecting and strengthening family relationships is furthered in the 'land and property' column through the jubilee legislation, discussed in chapter 9. It is important to stress that the content of each square in the table is not exhaustive, but illustrative.

The table is based on how Israel was established in the Old Testament. It is not possible to read off exactly how God wants every society to be organized in the twenty-first century. In particular, as stressed in chapter 5, in the New Testament it is not the task of government to compel the individual to acknowledge God, or Christ, in society today. So it is neither appropriate nor practical for countries like Britain, which have largely rejected belief in God, to depend for their military defence on God's intervention. Nor is God regarded today as the source of justice or ultimate political authority in the social order, however much these statements are true in some ultimate sense. Having said that, it is still a legitimate aspiration for Christians to seek to see God's role publicly acknowledged in public life, wherever that can be done through persuasion and consent rather than by force. This is easier to achieve in Africa and Latin America, which are largely Christian, than in Europe today. Formal acknowledgment of God's place in the social order can be reflected in the constitution, Parliamentary procedures, school curricula and the values undergirding the criminal justice system.

There are in fact many more interconnections between the columns and rows in Table 2 than it is possible to show in the table. For example, the protection of the individual, shown in the 'administration of justice' column does not just depend on specific laws such as those which protect the dignity of the offender (e.g. Deut. 25:3), but also depends on the rule of law being generally recognized and on the constraints on the king's power. These latter aspects of the system are shown in the 'political structure' column. The single provision of the Sabbath has an impact on family policy, as shown in the table, but also impacts on religious life, land and property, welfare and, indirectly, also affects capital utilization. Another example is the ban on interest. The primary impact is in the strengthening of family and community relationships (see ch. 11). However, the constraints this imposes on accumulation of wealth by an individual or family also is important in ensuring the continued strength and vitality of local communities in the political system: where there is a concentration of economic power, a concentration of political power is sure to follow.

The different parts of the system are mutually reinforcing, in ways the table cannot demonstrate. For example, the structure and roles of the extended family provide a key component of the system of welfare as shown, but at the same time the welfare system is set up on a basis that reinforces the role of the family rather than undermines it. The community, for example, is not encouraged to provide support for those who have close relatives available to them. Rather, gleaning laws, tithes and other forms of help are reserved for orphans, widows and foreigners. By the same token, specific interventions in a modern society, such as restoring the weekly day of rest, can potentially bring multiple social benefits across different sectors of public life.

The table helps to make clear the dangers of taking a principle from a specific law without having some idea of the wider context or framework within which that law was originally embedded. For example, to conclude from the biblical teaching that the family should be the major source of welfare provision in society is undoubtedly correct. But in early Israel the family's role was made possible by its economic resource-base in the land, the family-strengthening effects of the interest ban, and the family's role in a highly decentralized political structure. To increase the family's role in welfare today, in a very different political and economic setting, requires an understanding of how the contemporary wider political and economic environment can be adjusted to enable families to take on greater welfare responsibilities.

Conclusion

So how is it possible to bring about greater 'love' in society today, the kind of love which is concerned for somebody else rather than oneself, and promote the kind of society which prevents the exploitation and oppression of vulnerable minorities? The argument of this book is that the goals which led to people 'knowing' their families and their neighbours well in early Israel, in the wide sense of relational proximity, are the same goals as are needed in society today. It is important across all the various sectors of public life not just to inculcate relational values over against materialistic priorities, but to pursue the goal of sustaining the quality of all key relationships across all the sectors of political, economic and social life.

So the next question is how this can be done in society today, in societies which do not have the special relationship with God that Israel enjoyed in the Old Testament period. In a society where relatively few acknowledge the Lordship of Christ, what kind of 'translation strategy' is required to apply the biblical framework to the contemporary social order? The theory of such a translation strategy, and the experience of one small Christian charity in Britain in trying to turn theory into practice, will be the subject of Part 3.

How might the *Jubilee Manifesto* be implemented? Part 2 has shown how elements of a political, economic and social system combine to reinforce family and community relationships whilst offering important safeguards against parochialism and political discord. We examined these elements, not in order to find individual perspectives from which to criticize contemporary ideologies, but because they form a coherent model. Nonetheless, our criticisms have at times been far-reaching. This raises the urgent question of how the alternative could work in practice.

Chapter 16 explores how to translate biblical ideas into contemporary society. It considers a number of approaches to social reform, including political engagement, changing values, practical institutional reform and building a movement of people. In addressing the need to engage with those who do not share our faith if we are to bring about reform, we consider the ways in which the language and agenda of relationships can articulate common ground which is true to our faith.

In chapter 17 we present a series of case-studies from the work of the Jubilee Centre and its associated charities. We consider why specific projects were chosen, how they relate to our understanding of biblical teaching, how they operated and what was achieved. Valuable lessons can be learned from both successes and relative failures.

To close, chapter 18 sets out challenges that arise from this agenda for Christian social reform. This book is rooted in the experience of seeking social reform – we hope that further engagement will be its fruit.

16. The potential for Relationism

John Ashcroft

Strategies for social reform

Previous sections of the book have argued that the Bible provides an ethical paradigm which is relevant for all societies and which has a concern for relationships as a central theme. This paradigm embodies values which should guide our decisions as we seek to transform society. However, the agenda we propose will vary according to the political and social context in which the church operates and the nature of the church's position in society. The options where the church is a small and persecuted minority are different to those where Christian faith is the majority or where the church is an influential minority within an increasingly secular and plural society.[1]

This chapter begins by outlining five key forms of engagement in society before considering the ways in which the theme of relationships can be adopted as a mechanism for communicating the agenda described in Part 2. The various elements of a reform strategy are rooted in the need to develop, promote and apply a social and economic philosophy that prioritizes and sustains relationships.

---

1. Weithman (1997) is a good example of the extensive literature in theology and political theory on the appropriate modes of religious discourse and reasoning in a pluralistic secular liberal democracy. The strategies outlined in this chapter are informed as much by reflection on our experience of doing reform, as by theoretical reflection on the possibility of effective communication.

Political engagement to influence policy is one form of engagement that flows out of this. The second is persuading people to value relationships, recognizing that culture and values influence thinking and practice as well as the demand for, and acceptability of, specific reform proposals. Thirdly, organizational structures and working practices must be reformed. This gives people the opportunity to put changed values into practice as well as supporting the process of changing values. Change is not easy, but it is possible to create an environment that is conducive to the development of effective relationships. Creating the conditions for change and removing barriers to reform is therefore the fourth aspect of the strategy. Finally, any strategy for social reform must include a process for gathering, inspiring, supporting and resourcing a group of people who believe in the importance of relationships and are willing to use their opportunities for influence to build a more relational society.

Political engagement

How might a proactive minority seek to implement the *Jubilee Manifesto*? Reactive engagement allows others to set the agenda and easily becomes a defensive campaign against things we oppose rather than commending and promoting our positive vision for society. Where the majority share our faith, the debate can remain around the proper nature of a biblical vision for society. Theological differences within the church may still make for lively and contentious conversation, but this is a rather different challenge to political discourse with those who do not recognize the Lord we worship. In this context compromise can be legitimate. Our vision for a fallen society must offer hope but also be realistic. We must be clear when this involves compromise, and simultaneously support wider Christian involvement, including clear articulation of the gospel and the claims it makes upon all people.

There are different forms of political engagement covering debate about both the outcomes we should seek and the means of achieving them. Our involvement may focus on political structures and processes; the formation, agreement and implementation of specific policies; or influencing the broader themes which govern approaches to individual policy issues. Influencing a political party's policy themes requires political sponsorship as these are set in place well in advance of the publication of Green or White Papers. It is difficult to work as an influential 'insider' whilst also acting as a public critic – active involvement in shaping the broad policy agenda of any party cannot, in most cases, be done from a position of political independence. Christians may sometimes seek to exercise influence within an administration, or act as critical outsiders. Obadiah, Esther, Nehemiah and Daniel are examples of those who exercised influence within administrations, whilst Elijah and Jeremiah are examples of external critics. The different pattern of relationships makes it all but impossible for an individual or organization to fulfil both roles.

Examples of possible changes to political structures and processes include constitutional reform, decentralization to strengthen local government, and the reform of such international bodies as the European Union or World Trade Organization. These are important to the extent that they are perceived as obstacles to reform in other areas, or enshrine certain values. A key issue here is that many people and organizations participate in these structures, which can operate and be sustained only with some degree of consensus. While this consensus may, in part, be rooted in an equilibrium of competing powers and interests, participation in such processes and structures inescapably requires working with others.

It is also important to find ways in which a biblical vision can inform the Christian contribution to a shared vision for a community. For individual Christians political involvement can be seen as simply a responsibility of citizenship. There has been much recent concern about the extent of political disengagement in the UK, seen in terms of low turnout in elections and cynicism about party politics (Spencer 2004). Reasons for this may include the blurring of traditional ideological divides and the managerialism of pragmatic politics, perceptions of sleaze, a belief that 'spin' has become more important than substance, economic security, a sense of distance from where decisions are made and powerlessness (Spencer 2003a: 10–14). Political engagement in the UK should, however, be seen in much wider terms than simply participating in the centralized processes focused around Westminster. It includes involvement in the running of local public services – either actively, for example as a school governor, or through responding to consultation processes. It means sharing responsibility for the future of a local neighbourhood. And it includes being part of the process of holding others to account.

While political involvement is an important part of any commitment to social reform, we believe that this should not, in most cases, lead to the creation of 'Christian' political parties. There are times when no existing political party comes close to expressing the values that are at the heart of the biblical social vision and Christians have historically played a significant role in fostering new political movements or parties. Christian political parties risk compromising the witness of the church by linking the gospel to specific policies.[2] We have argued that the church has an important role in informing debate through the clear articulation of principles and in the practical expression of loving concern through various forms of social action. Specific policies, however, involve judgments where people may legitimately disagree and may be based on limited information, flawed theory, different time-horizons and constrained options. Linking the church itself to

---

2. A party based on relational principles would not face the same dangers.

policies which will inevitably result in imperfect outcomes and which will almost certainly work out more to the benefit of some groups than to others, also risks alienating people from the church. A political process divided along religious lines can also foster conflict.

Changing attitudes and values

A second element of any strategy for social reform involves changing people's thinking, culture and values. These have direct social and economic consequences and influence the policy agenda – not least through changing the political acceptability of various policy directions. Politics may shape people's aspirations but it must also reflect them. There were many factors behind the deregulation of Sunday trading.[3] The lobbying power of the large retail chains in favour of Sunday trading was certainly important, but in the end the large number of consumers who valued the convenience of shopping on Sundays more than the guarantee of a shared day off was decisive. Now that the full extent of weekend working and its negative social consequences are being felt, those values may be changing. It shows, however, that a vision of social reform dissonant with the values and priorities of much of the population is unlikely to succeed – at least in the short term. That is not to say that such battles should be avoided. Indeed, it can be argued that establishing the concept that Sunday is 'special' laid an essential foundation in the longer term campaign to change values and practice with regard to the importance of shared family time and the means by which such time may best be protected.

There are other examples where changing values and attitudes has been at the heart of social change. To a certain extent an environmental agenda can be imposed rather paternalistically by legislation and regulation. On issues where the spirit may be willing but the flesh is all too easily tempted by price and convenience, the discipline of enforcement through law and policy can be important. This requires consent, and, in the end, an environmental agenda requires people to live their lives in different ways, at a minimum in their purchasing habits and willingness to recycle, but more fundamentally by accepting constraints in such issues as the movement of goods and people.

Spiritual revival that does not reform those structures and institutions in society which influence social values may have little lasting legacy. And if we do not wish ideologies with corrosive values to shape our society, we must offer some alternative framework. The first task is to educate the church. Within the Christian community changing values is an educational and discipling process. We have argued that such values at the heart of our culture as justice, identity, security and autonomy, need to be significantly recast in the light of the biblical

---

3. This is discussed in more detail in the following chapter.

social vision. Paul's plea to the church in Rome to eschew conforming to the pattern of this world (Rom. 12:2) is as relevant for us today as when it was first written. The study and dissemination of the biblical paradigm is an essential part of this process. It provides a yardstick against which a society can be assessed, setting the reform agenda. It guides our understanding of why things are wrong and how we should approach reform. This is not a purely theological task and requires a combination of biblical and technical expertise. The paradigm can inspire the search for solutions, stretching our thinking beyond the assumptions instilled by our culture as well as motivating our engagement. In addition, studying the paradigm instils the wisdom and motivation that enable us to pursue a reforming vocation, whatever our walk of life. Within the community of the church, and possibly in new social institutions open to all, we need to develop and model new ways of living out those values.

Then we must seek to change the values and attitudes of those who do not yet share our faith (though we hope and pray that they will come to do so). Values are communicated in many ways – through the witness of our lifestyle, through the practical expression of our social concern, through artistic expression and through the various ways in which we participate in public debate. Social reform, evangelism and apologetics become closely linked at this point. Recent public debate about sexuality shows that a biblically informed position on such issues as marriage and homosexuality needs to be set in the context of a wider vision for the kind of relationships we seek in society as a whole if our voice is to be heard.

Organizational structures and working practices

Reforming organizational structures and working practices is a third element of a reform strategy. It directly addresses social needs and also offers a way into wider debates about ideology and values. Victorian reforms to working conditions, for example, were concrete expressions of wider concerns; similarly, reforming public services today reflects debates about social outcomes, the role of the state, personal responsibility and the deconcentration of political power. These debates will not be won if there are not successful examples of how values different from the prevailing ones can be put into practice. This kind of reform can come from within existing structures, with individual Christians pursuing their vocations, or from outside as a result of wider campaigns and movements. Churches, Christian organizations, organizations with Christian roots, and individuals in their personal or professional capacities all have a part to play in this aspect of social reform. This may be either explicitly faith-based engagement or involve working with, or as part of, other organizations and movements.

This kind of reform involves changing many sets of relationships. Distinctive Christian service provision is an important part of the overall witness to and service of society, but the church cannot address all the needs of society. Selected strategic involvement in neglected areas, pioneering new forms of service delivery and modelling best practice can have a wide impact. If, however, Christian involvement is not innovative, high quality and leading the field, it will not make a significant contribution to reform. And if Christian involvement is to influence the services which shape much of our society and have a profound influence on the lives of individuals and families, then it will need to be an integrated part of local systems as well as a national influence on policy and structures.

The financing, managing and delivery of public services involve many sets of relationships: central and local government; public, private and voluntary sector organizations; individual members of the public and whole communities; different professions, and so on. The current agenda of reform and modernization is fundamentally about the restructuring of these relationships. Indeed, getting the relationships right will be the critical factor in delivering the desired improvements. This will need to include long-term measures to address those changes to family and community relationships that put services under pressure. New relationships will need to arise between government, the public and professions, and will need to frame expectations and accountability without distorting activity.

Relationships are perhaps most immediately important for such vulnerable groups as children, the frail elderly, the homeless, or people with learning disabilities. They often have complex, interrelated needs requiring input from different organizations and professions and are less able to negotiate for themselves the cracks in the system. For them, the relationships within our public services can literally be a matter of life and death. The inquiry into the death of Victoria Climbié highlighted twelve missed opportunities to take action which might have prevented her death. Systemic failures of relationships within and between organizations were a major factor contributing to her death (Meads and Ashcroft et al. 2005). There are six main relationships for health and social-care professionals that are, increasingly, the key to both professional and organizational status and legitimacy. These are the relationship with your own profession, with other professions, with patients, with the wider public, with partners in delivery, and with policy actors (or their proxies).[4] This requires more than just good interpersonal skills; it also critically depends on the strategy, working practices and cultures of the organizations involved. If Christians, as part of their contribution to social reform, are to shape this collaborative environment, then they will need to find ways in which their vision for society, and for the services in which they work, can influence the definitions of quality, the outcomes

---

4. This is drawn from an international primary care project to which the Relationships Foundation, an associated charity of the Jubilee Centre, was a partner. See further, Meads and Ashcroft et al. (2005).

that are sought, and the patterns of accountability that are developed. Christian service provision can be distinctive, but cannot be disengaged from integrated local systems.

Peace-building[5]

Conflicts within and between nations make it all but impossible to address underlying social and economic concerns. Building a common vision for the future and creating just economic and political structures that remove the roots of conflict are important in creating the conditions for longer term developmental reform. Peacebuilding is, therefore, a fourth element of a strategy for social reform. For Christians involved in peace-building, the biblical paradigm offers a vision of a society designed to promote peace and well-being. Such a vision cannot be imposed on participants and needs to be articulated as a potentially shared vision.

Relief and conflict resolution are too easily seen as distinct categories. But if relief is delivered in a conflict situation, it can be co-opted by one or other side fuelling nascent conflict.[6] On the other hand, conflict can often not be resolved without a reciprocal and synchronized alleviation of the immediate needs of the affected populations. Development and peace-building differ from relief and conflict resolution in that they address the wider structural causal issues behind the immediate symptoms.

Peacemakers need to gain the trust of all the principal disputants, showing concern to each of them, even to those with whom they disagree. And while they cannot and must not remain morally neutral, they must be careful not to allow themselves to be co-opted into the political strategy of any party. Peacemakers can act as catalysts in gaining the trust of the principals and helping to create channels for dialogue in the pre-negotiation phase. They can continue to help maintain the channel for communications informally while negotiations are taking place, and then act to defuse tensions and help repair breakdowns of trust in the implementation of the settlement. At the same time, and in parallel, they can help to develop and disseminate a common framework for peace as a point of reference to transcend particular party demands, and as a way of suggesting a just

---

5. This section draws heavily on material originally prepared by Jeremy Ive. See also ch. 14, above.

6. In recognition of this, World Vision has embarked on the Local Capacity for Peace methodology within its complex humanitarian and relief programme. This is a set of tools for the design, implementation and evaluation stages to identify how 'dividers' and 'connectors' can be promoted or demoted within project interventions, thus supporting a 'do no harm' outcome.

basis on which diverse and conflicting concerns can be resolved. This can be available to the parties during the negotiation process, and in the implementation can contribute to the building-up of an ethos transcending racial, class or ideological differences.

For consensus-building, the backing of a number of key religious leaders and other public figures will be needed from across racial, social, ideological and religious divides. Just as vital, if not more so, will be the building upwards from within the communities themselves, of a general, and easily grasped set of concepts to inform the debate. Common frameworks of values applied to specific areas of the political, economic and social structures will need to be widely agreed as being the right basis for a future dispensation. Then, when negotiations take place, there will not be a vacuum, but basic concepts of sufficiently non-partisan character to be adopted by the respective principals without undermining their bargaining positions. Relationism can provide just these frameworks and concepts.

A movement of people

Recruiting, nurturing and resourcing 'agents of change' is perhaps the most important aspect of any strategy for social reform. This was the discipling approach taken by Jesus, with no particular concern to attract people in positions of influence. This is a long-term process as it may require changing habits and values, gaining knowledge and experience in a variety of academic disciplines and spheres of life, as well as building up the networks of personal relationships through which influence can be brought to bear.

There is a need for a group of Christians, guided and inspired by the biblical paradigm, at the heart of a movement. But there is also a case for nurturing a wider movement of people: this extends influence as well as creating opportunities for evangelism in the context of working together around shared concerns. This wider movement will be more diverse and inclusive, with less of a set agenda for change, relying on the quality and calibre of the people involved and the opportunities open to them. This may result in less control of the outcomes, but the outcomes may be greater than if we seek to retain too close control.

The potential for Relationism

Each of the aspects of social reform described above has illustrated that seeking to reform society, as opposed to seeking to act as disengaged witnesses, requires us at times to forge a shared agenda. This may not be the main role of the church, but for individual Christians and for para-church agencies it will be an important aspect of their everyday work.

This shared agenda may be developed in three stages. The first involves agreement on the importance of relationships as a point of connection. In this context it is then possible to offer a relational perspective on different areas of life, illustrating how the concern for relationships might influence policy and practice. So, for example, it is possible to talk about relational business, focusing on the contribution of relationships to competitive advantage, innovation, risk management and process improvement. At this level it does not include normative statements about business structure and operation. In a similar vein it is possible to talk about justice, health, education or family policy in relational terms. The second stage involves offering a normative account of relationships in each of these areas informed by the biblical paradigm. We may expect this to be supported by those of other faiths or none. The final stage is to show how these sets of norms can be drawn together into a coherent vision for society which can serve as an alternative to other '-isms' that hold sway.

A relational perspective

Relationships influence the psychological and physiological well-being of individuals. The psychological benefits of relationships are seen in their contribution to happiness, identity, self-worth and belonging (Argyle 1996). Good relationships are linked to healthier lifestyles, reduced stress levels (stress being clearly linked to a wide range of negative physiological consequences) and the positive benefits of social support. These benefits are interdependent, with committed relationships likely to offer security in a number of areas: emotional, physical and financial. The flip-side of this is, of course, the pain and costs of broken or dysfunctional relationships.

Research suggests that marriage, for example, provides as much happiness as an extra £60,000 in your bank account, increases life expectancy by three years and enables greater accumulation of wealth (Wilson & Oswald 2002). The benefits are not confined only to the marriage partners. The health, happiness, behaviour and educational achievement of children are affected by parental relationships. Family relationships in turn have significant implications for society, both social (e.g. through their capacity to affect anti-social and criminal behaviour) and financial (e.g. the value of informal care provided by the family). Further, to regard the importance of relationships with family and friends as pure 'motherhood and apple pie' risks missing their significant and, at times, challenging implications for personal lifestyle, public policy and service provision. The structure of relationships in a society, not simply the quality of individual interactions, must be attended to if the benefits of relationships are to be realized fully. The dividends of relationships cannot in the long run be divorced from the obligations and responsibilities they entail.

A relational perspective on place, roots and community illustrates how the biblical paradigm can open up a constructive discussion without necessarily taking it to the stage of offering relational norms. In Part 2 we suggested that an important aspect of biblical teaching on land was the concern to protect geographically rooted communities which were supportive of families, able to provide welfare, and both politically and economically strong. In the West today we are ambivalent about community, viewing it nostalgically but committed to a culture of choice and mobility that erodes it. Community sounds good, but in practice we may often use our wealth to buy more privacy and independence and less community – or at least settle for the comfortable community chosen on our own terms where the immediate personal benefits significantly outweigh any risks, costs and obligations.

Some have celebrated the anonymous freedom of the city as an antidote to the stifling conformity of close-knit communities. The link between place and relationship can have dangers when relationship divides become geographically expressed. The ghettoization of communities can reinforce separation and mutual suspicion. This may happen at a micro-level with 'gated communities' insulating themselves from the local community, or at a larger scale along ethnic lines. Yet the absence of community can mean loneliness, isolation and public spaces emptied through fear of crime. In so many little ways, dealing with acquaintances is easier than dealing with strangers or 'others', both through the positive pleasures of human interaction as well as the avoidance of friction in the cogs of daily life.

As well as the personal benefits, community presents the potential for effective collective action in response to local issues and problems. CCTV cameras are no substitute for community relationships in tackling crime and anti-social behaviour. Indeed a focus on relationships can deal with the causes of crime, not just deter people from offending. Living communities provide the networks of informal social care and support without which we face the prospect of a lonely atomized society. Without robust communities and a thriving civic society very little remains between the individual and state provision. Flexibility and effectiveness in response to local issues are lost as a result.

The physical attributes of places and our attachment to them are important for family, community and business relationships. Place influences who we meet and the nature of the encounter, as well as providing the roots and stability without which relationships can be difficult to sustain. In a society where hyper-mobility erodes geographical attachment and where planning has too often ignored the social context of place it is no surprise that relationships are under pressure. A lack of roots contributes to weaker communities, reduces levels of social support, makes neighbourhoods less safe, is less healthy and can increase exclusion and polarization (Spencer 2002b). It is worth noting here that community is an essential foundation for Christian mission. It is difficult to be a witness to neighbours we never see, to evangelize those we barely know. To be salt and light is not to be a temporary, uncommitted, fleeting and flickering presence. It means being rooted in and committed to communities. In a society that promotes the cultural and economic benefits of hyper-mobility, this can be hard to sustain (Spencer 2002b).

There are some signs of change, although mobility is still too often regarded as an economic good without regard to its social consequences. Architecture and town planning are rediscovering the importance of place, recognizing its influence on opportunities to meet. This is seen, for example, in the concept of 'defensible space' in response to the petty vandalism of spaces between buildings for which no-one has a sense of ownership. Pavements can be designed to encourage people to linger and meet. The horizontal relationships over the garden fence are less easy to replicate in the high-rise block unless careful attention is given to entrances and foyers.

Town planning can strengthen community identity or destroy its heart. The culture of the car can weaken neighbourhood attachment as we drive to the out-of-town store. Walking to the local shop increases the likelihood of meeting people you know, whether *en route* or in store. These 'multiplex' relationships with overlapping spheres do much to strengthen community. This is not to say that superstores are necessarily bad in relational terms. But it illustrates the point that even choices about where to shop influence relationships. We need to consider whether little by little we are eroding the relational environment.

Relational norms

Going beyond a relational perspective and drawing on the biblical paradigm, it is possible to offer a normative account for relationships in different areas of life. Examples of this include theories of relational justice, relational healthcare and relational finance. To treat these areas of public life normatively involves defining the goals in relational terms, as well as examining the ways in which key relationships need to operate in order to achieve these goals. So, for example, criminal justice can be defined not in terms of simply retribution or rehabilitation, but in terms of resolving the relationships between victims and offenders, and between offenders and society. In order for this to be achieved we need to look at how family and community relationship breakdown are conducted to address the relational causes of crime, as well as the relationships within and between all the various agencies (together with their relationships with the public) in preventing crime and solving crimes, in the judicial process, in punishing offenders, and in the course of their reintegration into society. Chapter 13 has set out the key biblical principles which should govern these relationships.

As chapters 11 and 12 have shown, money, finance and economics are not relationally neutral and lie at the heart of most political ideologies. Marx described the problem thus: 'The bourgeoisie . . . has left remaining no other nexus between man and man than naked self interest, than callous "cash payment"' (see Ferguson 2001: viii). Finance creates relationships between, for example, lenders and borrowers or investors and managers. Different forms of finance influence the nature of these relationships. Equity and debt finance, for example, lead to different distributions of risk and reward. Finance may also reflect the quality of the underlying relationships with, for example, trust and knowledge of the customer reducing the risk premium. Finance can also act as a relational amplifier. When relationships are strained, whether in businesses or families, financial issues can exacerbate conflict. On the other hand, financial reciprocity can strengthen relationships with common financial interests acting as a form of social glue.

At a personal level the use of money creates relationships, influences the nature of those relationships and can become a reductionist measure of value.[7] Most of us have many choices in the ways in which we use our money. We can use it in ways that strengthen both our immediate direct relationships as well as the wider network of contingent relationships we are drawn into through financial transactions. Barter depends upon personal interactions, but money enables more complex chains of relationships to be sustained that separate producer and ultimate consumer. The development of financial systems can also introduce greater distance in our relationships: a loan from a family member to help with a house purchase is very different from a loan from a building society that is backed up by many unknown people's savings. Money also shapes and reflects the power-dynamics of relationships. A personal loan can be a generous act to help those in need or become an instrument of oppressive control. The age-old nature of this problem is illustrated by warnings in the book of Proverbs about both debt and offering security for a neighbour, alongside praise for those who lend generously to the needy (e.g. Prov. 6:1; 22:7).

The structure of organizations is also important. There are significant relational consequences to separating ownership and responsibility through the mechanism of limited liability. Perhaps most obvious is the relationship between investors and directors, and the impact this has on other stakeholder relationships (see ch. 11 and Schluter 2000). At a higher level the relational impact of finance is seen most obviously in such issues as globalization and international debt. Part of the current concern about global Capitalism is the extent to which finance and relationships can become divorced. Protected by limited liability and technologically capable of instant transfer, capital can flow between countries and regions without regard to the relational consequences of the economic impact. A concern for relationships is not helped by economic naivety. Pragmatism as well

---

7. For a more extensive discussion, see Spencer (2003b).

as idealism is a necessary part of social reform. We can and should seek to build a concern for relationships into the economic equation, not simply leave them to evolve in response to decisions guided by other concerns and pick up the pieces afterwards.

The set of principles below is an illustration of how, informed by the biblical paradigm, an understanding of the impact of finance on relationships can be developed into norms.

Ten relational principles for corporate structure [8]

In a Judaeo-Christian understanding, personal relationships are the key to community, family and individual well-being. Flows of funds directly create certain relationships and indirectly influence a much wider network of relationships. The decisions of owners of capital, and the actions of the institutions that control these funds, are therefore not ethically neutral. They need to be evaluated by reference to their relational impact and, specifically, by reference to the following principles:

1. It is a fundamental human responsibility to ensure efficient and responsible use of resources. The exercise of choice in economic affairs is an expression of human dignity and responsibility.
2. The purpose of a business is to serve its stakeholders, including owners of capital, employees, customers, suppliers and the wider community, and in so doing to ensure an expected return which is sufficient to attract and retain the capital employed.
3. When owners of capital take risks, such rewards as they receive for their risk-taking are acceptable relationally because the prosperity of business serves the interests of society as a whole.
4. Those who own, control, have an interest in, or provide finance for an asset or a business have a moral responsibility regarding the way in which that asset is used or the business is conducted. In particular, they need to have regard for the relational impact of its use or conduct.
5. Owners of capital have a duty to pay employees the agreed remuneration on time and in the agreed manner, and to respect employees' religious and family commitments. However, they do not necessarily have a duty to share profits, although profit-sharing is often of mutual benefit.

---

8. These draft principles were written by a working group on relational finance as part of a series of discussions looking at reform of the PLC.

6. Risk-sharing in financial and business contracts is likely to promote parity, whereas contracts that seek to place all or most of the risk on one party are likely to have the reverse effect.[9]

7. It is important to promote parity in bargaining power so as to reduce the opportunity for exploitation and bullying in competitive business relationships, such as those with suppliers and customers.

8. In principle, all obligations, including debts and tax liabilities, should be honoured. Business practices that undermine this are likely to lead to a breakdown of trust within society.

9. A fair or just price requires a competitive market. So the rules governing corporate and market structure should protect and encourage a competitive market environment.

10. If society provides legal privileges for a specific corporate form (such as legal personality or limited liability), then reciprocal obligations are incurred by a business using that corporate form towards society as a whole.

Relationism

The main concern of this book has been to explore the potential of a paradigmatic understanding of biblical teaching in order to provide the basis for an alternative to Capitalism (the dominant economic and social philosophy) and its associated cultures of individualism and materialism. This goes beyond offering a relational perspective or individual relational norms and seeks to provide a more comprehensive and coherent alternative. The development of Relationism as an expression of the biblical paradigm is a continuing task.[10] In order to illustrate the potential for Relationism, a working example of how the *Jubilee Manifesto* might be presented as a relational manifesto is given below. Any attempt to do this is, of course, provisional and will rightly vary according to the different issues facing different societies.

---

9. In some circumstances, the imbalance in the relationship will be so great that the financial arrangement is unacceptable (cf. the biblical prohibition of interest) but this is not the inevitable consequence of a contract that transfers a significant amount of risk (cf. an insurance contract). In all cases, the totality of the relationship has to be considered (e.g. it is necessary to consider the impact of bankruptcy laws on lending relationships).

10. The term 'Relationism' was used in the Jubilee Centre's first articulation of the biblical paradigm in 1986 and first proposed as a theory of political economy in Schluter & Lee (1993).

A vision for a relational society

Personal and social well-being depends upon the quality of relationships within families and communities, and within and between organizations. We believe that building a society that sustains relationships requires recognizing the importance of:

1. **Family networks – for the love, support and welfare of the individual.**
   Stable family life benefits adults and children in terms of both emotional and practical support. Families have a wide range of care and welfare responsibilities, particularly for children, partners and elderly relatives. The extended family has a vital role in supporting marriage and the nuclear family, particularly when under pressure, and as a mediating institution between individuals and the state.
2. **Personal and family rootedness – to build strong communities.**
   Rootedness involves spending significant lengths of time in cities, towns and neighbourhoods, a sense of belonging and practical involvement. Rootedness is important for personal well-being, access to support networks, and for the ability to participate fully in community life.
3. **A shared culture – to foster inclusion and cohesion.**
   A shared culture which can embrace diversity and includes respect for liberty of conscience is needed to support both cohesion and inclusion.
4. **Justice and reconciliation – as the basis for achieving peace and social harmony.**
   This applies to personal, corporate, regional, ethnic and international relationships. Building peace requires encouraging reconciliation, restoring relationships, and addressing the many factors which contribute to their breakdown.
5. **The wide distribution of political power and economic assets – to promote accountability and community development.**
   Distant decision-making and financial dependence can inhibit both responsiveness to local needs and responsibility for addressing them. The desire for greater local responsibility can be in tension with the concern for ensuring quality and equity at a wider level. Where decisions or controls need to be located at higher levels, this should be done in ways that support local capacity and responsibility.
6. **The use of money and other resources, and the structuring of financial systems – to foster healthy commercial, social and international relations.**
   Finance shapes relationships in many ways, for example, through the impact of debt, capital flows, investment and spending patterns. Ownership involves responsibilities, and resources should be used in ways that strengthen relationships rather than undermining them.

7. **Influencing organizations to think relationally – to uphold an environment in which relationships thrive.**
   Relationships can be fostered or undermined by public and private sector organizations' policies and actions. The strategy, structure, culture and working practices of an organization should be conducive to the flourishing of relationships, both within that organization and in wider society.

8. **Fulfilling duties – particularly to those who are disadvantaged either relationally or materially.**
   Rights must be balanced by duties and obligations. People are responsible for their own relationships and for the impact of their actions on others. Relationship deprivation is as serious as material deprivation, and there is a particular duty of care to those who lack supportive relationships.

This vision carries with it a challenge to such ideologies as Socialism, Capitalism, individualism and Nationalism. The extent to which it might represent a distinctive body of thinking can be illustrated by contrasting Relationism and Capitalism.[11] Few countries today are wedded to Socialism. Capitalism is the dominant economic paradigm. It operates in a materialistic and individualistic culture where relationships are increasingly juridified, suggesting that political and legal philosophy, as well as sociological changes, are important drivers of society. Nevertheless, in highlighting a single counterpoint to a biblical framework for society, the global influence of Capitalism merits particular attention. The substance of the difference is set out in the chapters of Part 2, with chapters 11 and 12 offering the most direct contrast. Here, we simply summarize some of the reasons why a relational alternative is needed.

Capitalism is a difficult word to define. At its most limited, it may be used to describe a free and unhindered market economy, and, strictly speaking, Capitalism has nothing to say about the cultural context and institutions in which it is embedded. However, the emphasis on consumer choice, and the opportunity for entrepreneurial activity, both point to the need for parallel political freedoms. And it is surely no coincidence that the countries which gave rise to Capitalism at the same time tackled the hegemony of centralized political autocracy. Also, Capitalism requires not just free and unhindered product markets, but also free markets for the 'factors of production' – land, labour and capital. Allowing the exchange of land title to the highest bidder, and to allow or even facilitate the uprooting of families and individuals so as to relocate close to where work is available, inevitably leads to a

---

11. This section draws heavily on material drafted by Michael Schluter.

pattern of social relations fundamentally different from those in traditional societies.

While recognizing there are marked differences between societies such as the US and Sweden, both described as Capitalist but giving very different roles to government, we believe that a broad definition of Capitalism – including its culture – is helpful.

We might describe modern Capitalism as that societal structure:

- in which the legal order, the prevailing public morality, as well as the organization of socio-economic life grant unobstructed admission to the forces of economic growth and technological development; and
- in which those forces subsequently manifest themselves by way of a process of 'natural selection' as that is given shape by a continual competition in the market between independent production units organized on the basis of returns to capital. (Goudzwaard 1978: 11)

No definition of Capitalism is easily complete. Arguably, this definition fails to note the close association between economic and political freedoms, and thus does not address the form in which Capitalism is most frequently experienced today, that is 'democratic Capitalism'.

So if we need big ideas, what is wrong with 'democratic Capitalism'? It has Christian roots as it developed in Western Europe at a time when Christianity was the dominant religious belief-system. It embodies many important Christian ideas, such as the emphasis on stewardship of resources and the value of every individual in the sight of God. Capitalism has been so successful at generating wealth, and thus transforming the everyday life of huge numbers of people on the planet, that Francis Fukuyama believes that no other system is either necessary or feasible (Fukuyama 1993). Specifically, democratic Capitalism has been defended by Michael Novak (1990) as consistent with the teaching of the Judaeo-Christian on three main grounds:

1. Democratic Capitalism offers an economic system, based on competition under law to channel self-interest into the service of others and to promote human creativity as the key to ending poverty.
2. As a political system it emphasizes constitutional checks and balances to protect ordered rights and to avoid abuse of power.
3. It is a moral and cultural system which ensures a pluralistic, open, tolerant society with a vital and dynamic ethos.

Who could quarrel with any ideology which delivered such outcomes, and which is based on such values? However, the fruits of the Capitalist system seem far away from its Judaeo-Christian roots, such as they were, in a number of crucial respects. Mobility of labour, personal indebtedness and long working hours are some of the contributory factors in the gradual breakdown of family and community relationships, so fundamental to the Judaeo-Christian social vision, in every country which has embraced the Capitalist system on a long-term basis. The underlying cause of this relational disintegration arguably lies in an associated culture which attaches greater importance to material possessions than to human relationships.

The mechanics of this relational disintegration are not difficult to trace. The mobility of labour associated with the transformation of the economy from being predominantly agricultural to primarily industrial has resulted in a massive disruption to family and community relationships as people have moved in large numbers from the countryside to the towns. In the absence of effective constraints on land markets in rural areas, many families have been dispossessed of their land due to harvest fluctuations and debt, and the lack of long-term spatial planning in the cities to which such people move has exacerbated the relational disruption of this mobility. This social dislocation has tended to lead to a gradual weakening of religious belief-systems, and thus of the moral framework which underpins marriage and other close family relationships.[12] What is hard to discern is to what extent, and in what ways, modernization (sociologically and economically) could occur if the religious and philosophical framework were to be Relationist rather than Capitalist.

The time period over which family and community relationship-breakdown occurs depends on many factors, and is measured generally in centuries rather than decades. Relevant factors include the settledness of the population and the nature of the prevailing belief-systems prior to the onset of Capitalism, the degree of political upheaval associated with these social and economic changes, and the speed of transition from a village-based to an urban-based economy. The consequences of this damage to the relational infrastructure are only gradually being appreciated, but include a workforce often lacking relational and community-building skills, and without the emotional stability required for sustained productivity. In addition, the resulting lack of trust in society undermines the effective working of markets which depend on such trust, and adds to transaction costs such as legal fees (North 1990).

By establishing a set of social conditions that undermines family and community cohesion, Capitalism is, in effect, cutting off the branch it is sitting on. Not only will markets cease to operate as they should, but the growth of public spending required to meet the costs of social services, health services, education and criminal

---

12. Chs. 9 and 10 set out the alternative biblical vision for the nexus of family, land and welfare.

justice for a population which increasingly lacks core relational skills is likely to become unsustainable.

Chapters 11 and 12 demonstrate in more detail how biblical teaching on the ban on interest, treatment of debt and control of factor markets challenges some of the key assumptions of our current economic system. However, we should also ask whether the moral foundations on which Capitalism is built are sustainable. The growing list of scandals in major corporates over the past few years in Europe and the United States raises questions about the future of Capitalism as we know it today.[13] The extent to which management have looted companies, stealing from shareholders and employees, suggests that the problem is greater than a few loopholes in the structure of corporate governance. Arguably, without the moral imperative deriving from Christian theology and belief, it is impossible to derive a governance structure which provides effective protection against theft on a grand scale. Equally, the anonymity of shareholders and the short-term nature of most top-level corporate appointments fail to provide sufficient disincentives to prevent large Western corporates from abusing their power in low-income countries.

There are other concerns being expressed, too, about the sustainability of Capitalist economies, this time in terms of environmental issues. The emphasis on individual freedom and choice does not engender a culture that is willing to accept the self-restraint necessary for the long-term preservation of the planet. The number of environmentally induced catastrophes is likely to increase sharply in the years ahead, acting as a wake-up call that Capitalism and its culture need at the very least a significant overhaul to take more explicit account of their negative impact on the environment. In addition, the spread of wealth to countries currently classified as middle or low income will further increase pressure on the ecosystem. A very different pattern of economic and social organization will be needed to prevent further global warming, ensure sufficient water in hot climates for larger populations and reduce the dangers of terrorist attack using nuclear or biological weapons.

Conclusion

Christians need to be involved in social reform. There are many options for engagement, but where Christians are a minority (and arguably even when a majority) and seek to change society as a whole, a shared agenda must be forged. Buying into an agenda set by others risks undue distortion of the biblical

---

13. See, for example, the 'scandal sheet' as listed in *The Economist* on 28 June 2003 ('Survey of Capitalism and Democracy', p. 7).

framework for society. A minimalist option is to use the language of relationships to translate and engage. Offering a relational perspective on a wide range of issues opens up constructive possibilities for debate. However, in order to retain the coherence of the biblical framework it is possible to take a step further and seek to offer an integrated normative account of the relationships that we should seek in society and how they can be sustained. Examples of a number of these strategies can be found in the case-studies in the next chapter.

17. Case-studies

Michael Schluter

The framework of political, economic and social thought outlined in Part 2 is not simply a theory to be admired for its coherence and consistency. It is not a dead letter. Rather, it has been given by God as a source of inspiration to energize and guide the church in its search for solutions to the problems faced in societies in any place and at any stage in their history. As argued in Part 1, Jesus himself teaches his disciples that in the tradition of the prophets, they are to act as salt and light in society using 'The Law and the Prophets' as their agenda in seeking social change (Matt. 5:11–20). So from the beginning, the Jubilee Centre was established not just to study the biblical text, but to apply it.

In this chapter, the Jubilee Centre's experience of the process of that application will be explored. Why were specific projects chosen, how did they relate to the Centre's understanding of the biblical text, how were they funded, and what was achieved – and is still being achieved now? This is a story of taking biblical ideas and applying them to a specific society today. There were failures as well as successes. Christians are called to do what they can; granting success is God's prerogative.

The context for this endeavour has been a period of retrenchment for the church in the UK. Most denominations have been in steady decline during the period since 1983 when the Jubilee Centre was established. As a result, campaigns and initiatives were undertaken in a wider social environment increasingly indifferent, or even hostile, to Christian values – unlike much of the period of Christian social reform in the nineteenth century. However, there were other Christian initiatives running in parallel over this period providing increasing opportunities for co-operation and mutual support. These included, for example, CARE (originally established as the National Festival of Light in 1973), the renewed Evangelical Alliance, the London Institute for Contemporary Christianity, Maranatha, Family Matters and, more recently, the Christian Institute. There are also many Christian agencies and professional groups working in specific sectors. Each has its own theological framework informing its initiatives. Each has made an important contribution in its own way to Christian social reform, but as with the Jubilee Centre, each has found it difficult to have an impact on national social trends.

Criteria for issue selection

One obvious approach to implementing the broad social agenda set out in Part 2 would be to start a political party based on relational ideas, a 'Relationist party'.[1] This option was not seriously considered in the early 1980s, given the known difficulty of new political parties in Western democracies having much impact, and also because relational thinking was in its infancy. So the Jubilee Centre decided to start with specific policy issues: the problem was which to tackle first.

An ideal but impractical approach to setting reform priorities might be to spend a number of years studying the Bible to grasp both in broad contour and in detail the nature of the biblical framework, and then to spend a number of years analysing the ideologies, structures and operating practices of society today. This would make it possible to identify initiatives likely to have the greatest strategic impact in terms of transforming public life to conform more closely to the biblical pattern. It might also be possible to identify which initiative would have the greatest chance of success. A Christian reform group would then research in detail selected issues and seek funding to take action. In practice, of course, it would be impossible to assemble such an overview, although a committee of Christians from different parts of public life, with a group of specialists in biblical social teaching, might approximate to it.

The Jubilee Centre's experience was some way from this ideal. The initial team started with a shortlist of key issues which came from eight years of personal study of the biblical text which preceded the establishment of the Jubilee Centre. However, the choice of specific issues was driven by the immediate social and

---

1. A 'Relationist party' does not have the same problems inherent in Christian political parties, set out in the Jubilee Centre's magazine, *Engage* (October 2003). See Jubilee Centre website: <http://www.jubilee-centre.org>.

political situation faced at the time, with little attempt at a social overview. The Jubilee Centre was founded in 1983, but was galvanized into campaigning as early as 1985 by a parliamentary bill brought forward by the Conservative government to deregulate Sunday trading. This bill threatened a 1,000-year legal tradition in the UK of restricting commercial activity so as to keep one day each week free for religious and family priorities.

The Centre has focused its research over the last twenty years on issues that seemed most important to the long-term support and revitalization of family and community relationships. These issues included mobility of labour, ways to give extended families an economic role or function, criminal justice, health and healthcare and reform of corporate structures. As none of these presented obvious opportunities in the short-term for fundable projects, bringing about change has involved background research on both biblical teaching and the contemporary social and policy realities, consultation with those in positions of influence, and a search for opportunities for practical engagement. This research has led to a number of books and research papers, first by the Jubilee Centre and *Cambridge Papers* exploring the issues from a biblical perspective and then from the Relationships Foundation exploring the application to contemporary society from a relational perspective. A list of these publications is on the Jubilee Centre and Relationships Foundation websites.[2]

Organizational development

As explained in chapter 1, the first charity to be set up was the Jubilee Centre, established as a Christian research group in Cambridge in 1983. Its mission statement gradually evolved to the following: 'The Jubilee Centre believes there is a biblical pattern for society. Its goal is to study it, disseminate it, and apply it to specific issues in Britain and overseas.'[3] The 'application' aspect was later taken over largely by the Relationships Foundation, as described below.

Next in time sequence was the Keep Sunday Special Campaign, set up in 1985 but not registered as a charity because it was established to fight a campaign, in Parliament and in the courts. After the defeat of the Sunday trading deregulation bill in 1986, the Newick Park Initiative was developed as a consultation process to contribute to peace-building in South Africa. This was quickly followed by Familybase, registered as a charity with the goal of strengthening extended families. It had a broad agenda of six main objectives which were intended

---

2. <http://www.jubilee-centre.org>; <http://www.relationshipsfoundation.org>.

3. Ezra's goals, we discovered later, were remarkably similar (see Ezra 7:10).

to apply six major themes from the biblical paradigm. The six issues were as follows:

1. Debt trap action
2. Regions revitalized
3. Enforced mobility checked
4. Allowances for family carers
5. Mergers restricted
6. Sundays safeguarded for the whole family

The reasons for the shift from the Familybase theme and name to the Relationships Foundation in 1993 were twofold. First, the theme of 'families' did not reflect the biblical concern for all kinds of relationships in society; more specifically, it made it difficult to reflect the Christian understanding of the centrality of Christ in all things. Secondly, the theme of family did not resonate with large numbers of those we were meeting with, both inside and outside the Christian constituency, perhaps because their experience of family was often so negative.

To focus attention on the relationships dimension of public life, the first step was to set out a coherent social vision for a secular audience based on the research findings of the previous eighteen years. *The R Factor* was published in 1993, and was widely reviewed in the British press.[4] This new framework for public policy was named 'Relationism', as the aim was to set out in the broadest terms an alternative to Capitalism and Socialism, and to individualism and materialism. Rather than pointing explicitly to its biblical sources, it was written to reflect Christian values, so as to be as inclusive as possible. Likewise, the Relationships Foundation was established not as a Christian organization, but as an organization 'based on the ethical values of the Judaeo-Christian tradition'.

In 1994, the team made a strategic decision to develop a track-record of sector-specific initiatives before seeking to promote the wider relational vision and challenge contemporary ideologies in the media. The first project was to examine the criminal justice system from a relational perspective and explore ways to bring about change in key areas of policy and practice. The biblical case for doing this has been set out in chapter 13. In Jubilee House the team carried out the biblical research, and then 'translated' the results of that research so as to address in secular language the major issues confronting British criminal justice policy. A book entitled *Relational Justice* was published in 1994,[5] a series of essays on various

---

4. Schluter & Lee (1993); reviewed by *The Economist, Financial Times, Times Literary Supplement,* and *The Guardian,* amongst others.
5. Baker & Burnside (1994).

aspects of the criminal justice system, demonstrating that the goal as well as the ethos and working practices of the system could be defined in relational terms. This was followed by a quarterly *Relational Justice Bulletin*.[6]

The RF team then faced a choice. They could focus their limited resources for the next few years on different aspects of the criminal justice system, working alongside those promoting the similar but distinct concept of restorative justice,[7] or could move on to other sectors to demonstrate the general applicability of the relational approach to public life. This was a hard decision. However, given a fundamental commitment to 'Relationism' as the big idea to reflect the comprehensive nature of the biblical social paradigm, and with the encouragement of some key supporters, they chose to begin new work in the health sector.

Having demonstrated the relevance and power of the relational approach to both the criminal justice and health sectors, the team decided that it would be better to look at the future of public services as a whole rather than to multiply detailed case-studies in either sector. As primarily a 'think tank', there were not the necessary consulting skills in-house to seek out and implement consulting contracts using the relational audit tools developed for use in the justice and health care sectors.[8] There was also the danger that as the Relationships Foundation was a small group, Relationism could be lost within a huge institution like the NHS, and the rest of public life would never then come under relational scrutiny. So, building on experience in the criminal justice and health sectors, at the time of writing the Relationships Foundation is seeking next to address the relational issues that cut across all areas of the public services through a series of public-service consultations.

In addition to the work on public services, the Relationships Foundation has developed several practical projects to build relationships in a number of quite different contexts. The peace-building work described below considers inter-ethnic and inter-political group relationships and has developed into a new charity called Concordis International.[9] Another Relationships Foundation initiative to tackle urban unemployment is described below. To issue financial 'bonds' in such a way as to satisfy government regulatory requirements, it was necessary to set up an Industrial and Provident Society, which we called City*life*,[10] and which was

---

6. The *Relational Justice Bulletin* can be obtained from the Relationships Foundation website, at <http://www.relationshipsfoundation.org>.

7. For further information on restorative and relational justice, and the differences between them, see Burnside and Schluter (2003).

8. These relational health audit tools are discussed on pp. 321ff.

9. See <http://www.concordis-international.org>.

10. <http://www.citylifeltd.org>.

registered with the Inland Revenue as a charity. Most recently, the Relationships Foundation has started an initiative called Keep Time for Children,[11] which aims to focus the attention of both policy-makers and parents on the importance of time given to children, especially at weekends.

The Relationships Foundation has also carried out several significant research studies, such as an exploration into family associations, or savings syndicates, as a way to give a greater financial role to extended families and local communities. Also, research has started with a group of specialists in company law and finance into designing an alternative structure for large-scale business operations which will conform more closely to relational values than the public limited company (PLC).[12] Through all of these pieces of research and practical initiatives, it is gradually becoming possible to discern the contours of what a genuinely 'relational society' might look like today.

We shall now examine in more depth five case-studies of initiatives that find their origins in the agenda set out in Part 2, in each case exploring the theological rationale as well as the funding, strategic alliances and other pragmatic considerations.

Case-study 1: The Sunday campaign

Britain has had laws restricting commercial activity on Sundays since King Alfred in around AD970. The most recent law prior to recent 'reforms' was passed in 1950, and listed goods that could not be sold on Sundays (similar to the 'blue laws' in the US). In the mid-1980s, the Conservative government decided these laws should be repealed, partly because they represented, in their view, unnecessary regulation and perhaps partly in response to financial support from some large retailers. No-one disputed that the laws needed updating to reflect changes in trading conditions since 1950, but many did not think they should be abolished. Following a Committee of Enquiry which published its results in 1984 (The Auld Committee), legislation for total deregulation was brought forward in 1985.

Connection with the biblical framework

On the surface of it, the weekly day of rest appears central to the biblical social vision; the Sabbath is, after all, one of the Ten Commandments and thus at the heart of biblical law. However, it is not quite as simple as that. The Sabbath in the Old Testament was a sign of the unique covenant between God and Israel; hence the death penalty for its non-observance (Exod. 31:12–17). The New

---

11. <http://www.keeptimeforchildren.org.uk>.
12. See chapter 16 (p. 297) for 'Ten relational principles for corporate structure'.

Testament had different covenantal 'signs', such as the bread and wine of the Lord's Supper. However, the Sabbath also served a social purpose. On the seventh day, 'God rested, and blessed the seventh day and made it holy' (Gen. 2:2–3). Jesus had confirmed that 'the Sabbath was made for humankind' (Mark 2:28), meaning not just for the Jews, and the church throughout its history has tried to observe Sunday as a day of rest, worship and family time whenever it has been able to do so. To put it another way, while the ceremonial and exclusivity purposes of the law have been fulfilled in Christ, the moral and civil purposes of the law are still intended as a normative guide to both social and individual behaviour.

In terms of the broader paradigm of Relationism, the setting aside of one day in seven has always been a crucial check on preoccupation with the material aspects of life, and ensures the time and space necessary for relationship priorities. The seven-day week is the main division of time which is based directly on revelation rather than the lunar and solar calendars.[13] The statements of the Sabbath law in Exodus and Deuteronomy point to three specific relational concerns. In Exodus 20:11–15, the focus is first on keeping the seventh day as 'a sabbath to the Lord your God', that is, as a day set aside for society to give priority to its relationship with God. Secondly, the Exodus text emphasizes a shared day off in the family or household, with reference back to God's rest at the end of his work of creation. Thirdly, in Deuteronomy 5:15, the reference is back to the years of slavery in Egypt, suggesting a focus on the welfare of low-income employees who are those most at risk in a seven-day work culture.

Christians in the UK were divided in their response to the government's proposals. One view was that because 'Christ is the end of the law', the Old Testament Sabbath provisions no longer were binding on Christians. Another was the 'Sabbatarian' view that Sundays were the Christian equivalent of the Jewish Sabbath. The Jubilee Centre set out its mid-way, relational position in a booklet entitled, *Why Keep Sunday Special?* (Townsend & Schluter 1985), with discussion of the economic and social arguments as well as the biblical issues. The foreword was written by an eminent biblical scholar, Sir Norman Anderson, and John Stott amongst others provided a supportive quote. The booklet seems to have played a crucial role in giving the churches the confidence to resist the government's proposals for deregulation.

The campaign
The Jubilee Centre set up a new vehicle for the running of the campaign, realizing that many potential supporters would not support its theological position. The name 'Keep Sunday Special Campaign' (KSSC) was chosen to convey the heart of

---

13. For elaboration see Mills (1998, 2002).

the message, and to capture maximum support: after all, who did not want Sunday to continue to be kept 'special'? A campaign committee was formed from bodies representing sections of the smaller retailers, churches of all denominations and the shop-workers union, USDAW. A public-relations company offered advice, and eventually a way was found to pay them from one of the supporting retail organizations. Although the press completely ignored the campaign at this stage, it quickly gathered support throughout the churches and among a huge body of small retailers, shop-workers and the public.

The campaign strategy was to focus on about 200 back-bench Conservative constituencies, especially the marginals, as an election was approaching. The government's majority over all other parties was 144, so that with the government bill opposed by the other parties the challenge was to persuade over seventy Tories to vote against the party whip. Around 180 meetings were organized in these constituencies in the weeks leading up to the vote, with an average of 150 constituents turning out to each meeting, even in the middle of winter. MPs were bombarded with letters in what became the greatest letter campaign of the 1980s. Meanwhile, the retailers seeking change did nothing. They were convinced no-one could overturn such a huge government majority at the second reading of a bill; nobody had in living memory. The Keep Sunday Special Campaign won the key parliamentary vote in 1986 by fourteen votes (out of 600 votes cast) in an extraordinary victory.[14]

However, that was not the end of the battle. The retailers wanting Sunday trading did not give up. They broadened their coalition, bringing in the major food retailers who broke the law repeatedly by opening on Sundays, and appealed to the European Court which took two years each time to reach decisions. The Conservative government, now under John Major, colluded and refused to enable local authorities to enforce the law. Thus, for five years the Keep Sunday Special Campaign's position was being eroded week by week as major retailers flouted the law with impunity. On both sides, the campaign was funded mainly by retailers, although we estimated that those wanting Sunday opening spent at least 50 times more on their campaign than those opposed, if contributions in kind as well as in cash are included. So when the issue came back to Parliament in a fresh bill in 1993 it was not surprising that the Sunday-trading retailers won. However, they won by just eighteen votes out of 600 votes cast. Except on Easter Day, large shops could now open for six hours on a Sunday, provided those hours were between 10am and 6pm.[15] Small shops could open whenever they liked. Over the

---

14. For further details of the campaign see Schluter & Lee (1987).

15. The other exception was Christmas Day; if it fell on a Sunday, large shops must remain closed.

following ten years, Sunday has become the second busiest shopping day of the week after Saturday for two-thirds of all retailers.[16]

An important lesson from this single-issue campaign is the difficulty of seeking to apply the values of the biblical paradigm without a concerted attack on the values of the wider culture. The Sunday campaign was arguing for safeguards for vulnerable employees, time for families and protection of smaller shops against a culture which focused on individual rights, consumer convenience and 'freedom to shop'. Whereas in the nineteenth century the campaign against slavery took place against the background of a mass movement to bring the gospel to every segment of the population, with growing numbers attending church even amongst the most deprived communities, the Keep Sunday Special Campaign (KSSC) was operating in a culture of declining church attendance, and with only weak attempts by the churches to question the rights-based, self-centred consumer culture. In such an environment, the KSSC was bound to lose in the end; the only question was how long it could hold out. The answer was eight years, from 1986 to 1994.

Even though the campaign was lost, there was a long-term impact on national life. Media interest in the Sunday issue continued to be strong for the ten years following the change in the law, with KSSC asked to comment whenever some new statistic came to light. KSSC became a household name such that the change in quality of life arising from Sunday becoming a busy shopping day was recognized and noted. Whether this may provide the platform required to 'turn the clock back' is still an open question.

Case-study 2: International peace-building

Background

In 1986, the Jubilee Centre initiated what is now called a 'track 2 peace-process', facilitating high-level informal talks between the ANC and the white establishment in South Africa. The South Africa programme began against the backdrop of the Second State of Emergency, with little sign of the possibility of negotiation between the largely white government and the black-majority opposition. Nelson Mandela, the leader of the African National Congress, was responding on his own personal initiative to the first tentative overtures by the South African Government, but there was no agreed basis for his release, nor about the way in which a mutually acceptable transfer of power might take place. The meetings of the Newick Park

---

16. Figures produced by Bond Pearce, commercial law firm, cited in the *Daily Express*, 26 August 2004.

Initiative (NPI) took place over a four year period, with the first meeting in March 1987. The NPI's goals were to establish informal and confidential dialogue between leading members of the ANC and the white establishment, and to explore policy options on issues constituting major stumbling blocks to formal negotiations. At the same time, the secret initiative sponsored by Consolidated Goldfields was underway. The first meeting of this took place in October 1987, involving some of the same players, followed by further meetings where the detailed arrangements for the transfer of power were agreed upon, making possible the release of Mandela, announced on 2 February 1990.

Connection with the biblical framework

At the time, the reasons for taking on this issue were primarily those of 'calling' rather than an understanding arising from systematic biblical research. However, subsequent reflection has revealed how central peace-building is in a biblical framework based on the theme of relationships. Both ethnic and family conflict are the antithesis of the intended social order. No wonder Jesus promises, 'blessed are the peacemakers, for they shall inherit the earth' (Matt. 5:8). The great vision of the prophet Micah, of a time when 'the law would go out from Zion' to the nations, focused on an end to war and conflict (Mic. 4:1–4). Shalom, a description of social harmony, is one of the core values of the biblical social order (see ch. 6).

Peace takes obvious precedence over other economic and social priorities. It is not possible, generally, to reform land tenure or the criminal justice system, to tackle unemployment or to strengthen family and community networks, while a nation's attention and energy is focused on war or internal control. The most significant intervention for the most vulnerable, and the most effective use of scarce external resources, in most cases is the pursuit of peace-building initiatives.

Ironically, the Afrikaner argument for apartheid had been based on biblical justifications (for example on the 'division of nations' in Genesis 10 and Acts 17). While there is a biblical basis for the importance of family and lineage in defining individual identity, and the value of shared culture for political integration, there is no biblical foundation in either Old or New Testament for discrimination on the basis of colour, race or language, or for the concept of 'separate development'. Rather, the whole Bible insists on the fair treatment of all racial and ethnic groups, whether native or immigrant, and the cultural integration of those 'foreigners' who wish for it (see ch. 10).

The conference process

The first conference in 1987 involved just six senior South Africans, with no member of the ANC. By the tenth consultation in 1991, some of the most senior members of the ANC's economic policy team had attended, as well as the chairman of the ANC's constitution committee. From the white establishment, participants included the director-general of the department of finance, the chairman of the Broederbond[17] and a number of key players in the more informal pre-negotiation process. Among the international participants were a senior member of the US State Department and eminent political leaders from continental Europe and the UK. All these individuals attended in their personal capacities, but brought extensive political experience and influence in their constituencies.

Themes for discussion were selected on the basis of what was considered most likely at the time to contribute to the long-term peace process. These included federal and unitary systems of government, constitutional safeguards for individuals and cultural minorities, land reform and agricultural development, alternatives to bank and industry nationalization, and African participation in public administration and public sector activity. In each conference, one of the twelve or so papers would address ethical issues underlying the public policy discussion. These were generally prepared by the Jubilee House team, in discussion with South African theologians and academics. It is hard to determine what influence these theological papers had on policy outcomes, although they did influence the agreed final statements made at the end of each conference. On a later occasion, one of the members of the process gave the then white-led South African cabinet an extensive briefing drawing on what had been discussed in NPI meetings; the NPI documentation was also circulated at a senior level in the ANC.

So what was achieved, and at what cost? Much of the benefit is hard to measure. Confidence building is an intangible process, as is the creating of networks enabling those attending to contact each other informally between meetings as need arises. Probably the most tangible achievements were:

- To create one of the very few positive and safe environments in the period 1987–1991 where senior members of the ANC and the white establishment could meet together and debate policy issues with high-level research input.
- To build confidence amongst senior members of the ruling elite in South Africa that they could 'do business' with the ANC leadership.
- To identify areas of consensus in terms of values, goals and strategies for some of the most contentious issues and thus narrow down areas of conflict and disagreement.

---

17. An Afrikaner secret society closely linked historically to the then-ruling National Party.

- To help provide an acceptable policy framework for issues like land, industry and bank nationalization, and thus facilitate the movement towards formal negotiation. Twice NPI conference discussions appeared to be directly influential in enabling the ANC to identify how it would need to change its position for the sake of a broader accommodation with the major stakeholders.

The funding of this initiative was extremely difficult. Small donations were received from companies, including Anglo-American, BP and Consgold. Individual Christians and Christian-based trusts supported the initiative generously. By 1991, the Jubilee Centre, as the chief funding agency, had accumulated a substantial debt, and it was only the generosity of a Christian donor after the conferences finished which prevented more drastic survival measures being necessary.

From 1994 to 1999 NPI did five years of work in Rwanda. The aim initially was to bring together leaders of the government with Hutu leaders from outside Rwanda who had not been supportive of, or involved in, the genocide. However, it quickly became apparent that this attempt at dialogue was premature; the events of 1994 were too recent. So the team had to seek other ways to help build peace.

Analysis of the causes of the genocide revealed that from 1986 agricultural production per head had been falling as cultivation extended onto increasingly marginal land. With a population growth rate of over 3.5% per annum, and with no use of chemical fertilisers, there was a growing army of unemployed young men who could easily be mobilized for political purposes. Thus, one goal of NPI's involvement was to support the government's efforts to raise agricultural production and thus create employment opportunities on the land where 90% of the population eked out a living.

The other aspect of NPI's Rwanda involvement was to support the criminal justice system. One specific initiative was to explore with government and church leaders the possibility of a Truth and Reconciliation Commission, based on the South African model. Despite excellent papers presented at the workshop, and the active engagement of a commissioner from South Africa, at that time neither government nor church was prepared for the risks involved in such an undertaking. NPI's other primary objective was to help the churches prepare communities for the local 'gacaca' (community) courts; these local courts were being proposed to help tackle the huge backlog of genocide cases which were beyond the capacity of the formal court system to handle. The project was closed down in 1999, primarily due to funding difficulties.

In the same year, work slowly began in the Sudan with RFI (the new name for NPI), in partnership with the African Renaissance Institute (ARI), leading to a series of five conferences in 2001 and 2002. The initiative involved leaders from all the major political parties, as well as from civil society. The results of these consultations, based on research papers prepared mainly by the Sudanese themselves but with some international input, were fed into the formal IGAD[18] process organized by the 'troika' (US, UK and Norwegian governments). These and other governments generously helped to finance ARI/RFI meetings as well. It is too early now to assess the impact of these meetings on the overall peace process. However, the Southern Sudan political leadership have stated that the seeds of the ceasefire agreement of September 2002 had been sown at the conference ARI and RFI convened in July of that year on defence and security issues. Also, a Northern Sudanese negotiator has stated that the relationships built up in RFI conferences were crucial in facilitating trust and dialogue when the formal IGAD-sponsored talks got under way. More recently, Concordis International (the new name for RFI) has initiated a series of consultations on the crisis in Darfur in Western Sudan and other regional conflicts in Sudan.

Case-study 3: Consumer credit and debt

The Conservative Party came to power in 1979 on a platform of deregulation of business and financial services. The crescendo of this attack on 'red tape' in the City came with the so-called 'Big Bang' in 1986. Many of the former constraints on consumer lending such as minimum deposit requirements were swept away overnight. However, the public had not been prepared for this new freedom to borrow. In the context of a new 'wealth culture' being promoted by the government, there were many who did not resist the temptation to borrow heavily. The number of people with multiple debts escalated sharply.[19]

Connection with the biblical framework

Debt was an issue of major concern in the biblical social vision, as has been discussed in chapters 10 – 12. The regular cancellation of debts and the ban on interest discouraged speculative lending. The strong moral obligation to pay debts (debt forgiveness was never a right, except in the year of debt release) and the practice of bonded servitude for defaulters discouraged unnecessary borrowing. The language of debt plays a major part in New Testament teaching on sin.

---

18. IGAD stands for 'Inter-Governmental Authority on Development' in the Horn of Africa.

19. For details see Hartropp et al. (1988).

Why is debt such a big issue in a 'relational society'? First, debt is not conducive to a free society where people deal with each other as equals. The book of Proverbs states that the borrower is the slave of the lender (Prov. 22:7). Debt contributes to a concentration of economic power, and to the formation of an economic underclass. Secondly, debt imposes immense psychological burdens. A Jubilee Centre survey of over 1,000 multiple-debt cases showed how often debt is closely associated with depression, and with relationship breakdown in families, including divorce and child abuse (Lang 1988).

Implementation

The main difficulty with our 'Freedom from Debt' campaign was finding anyone to fund it. The main beneficiaries were people in debt; by definition, of course, they were not in a position to fund it! Many of those in a position to help had little sympathy for those in debt, believing it was the debtors' own fault and they needed to learn a lesson. The only solution we could find was to rename the initiative 'Credit Action', and to provide teaching materials in schools warning about the dangers of debt. Financial institutions were willing to pay for this. Thus NatWest, as sponsors, gained access to secondary school pupils, which gave them a competitive edge, while ensuring proper money education was available in schools. When the video and teaching pack was launched in 1988, it was purchased by one third of all secondary schools in Britain within six months.

Credit Action was launched as a separate charity in 1994,[20] and has continued over the last ten years to focus primarily on preventing students and young people from getting into debt, while providing debt-counselling to a small number of especially needy cases, mainly in the Christian community. Its national director, Keith Tondeur, through his energetic speaking programme in churches and Christian conferences, has also helped to keep the issue high on the churches' agenda over this period as well as feeding information and proposals into the national policy context.

Case-study 4: Tackling urban unemployment

Background

Unemployment in Britain is lower than in most of continental Europe, is low relative to the late 1980s, and is a huge improvement on the 1930s. So why focus on this issue? In fact, levels of unemployment are much higher than indicated by official statistics as the figures have been 'adjusted' by governments over the last

---

20. For further information, see <http://www.creditaction.org.uk>.

two decades: those over fifty, for example, who have taken early retirement and do not claim benefits are no longer included in the statistics.[21] So today, in 2004, the headline rate of unemployment claimants is at its lowest for thirty years at just over 3%, but adding the huge number of people who have moved onto sickness and disability benefits, and others who want to work, the number is at least twice the official figure. Indeed, the total number of economically inactive people who want to work and could work has remained virtually unchanged at about 2.2 million in 1995, 2000 and 2003.[22] In addition, unemployment is concentrated in certain inner-city wards of the larger cities characterized by large ethnic minorities and single-parent families, where unemployment is often as high as 25–50%.

Outline of the scheme

An initial survey by the Relationships Foundation revealed a large number of agencies tackling unemployment on the ground in different cities, often with innovative schemes. Their problem was not lack of ideas but access to financial resources, despite all the government money then available. With the help of a senior merchant-banker who was gradually reducing his professional work, the project team developed 'employment bonds' as a new financial product. This was based on wealthier citizens lending money interest-free for five years so that both the capital sum and the interest foregone by the bondholder could be used to help get the unemployed into work.[23] The capital sum has been used for property development, either for social housing, often built using, in part, long-term unemployed labour, or for 'incubator' space, enabling the long-term unemployed to start their own businesses. The interest foregone by the bondholders has been used partly to fund the marketing and administration of the bonds (about 20%), partly to give grants to charities helping unemployed people into work, and partly as a source of low-interest loans, with no collateral required, to help long-term unemployed to start their own small businesses. As mentioned above, the Relationships Foundation established an Industrial and Provident Society, called City*life*, to issue these bonds in order to satisfy the rules of the Financial Services Authority (FSA). As with the Relationships Foundation, City*life* is not a Christian organization but is based on the ethical values of the Judaeo-Christian tradition.[24]

---

21. Those over fifty may not choose to claim benefit because after thirteen weeks they have to take *any* job they could do within an hour's journey from where they live.
22. Social Trends 26, 31, 34, HMSO.
23. For more details on employment bonds and how they work, visit the City*life* website at: <http://www.citylifeltd.org>.
24. See p. 218 above.

Connection with the biblical framework

The approach taken to tackling unemployment grew out of reflection on a number of different biblical themes which had been the subject of earlier Jubilee Centre research:

- Biblical concern for the strength of family and community relationships makes tackling unemployment a priority. There is no question that unemployment puts pressure on close family relationships. At a community level, it is more difficult to prove the divisive effects of unemployment. However, in Old Testament times the jubilee land laws ensured the majority of the population had the resources necessary to grow their own food, and it was the responsibility of those who had land to provide work opportunities for those without (Lev. 25:8–17; Deut. 24:19–22). In New Testament times wealthier citizens were encouraged repeatedly by Paul to use their wealth for the common good (e.g. 1 Pet. 2:11–15; Rom. 13:3–4; 1 Tim. 5:3–16).[25]

- Capital has the potential to play a major role in building social relationships (see ch. 11). The ban on interest was concerned to ensure that any return on capital was either pecuniary and based on risk-sharing, or was a social return based on achieving a relational benefit. The employment bond is a product based on the kind of social return envisaged by biblical teaching.

- The responsibility to tackle a major social blight did not lie with the king, or some other representative of centralized power, but with the local people themselves. Cities were intended to be, as far as possible, self-governing entities rather than merely the outposts of larger political units (Crook 1996). Residents of cities were responsible for tackling their own problems rather than 'passing the buck' to a higher political authority.

It was taking these principles together which gave rise to the employment bond. This is a good example of the Jubilee Centre's experience that the creative application of the biblical social vision often requires that several laws are considered together to respond effectively to a situation today.

Implementation

In Sheffield, the first city to launch a bond, the team gained the support of leading Sheffield politicians such as David Blunkett, then Secretary of State for Education and Employment, the chief executive of the City Council and other prominent

---

25. Winter (1994).

individuals with a Sheffield connection such as the actor Sean Bean. In 1998/99 over 500 individuals, eighteen church groups and a small number of companies bought 'Sheffield employment bonds' with a total value of nearly £800,000, to be repaid in 2004. The second bond, issued in Newcastle in 2001, raised a larger sum (just over £2 million) but mainly from the corporate sector. It was thus more successful in helping unemployed people into work, but less successful in involving local citizens in the process of doing so.

However, in our City and East London Bond, launched in 2002, the Steering Committee set itself a highly ambitious target of £50 million, to fit in with fifty years of the Queen's rule. Despite an energetic marketing campaign, against a background of sharply falling stock markets and other factors, we 'only' raised £2 million. This led to our largest corporate backer withdrawing support. At the time of writing, City life is emerging from this difficult time into a period of rapid growth with research for five further bonds already well advanced, and a second Sheffield bond just launched.

Overall, after six years of work, City life has raised just under £5 million, has helped over 700 people into work at an average cost (in terms of interest forgone to the investor) of around £1,600 per job,[26] and has involved almost 800 individuals and sixty companies in contributing capital to the scheme. This provides an encouraging indication of what may be possible.

Case-study 5: Relational health audits

Background
The R Factor provides a framework of analysis ('relational proximity') for deconstructing social relationships. This is defined as 'a closeness of relationship between two individuals through which each is able to recognize the other more fully as a complete and unique human being' (Schluter & Lee 1993: 276). Relational proximity is not the same as compatibility; it is not a question of whether one person is suited to another person. Nor is it a matter of geographic proximity, although that may also influence the relationship between two people in a number of ways. Rather, relational proximity is best described as a set of preconditions for one person getting to know another person well. Where there is a high degree of relational proximity, people will know each other well, whether or not they happen to like each other.

There are five 'dimensions' of relational proximity set out in The R Factor (see also ch. 15, pp. 274–281). These may be summarized as follows:

---

26. City life Annual Report, 2004. These estimates exclude the costs of establishing City life as a charity and the initial research costs for each bond.

- *Directness*: proximity of contact – intensity/depth of communication in the relationship
- *Continuity*: proximity through time – length and stability of the relationship
- *Multiplexity*: proximity in diverse situations – breadth and scope of the relationship
- *Parity*: proximity in mutual respect and involvement – balance of power in the relationship
- *Commonality*: proximity of purpose – motivation driving the relationship

This framework can be used to 'deconstruct' relationships, whether in a personal, business or professional context.[27] It provides a language for discussing what is happening in a relationship, and this makes it easier in a business and public policy context especially, to analyse and debate the relational implications of decisions. There seem to be enormous areas of potential application.

Connection with the biblical framework

Arguably, all five dimensions of relational proximity are fulfilled perfectly in the relationships of the Godhead, as well as in God's relationship with us as human beings (see ch. 15). Jesus told an expert in the law that the greatest commandment is to love the Lord your God, and love your neighbour, because 'all the law and the prophets hang on these two commandments' (Matt. 22:37–40). So the question was how laws like the jubilee land provisions (see ch. 9), or the ban on interest (see chs. 11 and 12), were an expression of good or 'right' relationships between an Israelite and God, or an Israelite and his or her neighbour. This was not immediately obvious!

However, gradually it became clear that by encouraging roots in a particular locality for every citizen, the jubilee land laws would encourage greater *continuity* of relationships with extended family and neighbours. Because every family owned land in perpetuity (see ch. 9), there would also be a degree of *parity* between citizens; no families could become landless and land ownership could not become concentrated in the hands of a few. In the case of the ban on interest, the shared risk of borrower and lender would increase *commonality*, the sense of common purpose or shared goals in the relationship. The emphasis in Scripture on the significance of face-to-face relationships pointed towards the significance of *directness* in the communication aspects of a relationship.

This framework underlines the fact that communication skills influence only about 20% of the total communication process, both in personal and organizational contexts. The ability to interpret what the other person is saying, and decisions about

---

27. For a more detailed breakdown of these five dimensions into nineteen subdimensions, see Schluter and Lee (2003), ch. 4.

what to say (rather than the skill of how to say it), account for the other 80% of the process. Communication is like an iceberg; most of it lies unseen, beneath the surface.

Project development

In 1994 the Relationships Foundation team was commissioned by the Scottish Prison Service to develop a management tool based on the relational proximity framework to assess the quality of relationships between prison officers and prisoners inside prisons. With the help of Hans Toch, an eminent American social psychologist working in criminology and criminal justice administration, the first questionnaire was developed using this framework. KPMG, a leading accountancy and consulting partnership, then took an interest and over a number of years helped to refine the tool further. Since then it has been applied systematically in a wide range of organizational contexts including relationships between:

- a health authority and community trust in West London
- the lifer management unit in Prison Service HQ and the 'lifer governors' in prisons across England and Wales
- partners and senior solicitors in a leading international law firm in the City of London
- various groups involved in setting up primary-care groups in the NHS
- the national offices of a leading international public-relations company.

Members of the Relationships Foundation team undertook several consultancy assignments as part of an attempt to explore the concepts and their applicability in different work situations. Then in 1996 the Foundation attempted to set up a consultancy company to sell the tools on a commercial basis. However, the Foundation did not have the necessary consultancy skills in-house, or a sufficient track-record of successful applications of the new tools to call in evidence. Nor was it possible to attract an experienced management consultant to lead the team because salary scales were not sufficiently attractive.

A second attempt, to partner with one of the big five accounting firms, also did not succeed. Arguably, the relationship lacked parity! Perhaps, the potential profits of the consultancy contracts available from use of the tools was too small to be of commercial interest to such a large-scale consultancy group.

The solution was to make the tools available through working with a company that trains people in the use of psychometric tools.[28] Those wishing to use the

---

28. Information about the tools and accreditation courses may be found on the Relationships Foundation website: <http://www.relationshipsfoundation.org/relational_health_audit/Index.html>.

tools have to undergo a brief accreditation course. The hope is that this approach will lead to widespread use of the tools, and the opportunity eventually to test the validity of the tools statistically based on data generated by their application in diverse situations. At the same time, it provides the Relationships Foundation with the delivery capacity to support organizations wishing to explore relational thinking and assess different organizational relationships.

Over the last ten years, the concept of relational proximity has been widely used in the NHS. The tools were used as part of a 'Relational Health Care' (RHC) project, culminating in a book entitled *Relationships in the NHS*, published collaboratively with the Royal Society of Medicine.[29] Members of over 150 primary-care organizations and thirty health authorities/boards in England, Wales and Scotland have used RHC materials (Meads & Ashcroft 2000: 139). In addition to six national workshops or conferences hosted by the Relationships Foundation, organizations that have used RHC materials in their events have included the Association of Managers in General Practice (1997), the NHS Staff College, Wales (1997–98), the Health Education Authority (1998–99) and the European Multi-Professional Education Network (1998).

Similar success was not achieved in the Prison Services, either in Scotland or in England and Wales, despite a number of opportunities to use the tools in particular prisons. However, influence is evident at several points. It is likely that the 'relational audit' questionnaires developed for the Scottish Prison Service influenced the draft prison audit published by the International Centre for Prison Studies at Kings College London (Coyle 2003). Also, the recent emphasis on relationships in the management of the Prison Service may well be evidence of the influence of the earlier audits, as well as the 'drip-feed' of the *Relational Justice Bulletin*, published quarterly by the Relationships Foundation to promote relational best practice in the criminal justice system.

The relational audit methodology in principle could be used to evaluate the 'relational impact' of government (or corporate) policies, or of legislative proposals. Given the difficulties of weighing up the relational consequences of a specific policy for one group over against another, such analysis is unlikely to provide a definitive answer as to whether it is right to proceed with a proposal under consideration. However, as shown in the Relationships Foundation's analysis of the Job Seeker's Allowance legislation in Britain, a relational impact assessment often has the potential to highlight relational weaknesses in government's proposals and show ways these can be overcome (Clark 1996).

---

29. Meads & Ashcroft (2000).

Conclusion

Several observations can be made from this brief overview. Rightly or wrongly, the Jubilee Centre has not focused on one area of biblical research and public policy, such as criminal justice or finance, in order to make a significant impact. Rather, the primary goal has been to explore the framework as a whole, and the interrelation between its various components. The result has been greater clarity in distinguishing between Relationism and, say, Capitalism, but a less obvious impact on any specific policy area. The experience with the Sunday-trading legislation illustrates how much work is often required to influence policy decisively on just one issue.

A major limiting factor for the Jubilee Centre and its associated charities in seeking to bring about social change has been shortage of funding. Although financial resources have been accessed successfully from foreign governments (for international peace-building), from corporates and from government departments in the UK, as well as from many generous individuals, lack of resources has been a major constraint on the range and depth of the work undertaken. While this has undoubtedly limited the short-term impact on public policy, it has probably not affected very much the development of the understanding of the framework. Indeed, arguably a higher level of activity in the policy arena might have left less time for innovative thinking.

The importance of 'sector champions' has emerged as a key factor affecting the level of influence in a particular policy arena. Where an energetic, senior person took up relational ideas in a sector, the Relationships Foundation was able to have a much greater influence than where it had to rely on its own contacts to achieve influence. Thus, the influence of relational ideas has probably been greater in the health sector than in the criminal-justice system in Britain over the last ten years, even though the latter started first.

In trying to assess at this stage the overall impact of relational ideas on public (and private) life in Britain, two caveats must be borne in mind. First, the complexity of relationships makes it notoriously difficult to measure with certainty the reasons for changes in quality of relationships. To say that as a result of our work any particular relationship is now 'better' or 'more proximate' than it would have been is almost impossible to assess with confidence. However, it is possible to point to significant changes in the structure or working practices in organizations, for example resulting from Relational Health Audits, and to obtain subjective assessments from leading persons in the relevant field of activity affirming that important relational benefits have occurred through Relationships Foundation activity.

Secondly, it is still early days to assess the impact of a new 'ideology'. Despite it being now thirty years since the start of biblical reflection on these issues, twenty years from the founding of the Jubilee Centre, and ten years for the Relationships Foundation, this is not long for the development and dissemination of ideas. Seeds take time to grow, as Christ constantly reminded his disciples. So the jury is still out on whether Relationism, constantly renewed and refreshed by the biblical research of the Jubilee Centre, can significantly alter the course of British, or even international, cultures and policy in the twenty-first century.

18. Epilogue

Michael Schluter

Is it really possible to change the world? Could the *Jubilee Manifesto*, or its translation into Relationism, ever take hold as a significant framework for ordering society?

As we begin the third millennium, materialism dressed up in the economic institutions of the Capitalist economy seems not just ascendant but dominant on a global scale. The superficial offerings of luxury goods and services offer a better life not just to those in Western societies, but to the poor in Africa and Asia as well. Consumerism and economic growth seem to provide not just something to work for, but something to live for. The challenge posed by Marxism and Socialism has all but disappeared. Fukuyama (1992), for example, wrote after the fall of the Berlin wall that we have reached 'the end of history', where Capitalism holds uncontested sway as the only successful framework for organizing social and economic life.

However, there are clouds on the horizon, at present no bigger than a man's hand. The growing evidence of global warming raises questions about the sustainability of an economic system which relies so heavily on the movement of goods and people. Arguably an even more pressing issue is the breakdown of the *social* ecology in societies that have been under a Capitalist system for centuries rather than decades; the breakdown of family and community relationships undermines the moral order on which the social order rests. The ethical values that produce trust and integrity, which are the foundations on which a Capitalist system is built, have steadily been eroded. The building that stands upon them must eventually collapse. Scandals like the bankruptcy of Enron and other companies in 2002 may well be warnings of what is to follow.[1]

Looking at future possibilities from a more positive perspective, who would underestimate the power of God to intervene in world affairs? At a time when the Jewish temple seemed indestructible, both as a building and as a moral-political system, Jesus prophesied that it could be 'cast into the sea', such is the power of prayer (Mark 11:22–24). Jesus underlines in his ministry the central importance of God's word for human well-being (Matt. 4:4; cf. Deut. 8:4), and the creative power of the word to transform the life of individuals and society (Mark 4:1–20). Isaiah the prophet, writing hundreds of years before the coming of Jesus, gives the promise of God that his word will not return to him empty (Isa. 55:10–11). The potential of the biblical social vision, and Relationism if it remains tied to its biblical moorings, should not be underestimated.

Some will reject the idea of any biblically-based concept of bringing about global change as utopian, and point to texts suggesting the growing power and influence of evil leading up to the return of Christ. However, in the parable of the wheat and the weeds, Jesus tells his disciples that both the kingdom and its enemies will grow until the end of the age (Matt. 13:36–43); and it seems also from the parable that both what causes good to flourish and what 'causes sin' will also continue to grow until the end comes (Matt. 13:41).

An essential precondition for the transformation of society is going to be a willingness by Christians to think radically about society from a biblical perspective, to take the biblical social vision seriously. At root, this is an issue of confidence – confidence in the authority, trustworthiness and relevance of the Bible for the ordering of society, and confidence that Christians can once again set the agenda for national policy reform. Such confidence will point to the need for further research into the Bible's teaching on social issues and its contemporary applications.

There is a broad research agenda which urgently needs to be addressed. In part this needs to be done by theologians and specialists in the languages and cultures of the Ancient Near East. However, such study must be informed by the questions and issues facing us in the modern world and thus requires simultaneous engagement of social scientists, natural scientists and those involved in contemporary policy debate. The underlying assumption is that relational issues change little over the centuries, although the political, economic and technological contexts in which they are expressed may change profoundly. Thus, the concepts and values underpinning the criminal and civil law of Israel need more

---

1. See, for example, the 'scandal sheet' as listed in *The Economist* on 28 June 2003 ('Survey of Capitalism and Democracy', p. 7).

detailed examination. So, too, to give just a few examples, the goals and values of biblical teaching on education and wisdom, the nature of family and community relationships, and the organization and distribution of political power all need further examination. In addition, biblical teaching relevant to some of the major issues of our day needs to be explored. What can we learn from the Bible about the idea of corporate personality, the responsibilities of capital assets ownership, political correctness, genetic engineering, and the new communications technologies? This research will serve continually to refresh the Relationist agenda.

Relationism challenges not just the political and economic system, not just the way families and communities are structured, but also the priorities and lifestyle of each person as an individual. Its appeal to the individual to seek wisdom and to desire character above the pursuit of wealth or position resonates at the very deepest level with Christian truth. As with biblical law, its effect is to point the way to Christ who alone has the power to transform the human personality, and to bring ultimate peace to the nation, the community and the individual soul.

A Christian view of history is not determinist. As Christians, while we believe in the overruling providence of God, we believe also in the need to engage, to seek to change society in the ways God shows us. So the challenge at the end of this book is not just to read the *Jubilee Manifesto*, but to implement it. What does that mean in practice?

The opportunities occur at many levels. There are ways to introduce relational ideas in the family[2] and the local church.[3] Those in paid employment can also seek to transform their workplace with relational thinking, using, for example, Relational Health Audit tools.[4] Those employed in teaching, hospitals, primary health care, social services and criminal or civil law have special opportunities to challenge the current materialistic philosophies underpinning their areas of work with biblical and relational ideas. Although there is still much work to be done, a start has been made in chapters 6 to 15 to work through issues in each of these areas of public life. In the world of politics, too, Relationism offers a wide range of policy options which Christians can seek to incorporate into party political statements and actions.

The biblical approach to bringing about social change is not by violent revolution, nor by training a small political elite, but by every disciple of

---

2. See, for example, Schluter & Lee (2003).

3. See, for example, Brian Hathaway (1996) and the Relational Church Audit on the Jubilee Centre website: <http://www.jubilee-centre.org>.

4. Details of the Relational Health Audit tool can be found at: <http://www.relationshipsfoundation.org/relational_health_audits/index.html>.

Christ 'practising and teaching [communicating] the law' (Matt. 5:19), which is summarized by the commandments to love God and love neighbour (Matt. 22:37–40). For all of us who are Christ's disciples, the imperative is to transform society, so as to achieve greatness in the kingdom of God (Matt. 5:11–20, esp. 19). We are given the mandate, the incentive and the agenda. It is time to act.

Bibliography

ALEXANDER, T. D. and D. W. Baker (eds.) (2003), *Dictionary of the Old Testament: Pentateuch*, Leicester: IVP.

ALEXY, R. (2002), *A Theory of Constitutional Rights*, Oxford: Oxford University Press.

ALLEN, J. W. (1960), *A History of Political Thought in the Seventeenth Century*, London: Methuen.

ANDERSON, F. I. (1970), 'Israelite Kinship Terminology and Social Structure', *Biblical Translator* 20, pp. 29–39.

AQUINAS, T., *Summa Theologiae*.

ARGYLE, M. (1996), 'The Effects of Relationships on Well-being', in N. Baker (ed.), *Building a Relational Society*, Aldershot: Arena, pp. 33–48.

BAKER, N. (ed.) (1996), *Building a Relational Society*, Aldershot: Arena.

BAKER & BURNSIDE (eds.) (1994), *Relational Justice: Repairing the Breach*, Winchester: Waterside Press.

BALDWIN, J. (1978), *The Message of Daniel, Bible Speaks Today series*, Leicester: IVP.

BARTH, K. (1961), *Church Dogmatics* (III / 4), Edinburgh: T. & T. Clark.

BARTHOLOMEW, C. et al. (eds.) (2002), *A Royal Priesthood*, Carlisle: Paternoster.

BARTON, J. (1998), *Ethics and the Old Testament*, London: SCM.

BAUCKHAM, R. (1989), *The Bible in Politics: How to Read the Bible Politically*, London: SPCK.

__ (2003), *Bible and Mission: Christian WItness in a Postmodern World*, Grand Rapids: Baker Academic and Carlisle: Paternoster.

BEAUMONT, P. and K. WOTHERSPOON (2000), *Christian Perspectives on Law and Relationism*, Carlisle: Paternoster.

BECHTEL, L. M. (1991), 'Shame as a Sanction of Social Control in Biblical Israel: Judicial, Political and Social Shaming', *Journal for the Study of the Old Testament* 49: 47–76.

__ (1994), 'The Perception of Shame within the Divine-Human Relationship in Biblical Israel', in Lewis M. Hopfe (ed.), *Uncovering Ancient Stones: Essays in Memory of H. Neil Richardson*, pp. 79–92, Winona Lake, IN: Eisenbrauns.

BELL, J. (1992), *French Constitutional Law*, Oxford: Oxford University Press.

BERGER, P. L. (1990), *The Sacred Canopy: Elements of a Sociological Theory of Religion*, New York: Anchor Books.

BERGER, P. L. and R. J. NEUHAUS (1977), *To Empower People: The Role of Mediating Structures in Public Policy*, Washington: American Enterprise Institute for Public Policy Research.

BERMAN, H. J. (1983), *Law and Revolution: The Formation of the Western Legal Tradition*, Cambridge, MA: Harvard University Press.

BEVIR, M. and D. O'BRIEN (1999), *The Philosophy of John Macmurray*, found at < http://www.psa.ac.uk/cps/1999/bevir2.pdf>.

BIMSON, J. J. (1989), 'The Origins of Israel in Canaan: An Examination of Recent Theories', *Themelios* 15.1: 4–15.

___ (2003), *(When) did it happen?*, Cambridge: Grove Books.

BIRCH, B. C. (1991), *Let Justice Roll Down: The Old Testament, Ethics, and Christian Life*, Louisville: Westminster/John Knox.

BIRCH, P., S. WEED and J. OLSEN (2004), 'Assessing the Impact of Community Marriage Policies on US County Divorce Rates', *Family Relations*, 53(5), pp. 495–503.

BISHOP, S. (1999), 'Justice after genocide', *Relational Justice Bulletin* 3: 3.

BOBBITT, P. (2002), *The Shield of Achilles: War, Peace and the Course of History*, New York: Anchor Books.

BOFF, L. and C. BOFF (1989), *Introducing Liberation Theology*, Tunbridge Wells: Burns and Oates.

BORALEVI, L. C. (2002), 'Classical foundational myths of European Republicanism: the Jewish Commonwealth', in M. van Gelderen and Q. Skinner (eds.), *Republicanism: A Shared European Heritage*, vol. 1, *Republicanism and Constitutionalism in Early Modern Europe*, pp. 247–262, Cambridge: Cambridge University Press.

BOSSUET, J. (1709), *Politics Drawn from Holy Scripture*, edited by Patrick Riley, repr. *Cambridge Texts in the History of Political Thought*, Cambridge: Cambridge University Press, 1991.

BOTTOMS, A. E. (2003), 'Some sociological reflections on restorative justice', in A. von Hirsch et al. (eds.), *Restorative Justice and Criminal Justice: Competing or Reconcilable Paradigms?*, 79–113, Oxford: Hart.

BOWES, D. (2002), 'The Real Kindergarten Cop', *Relational Justice Bulletin* 16: 4–5.

BRAATEN, C. E. (1989), 'Introduction: Naming the Name', in C. E. Braaten (ed.), *Our Naming of God*, Minneapolis: Fortress Press.

BRIGGS, R. S. (2003), 'Getting Involved: Speech Acts and Biblical Interpretation', *Anvil* 20: 25–34.

BRITTAN, S. (2000), 'How to achieve a stake in the country for all', *Financial Times*, 16 March, p. 19.

___ (2003), 'Placing capital into the wallets of babes', *Financial Times*, 10 April, p. 17.

BRONK, R. (1998), *Progress and the Invisible Hand: The Philosophy and Economics of Human Advance*, London: Little Brown.

BROWN, J. C. (1992), 'Divine Child Abuse', *Daughters of Sarah*, Summer.

BRUBAKER, R. (1992), *Citizenship and Nationhood in France and Germany*, Cambridge, MA: Harvard University Press.

BRUEGGEMANN, W. (1994), *A Social Reading of the Old Testament: Prophetic Approaches to Israel's Communal Life*, Minneapolis: Fortress.

__ (1999), 'The Role of Old Testament Theology in Old Testament Interpretation', in E. Ball (ed.), *In Search of True Wisdom*, 70–88, Sheffield: Sheffield Academic Press.

BUBER, M. (1937), *I and Thou*, Edinburgh: T. & T. Clark.

BURNSIDE, J. P. (2000), 'Justice, Seriousness and Relationships', in P. Beaumont and K. Wotherspoon (eds.), *Christian Perspectives on Law and Relationism*, pp. 18–51, Carlisle: Paternoster.

__ (2001), *The Status and Welfare of Immigrants*, Cambridge: Jubilee Centre.

__ (2002), 'Licence to kill?', *Cambridge Papers* 11.2.

__ (2003), *The Signs of Sin: Seriousness of Offence in Biblical Law*, Journal for the Study of the Old Testament Supplementary Series 364, Sheffield, Sheffield Academic Press.

BURNSIDE, J. P. et al. (2004), *Religion and Rehabilitation*, Cullompton: Willan Publishing.

BURNSIDE, J. P. and M. SCHLUTER (2003), 'Relational Justice: Ten Years on', *Relational Justice Bulletin* 19: 627.

CARLISLE, T. (1888), *Oliver Cromwell's Letters and Speeches with Elucidations*, London: Richard Clay & Sons.

CARROLL, J. and W. DOHERTY (2003), 'Evaluating the Effectiveness of Pre-marital Prevention Programmes: A meta-analytic review of research', *Family Relations* 52(2): 105–118.

CARTER, A. (1990), 'On Individualism, Collectivism and Interrelationism', *Heythrop Journal*, vol. xxxi, pp. 23–38.

CHAPLIN, J. P. (1996), 'Subsidiarity as Political Norm', in J. Chaplin and P. Marshall (eds.), *Political Theory and Christian Vision: Essays in Memory of Bernard Zylstra*, Lanham MD: University Press of America.

__ (2002), 'Political Eschatology and Responsible Government: Oliver O'Donovan's Christian Liberalism', in C. Bartholomew, J. Chaplin, R. Song & A. Wolters (eds.), *A Royal Priesthood? The use of the Bible ethically and politically*, pp. 265–308, Carlisle: Paternoster.

CLARK, M. (1996), 'Relational Impact Statements: Measuring the effects of public policy on personal relationships', in N. Baker (ed.), *Building a Relational Society*, 249–266, Ashgate: Arena.

CLINES, D. (1997), *The Theme of the Pentateuch*, 2nd edn, Sheffield: Sheffield Academic Press.

COHN, Haim H. (1970), 'The Penology of the Talmud', *Israel Law Review* 5: 53–74.

COLE, G. and M. Schluter (2004), 'From Personalism to Relationism: Commonalities and Distinctives', Cambridge: Jubilee Centre, available online at: <http://www.jubilee-centre.org>.

CORNELL, D. (1998), 'Rethinking the Beyond of the Real', in S. Harasym (ed.), *Levinas and Lacan: The Missed Encounter*, pp. 139–181, Albany: SUNY Press.

COSTELLO, J. E. (2002), *John Macmurray: A Biography*, Edinburgh: Floris Books.

COWBURN, J., SJ (1996), 'A History of Personalism' (unpublished paper).

COYLE, A. (2001), 'An Unchristian Solution?', *Relational Justice Bulletin* 11: 1–3.

___ (2003), *Humanity in Prison: Questions of definition and audit*, London: International Centre for Prison Studies.

CRITES, S. (1971), 'The Narrative Quality of Experience', *Journal of the American Academy of Religion*, 39.3: 291–311.

CROOK, A. (1996), *Savings Syndicates*, Cambridge: Relationships Foundation.

CROSS, J. D. (1978), *The International Dictionary of the Christian Church*, Grand Rapids: Zondervan.

DANIELL, D. (2003), *The Bible in English*, London: Yale University Press.

DAVIES, E. W. (1999), 'Walking in God's Ways: The Concept of *Imitatio Dei* in the Old Testament', in E. Ball (ed.), *In Search of True Wisdom*, pp. 99–115, Sheffield: Sheffield Academic Press.

DE SOTO, H. (2000), *The Mystery of Capital*, London: Black Swan.

DE TOCQUEVILLE, A. (1972), *Democracy in America*, vol. 2, New York: Vintage Books.

DEVER, W. G. (2000), 'Biblical and Syro-Palestinian Archaeology: A State-of-the-Art Assessment at the Turn of the Millennium', *Currents in Research: Biblical Studies* 8: 91–116.

___ (2001), *What Did the Biblical Writers Know and When Did They Know It?*, Grand Rapids and Cambridge: Eerdmans.

DIGESER, P. (2000), 'Forgiveness and Political Restoration', unpublished paper for the Political Studies Association UK, 50th Annual Conference, 10–13 April 2000, London.

DONOVAN N. and D. HALPERN (2002), 'Life Satisfaction: The State of Knowledge and Implications for Government', London: Cabinet Office Strategy Unit, December.

DOOYEWEERD, H. (1969), *A New Critique of Theoretical Thought*, vol. 3, Philadelphia: Presbyterian and Reformed.

DUFF, R. A. (2001), *Punishment, Communication and Community*, Oxford: Oxford University Press.

DURHAM, J. (1987), *Exodus*, Waco: Word Books.

ELAZAR, D. J. (1996), *Covenant and Commonwealth: From Christian Separation through the Protestant Reformation, The Covenant Tradition in Politics*, vol. 2, New Brunswick: Transaction Publishers.

ELAZAR, P. and S. COHEN (1985), *The Jewish Polity*, Bloomington: Indiana State University Press.

FAULKNER, D. (2002), 'Turning prisons inside-out', *Relational Justice Bulletin* 16: 1–3.

___ (2003a), 'Crime, Citizenship and Community', *Relational Justice Bulletin* 18: 6–8.

___ (2003b), 'Sentencing Reform: Policy, Legislation and Implementation', *British Journal of Community Justice* 1.3: 9–21.

FEINBERG, J. (2001), *No One Like Him*, Wheaton: Crossway Books.

FERDON, G. (2004), 'New Modelling English Government: Biblical Hermeneutics, Jewish Polity and Constitutional Forms during the Interregnum 1649–1660', unpublished PhD thesis, University of Cambridge.

FORBES, B. C. (1922), *Forbes Epigrams*, New York: B. C. Forbes Publishing Co.

FORRESTER, D. B. (2001), *On Human Worth*, Canterbury: SCM.

FRASER, A. (1973), *Cromwell, Our Chief of Men*, London: Panther.

FROMM, E. (1970), *Psychoanalysis and Religion*, New Haven and London: Yale University Press.

FUKUYAMA, F. (1993), *The End of History and the Last Man*, London: Penguin.

— (1995), *Trust: The Social Virtues and the Creation of Prosperity*, New York: Free Press.

GALLIE, W. B. (1964), *Philosophy and the Historical Understanding*, New York: Schocken Books.

GARLAND, D. (2001), *The Culture of Control: Crime and Social Order in Contemporary Society*, Oxford: Oxford University Press.

GELLNER, E. (1983), *Nations and Nationalism*, Oxford: Blackwell.

GOLDINGAY, J. (1991), *Approaches to Old Testament Interpretation*, Leicester: Updated edn, Apollos.

— (1987), *Theological Diversity and the Authority of the Old Testament*, Grand Rapids: Eerdmans.

GORRINGE, T. (1995), *Discerning Spirit*, London: SCM.

GOTTWALD, N. (1979), *The Tribes of Yahweh: A Sociology of the Religion of Liberated Israel, 1250–1050 BCE*, London: SCM.

GOUDZWAARD, B. (1978), *Capitalism and Progress*, Toronto: Wedge.

GUNTON, C. E. (1993), *The One, the Three and the Many: God, Creation and the Culture of Modernity*, Cambridge: Cambridge University Press.

GUSTAFSON, J. M. (1984), 'The Changing Use of the Bible in Christian Ethics', in C. E. Curran & R. A. McCormick (eds.), *The Use of Scripture in Moral Theology*, New York: Paulist Press.

HALLARD, B. W. (2000), 'The Death Penalty: God's Timeless Standard for the Nations?', *Journal of the Evangelical Theological Society* 43.3: 471–487.

HALLER, W. (ed.) (1965), *Tracts on Liberty in the Puritan Revolution 1638*, 3 vols., New York: Octagon.

HAMILTON, C. (2003), *Growth Fetish*, London: Allen & Unwin.

HANSON, P. D. (1986), *The People Called: The Growth of Community in the Bible*, San Francisco: Harper & Row.

HARTROPP, A. et al. (1988), *Families in Debt*, Cambridge: Jubilee Centre.

HASTINGS, A. (1997), *The Construction of Nationhood*, Cambridge: Cambridge University Press.

HATHAWAY, B. (1996), *Living Below with the Saints we Know*, Guildford: Eagle.

HELD, D. (2002), *Governing Globalisation: Power, Authority and Global Governance*, Cambridge: Polity Press.

HELD, D. et al. (1999), *Global Transformations: Politics, Economics and Culture*, Cambridge: Polity Press.

HESLAM, P. S. (1998), *Creating a Christian Worldview: Abraham Kuyper's Lectures on Calvinism*, Carlisle: Paternoster.

HILBORN, D. (ed.) (2004), *Movement for Change: Evangelical Perspectives on Social Transformation*, Carlisle: Paternoster.

HILL, M. (2002), *The How and Why of Love: An Introduction to Evangelical Ethics*, Kingsford NSW: Matthias Media.

HINDE, R. (1997), *Relationships: A Dialectical Perspective*, Hove: Psychology Press.

HM TREASURY (2004), *Flexibility in the UK Economy*, Budget documents, March.

HOLLAND, J. (1994), 'Bank Lending Relationships and the Complex Nature of Bank-corporate Relations', *Journal of Business Finance and Accounting*, 21:3, 367–393. April.

HOMANS, G. C. (1951), *The Human Group*, London: Routledge.

HOUGH, M. et al. (2003), *The Decision to Imprison: Sentencing and the Prison Population*, London: Prison Reform Trust.

HUEGLIN, T. (1992), 'Have we studied the wrong authors: on the relevance of Johannes Althusius', *Studies in Political Thought* 1: pp. 75–93.

__ (1999), *Early Modern Concepts for a Late Modern World: Althusius on Community and Federalism*, Waterloo, Ontario: Wilfred Laurier University Press.

HUTTON, W. (1999), 'The Jubilee Line that Works', *The Observer*, 3 October.

IPPR/CASE (2003), *Wealth and Welfare: The Role of Assets over the Life Cycle*.

IVE, J. (1986), 'The Local Dimensions of Defence: The Standing Army and Militia in Norfolk, Suffolk and Essex, 1649–1660', Unpublished PhD thesis, University of Cambridge.

JACKSON, B. S. (1989), 'Ideas of Law and Legal Administration: A Semiotic Approach', in R. E. Clements (ed.), *The World of Ancient Israel: Sociological, Anthropological and Political Perspectives*, Cambridge: Cambridge University Press.

__ (1992), 'Practical Wisdom and Literary Artifice in the Covenant Code' in B. Jackson and S. Passamaneck (eds.), *Jewish Law Association Studies VI: The Jersualem 1990 Conference Volume*, pp. 65–92, Atlanta: Scholars Press.

__ (2000), *Studies in the Semiotics of Biblical Law*, Sheffield: Sheffield Academic Press.

JANZEN, W. (1994), *Old Testament Ethics: A Paradigmatic Approach*, Louisville: Westminster/John Knox.

JENSON, P. P. (1992), *Graded Holiness: A Key to the Priestly Conception of the World*, Sheffield: JSOT Press.

__ (2002), *The Problem of War in the Old Testament*, Cambridge: Grove Books.

JENSON, R. W. (1982), *The Triune Identity*, Philadephia: Fortress.

__ (1988), *America's Theologian: A Recommendation of Jonathan Edwards*, Oxford: Oxford University Press.

__ (1997), *Systematic Theology, Vol. 1: The Triune God*, Oxford: Oxford University Press.

__ (1999), *Systematic Theology, Vol. 2: The Works of God*, Oxford: Oxford University Press.

JOHNSON, D. and C. SAMPSON (1994), *The Missing Dimensions of Statecraft*, New York: Oxford University Press.

JOHNSTON, O. R. (1977) 'God and the Nations', *Evangelical Review of Theology*, 83–93.

JOHNSTONE, G. (2002), *Restorative Justice: Ideas, Values, Debates*, Cullompton: Willan Publishing.

KAISER, W. (1991), *Toward Old Testament Ethics*, Grand Rapids: Academic Books.

KARTVEIT, M. (1989), *Motive und Schichten der Landtheologie in 1 Chronicles 1 – 9*, Stockholm: Almquist & Wiksell International.

KASS, L. R. (1994), 'Educating Father Abraham: The Meaning of Wife', *First Things* 47: 16–26.

KAUFMAN, S. A. (1979), 'The Structure of the Deuteronomic Law', *Maarav* 1: 105–158.

KAY, J. (2003), *The Truth About Markets: Their Genius, Their Limits, Their Follies*, London: Allen Lane.

KAYE, J. S. (2003), 'Problem-Solving Courts', *Relational Justice Bulletin* 17: 1–2.

KENNEDY, R. (1968), Address, University of Kansas, Lawrence, Kansas, 18 March 1968.

KHALAF, S. (1971), 'Family Associations in Lebanon', *Journal of Comparative Family Studies*, vol. 2, no. 2.

KIDNER, D. (1964), *Proverbs: An Introduction and Commentary*, Leicester: IVP.

KIERKEGAARD, S. (1956), 'Either/or' in R. Bretall, *A Kierkegaard Anthology*, Princeton: Princeton University Press.

KING, M. (2002), 'The Inflation Target Ten Years On', Address to the London School of Economics, Bank of England, 19 November.

KLINE, M. G. (1972), *The Structure of Biblical Authority*, Grand Rapids: Eerdmans.

KNIERIM, R. (1995), *The Task of Old Testament Theology: Substance, Method and Cases*, Grand Rapids: Eerdmans.

KNOX, D. B. (1988), *The Everlasting God*, Homebush: Lancer.

__ (1992), *Sent By Jesus*, Edinburgh: Banner of Truth.

KOHN, H. (1985), *The Idea of Nationalism*, New York: Macmillan (excerpted in John Hutchinson and Anthony D. Smith, *Nationalism*, Oxford: Oxford University Press).

KOONINGS, K. & D. KRUIJT (2002), *Political Armies: The Military and Nation Building in an Age of Democracy*, London and New York: Zed Books.

KOYZIS, D. (2003), *Political Visions and Illusions*, Downers Grove: IVP.

KRAYNAK, R. (2001), *Christian Faith and Modern Democracy: God and Politics in the Fallen World*, Notre Dame IN: University of Notre Dame Press.

KUHN, T. S. (1970), *Structure of Scientific Revolutions*, 2nd edn, Chicago: University of Chicago Press.

KUYPER, A. (1931), *Lectures on Calvinism*, repr. Grand Rapids: Eerdmans, 1976.

__ (1950), *Christianity and the Class Struggle*, Grand Rapids: Piet Hein Publishers.

KYMLICKA, W. (1995), *Multicultural Citizenship*, Oxford: Clarendon Press.

LANG, R. (1988), 'Analysis of Individuals with Multiple Debt Problems', in A. Hartropp et al., *Families in Debt*, Cambridge: Jubilee Centre.

LAYARD, R. (2003), 'Happiness: Has Social Science a Clue?', Lionel Robbins Memorial Lecture, found at <http://cep.lse.ac.uk/events/lectures/layard/RL030303.pdf>.

LEDERACH, J. P. (1997), *Building Peace*, Washington, DC: United States Institute of Peace.

LEVINAS, E. (1969), *Totality and Infinity*, translated by A. Lingus, Pittsburgh: Duquesne University Press.

LIPTON, M. (1977), *Why Poor People Stay Poor: A Study of Urban Bias in World Development*, London: Temple Smith.

LOCKWOOD O'DONOVAN, J. (2004), 'Nation, State and Civil Society in the Western Biblical Tradition', in O. O'Donovan and J. Lockwood O'Donovan, *Bonds of Imperfection: Christian Politics Past and Present*, pp. 276–295, Grand Rapids: Eerdmans.

LOGSDON, B. (1991), 'Multi-polarity and Covenant: towards a biblical framework for constitutional safeguards', Cambridge: Jubilee Centre, unpublished paper.

LONG, V. P., D. W. BAKER & G. J. WENHAM (eds.) (2002), *Windows into Old Testament History: Evidence, Argument and the Crisis of 'Biblical Israel'*, Grand Rapids and Cambridge: Eerdmans.

LORBERBAUM, M. (2003), 'Making and Unmaking the Boundaries of Holy Land', in A. Buchanen and M. Moore (eds.), *States, Nations and Borders: The Ethics of Making Boundaries*, pp. 19–40, Cambridge: Cambridge University Press.

LUCKHAM, R. (1971), *The Nigerian Military: A Sociological Analysis of Authority and Revolt, 1960–1967*, Cambridge: Cambridge University Press.

LUKES, S. and A. SCULL (eds.) (1983), *Durkheim and the Law*, New York: St Martin's Press.

LUND, N. W. (1992), *Chiasmus in the New Testament*, Chapel Hill: University of North Carolina Press.

MacCORMICK, N. (1999), *Questioning Sovereignty*, Oxford: Oxford University Press.

MACFARLANE, A. (1978), *The Origins of English Individualism: the family, property and social transition*, Oxford: Basil Blackwell.

MacINTYRE, A. (1981), *After Virtue*, London: Duckworth.

__ (2003), *The Power of Institutions: Political Architecture and Governance*, Ithaca and London: Cornell University Press.

MACMURRAY, J. (1950), *Conditions of Freedom*, repr. Amberst, NY: Humanity Books, 1993.

__ (1961), *Persons in Relation*, repr. London: Faber, 1995.

MALCHOW, B. (1996), *Social Justice in the Hebrew Bible*, Minnesota: Liturgical Press.

MARITAIN, J. (1947), *Humanism Integral: Problèmes Temporels et Spirituals d'une Nouvelle Chrétienité*, 2nd edn, translated by J. Evan, New York: Scribner, 1968.

MARSDEN, G. (1997), *The Outrageous Idea of Christian Scholarship*, Oxford: Oxford University Press.

MARSHALL, C. (2001), *Beyond Retribution: A New Testament Vision for Justice, Crime and Punishment*, Grand Rapids: Eerdmans.

MARSHALL, I. M. (1978), *The Gospel of Luke*, Exeter: Paternoster.

MARUNA, S. (2001), *Making Good: How Ex-convicts Reform and Rebuild their Lives*, Washington, DC: American Psychological Association.

MARUNA, S. et al. (2002), 'The Prisoner's Beatitude', *Relational Justice Bulletin* 14: 1–3.

MARUNA, S. & T. P. LEBEL (2002), 'Revisiting Ex-prisoner Re-entry: A New Buzzword in Search of a Narrative', in M. Turney and S. Rex (eds.), *Reform and Punishment: The Future of Sentencing*, Devon, UK: Willan, pp. 158–180.

MATTHEWS, V. H. (1987), 'Entrance Ways and Threshing Floors: Legally Significant Sites in the Ancient Near East', *Fides et Historia* 19: 25–40.

MAYES, A. D. H. (1974), *Israel in the Period of the Judges*, London: SCM.

MAYS, J. L. (1969), *Amos: A Commentary*, London: SCM.

MCCONVILLE, G. (2002), 'Law and Monarchy in the Old Testament', in Bartholomew et al. (2002).

MCILROY, D. (2003), 'Subsidiarity and Sphere Sovereignty', *Law and Justice*, vol. 151, 111–136.

___ (2004), 'Style or Substance: Does the reputation of the Church matter?', *Cambridge Papers* 10.1.

MCKENZIE, J. L. (1959), 'The Elders in the Old Testament', *Biblica*, 522.

MEADS, G. & J. ASHCROFT (2000), *Relationships in the NHS: Bridging the Gap*, London: Royal Society of Medicine Press.

MEADS, G., J. ASHCROFT, with H. Barr, R. Scott and A. Wild (2005), *The Case for Interprofessional Collaboration*, Oxford: Blackwells.

MENDENHALL, G. E. (1955), *Law and Covenant in Israel and the Ancient Near East*, Pittsburgh: Biblical Colloquium.

___ (1958), 'The Census Lists of Numbers 1 and 26', *Journal of Biblical Literature* 77, pp. 52–66.

MIDGLEY, M. (2002), *Evolution as a Religion*, 2nd edn, London: Routledge.

MILGROM, J. (2001), *Leviticus 23 – 27*, New York: Doubleday.

MILLER, D. (1995), *On Nationality*, Oxford: Clarendon Press.

MILLS, P. (1998), 'A Brief Theology of Time', *Cambridge Papers* 7:1.

___ (2000a), 'Christians and Financial Security: Faith versus prudence?', in M. Schluter et al., *Christianity in a Changing World*, 191–203, London: Marshall Pickering.

___ (2000b), 'Investing as a Christian: Reaping where you have not sown?', in M. Schluter et al., *Christianity in a Changing World*, 204–215, London: Marshall Pickering.

___ (2000c), 'The Biblical Ban on Interest: Dead letter or radical solution?', in M. Schluter et al., *Christianity in a Changing World*, 176–190, London: Marshall Pickering.

___ (2002), 'A Brief Theology of Time (Part 2)', *Cambridge Papers* 11:4.

MILLS, P. S. and J. PRESLEY (1999), *Islamic Finance: Theory and Practice*, Basingstoke: MacMillan.

MOLTMANN, Jürgen (1981), *The Trinity and the Kingdom of God*, London: SCM.

___ (2000), *Experiences in Theology*, London: SCM.

MONTVILLE, J. (ed.) (1991), *The Psychodynamics of International Relations*, vol. 2, Lexington, MA: D. C. Heath and Company.

MOO, D. (1996), *The Epistle to the Romans*, New International Commentary on the New Testament, Grand Rapids: Eerdmans.

MOONEY, S. C. (1988), *Usury: Destroyer of Nations*, Warsaw, OH: Theopolis.

MOTYER, J. A. (1993), *The Prophecy of Isaiah*, Leicester: IVP.

MOUW, R. J. (1984), 'Commands for Grown-Ups,' in C. E. Curran & R. A. McCormick (eds.), *The Use of Scripture in Moral Theology*, pp. 66–77, New York: Paulist Press.

MUILENBURG, J. (1961), *The Way of Israel: Biblical Faith and Ethics*, New York: Harper.

NAUGLE, D. K. (2000), *Worldview: The History of a Concept*, Grand Rapids and Cambridge: Eerdmans.

NELSON, B. (1969), *The Idea of Usury: From Tribal Brotherhood to Universal Otherhood*, Chicago: Chigaco University Press.

NEUHAUS, R. J. (1984), *The Naked Public Square: Religion and Democracy in America*, Grand Rapids: Eerdmans.

NEWMAN, G. et al. (1997), *Rational Choice and Situational Crime Prevention: Theoretical Foundations*, Dartmouth: Ashgate.

NIEHAUS, J. (1992), 'The Central Sanctuary: where and when?', *Tyndale Bulletin* 43.1: 3–30.

NOLL, M. (2002), *America's God: From Jonathan Edwards to Abraham Lincoln*, New York: Oxford University Press.

NOONAN, J. T. (1957), *The Scholastic Analysis of Usury*, Cambridge, MA: Harvard University Press.

NORTH, D. C. (1990), *Institutions, Institutional Change and Economic Performance*, Cambridge: Cambridge University Press.

NORTH, R. (1954), *Sociology of the Biblical Jubilee*, Rome: Pontifical Biblical Institute.

NOTH, M. (1960), *The History of Israel*, translated by P. R. Ackroyd, Oxford: Blackwell.

NOVAK, M. (1990), *Morality, Capitalism and Democracy*, London: IEA Health and Welfare Unit.

O'DONOVAN, O. (1976), 'Towards an Interpretation of Biblical Ethics', *Tyndale Bulletin* 27: 54–78.

__ (1986), *Resurrection and Moral Order: An Outline for Evangelical Ethics*, Leicester and Grand Rapids: IVP and Eerdmans.

__ (1996), *The Desire of the Nations: Rediscovering the Roots of Political Theology*, Cambridge: Cambridge University Press.

__ (2003), 'Christianity and Territorial Right', in A. Buchanen and M. Moore (eds.), *States, Nations and Borders: The Ethics of Making Boundaries*, pp. 127–142, Cambridge: Cambridge University Press.

OFFICE FOR NATIONAL STATISTICS (ONS) (2002), *People's Perceptions of their Neighbourhood and Community Involvement: Results from the social capital module of the General Household Survey 2000*, London: The Stationery Office.

OKUMU, W. A. J. (2002), *The African Renaissance: History, Significance and Strategy*, Trenton, NJ: Africa World Press.

OLDHAM, J. H. (1942), *Real Life is Meeting*, London: Sheldon Press.

OLTHIUS, J. (1997), 'Face-to-Face: Ethical Asymmetry or the Symmetry of Mutuality' in James Olthuis (ed.), *Knowing Other-wise: Philosophy at the threshold of spirituality*, pp. 131–158, New York: Fordham University Press.

O'NEILL, O. (2002), *A Question of Trust*, Cambridge: Cambridge University Press.

O'NEILL, R. (2002), *Experiments in Living: The Fatherless Family*, London: Civitas.

OSWALD, A. J. (1997), 'Happiness and Economic Performance', *Economic Journal*, 107:445, pp. 1815–1831.

PAGDEN, A. (2003), 'The Christian Tradition' in A. Buchanen and M. Moore (eds.), *States, Nations and Borders: The Ethics of Making Boundaries*, Cambridge: Cambridge University Press.

PANNENBERG, W. (1977), *Jesus – God and Man*, 2nd edn, translated by L. Wilkens and D. Priebe, Philadelphia: Westminster Press.

— (1991), *Systematic Theology* vol. 1, translated by Geoffrey Bromiley, Edinburgh: T. & T. Clark.

— (1994), *Systematic Theology* vol. 2, translated by Geoffrey Bromiley, Edinburgh: T. & T. Clark.

— (1998), *Systematic Theology* vol. 3, translated by Geoffrey Bromiley, Edinburgh: T. & T. Clark.

PATRICK, D. (1981), *The Rendering of God in the Old Testament*, Overtures to Biblical Theology 10, Philadelphia: Fortress Press.

PENNELL, J. and G. BURFORD (1998), *Family Group Decision Making: After the Conference; Progress in Resolving Violence and Promoting Well-Being: Outcome Report*, 2 vols., St Johns, Newfoundland: Memorial University of Newfoundland, School of Social Work.

PERDUE, L. G. et al. (1997), *Families in Ancient Israel*, Louisville: Westminster/John Knox.

PETERS, T. (1993), *God as Trinity: Relationality and Temporality in Divine Life*, Louisville: Westminster/John Knox.

PHILLIPS, A. (1973), *Deuteronomy*, Cambridge: Cambridge University Press.

PLAMENATZ, J. (1973), 'Two Types of Nationalism', in E. Kamenka (ed.), *Nationalism: The Nature and Evolution of an Idea*, Canberra: Australian National University Press, pp. 22–37.

PLEINS, J. D. (2001), *The Social Visions of the Hebrew Bible: A Theological Introduction*, Louisville: Westminster/John Knox.

POYTHRESS, Vern S. (1988), *Science and Hermeneutics: Implications of Scientific Method for Biblical Interpretation*, Grand Rapids: Academic and Leicester: Apollos.

PRITCHETT, C. (1971), *The American Constitutional System*, New York: McGraw Hill.

PRYOR, S. (2001), *The Responsible Prisoner*, London: HM Inspectorate of Prisons.

PUTNAM, R. D. (2000), *Bowling Alone: the collapse and revival of American community*, London: Simon and Schuster.

RAMSBOTHAM, D. (1999), 'The Healthy Prison', *Relational Justice Bulletin* 3: 1–2.

RAMSEY, P. (1968), *The Just War: Force and Political Responsibility*, New York: Scribner.

REEVES, R. (2003), *The Politics of Happiness*, London: New Economics Foundation.

REIMER, D. J. (1997), 'Righteous[ness]' in W. A. VanGemeren (ed.), *New International Dictionary of Old Testament Theology and Exegesis*, Grand Rapids: Zondervan and Carlisle: Paternoster.

Relational Justice Bulletin. Archive of back issues at <http://www.relationshipsfoundation.org/relational_justice/RJ_bulletin_archives.html>.

REX, S. (2001), 'Rethinking Community Punishment', *Relational Justice Bulletin* 10: 4–5.

RICHARDS, M. (1998), *Censure Without Sanctions*, Winchester: Waterside Press.

RIVERS, J. (2004), 'The Moral Authority of Scripture', *Cambridge Papers* 13.3.

ROBERTS, C. (2003), 'The Nature, Extent and Consequences of Changes in Family Relationships', Relationships Foundation Conference, October 2003.

RODD, C. (2001), *Glimpses of a Strange Land: Studies in Old Testament Ethics*, Edinburgh: T. & T. Clark.

ROTH, M. T. (1997), *Law Collections from Mesopotamia and Asia Minor*, 2nd edn, Atlanta: Scholars Press.

RUTHERFORD, S. (1644), *Lex Rex. A Dispute for the Just Prerogative of King and People*, London: John Field.

SACKS, J. (2002), *The Dignity of Difference*, London: Continuum.

SAKENFELD, K. D. (1985), *Faithfulness in Action: Loyalty in Biblical Perspective*, Philadelphia: Fortress Press.

SCHLUTER, M. (2000a), 'Roots', in M. Schluter et al., *Christianity in a Changing World*, London: Marshall Pickering, pp. 81–91.

___ (2000b), 'Risk, Reward and Responsibility: Limited Liability and Company Reform', *Cambridge Papers*, 9.2.

SCHLUTER, M. and J. ASHCROFT (1988), 'Ethnicity and Nation-Building: Christian Norms, African Experience and a Possible Action Programme for South Africa', Cambridge: Jubilee Centre.

SCHLUTER, M. and R. CLEMENTS (1986), *Reactivating the Extended Family: From Biblical Norms to Public Policy in Britain*, Cambridge: Jubilee Centre.

___ (1990), 'Jubilee Institutional Norms: A Middle Way between Creation Ethics and Kingdom Ethics as the Basis for Christian Political Action', *Evangelical Quarterly* 62:1, 37–62.

SCHLUTER, M. and D. LEE (1988), *Keeping Sunday Special*, Basingstoke, Hants: Marshall Pickering.

___ (1993), *The R-Factor*, London: Hodder & Stoughton.

___ (2003), *The R-Option*, Cambridge: Relationships Foundation.

SCHMID, H. (1984), 'Creation, Righteousness and Salvation: "Creation Theology" as the Broad Horizon of Biblical Theology', in B. Anderson (ed.), *Creation in the Old Testament*, Philadelphia: Fortress.

SCHOLEFIELD, M. (2004), *A Guide to Trust*, Cambridge and Oxford: Relationships Foundation and the Career Innovation Group.

SCOTT, J. M. (1994), 'Luke's Geographical Horizon', in D. W. Gill and C. Gempf (eds.), *The Book of Acts in its First Century Setting*, vol. 2, pp. 454–483, Carlisle: Paternoster.

SCOTT, R. (2005), 'Crisis Prevention' in G. Meads and J. Ashcroft et al., *The Case for Interprofessional Collaboration*, Oxford: Blackwell.

SHERMAN, L. (1992), *Policing Domestic Violence*, New York: The Free Press.

SHRIVER, D. (2001), 'Forgiveness' in R. Helmick and R. Peterson (eds.), *Forgiveness and Reconciliation: Religion, Public Policy and Conflict*, Radnor PA: Templeton Foundation Press, 156–165.

SIMKINS, R. (1994), *Creator and Creation: Nature in the Worldview of Ancient Israel*, Peabody, MA: Hendrickson.

SKINNER, Q. (1978), *The Foundations of Modern Political Thought, Vol. 2: The Age of the Reformation*, Cambridge: Cambridge University Press.

SMIT, M. C. (2002), *Toward a Christian Conception of History*, edited by H. D. Morton and H. van Dyke, Lanham, NY and Oxford: Institute for Christian Studies and University Press of America.

SPENCER, N. (2002a), *Health and the Nation: A Biblical Perspective on Health and Healthcare in Britain Today*, Cambridge: Jubilee Centre.

— (2002b), *Where Do We Go from Here? A Biblical Perspective on Roots and Mobility in Britain Today*, Cambridge: Jubilee Centre.

— (2003a), *Apolitical Animal? A Biblical Perspective on Political Engagement Today*, Cambridge: Jubilee Centre.

— (2003b), *The Measure of All Things? A Biblical Perspective on Money and Value in Britain Today*, Cambridge: Jubilee Centre.

— (2004), *Votewise: Helping Christians Engage with the Issues*, London: SPCK.

SPOHN, W. C. (1995), *What Are They Saying About Scripture and Ethics?*, 2nd edn, New York and Mahwah: Paulist Press.

STEIN, S. (1953), 'The Laws on Interest in the Old Testament', *Journal of Theological Studies*, October: 161–170.

STEINMETZ, D. (1994), 'Vineyard, Farm and Garden: The drunkenness of Noah in the context of primeval history', *Journal of Biblical Literature* 113.2: 193–207.

STORKEY, A. (1979), *A Christian Social Perspective*, Leicester: IVP.

— (2004), *The Domestic Deficit: Work Pressures and the Welfare of Children*, Relationships Foundation, Camscope.

STORRAR, W. (1990), *Scottish Identity: A Christian Vision*, Edinburgh: Handsel Press.

STOTT, J. R. W. (1989), *The Cross of Christ*, 2nd edn, Leicester: IVP.

SUTTON, R. (1987), *That You May Prosper: Dominion by Covenant*, Tyler TX: Institute for Christian Economics.

TEMPLE W. (1942), *Christianity and Social Order*, repr. 1976, London: SPCK.

TOCH, H. (2000), 'Commonality in Prisons', *Relational Justice Bulletin* 7: 1–3.

TORRANCE, T. F. (2001), *The Christian Doctrine of God: One Being, Three Persons*, Edinburgh: T. & T. Clark.

TOWNSEND, C. J. (2002), 'Render Unto Caesar? The Dilemmas of Taxation Policy', *Cambridge Papers* 10.3.

TOWNSEND, C. and M. SCHLUTER (1985), *Why Keep Sunday Special*, Cambridge: Jubilee Centre.

TRAVIS, S. H. (1986), 'The Problem of Judgment', *Themelios* 11.2: 52–67.

TUCK, R. (2003), 'The Making and Unmaking of Boundaries from the Natural Law Perspective', in A. Buchanen and M. Moore (eds.), *States, Nations and Borders: The Ethics of Making Boundaries*, pp. 143–170, Cambridge: Cambridge University Press.

TWINING, W. & D. MIERS (1976), *How to Do Things with Rules*, London: Weidenfeld & Nicholson.

ULLMAN, E. (2002), 'Programming The Post-Human: Computer Science Redefines "Life"', *Harper's Magazine*, October, pp. 60–70.

UMHAU W. C. (1947), 'Traces of Primitive Democracy in Ancient Israel', *Journal of Near Eastern Studies* vol. 6, 98–108.

VAN PRINSTERER, G. (1989), *Lectures on Unbelief and Revolution*, ed. Harry Van Dyke, Ontario: Wedge.

VAN DER VYVER, J. (1999), 'Sphere Sovereignty of Religious Institutions: A Contemporary Calvinistic Theory of Church-State Relations', delivered at the Second European/ American Conference on Religious Freedom: Church Autonomy and Religious Liberty, Trier Germany, 27–30 May.

WADE, H. W. R. (1955), 'The Basis of Legal Sovereignty', *Cambridge Law Journal* vol. 13, 172–197.

WALDRON, J. (2002), *God, Locke and Equality*, Cambridge: Cambridge University Press.

WALKER, N. (1991), *Why Punish?* Oxford: Oxford University Press.

WARBURTON, P. (1999), *Debt and Delusion*, London: Penguin Books.

WARFIELD, B. B. (1968), 'The Biblical Doctrine of the Trinity', in *Biblical and Theological Studies*, Philadelphia: Presbyterian and Reformed.

WEBB, W. J. (2001), *Slaves, Women and Homosexuals: Exploring the Hermeneutics of Cultural Analysis*, Downers Grove: IVP.

WEBER, M. (1904–05; trans. Talcott Parsons 1930), *The Protestant Ethic and the Spirit of Capitalism*, London: Allen & Unwin 1985.

WEBSTER, N. (1787), *An Examination of the Leading Principles of the Federal Constitution*, Philadelphia.

WEINFELD, M. (1995), *Social Justice in Ancient Israel and in the Ancient Near East*, Jerusalem: The Magnes Press.

WEITHMAN, P. (ed.) (1997), *Religion and Contemporary Liberalism*, Notre Dame IN: University of Notre Dame Press.

WENHAM, G. J. (2000), *Story as Torah: Reading the Old Testament Ethically*, Edinburgh: T. & T. Clark.

WESTBROOK, R. (1986), 'The Prohibition on Restoration of Marriage in Deuteronomy 24:1–4', *Scripta Hierosolymitana* 31: 387–405.

WHITE, L. (2004), 'Turning Reparation Into Reality', *Relational Justice Bulletin*, 20: 6–8.

WILMOTT, P. (1986), *Social Networks, Informal Care, and Public Policy*, PSI Research Report 655, London: Policy Studies Institute.

WILSON, C. & A. OSWALD (2002), 'How Does Marriage Affect Physical and Psychological Health? A survey of the longitudinal evidence', available online at: <http://www.warwick.ac.uk/fac/soc/Economics/oswald/WilsonOswaldmarriagejan2002.pdf>.

WINTER, B. (1994), *Seek the Welfare of the City: Christians as Benefactors and Citizens*, Carlisle: Paternoster Press.

WOLTERSTORFF, N. P. (1983), *Until Justice and Peace Embrace*, Grand Rapids: Eerdmans.

WRIGHT, C. J. H. (1983), *Living as the People of God: The Relevance of Old Testament Ethics*, Leicester: IVP.

___ (1992), *Knowing Jesus through the Old Testament*, London and Downers Grove: Marshall Pickering and IVP.

___ (1995), *Walking in the Ways of the Lord: The Ethical Authority of the Old Testament*, Leicester and Downers Grove: IVP.

___ (1996), *Deuteronomy*, New International Biblical Commentary, Old Testament Series, Peabody and Carlisle: Hendrikson and Paternoster.

___ (2004) *Old Testament Ethics for the People of God*, Leicester: IVP.

WRIGHT, N. T. (1996), *Jesus and the Victory of God*, London: SPCK.

___ (2002), 'Paul and Caesar: A New Reading of Romans', in Craig Bartholomew, Jonathan Chaplin, R. Song and A. Wolters (eds.), *A Royal Priesthood? The Use of the Bible Ethically and Politically*, pp. 173–193, Carlisle: Paternoster.

___ (2003), *The Resurrection of the Son of God*, London: SPCK.

YODER, P. (1987), *Shalom: the Bible's Word for Salvation, Justice and Peace*, Institute of Mennonite Studies Series Number 7, Newton, Kansas: Faith and Life Press.

ZIZIOULAS, J. (1985), *Being as Communion: Studies in Personhood and the Church*, London: Darton, Longman and Todd.

Index of names

Index of subjects